Politics, Society and Government in the German Democratic Republic: Basic Documents

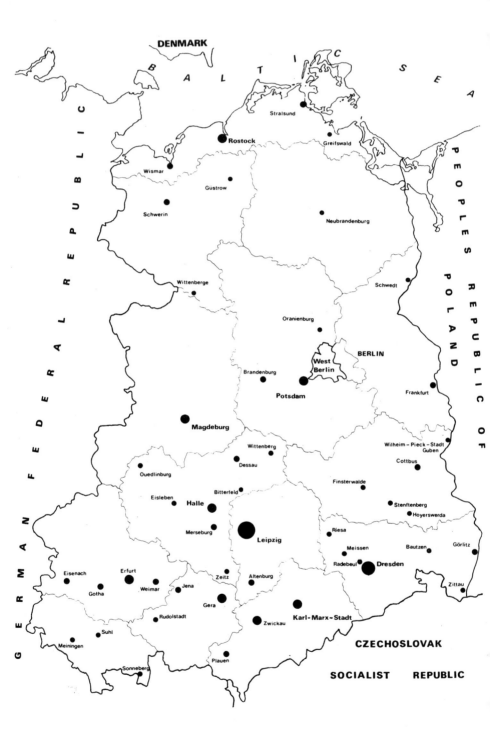

Politics, Society and Government in the German Democratic Republic: Basic Documents

Edited by
J.K.A. THOMANECK AND
JAMES MELLIS

BERG

Oxford / New York / Munich

Distributed exclusively in the US and Canada by
St Martin's Press, New York

Published in 1989 by
Berg Publishers Limited
Editorial Offices:
77 Morrell Avenue, Oxford OX4 1NQ, UK
165 Taber Avenue, Providence R.I. 02906, USA
Westermühlstraße 26, 8000 München 5, FRG

British Library Cataloguing in Publication Data

Politics, society and government in
    the German Democratic Republic : basic
    documents.
    1. East Germany. Politics, 1945–88
    I. Title   II. Thomaneck, J.K.A.
    III. Mellis, James
    320.9431
    ISBN 0–85496–247–6

Library of Congress Cataloging-in-Publication Data

Politics, society and government in the German Democratic Republic:
    basic documents / edited by J.K.A. Thomaneck and James Mellis.
        p.   cm.
        "Companion volume to Politics and government in the Federal
    Republic of Germany"—Editor's pref.
        Bibliography: p.
        Includes index.
        ISBN 0–85496–247–6 : $40.00 (est.)
        1. Germany (East)—Politics and government—Sources.
    2. Germany (East)—Social conditions—Sources.   I. Thomaneck, Jürgen
    II. Mellis, James
    JN3971.5.A2P65 1989
    320.943—dc19

Printed in Great Britain by Short Run Press Ltd, Exeter

JN
3971.5
.A2
P65
1989

Contents

of the German People's Council, 19 March — *D20:* From the proclamation on the October elections by the National Council of the National Front of democratic Germany, 15 May 1950. — *D21*: From the programme of the National Front of democratic Germany, 15 February 1950. — *D22*: From the report of the meeting of the Central Party Committee of the LDPD in Berlin, 13 May 1948. — *D23*: From the minutes of the meeting of the Principal Committee of the CDU, 5 October 1949. — *D24*: Internal file note from the SED party committee on the Democratic Farmers' Party, 18 June 1948. — *D25*: From the "Ten Demands" of the National Democratic Party of Germany, 19 June 1948. — *D26*: Internal file note from the SED party committee on the founding of the NDPD, June 1948. — *D27*: From the resolution of the 1st Party Conference: the SED becomes a "party of the new type", 28 January 1949. — *D28*: Law on the Constitution of the Provisional People's Chamber of the GDR, 7 October 1949. — *D29*: From the 1949 GDR constitution. — *D30*: From the Constitution of the German Democratic Republic, 8 April 1968. — *D31*: From the amendments to the Constitution, 7 October 1974. — *D32*: Law on Elections to the Representative Assemblies of the German Democratic Republic: Election Law of 24 June 1976. — *D33*: From the Constitution of the Socialist Unity Party of Germany. — *D34*: Law on the Local Elected Assemblies and their Organs in the German Democratic Republic, 12 July 1973. — *D35*: From an article on the SED and the Bloc parties, January 1974. — *D36*: Greetings from the Central Committee of the SED to the Twelfth Party Congress of the Democratic Farmers' Party of Germany, April 1987. — *D37*: Message of greeting from the Central Committee of the SED to the Thirteenth Party Congress of the National Democratic Party of Germany, May 1987. — *D38*: Message of greeting from the National Democratic Party of Germany to the Central Committee of the SED, May 1987. — *D39*: Report on Erich Honecker's meeting with leaders of the other political parties and the National Front, November 1987. — *D40*: Organizational structure of the SED. — *D41*: From the programme of the Socialist Unity Party of Germany. — *D42*: The construction of an advanced socialist society in the German Democratic Republic. — *D43*: Political parties and political representation, from *The German Democratic Republic*, the official handbook produced by the foreign press agency Panorama DDR. — *D44*: Resolution of the Central Committee of the SED and the Council of Ministers of the GDR on the Workers' and Farmers' Inspectorate of the GDR, 6 August 1974. — *D45*: Visit to the Politburo.

3. Public Opinion, Mass Organizations and the Organization of the Masses 123

D46: From Walter Ulbricht's speech on Socialism as a Socio-economic

Formation, 12 September 1967. — *D47*: From Walter Ulbricht's definition of the "Socialist Human Community", 22 March 1969. — *D48*: From Kurt Hager: speech on the Advanced Socialist Society, 14 October 1971. — *D49*: From the definition of "revolution" in the Dictionary of Marxist-Leninist Philosophy. — *D50*: Letter to Erich Honecker from the Democratic Women's Federation of Germany (DFD). — *D51*: Excerpt from Inge Lange's article "Policies on Women in the 35th Year of Our Republic's Existence", January 1984. — *D52*: Report by the Committee of the Democratic Women's League of Germany. — *D53*: From the general directive on the economic plan. — *D54*: From the president's speech at the Eleventh Congress of the League of Culture, June 1987. — *D55*: From the report on the Sixth Conference of the FDJ in *Neues Deutschland*. — *D56*: On the role of the Free German Youth Movement as a "helper and reserve of the Party", from Erich Honecker's report to the Tenth Party Congress of the SED. — *D57*: From the report by Harry Tisch to the Eleventh Congress of the Confederation of Free German Trade Unions, 23 April 1987. — *D58*: Report on a discussion between Harry Tisch and leading Gera trade unionists, 22 August 1987. — *D59*: From the closing statement by Harry Tisch to the Eleventh Congress of the Confederation of Free German Trade Unions, 25 April 1987. — *D60*: From Lenin's "Role and Function of the Trade Unions under the New Economic Policy". — *D61*: From the account of the Third FDGB Congress in the official history of the FDGB, 30 August–3 September 1950. — *D62*: Proclamation of the Founding of New Free Trade Unions, 15 June 1945. — *D63*: From Walter Ulbricht's speech at the First Trade Union Conference in Halle/Saale, 29 August 1945. — *D64*: From Walter Ulbricht's speech to the Second Party Congress of the Socialist Unity Party of Germany, Berlin, 20–4 September 1947. — *D65*: From Walter Ulbricht's speech to the FDGB committee conference, 6–7 July 1948. — *D66*: Extract from the constitution of the FDGB. — *D67*: From Walter Ulbricht's speech at the Second Party Conference of the SED, 9–12 July 1952. — *D68*: On the role and duties of the trade unions, from Erich Honecker's report to the Tenth Party Congress of the SED, April 1981. — *D69*: From the President's Report at the Ninth Congress of the Chamber of Technology (KDT), 5 December 1987. — *D70*: Promotion of television and radio in the directives for the Five-Year Plan 1976–1980. — *D71*: On increasing the impact of ideological work on the masses, from Erich Honecker's report to the Tenth Congress of the SED. — *D72*: Churches and other religious communities, from the foreign press agency's official handbook. — *D73*: From the Report on Erich Honecker's Talks with Church Leaders, 6 March 1978. — *D74*: From an interview with Erich Honecker on Luther and Church-State relations in the GDR, 6 October 1983. — *D75*: From the declaration by the leaders of the Evangelical Church in the GDR on the tenth anniversary of the Helsinki Agreement, 1 August 1985. — *D76*: From "Theses concerning Martin Luther: The 500th Anniversary of the Reformer's Birth"; the official quincentenary brochure.

4. Economic and Social Policy   167

D77: From the Programme of the SED: on the unity of economic and social policies, May 1976. — *D78*: From the handbook of the planned socialist economy published by the State Planning Commission of the GDR. — *D79*: From the statement by Willi Stoph, chairman of the Council of Ministers, in support of the Five-Year Plan for the GDR's national economic development 1986–1990 and the 1987 National Economic Plan, November 1986. — *D80*: From the GDR Central Statistical Office's report on the fulfilment of the economic plan in the first half of 1987. — *D81*: From the speech of the Chairman of the Council of Ministers of the GDR, Willi Stoph, Member of the Politburo of the Central Committee of the SED, to the Fifth Session of the People's Chamber of the GDR, introducing the Bill on the National Economic Plan for 1988, 18 December 1987. — *D82*: Law on the integrated socialist education system. — *D83*: From the Programme of the SED: on the development of education and the communist upbringing of youth. — *D84*: From the Five-Year Plan Act 1986–1990, adopted on 27 November 1986: on general and technical education. — *D85*: From the Law on the National Economic Plan for 1988, 19 December 1987. — *D86*: From Rudolf Bahro's *The Alternative*; an alternative view of education policies. — *D87*: From a speech made to the Third Congress of the FDGB in 1950. — *D88*: From the address by the Secretary of the Central Council of the FDJ to the Third Congress of the FDGB, 1950. — *D89*: From Walter Ulbricht's report and final address to the Second Party Conference of the SED, 9–12 July 1950. — *D90*: From Erich Honecker's report to the Ninth Party Congress: on the growing role of the trade unions and the further promotion of women. — *D91*: From the directives for the Five-Year Plan 1976–1980: on social policies in the enterprises. — *D92*: From the SED's programme: on the promotion of women. — *D93*: From Erich Honecker's report to the Tenth Party Congress of the SED: the women's policy of the SED, April 1981. — *D94*: From the Directives for the Five-Year Plan 1986–1990, on social policy in enterprises. — *D95*: From the Five-Year Plan Act 1986–1990, adopted on 27 November 1986: on catering and health care. — *D96*: From the Central Committee's report to the Eleventh Party Congress of the SED: on education and training, April 1986. — *D97*: From the report by Erich Honecker to the Eleventh Party Congress of the SED in April 1986: women in employment. — *D98*: From the Central Statistical Office's report for the first half of 1987: improvements in provision for children. — *D99*: Law on the participation of young people in shaping the advanced socialist society, and on their all-round promotion in the German Democratic Republic: Youth Law of the GDR, 28 January 1974. — *D100*: From the Labour Code of the GDR of 16 June 1977. — *D101*: From the decree on the promotion of women students with a child and expectant mothers studying at colleges and technical schools of 10 May 1972. — *D102*: From the regulation on apprenticeship of 15 December 1977. — *D103*: From the foreign press agency's official handbook *The German Democratic Republic*: on social policies for the promotion of families and working women. — *D104*: From Erich Honecker's address during consultations between the Secretariat of the Central Committee of the SED and the First Secretaries of the District Party Organizations, 12 February 1988.

5. The Judiciary, Security and Defence — 238

D105: From the official handbook *The German Democratic Republic*: on the administration of justice. — *D106*: From the foreign press agency's booklet on the GDR legal system. — *D107*: Report on the Plenary Meeting of the Supreme Court of the GDR, 16 December 1987. — *D108*: Court report from *Neues Deutschland*. — *D109*: From Werner Felfe's address to the Fifth Meeting of the Central Committee of the SED, 16 December 1987. — *D110*: From the Central Committee's report to the Eleventh Party Congress of the SED, April 1986. — *D111*: From the preamble to the decree by the Council of Ministers on the People's Police, 9 December 1964. — *D112*: From the Central Committee of the SED's congratulations to Erich Mielke. — *D113*: From Deputy Prime Minister Willi Stoph's declaration on the law setting up the National Peoples's Army, 18 January 1956. — *D114*: Law on the Creation of the National People's Army and of the Ministry for National Defence, 18 January 1956. — *D115*: From the Law on General Compulsory Military Service, 24 January 1962. — *D116*: From an article in *Neues Deutschland* by Colonel H. Herbel, 3 February 1962. — *D117*: From the Constitution of the German Democratic Republic, 8 April 1968. — *D118*: From the programme of the SED: on national defence, May 1976. — *D119*: From the official handbook *The German Democratic Republic*: on the National People's Army. — *D120*: From Werner Felfe's report on behalf of the Politburo to the Fifth Meeting of the Central Committee of the SED, 16 December 1987. — *D121*: Report on the verification agreement for intermediate-range missiles, 23 December 1987.

6. Foreign Relations — 265

D122: Bundestag Declaration, 28 June 1956: The Hallstein Doctrine. — *D123(a)*: Treaty on the basis of relations between the Federal Republic of Germany and the German Democratic Republic —

D123(b): Letter from the government of the FRG to the government of the GDR on German unity, 21 December 1972. — *D123(c)*: Supplementary protocol to the treaty on the basis of relations between the FRG and the GDR. — *D123(d)*: Statements on record. — *D124*: Declaration of the governments of the US, France, the USSR and GB, 18 June 1973. — *D125(a)*: Art. I of the Constitution of 1949. — *D125(b)*: Amendment to the Constitution, 1968. — *D125(c)*: Amendment to the Constitution, 1974. — *D126(a)*: The Law on Citizenship (Gesetz über die Staatsbürgerschaft der Deutschen Demokratischen Republik, Staatsbürgerschaftensgesetz), 20 February 1967. — *D126(b)*: Additional law on questions of citizenship (. . . zur Regelung von Fragen der Staatsbürgerschaft), 16 October 1972. — *D127*: Speech by Erich Honecker, General Secretary of the SED and Chairman of the Council of State (Staatsratsvorsitzender), on "Topical Questions of the Domestic and Foreign Policy of the GDR", at Gera, 13 October 1980. — *D128*: From the toast by Erich Honecker at a dinner in the "Redoute", Bonn, with Federal Chancellor Helmut Kohl in September 1987. — *D129*: Joint Communique on the official visit of the General Secretary of the Central Committee of the Socialist Unity Party of Germany and Chairman of the Council of State of the GDR, Erich Honecker, to the FRG from 7–11 September 1987. — *D130*: From the Programme of the SED: on relations with the FRG, May 1976. — *D131*: From the Politburo's report to the Fifth meeting of the Central Committee: on co-operation with socialist and social democratic parties, 16 December 1987. — *D132*: The West German Undersecretary of State for Foreign Affairs (Staatssekretär Walter Hallstein, speaking in the Bundestag on the special trade relationship between the two German states, 21 March 1957. — *D133*: From the directives for the Five-Year Plan 1981–1985 issued by the Tenth Party Congress of the SED, April 1981. — *D134*: From the Constitution of the GDR, 8 April 1968. — *D135*: From the programme of the SED: on foreign policy. — *D136*: From the Politburo report by Werner Felfe to the Fifth meeting of the Central Committee of the SED: co-operation with other socialist countries. — *D137*: From the Politburo report by Werner Felfe to the Fifth meeting of the Central Committee of the SED: co-operation with countries in Asia, Africa and Latin America. — *D138*: From the official handbook *The German Democratic Republic*: on friendship and co-operation with nations in Asia, Africa and Latin America. — *D139*: The GDR and Albania agree to exchange ambassadors. — *D140*: Albanian delegation's visit to Minister of Health, 16 December 1987.

7. Literature and Culture 297

D141: From Anna Seghers' speech on "Literature's share in forming the consciousness of the people", given at the Fourth Writers' Congress in

1956. — *D142*: From the speech by Wilhelm Pieck at the first cultural conference of the KPD, 3–5 February 1946. — *D143*: From the proclamation founding the "League of Culture for the Democratic Renewal of Germany", 4 July 1945. — *D144*: From Walter Ulbricht's speech at the "Working Meeting of Party Writers and Artists" in September 1948. — *D145*: Cultural tasks under the Two-Year Plan, from the First Party Conference of the SED, 25–28 January 1949. — *D146*: Prime Minister Otto Grotewohl on the relation between politics and art, August 1951. — *D147*: From the Central Committee of the SED's resolution on writers and authors accepted at the Twenty Fifth Plenum, 27 October 1955. — *D148*: Alexander Abusch on the role of writers and artists (1957). — *D149*: From Walter Ulbricht's address to the Fifth Party Congress of the SED, 10–16 July 1958. — *D150*: From the resolutions of the Fifth Party Congress of the SED, 10–16 July 1958. — *D151*: From V.I. Lenin, "On Party Organization and Party Literature". — *D152*: From Walter Ulbricht's closing speech at the Authors' Conference of the Mitteldeutscher Verlag Halle/Saale, held in the Palace of Culture of the Bitterfeld Electrochemical Combine, 24 April 1959. — *D153*: Resolutions passed at the Bitterfeld Conference. — *D154*: From Kurt Hager's speech to the Tenth meeting of the Central Committee of the SED, 28–9 April 1969. — *D155*: From Erich Honecker's speech to a mass meeting of the Leipzig Region Party Organization, 10 March 1972. — *D156*: From Erich Honecker's speech to the 9th Plenum of the Central Committee of the SED, May 1973. — *D157*: The socialist state and culture. — *D158*: From the Act relating to the local assemblies and their agencies in the GDR of 12 July 1973. — *D159*: Nationalized industries and culture. — *D160*: Youth and culture. — *D161*: From the programme of the SED: on the development of a socialist national culture, May 1976. — *D162*: From the Central Committee's report to the Eleventh Party Congress of the SED, April 1986. — *D163*: From the Directives for the Five-Year Plan, 1986–1990. — *D164*: From the report on the Tenth Writers' Congress of the GDR in *Neues Deutschland*, 27 November 1987. — *D165*: From the speech by Christoph Hein at the Tenth Writers' Congress of the GDR, November 1987. — *D166*: From the catalogue of the Tenth Art Exhibition of the GDR 1987/88.

Editors' Preface

The aim of this book is to serve as a companion volume to *Politics and Government in the Federal Republic of Germany: Basic Documents* (ed. by C.C. Schweitzer, D. Karsten, R. Spencer, R.T. Cole, D.P. Kommers, A.J. Nicholls; Berg Publishers, Leamington Spa, 1984). The book attempts to give English-speaking readers interested in present-day Germany access to major source materials relating to the politics, government, and society of the German Democratic Republic. It describes the GDR societal and political system of the 1980s but emphasizes the historical development of the various parts of this system. It is in the nature of such a collection that the documents present the GDR's own view of itself; the chapter introductions place the documents in context, but readers are referred to the bibliography for critical analysis and background.

Interest in the German Democratic Republic has been growing worldwide, stimulated by the leading part that country is now playing in the community of states embracing socialism. It is regarded very much as the most important junior partner of the USSR, and its presence can be seen all over the world, be it in Cuba, Ethiopia, Angola, or Vietnam. Interest has also been stimulated by the GDR's undoubted economic achievements. While a number of introductory accounts of the history and society of the GDR are available for the English-speaking world, the documentary basis needed to complement such explanatory works is lacking. In the present edition, the editors have attempted to set out the documents in such a way that each section forms a self-contained unit. Inevitably it was necessary to be highly selective and therefore, as with any anthology or selection of documents, it is possible to take issue with the choice of documents and topics. Ideally speaking, a bilingual presentation of documents would meet the demands of interpretative methodology much better; nevertheless, we hope that teachers and students of political science, recent history, international relations, and German studies will find this volume of assistance in their course work and also of use in stimulating interest in the subject as a basis for further research. The editors of this volume have had considerable experience of teaching GDR studies at British universities and have themselves felt the need for a book of this kind.

The documents printed in this volume are taken from original German sources. Where a suitable English translation already existed, we have utilized and acknowledged this.

Finally, we would like to express our indebtedness to the editors of the volume on West Germany who have provided us with a model for the layout and many of the selection criteria.

Abbreviations

ABI   Arbeiter- und Bauern-Inspektion: Workers' and Farmers' Inspectorate (Control body in matters economic)

CDU   Christlich-Demokratische Union: Christian Democratic Union

CMEA   Council for Mutual Economic Assistance (Comecon)

DBD   Demokratische Bauernpartei Deutschlands: Democratic Farmers' Party of Germany

DDR   Deutsche Demokratische Republik: German Democratic Republic

DFD   Demokratischer Frauenbund Deutschlands: Democratic Women's Federation of Germany

DTSB   Deutscher Turn- und Sportbund: German Gymnastics and Sports Federation

FDGB   Freier Deutscher Gewerkschaftsbund: Free German Trade Union Congress

FDJ   Freie Deutsche Jugend: Free German Youth

GST   Gesellschaft für Sport und Technik: Society for Sport and Technology

KB   Kulturbund: League of Culture

KPD   Kommunistische Partei Deutschlands: Communist Party of Germany

LDPD   Liberal-Demokratische Partei Deutschlands: Liberal Democratic Party of Germany

LPG   Landwirtschaftliche Produktionsgenossenschaft: Agricultural Production Co-operative

MfS   Ministerium für Staatssicherheit: Ministry for State Security

ND   Neues Deutschland ("New Germany"; SED party newspaper)

NF   Nationale Front: National Front

NVA   Nationale Volksarmee: National People's Army

RGW   Rat für gegenseitige Wirtschaftshilfe: Council for Mutual Economic Assistance (as CMEA)

SED   Sozialistische Einheitspartei Deutschlands: Socialist Unity Party of Germany

SMAD   Sowjetische Militäradministration in Deutschland: Soviet Military Administration in Germany

SPD   Sozialdemokratische Partei Deutschlands: Social Democratic

	Party of Germany
SSD	Staatssicherheitsdienst: State Security Service (Also known as SD or Stasi)
VdgB	Vereinigung der gegenseitigen Bauernhilfe: Farmers' Association for Mutual Assistance
VEB	Volkseigener Betrieb: Nationally Owned Enterprise
ZK	Zentralkomitee: Central Committee (usually of the SED)

Introduction

The German Democratic Republic evolved in the immediate post-war years and formally came into existence in 1949. Like the Federal Republic, it is yet another state in the course of German history whose creation was determined neither by ethnic criteria, nor by the notion of a nation state, nor by "natural" boundaries.[1] Together with the Federal Republic, the GDR resulted from the global political conditions prevailing at the time. The GDR was, of course, created out of the Soviet Occupation Zone. Although its original constituent parts had some historical and political tradition, with such former German states as Sachsen-Anhalt or Mecklenburg persisting as *Länder* until 1952, the present constituent parts (the *Bezirke* or regions) are arbitrary and artificial in the sense of being totally new creations. Such an artificial creation of a new state both as a whole and in respect of its constituent parts puts the legitimacy of such a state into question both internally and externally. The question of legitimacy was compounded by the fact that internally the German Democratic Republic could not rely on a population consensus, a factor constantly highlighted by West German propaganda which emphasized that the citizens of the GDR had never elected their own government in free elections, and which branded the GDR as a dictatorship.[2] Externally, the GDR lived in diplomatic purdah until the advent of Brandt's *Ostpolitik* at the beginning of the 1970s. The Federal Republic claimed the right to speak for all Germans, and in international terms the GDR was seen by the West as a mere satellite of the Soviet Union.[3] The GDR attempted to tackle the question of legitimacy by claiming to be the true anti-fascist democratic Germany where, in line with the Potsdam agreements, the Nazi past and the remnants of Nazism had been eradicated. By contrast the Federal Republic, in order to legitimize itself as a state, initially took recourse to the propagation of the so-called continuity theory, which saw West Germany as the constitutional successor to pre-1945 Germany. Clearly, the German Democratic Republic could not pursue such a path; and the question of legitimacy remains very much alive to date. The most recent attempt to

1

address this question was Honecker's differentiation between "nation" and "nationality" with the proclamation that the GDR had created a new type of nation, the socialist nation, where the socialist nation in the GDR is of German nationality. This differentiation stems from Stalin's distinction between socialist and bourgeois nations. Nevertheless, it is interesting to note that recently great emphasis has been placed on German national traditions, culminating in the review of attitudes towards Prussia and Martin Luther.

The German Democratic Republic is the first socialist state in German history. It has also, since its creation in 1949, shown itself to be a very successful one. The stability it has exhibited thus far has been remarkable. The peril of internal de-stabilization has manifested itself on a number of occasions, in particular in the events of June 1953 and of August 1961, and in the continuous stream of people who until 1961 voted with their feet. The peril of internal de-stabilization is compounded by the potential danger of external attempts at de-stabilization. The German Democratic Republic is a front-line state. It has a shared border with the Federal Republic, the West's front-line state in Europe, which with its successful Western democracy and material affluence is one of the great advertizements of Western capitalism. The potential for mutual de-stabilization is infinitely enhanced by the existence of a common language, cross-border family connections, and a common cultural tradition. Together with the particular position of Berlin, this provides for a unique situation.

An important factor in West Germany's political stability has been economic growth. The same can be said about the German Democratic Republic. It is often not generally recognized that the GDR too experienced an "economic miracle", albeit within the Eastern European context. Its citizens enjoy full employment and a considerable social wage. The GDR has become very much a junior partner of the Soviet Union. It can no longer be described with ease as a satellite state; its true position is more that of an ally. Furthermore, its successes in sport, with the GDR ranking among the top three in the world, have done much to create a separate East German consciousness.

Although the German Democratic Republic is a new creation both constitutionally and as a state, this does not mean that 1945 or 1949 represented absolute zero positions. The GDR could build on a continued working-class movement and consciousness. It could harness the traditional (predominantly Prussian) codes of values and attitudes, and the traditional Protestant ethic. When the division of Germany is being discussed, it is often forgotten that Mecklenburg, Brandenburg, Saxony, and Thuringia represent very different cultural attitudes from the western parts of Germany, and that Bavaria was formerly at least as remote from Schleswig as it was from Hither Pomerania.

On the other hand, despite factors of continuity, the GDR is a new and unprecedented venture in German history. In presenting an analysis of that state's history through documents, there is an evident risk of equating terms of Western constitutional and social theory with the terms used in the East. Nowhere is this more evident than, e.g. in the discrepancy perceived by Western observers between the letter of the first GDR Constitution and what actually happened in political reality. But the same conceptual gap emerges when one discusses the GDR parliament, the party system, the government, public opinion, and the media. The relationships between state and government, between state and parliament, and between government and parliament are fundamentally different from those obtaining in the UK, the FRG, or the USA. There is no equivalent in Western democracy for the role and function of the Socialist Unity Party (SED), now enshrined in the new constitution. Even students familiar with the Soviet Union will find considerable differences on close inspection.

Within the world system of "real existing socialism", the GDR provides an interesting "German" path towards socialism. It is very much a case of "Socialism with a German Face: The State that Came in from the Cold".

Notes

1. As evidenced by historical accounts, there is still considerable debate on the question whether the division of Germany is due entirely to the global political constellation and the rift between East and West in particular, or whether leading German politicians on either side played a significant role in the partitioning of Germany.
2. For a radical approach to the question of political consensus and the role of the allies cf. J.K.A. Thomaneck, 'The relationship between the GDR and the FRG: The origins', *GDR Monitor* 2 (1979/80), pp. 7–14.
3. Cf. the title of a recent book by David Childs, *The GDR: Moscow's German Ally* (London; George Allen & Unwin, 1983), which indicates a considerable shift in assessing the GDR in this respect.

1 The Origins of the German Democratic Republic, 1945–1949

When the fighting was over in Europe in May 1945, and all German soil was occupied by foreign troops, Germany was at war with nearly 60 countries. Three of these countries, however, dominated the scene: the United States of America, the Soviet Union, and Great Britain. They were broadly agreed that the most urgent task was to demilitarize Germany, to dismantle her industries, and to assume supreme power over her. At the conferences of Teheran and Yalta, where Roosevelt, Churchill, and Stalin met in person, agreements were reached on the Polish question, the division of Germany into occupation zones, and the mode of administration to be imposed. Germany westward of the rivers Oder and Neisse was to be split into three zones, and each of the great powers was to control the administration of one of these zones.[1] Berlin, however, was to be administered jointly by the three powers. Later, France was added to the three, and was assigned an occupation zone which had originally been part of the American zone.

Early in May, the unconditional surrender of Germany was signed, and one month later, on 5 June, the allied powers formally assumed supreme authority in Germany; German central authority was abolished by the Declaration of the Occupying Powers. The occupying powers were "to assume supreme authority with respect to Germany, including all the powers possessed by the German Government, the High Command, and any state, municipal or local government or authority". A Control Council consisting of the Commanders-in-Chief of the zones of occupation was established to decide on questions affecting Germany as a whole.

Despite its notes of dissonance, the Potsdam Conference in July and August 1945 did reach a number of agreements. Its joint report advocated (1) the decentralization of the political structure, with a view to rebuilding German political life according to democratic principles on a federal basis; (2) the elimination of Nazism from all areas of public life; (3) the abolition of central government, except

5

for administrative departments in the areas of finance, transport, communication, industry and foreign trade, which would form part of the work of the Allied Control Council; (4) the decentralization of German industry; (5) the punishment of prominent Nazis and war criminals; (6) the transfer westwards of 10 million Germans from east of the rivers Oder and Neisse; (7) the dismantling of German industries, primarily for purposes of reparation payments.

Each zone had its commander-in-chief, and each zone consisted of several *Länder*. Many of these, especially in the western zones, were artificial creations.[2] At zonal and *Land* level, the military authorities acted like regular governments. A further tier of administration at district level was carried out usually by a younger generation of officers. Apart from the Potsdam remits of demilitarization, decentralization of industry, denazification, and dismantling, the military authorities were faced with other urgent responsibilities. These included the tasks of dealing with ruined buildings, finding accommodation for refugees and displaced persons, distributing food, ensuring medical care, finding jobs, and providing education. For these purposes the help of the German population had to be enlisted, especially at municipal level. Within this context, political life developed again, and the first political parties emerged in the Soviet Zone.[3]

Largely due to the increasing global rift between East and West, the Control Council soon became inactive. Initially, it had decided on a proportional distribution of the refugees, it passed some labour legislation, and it agreed on the abolition of the State of Prussia. *De facto* it ceased operation in March 1948, when the Soviet Marshal Sokolovski left the Council in protest against the separatist developments in the three western zones. Following on the declaration of the Federal Republic of Germany in September 1949, the German Democratic Republic came into existence on 7 October 1949. Like its West German counterpart, it saw itself at the time as a provisional creation; it was in fact a counter creation to the Federal Republic, emerging from the People's Congress Movement (*Volkskongressbewegung*), a movement for the unity of Germany inspired and led by the Soviet Zone. The People's Congress Movement had been set up to counteract the separatist formation of a West German state.

Both the GDR and the FRG had German and non-German origins. Both states were the product of the Second World War and the ever-increasing rift between East and West. It can justifiably be argued, as indeed GDR historians argue to this day, that political, economic, and societal developments in the Soviet Zone between 1945 and 1949 were not only congruent with the Potsdam agreements but in fact constituted a proper implementation of them. It is more generally accepted nowadays that neither the Soviet Union nor political leaders in the Soviet Zone were interested in a separatist state in those years. It is more likely that there was a genuine belief in building a new society in the Soviet Zone of a kind which would look convincingly attractive at least to the working classes in the western zones. Within such a framework, developments in the Soviet Zone become more comprehensible, for a number of these developments are not only congruent with the Potsdam agreements but also laid the foundations for the establishment of a Marxist-Leninist state in the GDR. These so-called "anti-fascist democratic" measures also in some instances met the aspirations of political leaders and of the populace at large.[4]

Developments in the Soviet Zone were rapid, at times breathtakingly so in some specific areas. On 30 April 1945, the day Hitler committed suicide, a group of ten Germans known as the *Gruppe Ulbricht* landed at Frankfurt/Oder airport. Another group of Germans, the *Gruppe Ackermann*, soon followed. Both groups were led by established communist leaders, Walter Ulbricht and Anton Ackermann, but consisted of predominantly non-communist antifascists. The remit of these groups was to assist the Soviet Military Administration in its formidable task of running the Soviet Zone. The SMA encouraged the rapid development of political and trade-union life. The Communist Party published its manifesto on 11 June 1945, just over a month after Germany's surrender and before the Potsdam conference. The Social Democrats followed suit within a matter of days. The Christian Democrats issued their proclamation on 26 June, followed by the Liberals. Neither the spectrum of the parties nor their programmes differed from those which were to emerge in the western zones. Even the concept of close inter-party co-operation in the face of the total collapse of Germany and the consequences this entailed was a popular one in all zones. In the Soviet Zone, however, it assumed a much more stringent manifestation on 14 July 1945, with the formation of a United Front, the *Einheitsfront der antifaschistisch-demokratischen Parteien*, at state, district, municipal, and village level. Of course, the united front is a tactically fundamental strategic device of a Leninist party, but the *Einheitsfront* was also welcomed by the non-communist parties and the trade-union movement.[5] In the so-called *Blockausschüsse*, committees which were formed at all levels, all parties had equal representation and the right of veto. However, with the formation of the Socialist Unity Party (SED) in April 1946, the situation began to shift considerably. This fusion of the Social Democrats and the Communists understandably met the sentiments of many working-class people who had experienced the split of the labour movement in 1917 and saw labour disunity as one of the factors in Hitler's rise to dictatorial dominance. But the manner of the fusion met with disapproval, not only from the western Social Democrat leaders but also from members in the Soviet Zone. With the formation of the SED a shift took place within the United Front, for the SED proclaimed itself in favour of a socialist society, beyond an anti-fascist democratic order. Furthermore, the trade-union movement was accepted into the United Front, as also were other new parties which were *de facto* communist-led, such as the National Democrats and the Democratic Farmers' Party.

Party-political developments were underpinned by revolutionary changes in society and the economy. A major event was the land reform (*Bodenreform*) of September 1945, a programme initiated by all parties in Saxony, although two leading Christian Democrats would not agree to the expropriation of the landed gentry without compensation. A further major reconstruction of the economy was begun with the large-scale expropriation of industries in October 1945, which originated in Saxony and was overwhelmingly supported by the population in a plebiscite.[6] In June 1948 there followed the adoption of the concept of a centrally planned economy.[7] By 1948, the course was truly set for a Marxist-Leninist state; and with radically different developments in the western zones, the division of Germany had become inevitable. In the course of the implementation of the Potsdam agreements, changes in the Soviet Zone had also followed the letter of the then current handbook of socialist political economy.

Documents

D1 Protocol Between the Governments of the United Kingdom, the United States of America, and the Union of Soviet Socialist

Republics, and the Provisional Government of the French Republic
on the Zones of Occupation in Germany and the Administration of
"Greater Berlin", 12 September 1944, as amended by the Agreements
of 14 November 1944 and 26 July 1945:

The Governments of the United Kingdom of Great Britain and Northern
Ireland, the United States of America, and the Union of Soviet Socialist
Republics and the Provisional Government of the French Republic, have
reached the following agreement with regard to the execution of Article 11
of the Instrument of Unconditional Surrender of Germany:

(1) Germany, within her frontiers as they were on the 31 December 1937,
will, for the purposes of occupation, be divided into four zones, one of
which will be allotted to each of the four Powers, and a special Berlin
area, which will be under joint occupation by the four Powers.
(2) The boundaries of the four zones and of the Berlin area, and the
allocation of the four zones as between the UK, the USA, the USSR,
and the Provisional Government of the French Republic will be as
follows:

Eastern Zone . . .

The territory of Germany (including the province of East Prussia) situated
to the East of a line drawn from the point on Lübeck Bay where the
frontiers of Schleswig-Holstein and Mecklenburg meet, along . . . the western frontier of the Prussian province of Saxony and the western frontier of
Thuringia to where the latter meets the Bavarian frontier; then eastwards
along the northern frontier of Bavaria to the 1937 Czechoslovakian frontier, will be occupied by armed forces of the USSR, with the exception of
the Berlin area, for which a special system of occupation is provided below.

(*Selected documents on Germany and the question of Berlin, 1944–1961*,
London, HMSO 1961, Cmnd. 1552, pp. 27–30)

**D2 Statement by the Governments of the United Kingdom, the
United States of America, and the Union of Soviet Socialist
Republics, and the Provisional Government of the French Republic
on control machinery in Germany, 5 June 1945:**

(1) In the period when Germany is carrying out the basic requirements of
unconditional surrender, supreme authority in Germany will be exercised, on instructions from their Governments, by the British, United
States, Soviet and French Commanders-in-Chief, each in his own zone of

occupation, and also jointly, in matters affecting Germany as a whole. The four Commanders-in-Chief will together constitute the Control Council. Each Commander-in-Chief will be assisted by a Political Adviser.

(2) The Control Council, whose decisions shall be unanimous, will ensure appropriate uniformity of action by the Commanders-in-Chief in their respective zones of occupation and will reach agreed decisions on the chief questions affecting Germany as a whole.

(3) Under the Control Council, there will be a permanent Co-ordinating Committee composed of one representative of each of the four Commanders-in-Chief, and a Control Staff organized in the following Divisions (which are subject to adjustment in the light of experience): Military; Naval; Air; Transport; Political; Economic; Finance; Reparation, Deliveries and Restitution; Internal Affairs and Communications; Legal; Prisoners of War and Displaced Persons; Manpower.

There will be four heads of each Division, one designated by each Power. The staffs of the Division may include civilian as well as military Personnel, and may also in special cases include nationals of other United Nations appointed in a personal capacity.

(4) The functions of the Co-ordinating Committee and of the Control Staff will be to advise the Control Council, to carry out the Council's decisions and to transmit them to the appropriate German organs, and to supervise and control the day-to-day activities of the latter.

[. . .]

(7) The administration of the 'Greater Berlin area' will be directed by an Inter-Allied Governing Authority, which will operate under the general direction of the Control Council, and will consist of four Commandants, each of whom will serve in rotation as Chief Commandant. They will be assisted by a technical staff which will supervise and control the activities of the local German organs.

(8) The arrangements outlined above will operate during the period of occupation following German surrender, when Germany is carrying out the basic requirements of unconditional surrender. Arrangements for the subsequent period will be the subject of a separate agreement.

(Source as above)

D3 From a report on the "Ulbricht Group" by Wolfgang Leonhard, 2 May 1945:

On the morning of 2 May, the whole motorized convoy with the members of the "Ulbricht Group" and several high Soviet political officers from the central administration, all of whom spoke fluent German, started out from Bruchmühle. It was only then, on our drive to Berlin, that we experienced the full extent of the destruction and the horror. Fires, rubble, people wandering about in ragged clothing; German soldiers who were completely at a loss and no longer seemed to understand what was going on. Singing, celebrating, often drunken soldiers of the Red Army; Berlin women carrying out the first stages of clearing-up work under the supervision of Soviet soldiers. From the buildings there fluttered white flags as a token of surrender or red flags as a greeting to the Soviet troops. Many people wore white or red armbands; the particularly cautious wore both at once.

After a brief visit to the headquarters in the Lichtenberg district of Berlin we were split up; two members of the Ulbricht Group to each Berlin district. Ulbricht invited me to drive with him to the Neukölln district. That same evening, in an ordinary room in a working-class flat, lit by a flickering oil lamp, we met with a group of Neukölln communists. Although I was extremely pleased to be sitting together with real German communists for the first time, I was extremely upset even on this first evening by Ulbricht's high-handed manner. This was not a reunion with political friends but the man in charge meeting with his subordinates. Ulbricht asked the Neukölln communists a number of questions and in a brief, sober and harsh manner gave them the guidelines for their work.

(*Die Zeit* vol. 20 no. 22 of 7 May 1965)

D4 From Order No. 2 by the Head of the Soviet Military Administration in Germany, 10 June 1945:

(1) On the territory of the Soviet Occupation Zone in Germany, permission is to be given for the formation and activities of all anti-fascist parties having as their aim the final eradication of the remnants of fascism, the consolidation of the foundations of democracy and civil liberties in Germany, and the development of the involvement and participation of the broad masses of the population in this direction.

(2) The working population of the Soviet Occupation Zone in Germany is to be given the right to associate in free trade unions and organizations for the purpose of protecting the interests and rights of working people. The trade-union organizations and associations are to be given the right to conclude collective contracts with employers and to form social insurance associations and other institutions for mutual assistance, as well as cultural, educational, and other informational institutes and organizations.

(3) All the anti-fascist party organizations and free trade unions are to register their rules and programmes of activity with the municipal adminis-

tration authorities and with the military commandant and are at the same time to supply them with lists of the members of their controlling bodies.

(4) It is laid down that for the duration of the occupation government the activities of all organizations listed under points (1) and (2) shall be carried out under the supervision of the Soviet Military Administration and according to the instructions given by it.

(5) On the basis of the above, all fascist laws together with all fascist decrees, orders, commands, instructions, etc. forbidding the activities of the anti-fascist political parties and free trade unions and organizations and directed against the democratic freedoms, civil rights and interests of the German people are to be revoked.

(W. Ulbricht: *Zur Geschichte der neuesten Zeit*, vol. I.1, Berlin 1955, pp. 368 f.)

D5 From the Proclamation of the Social Democratic Party of Germany (SPD), 15 June 1945:

(4) . . . the Social Democratic Party of Germany demands:
  (1) Total eradication of all traces of the Hitler regime in legislation, dispensation of justice, and administration . . .
  (2) Security and food supply. Workers put on stand-by and formation of co-operatives in agriculture . . .
  (4) Reconstruction of the economy with the assistance of the local administrative bodies and the trade unions. Restitution of transport services as a matter of urgency. Procurement of raw materials. Removal of all restraints on the initiative of private enterprise while ensuring the protection of social interest . . .
  (6) Reorganization of social law. Liberal and democratic reform of employment law. Integration of works councils into the economy. Participation of the trade unions and consumer co-operatives in the organization of the economy . . .
  (7) Splitting-up of major landholdings to make land available for city-dwellers who want to resettle. Removal of small and medium-sized industrial enterprises to economically well-situated rural districts . . .
  (8) Nationalization of the banks, insurance companies, and mineral deposits. Nationalization of the mines and the energy supply industry. Seizure of major landholdings, viable large industrial concerns, and all war profits to be used for reconstruction. Abolition of unearned income from land ownership and rented property. Strict limitation on interest rates on mobile capital . . .
We want to conduct the struggle for the reformation of Germany primarily on the basis of organizational unity of the German working class.

We see this as a moral reparation for past political errors, intended to place a unified organization for political struggle in the hands of the younger generation. The banner of unity must be carried forward as a shining symbol in the workers' political campaign! We offer our hand in fraternal greeting to all who are for the struggle against fascism and for the people's freedom, for democracy, for socialism! . . . .
Berlin, 15 June 1945

(*Dokumente der Deutschen Politik und Geschichte von 1848 bis zur Gegenwart*, vol. VI, Berlin n.d., p. 16)

D6 From the Proclamation of the Communist Party of Germany, 11 June 1945:[8]

Not only the rubble of the destroyed cities but also the reactionary rubble from the past must be cleared away thoroughly. Let the reconstruction of Germany take place on a solid foundation so that a third repetition of catastrophic imperialist policies becomes impossible.

With the destruction of Hitlerism it is now also time to carry to its conclusion the democratization of Germany begun in 1848 in the democratic bourgeois reorganization, to remove completely the remnants of feudalism, and to eliminate the reactionary old Prussian militarism with all its political and economic ramifications.

We are of the opinion that to impose the Soviet system on Germany would be the false path, for this path is not appropriate to the present circumstances of development in Germany.

We are rather of the opinion that the decisive interests of the German people in the present situation prescribe another path for Germany, namely the path of setting up an anti-fascist, democratic government, a parliamentary democratic republic with all democratic rights and freedoms for the people.

At the present turning-point in history we communists call on all working people and all the democratic and progressive elements in the population to join in this great struggle for the democratic renewal of Germany and for the rebirth of our country.

(W. Ulbricht: *Zur Geschichte der neuesten Zeit*, vol. I.1, Berlin 1955, pp. 370 f.)

D7 Communique on the formation of a United Front of the anti-fascist democratic parties, 14 July 1945:

On 14 July 1945 the representatives of the anti-fascist democratic parties met for a first joint discussion.

The participants in the discussion were:

From the Central Committee of the Communist Party of Germany, Wilhelm Pieck, Walter Ulbricht, Franz Dahlem, Anton Ackermann, Otto Winzer;

From the Central Committee of the Social Democratic Party of Germany: Erich W. Gniffke, Otto Grotewohl, Gustav Dahrendorf, Helmut Lehmann, Otto Meier;

From the Committee of the Christian Democratic Union of Germany: Andreas Hermes, Walther Schreiber, Jakob Kaiser, Theodor Stelzer, Ernst Lemmer;

From the Committee of the Liberal Democratic Party of Germany: Waldemar Koch, Eugen Schiffer, Wilhelm Külz, Artur Lieutenant.

In an exchange characterized by the will to genuine co-operation it was agreed:

Hitler has plunged Germany into the deepest catastrophe in its history. Germany's war guilt is obvious. Large sections of the German people were under the spell of Hitlerism and its ideology and supported its wars of conquest to the bitter end. There were very many Germans who followed Hitler's policies without evidence of a will of their own and who have thus made themselves accomplices. In this way Hitler has plunged our whole people into a chaos of guilt and shame.

Only by a fundamental change in our whole people's way of life and in their attitudes, only through the creation of an anti-fascist democratic order can the nation be saved. The representatives of the four parties, while recognizing their mutual independence, have agreed the formation of a strong united front of the anti-fascist democratic parties in order to deal with the great tasks facing us with united strength. This opens up a new chapter in Germany's history.

A joint committee was formed, to which each of the four parties will send five representatives. This committee will meet at least twice a month with a changing chairman. A liaison office will organize the joint discussions and look after the exchange of material.

The joint committee has set itself the following major tasks:

(1) Co-operation in the struggle to purge Germany of the remnants of Hitlerism and to reconstruct the country on an anti-fascist democratic basis. Struggle against the poison of the Nazi ideology and against all militaristic and imperialistic ideas.

(2) Joint efforts towards reconstructing the economy as quickly as possible, to make work, bread, clothes and housing available for the population.

(3) Establishment of complete legal security on the basis of a democratic state subject to the rule of law.

(4) Guarantee of intellectual freedom and freedom of conscience, and

respect for all religious convictions and moral philosophies.

(5) Recovery of the trust of all nations, and achievement of a relationship with them based on mutual respect. Prevention of all incitement against other nations.

Genuine willingness to carry out the measures imposed by the occupation authorities and recognition of our duty to make reparations.

The parties agree to work out a common programme of action. It is recommended that the organizations of the anti-fascist democratic parties in all areas, regions, districts, and communities should join together for mutual reconstruction, as has happened centrally.

(*Deutsche Volkszeitung*, vol. 1 no. 1, 15.7. 1945)

D8 From the Programme founding the Liberal Democratic Party of Germany, 5 July 1945:

(1) External and internal liberation of the German people from the last traces of the shame and humiliation of National Socialism. Punishment of all who during the war and in the pre-war period transgressed against the law and against the principles of humanity, and also of those who bear the political responsibility for the tyranny of the National Socialists since 1933.

(2) Respect for human dignity without distinction of race or class, age or sex.

(3) Securing the elementary needs of the German people, food and clothing, national health and recreation, appropriate housing.
Reinstatement of public transport services as an essential precondition for the re-establishment of human community and order.

(4) Reordering of German communal life on a truly democratic basis with the object of political, economic, social, and cultural justice.

(5) Regaining of internal and external freedom with the rejection of all nationalistic arrogance. "No one is merely a citizen of the polity to which he belongs. Human nature rises from, and above, national bounds."

(6) Sincere participation in consolidating the peaceful coexistence of peoples and Germany's adoption into the family of nations.
Elimination of militarism and promotion of all efforts to banish war with all its misery and distress from the communal life of the nations, so that the primary ethical rule may come to be not the right of force, but the force of right.

(7) Creation of a true social ethos.

(8) Protection and promotion of all productive work in trades, crafts, art, commerce, industry, and agriculture, in office and in workshop. Right of

unhindered combination for occupational and trade-union representation.

The retention of a unified German national economy, of private property and of the free market is a prerequisite for initiative and for successful economic activity. Subordination of businesses to public control is justified only if the enterprises concerned are suitable and ready for this, and if this is required in the overwhelming interest of the common good. This also applies to agricultural enterprises of an excessive size.

[. . .]

(14) Simplification of the apparatus of state, reinstatement of an independent and efficient professional civil service as well as honorary appointments.

(15) Ordering of community life is unimaginable outside the rule of law. Therefore creation of a state governed by the rule of law, in which everyone is protected against force and injustice.

An independent judiciary is the competent body for upholding the law.

(16) The community life of our nation requires expressive and representative bodies. Our aim is a popular assembly based on universal suffrage and secret ballots. We, who come from all the productive strata of the German people, begin from this basic concept in our effort to create a new German nation and a new German state.

What unites us is the philosophy of liberalism and belief in democratic government. Everyone who shares these beliefs and rejects fascism is welcome in our work.

The necessity of co-operation with the other anti-fascist parties is self-evident to us.

(*Vorwärts und aufwärts. Wege und Ziele der Liberal-Demokratischen Partei*, Berlin 1945, pp. 54 ff.)

D9 Extract from the Order on Land Reform of the Province of Saxony, 3 September 1945:

Article 1

(1) Democratic land reform is a pressing national, economic and social necessity. Land reforms must ensure the dissolution of the extensive landholdings of the feudal nobility and gentry and put an end to the rule of the junkers and major landowners over the villages, because this rule always represented a bastion of reaction and fascism in our country and was one of the main sources of aggression and wars of conquest against other people.

The centuries-old dream of landless farm-workers and small farmers that the large landholdings should be transferred into their hands will be made reality by land reform. Thus land reform is the most important precondition for the democratic reordering and the economic improvement of our country.

Land ownership in Germany should be based on solid, healthy and productive farming units which are the private property of their owner.

(2) The aim of land reform is:

a) to increase the arable land of already existing farms under five hectares;

b) to create new, independent farming units for landless farmers, agricultural workers and small tenant farmers;

c) to give land to resettled people and refugees who have lost their land and possessions through Hitler's criminal war policy;

d) to create farms near the towns and under the control of the town administration to supply manual and office workers and tradesmen with meat and dairy products, and also to make small plots of land (allotments) available to manual and office workers for the purpose of growing vegetables;

e) to retain the existing farms used for scientific research and experimental purposes by the agricultural colleges or serving other government requirements, and to set up new ones.

Article 2

(1) To enable these measures to be carried out a land reserve will be set up from the landholdings listed under paragraphs (2), (3), and (4) of this article.

(2) The following landholdings, together with all buildings, livestock and fixtures and other agricultural property thereon, are expropriated, regardless of the size of the farm:

a) landholdings of war criminals and those responsible for the war, together with all agricultural property thereon:

b) landholdings, together with all agricultural property thereon, which belonged to the Nazi leaders and the active advocates of the Nazi party and its organizations and to the leading personalities of the Hitler state, including all those who during the period of Nazi rule were members of the Reich government and of the Reichstag.

(3) Likewise all the land and major landholdings of the feudal aristocracy and gentry extending to more than 100 hectares, together with all buildings, livestock and fixtures and other agricultural property are expropriated.

(4) The landholdings belonging to the state are also included in the land reserve for the land reform except where they are used for purposes listed under the following paragraph (5) of this article.

(5) The following landholdings and agricultural property are not subject

to expropriation:
   a) land belonging to the agricultural and scientific research institutes, experimental stations and teaching institutions;
   b) land belonging to town administrations and required for the production of agricultural produce to supply the town's inhabitants;
   c) common land and landholdings of agricultural co-operatives and schools;
   d) landholdings of monasteries, church institutions, churches and dioceses.

(*Volks-Zeitung* no. 19, 4 Sept 1945)

D10 From Order no. 124 of the Head of the Soviet Military Administration in Germany, 30 October 1945:

(1) Property located on the territory of Germany occupied by the troops of the Red Army and belonging to:
   a) the German state and its central and local authorities;
   b) the officials of the National Socialist Party, its leading members and influential supporters;
   c) the German military authorities and organizations;
   d) those societies, clubs, and associations forbidden and dissolved by the Soviet Military Command;
   e) the governments and subjects (both individuals and legal entities) of the countries participating in the war on Germany's side;
   f) persons indicated by the Soviet Military Command in special lists or in other ways, to be declared confiscated.

(2) Ownerless property located on the territory of Germany occupied by the troops of the Red Army to be taken into the temporary control of the Soviet Military Administration.

(3) All German official bodies, organizations, companies, businesses, and all private persons at present having the use of property listed in points (1) and (2) of this order, or having knowledge of such property, are required to submit a written declaration of this property to the local administrative bodies (municipal, regional, or district administration) within 15 days commencing from the day of publication of this order.

This declaration must state precisely: kind of property, its precise location, who owns it, and its condition on the day the declaration is made.

(4) The local administrative bodies are required to check the correctness of declarations submitted concerning the property listed in points (1) and (2) of this order and to take the necessary steps to register and secure all property located in their region or locality liable to confiscation or temporary control.

On the basis of the declarations submitted and material on the property they have received directly, the local administrative bodies will draw up a complete list of property liable to confiscation or temporary control and will submit this list to the appropriate military commandant by 20 November 1945 at latest.

(5) The military commandants have to supervise the work of the local bodies in receiving and collecting statements on the property listed in points (1) and (2) of this order, and after checking the lists submitted by the administrative bodies have to pass on these lists to the head of the Soviet Military Administration in the relevant province or state by 25 November 1945 at latest.

(6) The heads of the Soviet Military Administration in the provinces and states have to check the completeness and correctness of the statements on registration of property liable to confiscation or temporary control in the provinces and states, and send the lists received from the military commandants together with their own proposals for the future use of this property to the Head of the Economic Office of the Soviet Military Administration in Germany by 10 December 1945 at latest.

(7) The Head of the Economic Office of the Soviet Military Administration in Germany, Major-General Shabalin, has to present the proposals for the future use of the property declared to be confiscated or under temporary control by 25 December 1945 at latest.

(W. Ulbricht: *Zur Geschichte der neuesten Zeit*, vol. I.1, Berlin 1955, pp. 425 ff.)

D11 From the Resolution of the Unification Party Congress, 22 April 1946:

III.   The nature of the Socialist Unity Party of Germany

It is the historical task of the unified workers' movement to organize the struggle of the working class and all constructive elements of the population in a conscious and uniform manner. The Socialist Unity Party of Germany must direct the present endeavours of the working class towards the struggle for socialism and must lead the working class and all constructive elements of the population in the achievement of this, its historical mission.

The Socialist Unity Party of Germany can pursue its struggle successfully only if it unites the best and most progressive forces of the working population and by representing their interests becomes the *party of the constructive elements of the population.*

This campaign organization is founded on the democratic right of its members to make resolutions, the democratic election of all party officers, and the obligation of all members, deputies, representatives, and officers to be bound by democratically agreed resolutions.

The interests of working people are the same in all countries where the capitalist mode of production is found. The Socialist Unity Party of Germany therefore declares itself at one with the class-conscious workers of all countries. It feels solidarity with peace-loving and democratic peoples all over the world.

The Socialist Unity Party of Germany, as an independent party, campaigns in *its own* country for the true national interests of *its own* people. As a German socialist party it is the best and most progressive national force; it stands with all its strength and all its energy against all particularist tendencies and for *the economic, cultural, and political unity of Germany*.

The Socialist Unity Party of Germany will draw up a programme based on these principles and demands, which is to be presented to the membership by the committee and to be adopted at the next full party congress.

The Socialist Unity Party of Germany is the best guarantee for the unity of Germany! It will ensure victory for socialism! Socialism is the banner of the future!

Under this flag we shall be victorious!

(*Dokumente der Sozialistischen Einheitspartei Deutschlands* 1, pp. 9f.)

D12 From the basic principles and aims of the Socialist Unity Party of Germany, 22 April 1946.

The safeguarding of peace, the reconstruction of the German economy and the retention of the unity of Germany demand the destruction of the remnants of Hitler's fascism and the elimination of militarism and imperialism.

Reactionary forces must never again come to power! The unity of the labour movement and the bloc of all anti-fascist democratic parties is the prime requirement to prevent this . . .

With this considerations in mind, the Socialist Unity Party of Germany is founded on the basis of the following principles and aims:

I. Present Demands

(1) Punishment of all responsible for the war and of all war criminals. Removal of the remnants of the Hitler regime in legislature and administration. A complete purge of fascists and reactionaries anywhere in public life, in all official positions, and in economic management.

(2) Removal of capitalist monopolies, transfer of the enterprises belonging to those responsible for the war, fascists, and those with interests in the

war into the hands of the German administrative bodies.

(3) Eradication of reactionary militarism, deposition of major land-owners, and enforcement of democratic land reform.

(4) Extension of self-administration on the basis of democratically held elections. Management of the economy and of all public institutions by genuine democrats and proven anti-fascists. Systematic training of suitable working people to become officials of the self-administrative bodies, teachers, lay judges, and works' managers, with special attention to the advancement of women.

(5) Transfer of all public enterprises, of mineral resources and mines, of banks, savings banks and insurance companies into the hands of the local authorities, provinces and states or to the government of all Germany. Combination of economic enterprises in chambers of commerce with participation on equal terms by trade unions and co-operatives. Fullest promotion of co-operative principle. Limitation on employers' profits and protection against capitalist exploitation for the working population.

(6) Reconstruction of the economy and safeguarding of the currency on the basis of economic planning. Planned promotion of consumer goods production by industry and trades, with the involvement of private initiative. Fullest intensification and promotion of agriculture. Reconstruction of the ruined towns and cities and accelerated re-establishment of transport and traffic safety. Creation of the basis for Germany's reintegration into international trade by the export of consumer goods and the import of necessary raw materials and foodstuffs, with the assistance of international trade credit where necessary. Reconstruction of the credit system through public credit institutes. Provision of work for all working people. Ensuring the supply of the necessities of life, food, clothing, housing, and heating, for the broad mass of the population.

(7) Democratic tax reform. Simplification of the taxation system by combining taxes of various kinds. Increased consideration of social situation in tax assessment. The better-off are to bear the greater war burdens.

(8) Safeguarding of the democratic rights of the people. Freedom to express opinions in words, pictures, and writing, subject to the preservation of democratic government from reactionary attacks. Freedom of thought and religion. Equality of all citizens before the law irrespective of race or sex. Equal rights for women in public life and at work. State protection for the individual. Democratic reform of the legal system and the courts.

(9) Safeguarding of the rights to form coalitions, to strike, and to collective bargaining. Recognition of works councils as the legal representation of workers and employees in an enterprise. Participation of works councils on equal terms in all questions relating to the enterprise and production . . .

II. The struggle for socialism

However the realization of these present demands does not in itself mean the removal of the system of capitalist exploitation and oppression and the abolition of the anarchy of the capitalist mode of production, or the final guarantee of peace.

The aim of the Socialist Unity Party of Germany is liberation from all kinds of exploitation and oppression, from economic crises, poverty, unemployment, and imperialistic threats of war. This aim, the solution of the national and social questions affecting the life of our people, can only be achieved through socialism.

The Socialist Unity Party of Germany is fighting to transform capitalist ownership of the means of production into social ownership, to transform capitalist goods production into a socialist production carried on by and for society. In bourgeois society the working class is the exploited and oppressed class. It can free itself from exploitation and oppression only by at the same time freeing all of society from exploitation and oppression for ever and setting up a socialist society. Socialism ensures that all nations and all individuals can freely exercise their rights and develop their potential. It is only with socialism that humankind enters into the era of freedom and universal welfare.

The basic precondition for the institution of a socialist society is the seizure of political power by the working class. In this it allies itself with the remainder of the working population.

The Socialist Unity Party of Germany is fighting for this new state on the soil of the German Democratic Republic.

The present unique position in Germany which has arisen from the break-up of the reactionary apparatus of state power and the construction of a democratic state on a new economic basis offers the possibility of preventing the reactionary forces from using the means of force and civil war to oppose the final liberation of the working class. The Socialist Unity Party of Germany wishes to take the democratic path to socialism; however, it will have recourse to revolutionary methods if the capitalist class goes beyond the bounds of democracy.

III. The nature of the Socialist Unity Party of Germany

It is the historical task of the unified workers' movement to organize the struggle of the working class and all constructive elements of the population in a conscious and uniform manner. The Socialist Unity Party of Germany must direct the present endeavours of the working class towards the struggle for socialism and must lead the working class and all constructive elements of the population in the achievement of this, its historical mission.

The Socialist Unity Party of Germany can pursue its struggle successfully only if it unites the best and most progressive forces of the working population and by representing their interests becomes the party of the constructive elements of the population.

This campaign organization is founded on the democratic right of its members to make resolutions, the democratic election of all party officers, and the obligation of all members, deputies, representatives, and officers to be bound by democratically-agreed decisions.

The interests of working people are the same in all countries where the capitalist mode of production is found. The Socialist Unity Party of Germany therefore declares itself at one with the class-concious workers of all countries. It feels solidarity with peace-loving and democratic peoples all over the world.

The Socialist Unity Party of Germany, as an independent party, campaigns in its own country for the true national interests of its own people. As a German socialist party it is the best and most progressive national force; it stands with all its strength and all its energy against all particularist tendencies and for the economic, cultural, and political unity of Germany.

(Protokoll des Vereinigungsparteitages der SPD und der KPD am 21. und 22. April, Berlin 1946, pp. 173 ff., 177 ff.)

D13 From the Saxony Law on the Transfer of Enterprises owned by War and Nazi Criminals to the Property of the People, 30 June 1946:

Article 1

All property of the Nazi Party and its groupings, and the factories and enterprises of war criminals, leaders and active supporters of the Nazi state, and also those factories and enterprises which actively assisted the war criminals and were handed over to the Administration of the State of Saxony, are declared to be expropriated and transferred to the property of the people.

Article 2

The commercial enterprises declared by this law to be property of the people and listed in a separate list are transferred by this law to the property of the Administration of the State of Saxony or to the self-administrative bodies of the municipal and rural districts, the towns and villages, or the co-operatives or trade unions.

(Die Deutsche Demokratische Republik auf dem Weg zum Sozialismus I, p. 96)

D14 Extract from the Proclamation of the German People's Congress, 26 November 1947:

Unfortunately all efforts to set up a consultative body of all the German parties to discuss the representation of the interests of the German people at the Foreign Ministers' Conference have failed due to the resistance of leading representatives of the Social Democratic Party of Germany and of bourgeois parties in the western occupation zones. Finally the leader of the Christian Democratic Union in the Soviet occupation zone has also refused his agreement. At one of the most decisive moments, the leaders of these parties have proved to be inadequate and have abandoned the German people.

The Socialist Unity Party of Germany is unable and unwilling to accept this state of affairs. It considers it to be its duty to give the German people the opportunity of making its will known to the London conference and ensuring that its voice is heard. The Socialist Unity Party of Germany issues a last-minute appeal to put aside all that separates us.

This is not a party issue; it is the central issue of our people!

On the basis of the agreement which already exists among many organizations, we suggest that all the anti-fascist democratic parties, trade unions and other mass organizations, enterprise committees and the workforces of large enterprises, farmers' organizations, and representatives of the arts and sciences in the whole of Germany should speak out together for the German people.

We issue an invitation to a *German People's Congress for Unity and a Just Peace* on 6 and 7 December 1947 in the State Opera House, 101-102 Friedrichstrasse, Berlin.

Agenda

(1) The German people's will for a just peace, for democracy and the unity of Germany: speeches and discussion

(2) *Election of a delegation to the London Foreign Ministers' Conference.*

We recommend that all parties, organizations and large enterprises should immediately respond to our proposal and should make arrangements for sending delegates to this people's congress. Further consultation among the organizations prepared to participate is to follow immediately.

(*Dokumente der Sozialistischen Einheitspartei Deutschlands 1*, pp. 260f.)

D15 Formation of the German People's Council, 19 March 1948:

The German People's Congress resolves that a German People's Council consisting of 400 members should be elected.

The German People's Council is the body which holds consultations and passes resolutions between sessions of the People's Congress.

The German People's Council carries on the struggle for the unity of Germany and for a just peace settlement.

The German People's Council plays an active part in all questions arising from the programme of aims adopted by the German People's Congress.

For this purpose specialist committees of the People's Council, consisting of circa 30 members, will be formed; initially these will be: the committee for the peace settlement, constitutional committee, economic committee, justice committee, cultural committee, committee for social policy.

The German People's Council will lay down standing orders for itself in its work. It will maintain regular contact to government and economic bodies in all parts of Germany and to the state parliaments and democratic mass organizations. The medium for publications of the People's Congress and the German People's Council is the newspaper *Deutschlands Stimme* (Germany's Voice).

The activities of the German People's Council will be directed by a presidium consisting of 29 members and headed by 3 presidents.

A secretariat to the presidium of the People's Council will be formed.

(*Die Deutsche Demokratische Republik auf dem Weg zum Sozialismus I*, p. 164)

D16 From the justification of the Two-Year Plan for 1949-50, 30 June 1948.

The expropriation of the war criminals and Nazi criminals transferred the key positions of the economy of the Zone into the hands of the people. The industrial base now consists of the nationally-owned enterprises, which in the first quarter of 1948 represented only eight per cent of the total number of industrial enterprises subject to registration but which produced almost 40 per cent of the industrial output of the major sectors of industry in the zone. Therefore although the majority of enterprises remained in private hands, the controlling position of the monopolies had been ended.

The proportion of the total output of German industry produced by the nationally-owned enterprises in the major sectors of industry in the first quarter of 1948 is shown in the following table:

sector of industry	proportion of output from nationally-owned enterprises (per cent)
1. Mining	99
2. Metallurgy	54
3. Mechanical engineering and metalworking industry	41
4. Electrical engineering industry	33
5. Precision engineering and optics	16
6. Chemical industry	35
7. Building supplies	29
8. Timber processing industry	13
9. Textile industry	32
10. Light industry	11
11. Cellulose and paper industry	44
12. Electrical energy and gas	40
Overall average of production:	39%

This shows that the people control important positions in the economy of the Soviet Zone of Occupation. The great German monopoly industrial and financial groupings were dealt a severe blow by being expropriated in one part of Germany. This transferred into the hands of the people: 38 brown coal mines, metallurgical plants, and other enterprises of the Flick Group; 59 enterprises belonging either to the Siemens or AEG electrical combines; 38 separate enterprises of the Continental Gas AG; 9 factories belonging to Mannesmann; 14 enterprises of the Rütgers Group; 11 enterprises of the Christian Dierig AG textiles group; 7 chemical works belonging to Henkel AG; 8 enterprises of the Reemtsma Group; and other important production plant belonging to a series of major German industrial combines.

The key positions in transport and communications are also in the hands of the people. 3328 kilometres of railway lines belonging to private companies, including the Pommern, Mühlhausen, Lüben, Graf von Arnim companies, the Bachstein Group etc. were transferred to popular ownership. At present 98.6 per cent of the railways are nationally owned and 1.4 per cent in the hands of private companies.

However, road and inland waterway transport are for the main part in private hands, 85 per cent of all motor vehicles and tugs are in private ownership and only 15 per cent are national property. Only 12 per cent of inland shipping belongs to the people . . .

In agriculture too, where the junkers and landed gentry were formerly in command and formed the principal support for German imperialism and fascism, the scene has changed radically. As a result of land reform the junkers, landed gentry, and other war and Nazi criminals have forfeited the whole of their land and other means of production. A stop has been put to the rule of the junkers and the landed gentry in rural areas. 6837 enterprises belonging to junkers and landed gentry in the zone, with a total landholding of 2,472,000 hectares, were expropriated. Together with the land belonging to war criminals and active Nazi-party members and with part of the national and municipal estates, a total of 3,147,000 hectares was transferred into farmers' hands. This land was divided among 204,530 families, principally landless farmers and resettled people, 79,700 enterprises belonging to farmers until then short of land, and 191,700 enterprises run by small tenants and industrial workers, a total of 475,930 enterprises. To this must be added 38,000 farms which were given forest land, so that the number of those receiving land comes to 514,730. Additionally rural communities and local administration bodies were given land and forest belonging to the landed gentry. Land reform changed the picture of rural social relationships in the Soviet Zone of Occupation; an impression of this is given by the following table:

Groups of enterprises by productive land in hectares	number of concerns		land owned	
	1939 (%)	1946 (%)	1939 (%)	1946 (%)
from 0.5 to 5.0	56	44.5	10	11.7
from 5.0 to 20.0	33	47.5	30	49
from 20.0 to 50.0	8.5	6.8	21	22.2
from 50.0 to 100.0	1.4	1	9	8.1
over 100	1.1	0.2	30	9
Total	100	100	100	100

The small- and medium-sized agricultural enterprises possessed only 40.2 per cent of the total land in 1939, as against 60.7 per cent in 1946. The proportion of large concerns has been reduced sharply — particularly in terms of land area. In 1939 there were 6300 (1.1%) large enterprises of over 100 hectares with 29.8 per cent of the total land, whereas since the completion of land reform large private enterprises no longer exist.

Farmers' land holdings remain untouched

The removal of the rule of the junkers and major landowners in rural areas consolidated the position of the working sectors of the rural population, and those with medium-sized and small farms moved into first place. As befits their position, these medium-sized and small farmers must take the leading positions in the farmers' mutual aid associations, in the agricultural co-operatives and in other agricultural bodies. However, although small in number, the farmers with large farms are still playing an important part in rural life. The medium-sized and small farmers and the new farmers must fill the leading positions from among their ranks and must carry on a struggle to maintain the democratic character of their organizations. The farmers' mutual aid association must be used to prevent new farmers, small amd medium-sized farmers selling land, cattle, and equipment and to carry on an earnest struggle to consolidate them still further economically.

The rumours spread by the junkers and landed gentry and their advocates of a further imminent land reform which could affect farmers' property are a deliberate lie and a slander. Farmers' landholdings were and will remain untouched, but the power of the major landowners and junkers over rural areas will never return.

(*Dokumente der Sozialistischen Einheitspartei Deutschlands*, Vol. II, pp. 22–25)

D17 The Construction of Socialism in the Peoples's Democracies:[9]

(1) The people's democratic revolution in the countries of central and southern Europe — in Poland, Czechoslovakia, Hungary, Romania, Bulgaria, and Albania — first fully achieved the aims of the bourgeois democratic revolution. The revolution's anti-feudal character was expressed in the implementation of a revolutionary transformation in agriculture; estate owners' land was confiscated and divided up among small and landless farmers. The anti-imperialist character of the revolution was expressed by the liberation of the peoples of central and southern Europe from the yoke of imperialism and the safeguarding of their national independence. As its anti-feudal aims were achieved, the bourgeois democratic revolution developed into a socialist revolution; this was expressed in the socialist nationalization of major industry, transport, banks, foreign trade and large-scale internal commerce. The People's Democracy began to carry out successfully the functions of the dictatorship of the proletariat. The power of the People's Democracy is based on the close alliance of the working class with working farmers under the leadership of the working class.

(2) It is characteristic for the economies of the People's Democracies in

the transition from capitalism to socialism that three fundamental forms of the economy exist side by side; the socialist sector, the sector of small-goods production, and the capitalist sector. The socialist sector plays the leading role. On the basis of objective economic laws and with the support of the socialist sector, the People's Democracies in their struggle against the capitalist elements pursue a policy aimed at the construction of socialism.

(3) The socialist industrialization of the People's Democracies is an essential condition for overcoming their technological and economic backwardness, for the construction of socialism and for increasing the prosperity of the population. Thanks to the advantages of socialist economic structures and the mutual help and co-operation within the socialist bloc, the People's Democracies have been transformed from agricultural or agricultural-industrial countries into industrial-agricultural countries.

(4) Socialist reorganization of agriculture is necessary for socialism to triumph in the People's Democracies. Socialist reorganization of farms is taking place in these countries through the gradual combination of these farms to form production co-operatives on a voluntary basis and with the retention of the farmers' private ownership of the land. Socialization of all the land will come about with the development of higher forms of production co-operatives.

(5) The construction of socialism in the People's Democracies has led to a considerable rise in working people's material and cultural standard of living. It has resulted in the abolition of unemployment and increases in workers' real wages and farmers' real income. To ensure a continued increase in working people's prosperity it is necessary to remove the disproportion between the rapid growth in industry and the slower development of agriculture. The upswing in agriculture will be ensured by the further extension of production co-operatives and by the exploitation of all reserves and the still unexhausted development possibilities of individual farms.

(Akademie der Wissenschaften der UdSSR, Institut für Ökonomie: *Politische Ökonomie: Lehrbuch*, Berlin 1955, pp. 664 f.)

Notes

1. The assessment of the Potsdam Conference is still a matter of considerable historical debate, in the sense that some historians argue to this day that the Potsdam agreements were a binding blueprint for further developments whereas others contend that they were no more than broad consensus statements.
2. For example: Bavaria was very much a traditional land or state with its own centuries-old history; Schleswig-Holstein had historically been a clearly defined entity although by the 1940s it had been a province of Prussia for eight decades; and North Rhine Westphalia was a totally new creation.

3. It is still to some extent a matter for historical speculation why the Soviet Union encouraged the very early formation of political parties and other organizations. On the other hand, the reasons for France's considerable reluctance to permit political activity are well established.

4. It must be borne in mind that land reform was also envisaged in the West, especially by the British. Cf. John Farquharson, "Land Reform in the British Zone, 1945–1947", *German History* 6 (1988), pp. 35–6.

5. Attempts at an *Einheitsfront* were not tolerated by the occupying powers in the West. *Antifa* committees were forbidden after their emergence.

6. Again, the British in particular, were in favour of industrial expropriation.

7. Again, the concept of a centrally planned economy had much initial support in the West, especially from the British.

8. One has to remember that German history is a history of some spectacular revolutionary failures. 1848 is generally agreed to have been a failed bourgeois revolution (in contrast to the French revolutions of 1789, 1830, and 1848), and the 1918/19 Revolution in Germany is now seen by GDR historians to have been a bourgeois revolution propelled by the proletariat which ultimately failed in 1933 with the advent of the Third Reich. It is in this context that the KPD intended to pick up German history in 1848 and complete the process of democratization.

9. Bearing in mind the initial plans, especially by the British, for land reform, industrial reorganization, and a planned economy, it is very dubious whether developments in the Soviet Occupied Zone can be classified in retrospect as a (socialist) revolution.

2 The State, the Constitution and Party Political Life

The formation of the United Front in the summer of 1947 did not prevent or inhibit the individual parties from standing for local elections on separate platforms. Until October 1946 a multi-party situation prevailed in elections within the five *Länder* of the Soviet Occupied Zone. Despite the possibility that some parties were inhibited in their election campaigns, the *Länder* elections of 20 October 1946 provide an indication of the relative strengths of the individual parties, with the Socialist Unity Party narrowly missing an absolute majority in three of the states, i.e. Mecklenburg, Thuringia, and Saxony. A further interesting feature of these elections is the participation of two mass organizations, the VdgB and the *Kulturbund*. The *Vereinigung der gegenseitigen Bauernhilfe* (Farmers' Mutual Aid Association) had been formed in the wake of the land reform in order to provide technical and financial aid and advice for the newly created farms. Organizationally, its leadership was in the hands of the Socialist Unity Party. The *Kulturbund zur Demokratischen Erneuerung Deutschlands* (League of Culture for the Democratic Renewal of Germany) was founded on the initiative of the Soviet Military Administration in July 1945 as part of the democratization process in Germany with the object of eliminating fascism in the cultural sphere. Both the VdgB and the *Kulturbund*, along with the Trade Union movement and the Free German Youth, became part of the United Front. Within the remit of the anti-fascist bloc, and in the historical context of the fight against the remnants of fascism and the creation of a new Germany, such an inclusion of the mass organizations made sense. But in the context of party political tradition this phenomenon constituted a radical innovation and a contrast to developments in the western zones. It was to prove an important initiative for the organization of political life in the German Democratic Republic.

The People's Congress Movement is of prime importance for an understanding of constitutional and political life in the GDR today.

In order to counteract separatist developments in the western zones and in anticipation of the London Conference of Foreign Ministers in November/December 1947, the leadership of the Socialist Unity Party issued a call to all political parties, trade unions, and other mass organizations to form an all-German "People's Congress Movement for Unity and a Just Peace" in order to avert the threat of a permanently divided Germany. The Socialist Unity Party attempted to place itself at the head of a movement with a potentially vast appeal throughout Germany. The actual first congress was timed to coincide with the London Conference and took place on 6–7 December 1947 in Berlin. It was attended by 2215 delegates, of whom 664 came from the western zones. The second congress met on 18 March 1948, the anniversary of the 1848 bourgeois-democratic revolution with its aim of a new unified Germany. The second congress elected a People's Council (*Volksrat*) of 400 members to act as an all-German representative assembly. In the meantime the People's Congress Movement had been outlawed in the western zones. The second congress also established six committees, one of which under Otto Grotewohl was to work out a constitution for a German (i.e. all-German) Democratic Republic. The People's Congress Movement also initiated a signature campaign in May/June 1948 calling for a plebiscite on the question of German unity. This campaign resulted in 14 million signatures, representing 37 per cent of the German electorate. In March 1949, the People's Council decided to hold a third congress. This was at a time when West Berlin was subject to the Berlin Blockade and preparations for a West German constitution were well under way.[1] Elections for this third congress were to be held in May 1949, and were to take place on the basis of so-called "unified lists" (*Einheitsliste*) whereby candidates were nominated by the individual parties and mass organizations, and the total membership of the People's Council was distributed according to a predetermined key. The SED was to be allocated 25 per cent of the seats, the CDU and LDPD 15 per cent each, the NDPD and the DBP 7.5 per cent each, the Free German Trade Unions 10 per cent, the Free Youth Movement and the League of Culture 5 per cent, and the rest was to go to other mass organizations. On 15 and 16 May 1949 elections were held consisting of a yes or no vote for the lists and the aims of congress: 61.8 per cent of the population in the Soviet Occupied Zone and 51.7 per cent of the population of the Soviet sector of Berlin voted yes. The third congress on 30 May 1949 accepted the proposed constitution for a German Democratic Republic. On 7 October 1949 this constitution became the constitution of the newly formed German Democratic Republic, and the second People's Council became the parliament (*Volkskammer*, People's Chamber) of the GDR. The first elections for the People's Chamber took place on 15 October 1950, again on the basis of a unified list with seats distributed according to a predetermined key; the People's Congress Movement had been renamed the National Front of a Democratic Germany. The principles of unified list and predetermined distribution have remained in force to this day; they were finalized in 1963. The key allots 127 members to the SED, 52 each to the LDPD, CDU, NDPD, and DBD, 68 members to the trade union movement, 40 to the Free German Youth movement, 35 to the Democratic Women's League, and 22 to the League of Culture. These principles were by no means uncontested and at the least constituted bargaining points between the SED on the one hand and the other parties on the other hand. Naturally, the other parties were aware that the mass organizations were either led by SED members, dependent on the Socialist Unity Party, or indeed had already declared themselves as comrades-in-arms of the SED. Furthermore, developments had taken place which had changed the party political scene substantially. Party formation had merely been a first stage in this shift. The formation of the DBD and the NDPD had been initiated under the auspices of the SED, and both the new parties declared themselves as partners of the SED. Significantly, they were a departure from the existing party framework, inasmuch as they were conceived as interest groupings. The DBD was to mobilize and enlist the support of the farmers, and the NDPD was to mobilize and enlist the middle classes, including the small entrepreneurs, former professional soldiers, and ex-Nazis. In the meantime, the SED had declared itself a party of the new type in January 1949, i.e. it had become a Marxist-Leninist party.

With these developments the new constitution of 7 October 1949 was already at variance with political reality. In the economy developments were moving rapidly towards a socialist mode of production, and in party politics the primacy of the SED had already been established. The 1949 constitution was closely modelled on the Weimar constitution, and the word "socialism" is nowhere to be found. This can of course be easily explained by the history of the constitution which was after all intended to serve the whole of Germany. During the 18 years of its life the gap between the letter of the constitution and political practice widened considerably, due partly to internal and partly to external developments. Finally in 1967, on the occasion of the 7th Party Congress of the SED, Walter Ulbricht announced that a new constitution would be drafted, and this was duly implemented by the setting up of a constitutional committee of the People's Chamber. The new constitution of 1968 refers to itself as a "socialist constitution"; the primacy of the SED is laid down constitutionally; all power is exercised by the working people; compared with 1949, the new constitution omits a number of inviolable basic rights, such as the right to strike; the concept of an-indivisible Germany no longer features, instead the GDR defines itself as a "socialist state of the German nation". This phrase was amended in the 1974 version where the reference to "the German nation" was eliminated. Whereas the 1968 constitution does not refer to "communism", this was changed by the 1974 amendments.[2] Finally, the 1974 amendments strengthened constitutionally the bond with the Soviet Union.

It is extremely difficult to apply western concepts of the state and constitutional concepts such as the division of powers to the GDR. It is more appropriate to attempt to answer a number of questions: Who is responsible to whom? What are the functions of the People's Chamber? Who introduces bills? Who is involved in the making of laws? Who controls whom? What is the role of the parties? Who has executive powers? Who elects whom? According to Article 48 of the constitution, the People's Chamber is the embodiment of the principle of the people's sovereignty, and it is the highest organ of power. The people exercise their sovereignty through the election of its 500 members every five years. The members of the People's Chamber are not professional politicians; they are otherwise gainfully employed, and merely receive attendance allowances and a free rail card. According to GDR statistics, in 1981–86 47.2 per cent of the members were workers, 10.4 per cent farmers, farm workers, etc., 17.8 per cent public service employees, and 23 per cent were members of the intelligentsia. 32.4 per cent were women. Members are organized in groups either according to their party or mass organization. Each group has the right to put questions and motions and the right to make statements. Each group has the right to initiate laws, a right also held by the council of group leaders, any 15 members, and the leadership of the trade union movement. However this right has hitherto only ever been exercised by the council of ministers and the council of state. The council of group leaders is responsible for the proper running of the chamber according to standing orders. The actual participation in the decision-making processes takes place in 15 committees dealing with foreign affairs, defence, industry, housing, transportation, etc. Each committee works according to an annual plan; each committee has a right to information and control. The council of ministers is obliged to inform committees about governmental action, and must consider the conclusions arrived at in the work of the committees. Committees can demand that the minister be present during their deliberations. One of the committees' major tasks is to deliberate on bills and to discuss these with the public. Plenary sessions of the People's Chamber have been decreasing steadily; between 1976 and 1981 the chamber met only 13 times in plenary session. The People's Chamber decides on fundamental questions of government policy, and combines legislative and executive powers. Its executive organs are the Council of State, the Council of Ministers, the National Council for Defence, and the highest organs of the judiciary. The fundamental decisions of the People's Council form the basis of the activities of the state apparatus. The overwhelming majority of these decisions are taken unanimously. The People's Chamber also appoints the Council of State and its Chair, the Chair of the Council of Ministers and on his or her nominations the ministers, the Chair of the National Council for Defence, the President and judges of the High Court, and the Chief Public Prosecutor.

Elections in the GDR are in the hands of the National Front of the GDR. Parties and mass organizations suggest candidates' names which are then placed on the unified list, which in turn is decided on by the SED. Candidates are then presented to the public at meetings organized by the National Front. At this stage the electorate can propose the rejection of a candidate; however the final decision rests with the National Front. The same procedure applies at district and regional (county) level. The actual elections are mere approbations, although it is possible to score out the name of a candidate; however it would require more than 50 per cent of the electorate to do so to stop a candidate from being elected.

Neither the elections nor the numerical allocation of seats reveals anything about the actual decision-making power. It is interesting to note, for instance, that out of the 68 trade union members in the People's Chamber 61 are also enrolled members of the SED, and that the vast majority of the members from the Free Youth Movement, the Democratic Women's League and the League of Culture are also SED members and thus bound by the SED party statute. This gives 281 SED members in the People's Chamber subject to party discipline, so that the majority of members of parliament are accountable to the SED. The same, of course, applies for regional and district councils, and most importantly at National Front level. Furthermore, the constitution itself establishes the primacy of the working class and its Marxist-Leninist party. Close co-operation and personnel overlap also exists between the state apparatus, the apparatus of the mass organizations, and the SED party organization. There is therefore *de facto* a high concentration of power within the SED. Concomitantly, the state apparatus follows the SED's lead as the executive arm of the party's policies. The SED is not just a party within the state, the state itself is part of the party. According to the constitution, the multi-party system has as its aim the integration of the dynamics of the people. The other four parties thereby become channels of communication and mobilization, fulfilling Lenin's concept of the transmission belt. The multi-party system also shifts the burden of responsibility away from the SED, not only internally where the SED could utilize the DBD in the farm collectivization programme, but also externally when, e.g. members of the CDU can act as unofficial ambassadors for the GDR. Nevertheless, possibly because of the political if not organizational dependence on the SED, the membership of the four other parties has declined since 1949.

The SED, according to its party statute, is structured on and functions according to the principle of democratic centralism. Among other things this means that the Politburo is *de facto* the chief policy making body of the GDR. The structure of the SED shows a clear congruence with the state apparatus along governmental and administrative lines. This is consolidated by personnel overlap between the state and party apparatus. Members of the Politburo and the Central Committee Secretariat are also often members of the Council of State, the Council of Ministers, and Chairs of the committees of the People's Chamber. However, despite the hierarchical decision-making processes and accountability structures, it must be pointed out that a high proportion of citizens are involved in social and political activities. It is also true to say that when major bills are sent out for discussion, a vast number of members of the public participate in the consultative process.

Nevertheless, in terms of decision-making the GDR system of government is characterized predominantly by the issuing of directives which originate in the higher echelons of the party hierarchy and proceed via party congresses to the apparatus of state such as the People's Chamber.

Documents

D18 Results of the State Elections, 20 October 1946:

Votes:

	SED	CDU	LDP	Mutual Farmers' Aid Assoc.	League of Culture
Mecklenburg	547,633	377,808	138,572	43,260	—
	49.5%	34.1%	12.5%	3.9%	
Thuringia	816,864	313,824	471,415	55,093	—
	49.3%	18.9%	28.5%	3.3%	
Saxony	1,595,281	756,740	806,163	57,229	18,565
	49.1%	23.3%	24.7%	1.7%	0.6%
Brandenburg	634,786	442,206	298,311	83,271	—
	43.9%	30.6%	20.6%	4.9%	
Saxony-Anhalt	1,063,889	507,397	695,685	56,630	—
	45.8%	21.8%	29.9%	2.5%	
Total	4,658,483	2,397,975	2,410,146	295,483	18,565

Seats:

	SED	CDU	LDP	Mutual Farmers' Aid Assoc.	League of Culture
Mecklenburg	45	31	11	3	—
Thuringia	50	19	28	3	—
Saxony	59	28	30	2	1
Brandenburg	44	31	20	2	—
Saxony-Anhalt	51	24	33	2	—

(Hermann Weber: *DDR: Dokumente zur Geschichte der Demokratischen Republik 1945–1985*, Munich 1986, p. 89)

D19 Formation of the German People's Council, 19 March 1948:

The German People's Congress resolves that a German People's Council consisting of 400 members should be elected.

The German People's Council is the body which holds consultations and passes resolutions between sessions of the People's Congress.

The German People's Council carries on the struggle for the unity of Germany and for a just peace settlement.

The German People's Council plays an active part in all questions arising from the programme of aims adopted by the German People's Congress.

For this purpose specialist committees of the People's Council, consisting of circa 30 members, will be formed; initially these will be: the committee for the peace settlement, constitutional committee, economic committee, justice committee, cultural committee, committee for social policy.

The German People's Council will lay down standing orders for itself in its work. It will maintain regular contact to government and economic bodies in all parts of Germany and to the state parliaments and democratic mass organizations. The medium for publications of the People's Congress and the German People's Council is the newspaper *Deutschlands Stimme* (Germany's Voice).

The activities of the German People's Council will be directed by a presidium consisting of 29 members and headed by 3 presidents.

(*Um ein antifaschistisch-demokratisches Deutschland. Dokumente aus den Jahren 1945-1949*, Berlin 1968, pp. 505 ff.)

D20 From the Proclamation on the October Elections by the National Council of the National Front of Democratic Germany, 15 May 1950:

The campaign programme for the national liberation of the German people was announced three months ago by the National Front of democratic Germany.

In the meantime the worldwide forces of peace and international friendship have grown in unity and strength. But the opponents of peace and national freedom are moving towards ever more open and brutal measures in the enslavement of nations and war preparations.

In this political struggle, the German Democratic Republic has achieved a new success of extraordinary importance through its consistent policy of friendship with the Soviet Union and the People's Democracies. The request for a reduction in reparations payments which our government directed to the government of the USSR was complied with in a most generous manner in a letter from Generalissimo Stalin, despite the fact that even the reparations agreed in Potsdam were not at all in proportion to the enormous damage inflicted on the peoples of the Soviet Union by Hitler's troops.

The reduction in reparations payments will make a decisive contribution to the rapid development of our peace-time economy and to the raising of the standard of living. This historical deed, together with the generous aid deliveries the Soviet Union has already supplied us with, will give the population of West Germany additional proof that our peaceful democratic path is in the interests of the German people.

By contrast, the criminal war policies of the Western occupation powers, assisted by their agents in Bonn, is leading West Germany and West Berlin ever deeper into crisis and to the threshold of ruination . . .

The German people, whose national honour and national rights have been trampled underfoot by the English, American, and French colonialists, will make its reply through the still closer union of all honourable Germans in the National Front of democratic Germany. And it will not let any talk of so-called free elections under pressure from occupying troops hold it back from organizing still closer co-operation in the National Front.

The successful policies of the government of the German Democratic Republic form the basis which made it possible for the October elections to take place in the context of the programme of the National Front of democratic Germany. This will carry our struggle for the consolidation of peace, the strengthening of the democratic order, and the unity and independence of the whole of Germany a significant step forward. Accordingly the National Council of the National Front of democratic Germany welcomes the Democratic Bloc's decisions to put forward a common election programme and a common list of candidates from the National Front of democratic Germany for the elections on 15 October. The National Council calls on the many thousand active members of the committees of the National Front of democratic Germany to prepare for the coming elections by convincing every single citizen of the correctness of our path, the struggle for a single, free, democratic Germany, for the conclusion of a peace treaty and the re-achievement of Germany's independence.

(*Vom Deutschen Volkskongress zum Nationalkongress. Herausgegeben vom Sekretariat der Nationalen Front des demokratischen Deutschland.* Berlin 1950, pp. 54 f.)

D21 From the Programme of the National Front of Democratic Germany, 15 February 1950:

The manifesto issued by the National Front of democratic Germany on 7 October 1949 has called forth a response in all parts of our German fatherland and has been warmly welcomed by the patriotic forces from the most varied circles of our people.

The National Front of democratic Germany is fighting for a lasting peace; for the unity of democratic Germany; for the conclusion of a just peace treaty and the withdrawal of all occupation troops within a period to be determined.

This is the way to obtain the unity and national independence of Germany.

(1) The formation of the German Democratic Republic is a turning-point for all Germany.

The formation of the Republic and the creation of the great National Front of democratic Germany has once and for all blocked the way towards the enslavement of all Germany by the Anglo-American imperialists and their German accomplices.

The co-operation of all patriot forces in the National Front of democratic Germany and their common struggle will make it possible to safeguard peace in central Europe and will guarantee the rise of a peaceful, independent, and democratic Germany.

All German patriots should be aware that the goal of liberating Germany and saving the nation can only be achieved through the struggle against the principal enemies of the true peaceful interests of the nation, through the struggle against the Anglo-American and French imperialists. They have split Germany and set up the Protectorate Administration in Bonn as their German tool. They have ripped up the international treaties of Yalta and Potsdam, are denying us Germans the guaranteed right to national independence and are organizing a German mercenary army. They want to turn West Germany into a colony, a strategic deployment zone for the criminal American plan of world conquest. From West Germany they are planning the war to destroy Europe. To this end they are mounting a savage propaganda attack on the Oder-Neisse Line, which is recognized by the German Democratic Republic as a border for peace.

The National Front of democratic Germany has taken on the decisive task of mobilizing and organizing the German people for the liberation of Germany from the presence and the machinations of the Anglo-American imperialists. All Germans in the east, west, south and north of Germany who love their native land and peace should be active in this struggle as members of the National Front.

(*Nationale Front des demokratischen Deutschland. Informationdienst*, Berlin, vol. 3 1950, no. 9, pp. 3 ff.)

D22 From the report of the meeting of the Central Party Committee of the LDPD in Berlin, 13 May 1948:

On 13 May 1948 the Central Party Committee of the LDPD held a regular meeting which was chaired by Professor Kastner, the vice-president of the party. At the start of the meeting, Professor Kastner gave a general account of the present political situation and stated that sequestration, denazification and land reform had been carried through and were now completed. Assurances had been given by the German Economic Commission and the SMA that there was no question of a new land reform. Regarding the forthcoming local elections, the following resolution on setting up lists of the supra-party organizations was passed by the committee:

"With regard to the forthcoming local elections, the Central Committee reconfirms the LDPD's position that the parties alone are the representatives of political will and of political parliamentary responsibility. The LDP expects that in the coming elections the supra-party organizations will not put up any separate lists, as has until now been the practice of the Confederation of Free German Trade Unions. The LDP instructs its members to make themselves available only for the election proposals of the LDP and not for any other separate lists which may now after all be set up, and expects all its supporters to continue to canvass for the LDP's election proposals."

(Quoted by: B. Itzerott: "Die Liberal-Demokratische Partei Deutschlands (LDPD)", in: H. Weber: *Parteisystem zwischen Demokratie und Volksdemokratie*, Cologne 1982, pp. 197 f.)

D23 From the minutes of the meeting of the Principal Committee of the CDU, 5 October 1959:

Present: Otto Nuschke, Reinhold Lobedanz, Hugo Hickmann, Karl Grobbel, Erich Fascher, Siegfried Trommsdorff, Arnold Gohr, Heinrich Albert, Carl Garz, Fritz Brauer, Hans-Paul Ganter-Gilmanns, Ilse Schmidt, August Hillebrand, Paul Nowak, Hermann Geiger, Josef Collett, Gerald Götting, Otto Freitag, Siegfried Witte, Gerhard Rohner, Ilse-Ruth Bubner, (Georg Dertinger)

Agenda: the political situation

Otto Nuschke reports on the political situation and the plans concerning restoration of German sovereignty, the coming into force of the Constitution of the People's Council, and the formation of a provisional government, and requests authorization to undertake the appropriate steps. A resolution to the contrary would mean abandoning the continuation of the CDU's work. Georg Dertinger follows with a report on details of the measures planned.

Professor Hickmann casts doubts on the usefulness of transforming the People's Council into a People's Chamber and suggests:

(1) A provisional German Government should be set up in Berlin.

(2) For this, a provisional People's Chamber should be formed from the state parliaments.

(3) The constitution prepared by the People's Council for the Democratic German Republic should be brought into force immediately for the Soviet Occupation Zone.

(4) The dates of the constitutionally prescribed elections for the People's Chamber and for the state parliaments should be determined at once.

The declaration of Government should state that additional elections to the local assemblies are permissible if a particular emergency situation (such as incomplete representation) makes them necessary. (The request is withdrawn if the People's Council is authorized as People's Chamber by the SMAG.)

Lobedanz puts forward the bloc principle as the basis for the provisional government. Demand: specific date for elections, run-up time allowed for government.

Personnel within the government: every minister shall staff his department with his own team.

Further demand: urgently necessary to set up a central unit for political scrutiny of the cabinet.

Gohr emphasizes the points made by Nuschke and Dertinger, supports Hickmann's proposals, raises the claim for the appointment to the ministry of agriculture.

(Hickmann re-emphasizes that Grotewohl has accepted the CDU's demands on the appointment to the ministry of agriculture)

Albert agrees with the points made by Nuschke and Dertinger and, like the previous speakers, points out that the bloc principle must be carried over into the cabinet.

As representative of the Mecklenburg CDU he also emphasizes the demands on appointments to the agriculture and finance ministries.

On the various questions concerning the bloc principle, Nuschke points out that Grotewohl had agreed to apply this bloc principle to the cabinet. (Grotewohl had also emphasized that he wished the standing orders of the old Weimar cabinet also to be used for his cabinet.)

Brauer: Demand for appointment to ministry of agriculture, indicates in his remarks, e.g. the importance of forestry, on this topic underlines the considerable measures so far undertaken by the CDU and at the same time justifies the demands for appointment to the above-mentioned ministry.

(Nuschke announces for information that the actual negotiations on appointment to individual posts will be carried out in the parties during the period 7–12 October.)

Witte refers to the CDU's special responsibility as an all-German party and also argues that the government is a provisional one; sovereignty could be regarded as complete only after an election. The party's demand, the importance of which could not be ignored, is for a firm date for elections to be set. The party must put forward as non-negotiable the demand that it should be given the appointments to the finance and agriculture ministries.

Ganter-Gilmanns also places the appointments to the finance and agriculture ministries in the forefront of his demands, and particularly emphasizes the remarks made by Minister Witte.

Fascher: Agreement with the statements made by Nuschke and Dertinger, indeed sees the gift of sovereignty a strong propaganda basis, points out however that a clear formulation of the provisional nature of this zonal government would have to be produced.

Legal basis — People's Council — People's Council constitution

Major differentiation from the Western formation of a government by the establishment of a foreign ministry.

Demand: set date for elections. Fascher further indicates that the following pairs of ministries should each be combined to form one ministry: Labour and Reconstruction, Internal and Foreign Trade, Post and Communications.

He further emphasizes that if the SED is already supplying a prime minister, it should be dissuaded from its demand to supply a vice-premier as well. Additionally the CDU should claim the state secretaryship in the national education ministry, since the LDP nomination was meaningless. He also demands finance and agriculture ministries.

Freitag: Places in the foreground as principal demand a clear decision to be given as a guideline to the working group of the People's Council (bloc principle).

Hillebrand: Formation of government replied to positively. Demand for agriculture ministry underlined, wants our candidates put forward by name.

Nowak: emphasizes the urgency of personnel appointments. Siegfried Trommsdorff sums up the general reservations, in general accepts the necessity of the new order.

Then the following resolutions are adopted unanimously: "The Principal Committee expresses its thanks to the presidents of the party in the Zone for their conduct in the present difficult situation in Germany, and expresses its complete confidence in them. It authorizes them to bring the unfinished negotiations to a conclusion taking into consideration the views which have emerged from committee deliberations.

"The conclusion of the setting-up of a separate West German state through the formation of a government and a parliament, together with the fact of the hitherto unbridgeable differences between the occupying powers on the German question face the German people with a new situation . . .

"The democratic forces in Germany, which have proved the viability and will to peace of a young German democracy, may today raise their voices as the chosen spokesmen of a new Germany and demand the re-establishment of German sovereignty, self-government and a free democratic order.

"The realization of these demands would guarantee both the re-establishment of German unity and the safeguarding of peace. The Christian Democratic Union sees the speedy introduction of such a development as the major requirement of the moment and is ready to co-operate with all democratic forces in such a work of liberation, of re-establishment of German sovereignty, and of safeguarding a parliamentary democratic order on the basis of the constitution arrived at by the People's Council, and it requests the Soviet Occupying Power to crown the policy of friendship between Germany and the Soviet Union by permitting such a development.

"We proclaim to our members and supporters in the Zone that at this time they may be proud of having held firm and participated tenaciously and faithfully in working to achieve a decisive stage in the post-war development of Germany. It is now important to enter courageously and confidently into the next stage, which has as its goal: re-establishment of the unity of Germany, the election of a German national assembly, the formation of a German government, the conclusion of the peace treaty and the withdrawal of the occupying troops."

(Hermann Weber: *DDR: Dokumente zur Geschichte der Deutschen Demokratischen Republik 1945–1985*, Munich 1986, pp. 143–7)

D24 Internal file note from the SED Party Committee on the Democratic Farmers' Party, 18 June 1948:

                                                                    Strictly confidential
copies: Comrade Dahlem
        Comrade Gniffke
        filing

Comrade Major Malish of the Information Department (of the SMAG) was only able to give a short report on the composition of the Zone committee. He stated that Goldenbaum as Zone president was practically on his own and therefore exposed to great difficulties. Comrade Malish asked that all steps should be taken to assist him (Goldenbaum) in his work. Above all, a chief editor was needed for the newspaper "*Das Bauern-Echo*" (Farmers' Echo), for which a licence has already been sought. It was also necessary to determine a reliable deputy for Goldenbaum, since Comrade Albrecht of the Mutual Farmers' Aid Association was not up to his task and should therefore only be responsible for work in Brandenburg. Comrade Goldenbaum will be in Berlin on Monday and will be directed by Comrade Malish to visit the Central Building. I urgently recommend that he should then have a discussion with Paul Merker on his present plans and his difficulties.

In Comrade Malish's opinion it is particularly important that the appropriate instruction should be given to the Personnel Policy Department to make available a chief editor and a secretary for the party.

The Zone committee consists of ten members. These are: Goldenbaum (SED), Albrecht (SED), Steffens (no party), Martin (SED), Hoffmann (SED), Fräulein Walter (no party), Richter (SED), Voss (?), Bauberg (?), Dulanski (?), — (SED).

Further details of the activity and composition of the Farmers' Party must be obtained from Comrade Goldenbaum.

(Source as above, p. 111)

D25 From the "Ten Demands" of the National Democratic Party of Germany, 19 June 1948:

(1) We National Democrats are a national party, therefore our first demand is: the unity of Germany as an indivisible republic.

(2) We demand the immediate conclusion of a just peace for the whole of Germany, and public announcement of the reparations so far paid by Germany and the reparation debts outstanding.

(3) We demand an increased expansion of peaceful German industry, particularly processing industries.

In common with all other industrial nations, Germany cannot feed itself completely from its own land resources, therefore we demand to be an equal partner in international trade to secure the foodstuffs and raw materials we need.

(4) We are in accord with the bloc of anti-fascist democratic parties in demanding the implementation of democratic land reform and the expropriation of the trusts and concerns in the whole of Germany, since the major landowners and the controllers of the trusts were the main forces behind the war . . .

(5) We stand for the protection of fundamental rights and for the improvement of the standard of living of ordinary people.

We demand that industrial production be tailored to the needs of the population.

We stand for the preservation of property earned by honourable work. In the interests of a democratic economy we support the promotion of private initiative. We demand social and humane working conditions for the working population.

We stand for the safeguarding of the way of life of the middle classes, the promotion of trades and crafts, and healthy economic conditions for the small businessman.

Former professional government employees who play a committed part in the construction of a democratic Germany must be given the opportunity to be reintegrated into their profession.

We demand adequate government financial support for orphans, widows with school-age children, invalids and the sick. In any currency reform affecting the whole of Germany we demand particular consideration be given to the interests of small savers.

(6) We stand for completely equal rights for all enfranchised Germans. We therefore demand that former National Socialists who are not guilty of any crimes should no longer be branded as "former party members" in public life. We demand that all young people covered by the political amnesty for youth should be admitted to all occupations, including the courts, the police, and as new teachers.

(7) We make the demand "Democracy only for democrats!" We want a strong democracy which, in contrast to the Weimar Republic, does not protect its enemies or allow them to camouflage themselves as democrats.

(8) We demand immediate legally-defined equal rights for women in the family and in working life.

(*Nationalzeitung* vol. 1 no. 55, 19.6.1948)

D26 Internal file note from the SED Party Committee on the founding of the NDPD, June 1948:

Strictly confidential!

copies: Comrade Dahlem
       Comrade Gniffke
      filing

Report on the National Democratic Party

The zone committee of the party consists of 11 members. These are: Professor Heilmann, formerly LDP, Halle, Senior civil servant Rühle, Halle, in practice SED, Civil servant Dallmann, Halle, former Nazi party member (not admitted to SED because of this party membership, but counts as SED in practice), Engineer Hauptmann, Thuringia, no party, previously LDP, very progressive, Frau Hochkeppler, housewife, no party, formerly KPD, in practice SED, Thuringia, Author Korn, sympathizer, no party, Saxony, League of Culture secretary Reinwarth (the only man of whom no precise estimate can be given), Saxony, Office-worker Kubitza,

Saxony, in practice SED, Director Dr Koltzenburg, Brandenburg, CDU, formerly a democrat, Herr Arlt, sympathizer, in practice SED and as executive secretary: Journalist Schneider, SED, Berlin.

State committees already exist in all states with the exception of Mecklenburg. No further details on the persons involved could be obtained either from Comrade Major Konyets (SMAD) or from Schneider, the secretary.

Schneider indicated that organizational preparations are in progress in all states of the Zone, but that adequate supervisory arrangements are at present not yet available. He did not even have a clear picture of what local and district committees of the party had already come into existence. As a partial report he mentioned four district committees in the state of Saxony, four district committees in Brandenburg, 10 or 11 local and district committees in Saxony-Anhalt.

He could give no details about the other states. The basic principles and demands of the party will be published in the *National-Zeitung* on 19 June and will simultaneously be distributed as a pamphlet with a large printing. Background materials are also being prepared for transmission to the existing groups.

Schneider refers to the great technical difficulties. He accordingly requests that some politically reliable assistants, including a secretary, two shorthand typists, and two drivers, should be made available to him by the Personnel Policy Department of the Central Secretariat. Given the danger that agents of the western occupying powers might be attached to the party leadership by way of the technical apparatus being set up, this request should definitely be complied with. Schneider intends to set up a limited central office at first, to include the Propaganda and Training Departments, the Economics Department and also the Personnel Department, which he himself will supervise. A concluding judgement of the party's growth in numbers and its political groupings cannot yet be given as the situation stands.

(Hermann Weber: *DDR: Dokumente zur Geschichte der Deutschen Demokratischen Republik 1965–1985*, Munich 1986, p. 118)

D27 From the resolution of the 1st Party Conference: the SED becomes a "party of the new type", 28 January 1949:

It must be stated self-critically that the struggle for ideological clarity within the party after the unification was not carried on actively enough. In particular, the important step towards ideological clarification taken by the second party assembly was not sufficiently analysed within the party as a whole. There were also serious weaknesses in the ideological struggle which encouraged certain elements to undertake attempts to turn the SED into an opportunistic party of the western type. These attempts were assisted by the class enemy using its Schumacher agency to send spies and agents into the ranks of our party with the task of creating anti-Soviet and nationalistic tendencies and attitudes within the SED.

The danger thus raised was averted when the party committee at its 11th assembly in June 1948 took a decisive turn and linked the task of developing the SED into a party of the new type to the acceptance of the Two-Year Plan. This work was continued in the 12th and 13th assemblies of the party committee and in particular the question of the ideological struggle was brought to the forefront of party activity. It has been shown by the party discussion which followed the 13th assembly, in which a series of fundamental questions were settled (our relationship to the Soviet Union, to Marxism-Leninism, the path to socialism, the false theory of a special German path, the degeneration of the Yugoslavian leadership, the alliance with the farming population, the role of the party, the importance and aims of work in factory groups, etc.), that the party has already achieved a high theoretical standard and far-reaching ideological unity. The differences in opinion which were resolved showed that the previous ideological difference between communists and social democrats has largely disappeared and that the party has many new members who belonged to neither of the old parties. Party discussion and practical party work have proved that the hitherto obtaining parity principle in filling all major positions has outlived its usefulness and has become an impediment to the effective deployment of members.

The party discussion has also made clear that we are on the way to becoming a party of the new type, that is a campaigning Marxist-Leninist party.

The characteristics of a party of the new type are:

The Marxist-Leninist party is the conscious vanguard of the working class. That is, it must be a workers' party which primarily has in its ranks the best elements of the working class, who are constantly heightening their class consciousness. The party can only fulfil its role as the vanguard of the proletariat if it has mastered Marxist-Leninist theory, which gives it insight into the laws of development of society. Therefore the first task in the development of the SED into a party of the new type is the political and ideological education of the membership and particularly of the office-bearers in the spirit of Marxism-Leninism.

The role of the party as vanguard of the working class is realized in the day-to-day strategic guidance of party activity. This makes it possible to direct all aspects of party activity in the areas of government, economy, and cultural life. To achieve this it is necessary to form a collective strategic party leadership by electing a Political Bureau (Politburo). . . .

The Marxist-Leninist party is founded on the principle of democratic centralism. This means strictest adherence to the principle that leading bodies and officers are subject to election and that those elected are accountable to the membership. This internal party democracy is the basis for the tight party discipline which arises from members' socialist consciousness. Party resolutions are binding on all party members, particularly for those party members active in parliaments, governments, administrative bodies, and in the leadership of the mass organizations.

Democratic centralism means the development of criticism and self-criticism within the party and supervision to ensure that resolutions are rigorously carried out by the leadership and by members.

Toleration of factions and groupings within the party is not consistent with its Marxist-Leninist character.

The Marxist-Leninist party is strengthened by the struggle against opportunism. The working class is not a closed group. The spirit of opportunism is constantly being imported into it by bourgeois elements and calls forth uncertainty and vacillation in its ranks.[3] Therefore the remorseless struggle against all opportunistic influences is an indispensable precondition for strengthening the party's campaigning power.

The highest class vigilance is the absolute duty of every party member. It is also necessary to prevent the infiltration of spies and agents of the secret services and of Schumacher's Eastern Bureau into the party and the democratic bodies.

The Marxist-Leninist party is permeated with the spirit of internationalism. This internationalism determines its place in the worldwide conflict between the war propagandists and the forces of peace, between reaction and progress, between capitalism and socialism. In this struggle the Marxist-Leninist party is firmly allied with the forces of peace and democracy, side by side with the People's Democracies and the revolutionary workers' parties all over the world. It recognizes the leading role of the CPSU(B) in the struggle against imperialism and declares it to be the duty of all working people to support the socialist Soviet Union with all their might.

(*Die nächsten Aufgaben der SED. Entschließungen der 1. Parteikonferenz der Sozialistischen Einheitspartei Deutschlands*, Berlin 1949, pp. 524 ff.)

D28 Law on the Constitution of the Provisional People's Chamber of the GDR, 7 October 1949:

Article 1

The Provisional People's Chamber of the GDR is constituted in the composition of the German People's Council elected on 30 May 1949 by the Third German People's Congress, on the basis of the Constitution of the German Democratic Republic passed by the German People's Council on 19 March 1949 and confirmed by the Third German People's Congress on 30 May 1949.

Article 2

This law comes into force on its adoption. It will be drawn up and proclaimed by the President of the Provisional People's Chamber.

(*Neues Deutschland* vol. 4 no. 236 of 8 October 1949)

D29 From the 1949 GDR Constitution, 7 October 1949:

A. Foundations of state authority

Article 1

Germany is an indivisible democratic republic; it is based on the German states.

The Republic decides on all matters essential for the existence and development of the German people in its totality; all other matters are decided on independently by the states.

The Republic's decisions are implemented by the states as a matter of principle.

There is only one single German nationality.

Article 2

The colours of the German Democratic Republic are black-red-gold.

The capital of the Republic is Berlin.

Article 3

All state power proceeds from the people.

Every citizen has the right and the duty to participate in decisions in his locality, his district, his state, and in the German Democratic Republic.

Citizens' participation in decision-making is carried out through: participation in petitions and referendums; exercise of active and passive voting rights; assumption of public positions in administration and justice.

Every citizen has the right to make submissions to the people's assembly.

State authority must serve the good of the people, freedom, peace, and democratic progress.

Those active in public service are servants of the totality and not of a party. Their activities are supervised by the people's assembly.

Article 4

All measures of state authority must be in line with the principles declared in the constitution as the content of state authority. The people's assembly decides on the constitutionality of such measures in accordance with article 66 of this constitution. Everyone has the right and the duty to resist measures which contravene the decisions of the people's assembly.

Every citizen is bound to act in accordance with the constitution and to defend it against its enemies.

Article 5

The generally recognized rules of international law are binding on the state authority and on every citizen.

It is the state authority's duty to uphold and preserve friendly relations with all nations.

No citizen may take part in acts of war serving the oppression of a nation.

B. *Content and limits of state authority*

I. *Rights of the citizen*

Article 6

All citizens have equal rights before the law.

Agitation to boycott democratic institutions and organizations, murderous agitation against democratic politicians, expressions of religious, racial, or national hatred, military propaganda and incitement to war, and all other actions directed against the principle of equal rights are crimes falling under the Criminal Law Code. Exercise of democratic rights under the constitution is not agitation to boycott.

Anyone punished for commiting these crimes may not be active either in public service or in leading positions in economic and cultural life. He loses the right to vote and to stand for election.

Article 7

Men and women have equal rights.

All laws and decrees forming an obstacle to equal rights for women are revoked.

Article 8

Personal freedom, the inviolability of the home, postal privacy and the right to settle in any chosen place are guaranteed. The state authority can limit or remove these freedoms only on the basis of the laws applying to all citizens.

Article 9

All citizens have the right within the limits of the laws applying to everyone to express their opinions freely and publicly, and to assemble peacefully and without weapons for this purpose. This freedom is not limited by any relationship of service or employment; no one may be disadvantaged for making use of this right.

There is no censorship of the press.

Article 10

No citizen may be extradited to a foreign power. Foreign nationals will neither be extradited nor expelled if they are persecuted abroad for their struggle for the principles laid down in this constitution.

Every citizen has the right to emigrate. This right may be limited only by a law of the Republic.

Article 11
The parts of the Republic where a foreign language is spoken are to be furthered in the free development of their national traditions by legislature and administration; in particular they may not be prevented from using their native language in schools, in internal administration, and in the courts.[4]

Article 12
All citizens have the right to form associations or societies for purposes which are not in conflict with criminal law . . .

Article 14
The right to belong to associations for the improvement of wages and working conditions is guaranteed for all. All agreements and measures which restrict this freedom or seek to prevent it are illegal and forbidden.

The trade union right to strike is guaranteed.

Article 15
The worker is protected by the state.

The right to work is guaranteed. By managing the economy, the state ensures work and livelihood for every citizen. Where no appropriate possibility of work can be shown to exist for a citizen, the necessary maintenance will be provided . . .

II   Economic order

Article 19
The order of economic life must be in accordance with the principles of social justice; it must ensure everyone an existence fit for human beings.

The economy has to serve the good of the whole people and the supply of its needs; it has to ensure everyone a share in the results of production commensurate with his input. Within the framework of these requirements and aims the economic freedom of the individual is guaranteed.

Article 20
Farmers, merchants and tradespeople are to be supported in developing their private initiative. Co-operative self-help is to be encouraged.

Article 21
To secure the necessities of life and to increase the prosperity of its citizens, the state draws up the public economic plan in the legislative organs with the direct participation of its citizens. Supervision of its implementation is the duty of the elected assemblies.

Article 22
Private property is guaranteed by the constitution. Its content and its limitations are set by the laws and by social duties to the community. . . .

V Religion and religious communities

Article 41
Every citizen enjoys full freedom of belief and of conscience. The right to carry on one's religion undisturbed is protected by the Republic. Institutions of religious communities, religious events and the teaching of religion may not be misused for unconstitutional or party-political ends. However, the right of the religious communities to take up a position from their own viewpoint on the major questions facing the people remains uncontested . . .

Article 43
There is no state church. The freedom of association in religious communities is guaranteed . . .

C. Structure of state authority

I People's representation in the Republic

Article 50
The supreme organ of the Republic is the People's Chamber.

Article 51
The People's Chamber consists of the deputies of the German people. The deputies are elected for a period of four years in general, equal, direct and secret elections on the principles of proportional representation.

The deputies are the representatives of the whole people. They are subject only to their conscience and not bound by mandate.

Article 52
All citizens having completed their 18th year are entitled to vote.

Any citizen having completed his 21st year may stand for election. The People's Chamber consists of 400 deputies.

Details are laid down in an election law . . .

Article 63
The competence of the People's Chamber covers:
determining and implementation of the principles of government policy;
confirmation, supervision, and recall of the government;
determining the principles of administration and supervision of all state activities;
the right of legislature, where no referendum is held;
passing resolutions on the state budget, the economic plan, the Republic's loans and borrowings, and the approval of international treaties;

the pronouncement of amnesties;

the election of the President of the Republic, together with the Chamber of States;

the election and recall of the members of the Supreme Court of the Republic and the Chief Public Prosecutor of the Republic . . .

II   Representation of the states

Article 71

A Chamber of States is formed for the representation of the German states. In the Chamber of States each state has one deputy per 500,000 inhabitants. Every state has at least one deputy.

Article 72

The deputies of the Chamber of States are elected by the state parliaments for the lifetime of that parliament and in proportion to the parties' strengths. The deputies of the Chamber of States should as a rule be members of the state parliament.

The state parliaments determine their state's attitude towards matters to be discussed in the Chamber of States. This does not affect the regulations on freedom of conscience of deputies in the individual state constitutions . . .

IV   Government of the Republic

Article 91

The government of the Republic consists of the Prime Minister and the ministers.

Article 92

The strongest party in the People's Chamber names the Prime Minister; he forms the government. All parties having at least 40 members are represented in proportion to their strength by ministers or secretaries of state. Secretaries of state participate in an advisory capacity at government meetings. If a party excludes itself, the government is formed without it.

The ministers should be deputies of the People's Chamber.

The People's Chamber confirms the government and approves the programme it submits . . .

V   President of the Republic

Article 101

The President of the Republic is elected for a four-year term in a joint session of the People's Chamber and the Chamber of States. The joint session is convened and chaired by the president of the People's Chamber.

Any citizen having completed his 35th year may be elected . . .

VI   Republic and states

Article 109
Every state must have a constitution conforming to the principles of the constitution of the Republic. The state parliament is the highest and sole representative assembly of the state.

The representative assembly must be elected in a general, equal, direct and secret election of all enfranchised citizens according to the principles of proportional representation laid down in the election law for the Republic . . .

VIII   Administration of justice

Article 126
Jurisdiction is carried out by the Supreme Court of the Republic and by the courts of the states.

Article 127
The judges are independent in their dispensation of justice and subject only to the constitution and the law . . .

IX   Self-administration

Article 139
Communities and groups of communities have the right of self-administration within the laws of the Republic and of the states. The tasks of self-administration include the agreement and implementation of all public matters affecting the economic, social and cultural life of the community or group of communities. Every task is to be carried out by the most local suitable group.

(*Die Verfassung der DDR*, Berlin 1949, pp. 13 ff)

D30 From the Constitution of the German Democratic Republic, 8 April 1968:

Section I   Principles of socialist society and state order

Chapter 1   Political principles

Article 1
The German Democratic Republic is a socialist state of the German nation. It is the political organization of working people in town and country who

are together realizing socialism under the leadership of the working class and its Marxist-Leninist party.

The capital of the German Democratic Republic is Berlin.

The state flag of the German Democratic Republic consists of the colours black-red-gold and carries in the centre of both sides the state coat of arms of the German Democratic Republic.

The state coat of arms of the German Democratic Republic consists of hammer and compasses surrounded by a wreath of corn, the lower part of which is wound with a black-red-gold ribbon.

Article 2

(1) All political power in the German Democratic Republic is exercised by the working people. The individual human being forms the focus of all efforts of socialist society and its state. The social system of socialism is constantly being perfected.

(2) The firm alliance of the working class with the class of co-operative farmers, the members of the intelligentsia and the other sections of the population, socialist ownership of the means of production, planning and management of social development in accordance with the most progressive scientific findings are inviolable principles of the socialist order of society.

(3) The exploitation of man by man is abolished for ever. What is made by the people's hands is the people's property. The socialist principle "From each according to his ability, to each according to his work" is being realized.

(4) The correspondence between the political, material and cultural interests of working people and their collectives and the requirements of society is the most important driving force of socialist society.

Article 3

(1) The alliance of all forces of the people finds its organized expression in the National Front of democratic Germany.

(2) In the National Front of democratic Germany the parties and mass organizations unite all forces of the people for common action to develop the socialist society. Thus they realize the mutual involvement of all citizens in the socialist community according to the principle that everyone bears responsibility for the whole.

Article 4

All authority serves the good of the people. It ensures their peaceful life, protects socialist society and guarantees the planned increase in the standard of living and the free development of the individual, preserves his dignity and guarantees the rights established in this constitution.

Article 5

(1) Citizens of the German Democratic Republic exercise their political power through democratically elected assemblies.

(2) The elected assemblies are the basis of the system of state authorities.

They base their activity on citizens' active participation in the preparation, implementation, and supervision of their decisions.

(3) At no time and under no conditions may bodies other than those specified in the constitution exercise state authority.

Article 6
(1) In keeping with the interests of the German people and the international obligation of all Germans, the German Democratic Republic has eradicated German militarism and Nazism on its territory and conducts a foreign policy serving peace and socialism, international understanding and security.

(2) In accordance with the principles of socialist internationalism, the German Democratic Republic cultivates and develops all-round co-operation and friendship with the Union of Soviet Socialist Republics and the other socialist states.

(3) The German Democratic Republic supports the strivings of the nations for freedom and independence and maintains co-operation with all states on a basis of equality and mutual respect.

(4) The German Democratic Republic is working for a system of collective security in Europe and a stable peace order in the world. It supports general disarmament.

(5) Militaristic and revanchist propaganda in any form, incitement to war and expression of religious, racial or national hatred will be punished as crimes.

Article 7
(1) The state authorities guarantee the inviolability of the territory of the German Democratic Republic including its airspace and territorial waters and protection and exploitation of the continental shelf.

(2) The German Democratic Republic organizes the defence of the country and the protection of the socialist order and the peaceful life of citizens. The National People's Army and the other national defence forces protect the socialist achievements of the people against all external attacks. The National People's Army carries on a close military co-operation with the armies of the Soviet Union and other socialist states in the interests of preserving peace and security.

Article 8
(1) The generally recognized rules of international law serving peace and peaceful co-operation between nations are binding on the state authority and on every citizen. The German Democratic Republic will never undertake a war of aggression or employ its armed forces against the freedom of another nation.

(2) The creation and maintenance of normal relations and the co-operation of the two German states on the basis of equality are the national concern of the German Democratic Republic. In addition the German

Democratic Republic and its citizens aspire to the surmounting of the division forced on the German nation by imperialism, the step-by-step rapprochement of the two German states, and their ultimate union on the basis of democracy and socialism.

Chapter 2   Economic principles, science, education and culture

Article 9

(1) The national economy of the German Democratic Republic is based on socialist ownership of the means of production. It develops in accordance with the economic laws of socialism on the basis of the socialist relations of production. The socialist relations of production arose as a result of the struggle against the economic system of monopoly capital, whose aggressive and adventurous policies have to date brought only misfortune on the German nation. By depriving the monopolies and major landowners of power and by the abolition of the capitalist profit economy the source of war policies and the exploitation of man by man was removed.

Socialist property has proved itself in practice.

(2) The national economy of the German Democratic Republic serves the strengthening of the socialist order, constantly improving satisfaction of the material and cultural needs of the people, the development of their personalities and their socialist social relationships.

(3) In the German Democratic Republic the principle of planning and management of the economy and of all other areas of society applies. The national economy of the German Democratic Republic is a planned socialist economy. The economic system of socialism links the central state planning and management of the basic questions of social development with individual responsibility for socialist manufacturers and local government bodies.

(4) The determination of the currency and finance system is a matter for the socialist state. Taxes are levied on the basis of laws.

(5) Foreign trade including exports and imports and dealings in foreign currency is a state monopoly.

Article 10

(1) Socialist property exists
   as national property of society as a whole,
   as co-operative common property of working collectives and
   as property of citizens' social organizations.

(2) It is the duty of the socialist state and its citizens to protect and increase socialist property.

Article 11

(1) Citizens' private property and the right of inheritance are guaranteed. Private property serves to satisfy citizens' material and cultural needs.

(2) Copyrights enjoy the protection of the socialist state.

(3) The use of property and of copyrights may not run counter to the interests of society.

Article 12

(1) Mineral wealth, mines, power stations, dams and large stretches of water, the natural resources of the continental shelf, larger industrial enterprises, banks and insurance institutions, the state farms, the highways, the transport systems of the railways, sea shipping and air traffic, post and communication systems are national property. Private possession of them is not permitted.

(2) The socialist state guarantees the exploitation of national property with the aim of achieving the best results for society. This is served by the planned socialist economy and socialist economic law. The exploitation and management of national property is carried out in principle by the nationally owned enterprises and state institutions. The state can transfer its exploitation and management by contract to co-operative or social organizations and associations. Such a transfer must serve the interests of the generality and the increase of social wealth.

Article 13

The tools, machines, equipment and buildings of the agricultural, craft, and other socialist co-operatives, and the livestock of agricultural co-operatives and the produce achieved from co-operative exploitation of the soil and from co-operative means of production are co-operative property.

Article 14

(1) The exploitation and running of private enterprises and institutions for gain must satisfy social needs and serve to raise national prosperity and increase social wealth.

(2) Close co-operation of socialist and private enterprises and institutions is promoted by the state. In accordance with the demands of society, private enterprises may on application incorporate state participation.[5]

(3) Associations in the private economy to establish economic power are not permitted.

Article 15

(1) The land of the German Democratic Republic is one of its most valuable national resources. It must be protected and used rationally. Land used for agriculture or forestry may have its intended use changed only with the approval of the government bodies responsible.

(2) In the interests of citizens' welfare state and society attend to the protection of nature. Preservation of the purity of the waters and the air and the protection of plants and animals and the scenic beauty of our country are to be guaranteed by the relevant bodies and are also a matter for every citizen.

Article 16

Expropriations are permitted only in the common interest on the basis of law and against appropriate compensation. They may only take place if the common interest being pursued cannot be achieved in another way.

Article 17
(1) Science and research and the application of their findings form an important basis of socialist society and enjoy all-round promotion by the state.

(2) By its integrated socialist education system the German Democratic Republic ensures a high level of education for all citizens, corresponding to the constantly increasing demands of society. It enables citizens to shape socialist society and to take a creative part in the development of socialist democracy.

(3) The German Democratic Republic promotes science and education with the aim of protecting and enriching society and the life of its citizens, mastering the scientific and technological revolution and guaranteeing the constant progress of socialist society.

(4) Any misuse of science directed against peace, international understanding, or against human life and dignity is forbidden.

Article 18
(1) Socialist national culture is one of the foundations of socialist society. The German Democratic Republic promotes and protects socialist culture, which serves peace, humanism, and the development of socialist society. It combats imperialist anti-culture, which serves psychological warfare and the degradation of humankind. Socialist society promotes the cultural life of the working people, cultivates all the humanist values of our national cultural heritage and of world culture, and develops socialist national culture as the concern of the whole nation.

(2) The promotion of the arts, the artistic interests and abilities of all working people, and the dissemination of artistic works and creations are the obligation of the state and of all social forces. Artistic activity is based on the artist's close contacts with the life of the people.

(3) Physical training, sport and tourism as elements of socialist culture serve citizens' all-round physical and intellectual development.

Section II   Citizen and community in the socialist society

Chapter 1   Basic rights and basic duties of the citizen

Article 19
(1) The German Democratic Republic guarantees all citizens the exercise of their rights and participation in guiding social development. It guarantees socialist legality and legal security.

(2) Respect for and protection of the dignity and freedom of the individual are mandatory for all state organs, all social forces and each individual

citizen.

(3) Free of exploitation, oppression and economic dependence, every citizen has equal rights and manifold opportunities to develop his abilities to their full extent and to develop his powers voluntarily and unhindered for the good of society and for his own advantage within the socialist community. In this way he realizes personal freedom and dignity. Citizens' relations to each other are characterized by mutual respect and assistance and by the principles of socialist morality.

(4) Conditions for acquiring and forfeiting citizenship of the German Democratic Republic are laid down by law.

Article 20
(1) Every citizen of the German Democratic Republic has the same rights and duties irrespective of nationality, race, philosophy or religious confession, social origin or position. Freedom of conscience and freedom of religion are guaranteed. All citizens are equal before the law.

(2) Men and women have equal rights and have the same legal position in all spheres of social, political and private life. The promotion of women, particularly in vocational qualification, is a social and government objective.

(3) Young people are particularly promoted in their social and vocational development. They are given all opportunity to take part responsibly in the development of the socialist order of society.

Article 21
(1) Every citizen of the German Democratic Republic has the right to help shape all aspects of the political, economic, social and cultural life of the socialist community and the socialist state. The principle of participation in working, planning, and government applies.

(2) The right to participate in decision-making and development is guaranteed in that citizens:

elect all official bodies democratically and take part in their activity and in the planning, guiding and shaping of social life;

can demand that the elected assemblies, their deputies, and the managers of state and economic bodies account to them for their actions;

express their wishes and demands through the authority of their social organizations;

can address their requests and proposals to the social, state and economic bodies;

make their will known in referendums.

(3) The realization of this right to participate in decision-making and development is at the same time a high moral obligation for every citizen. The performance of social or government functions has the recognition and support of society and the state.

Article 22
(1) Every citizen of the German Democratic Republic who has completed

his 18th year by the election day is entitled to vote.

(2) Every citizen can be elected to the local assembly if he has completed his 18th year by the election day. He can be elected to the People's Chamber if he has completed his 21st year by the election day.

(3) The conduct of elections by democratically formed election commissions, public discussion on the basic policy issues, and the nomination and scrutiny of candidates by the voters are indispensable socialist election principles.

Article 23
(1) The protection of peace and the socialist fatherland and its achievements is the right and honourable duty of the citizens of the German Democratic Republic. . .

Article 24
(1) Every citizen of the German Democratic Republic has the right to work. He has the right to a workplace and free choice of it in accordance with social needs and personal qualification. He has the right to wages according to quality and quantity of work. Men and women, adults and young people have the right to equal pay for equal work.

(2) Socially useful activity is an honourable duty for every citizen. The right to work and the duty to work form a unity.

[. . .]

Article 25
(1) Every citizen of the German Democratic Republic has equal rights to education. The educational establishments are open to all. The integrated socialist education system guarantees every citizen a continuous social education, training, and further education.

[. . .]

Article 27
(1) Every citizen of the German Democratic Republic has the right to express his opinion freely and publicly within the principles of this constitution. This right is not limited by any relationship of service or employment. No-one may be disadvantaged for making use of this right.

(2) The freedom of the press, of radio and of television is guaranteed.

Article 28
(1) All citizens have the right to assemble peacefully within the bounds of the principles and aims of the constitution.

[. . .]

Article 29
The citizens of the German Democratic Republic have the right to combine to realize their interests by common action in political parties, social organizations, associations and collectives, in accordance with the principles and aims of the constitution.

[. . .]

Chapter 2   Enterprises, towns and communities in the socialist society

Article 41
The socialist enterprises, cities and towns, communities and groups of communities are in terms of central state planning and management independent communities in which citizens work and shape their social circumstances. . .

Chapter 3   The trade unions and their rights

Article 44
(1) The free trade unions, united in the Confederation of Free German Trade Unions, are the comprehensive class organization of the working class. They look after the interests of workers, employees and members of the intelligentsia by their comprehensive participation in state, economic, and social decision-making.

(2) The trade unions are independent. No one may limit or hinder them in their activity.

[. . .]

Chapter 4   The socialist production co-operatives and their rights

[. . .]

Section III   The representative assemblies

Chapter 1   The People's Chamber

Article 48
(1) The People's Chamber is the supreme organ of state power in the German Democratic Republic. In its plenary meetings it decides basic issues of state policy.

(2) The People's Chamber is the sole organ in the German Democratic Republic with powers to amend the constitution and pass legislation. No one can limit its rights.

[. . .]

Article 50
The People's Chamber elects the chair and members of the Council of State, the chair of the National Defence Council, the president and judges of the Supreme Court and the Public Prosecutor General. They may at all times be recalled by the People's Chamber.

Article 51
The People's Chamber confirms state treaties of the German Democratic Republic and other international treaties in as far as they affect laws of the People's Chamber. It decides on the termination of these treaties.

Article 52
The People's Chamber makes the decision to place the German Democratic Republic on a defence footing. In cases of emergency the Council of State has the right to decide on the defence alert. The chairman of the Council of State proclaims the defence alert.

Article 53
The People's Chamber can decide to conduct referendums.

Article 54
The People's Chamber consists of 500 deputies elected by the people in free, general, equal and secret elections for a four-year term.

Article 55
(1) The People's Chamber elects a presidium for the duration of its elected term.

The presidium consists of the president of the People's Chamber, a vice-president and further members.

(2) The presidium's duties are to conduct the daily business of the plenary sessions. Further duties are regulated by the agenda of the People's Chamber.

[. . .]

Article 61
(1) The People's Chamber forms committees from its members. Their duty is to discuss draft laws and carry on constant supervision of the implementation of the laws in close co-operation with the voters.

[. . .]

Article 63
(1) The People's Chamber is quorate if more than half the deputies are present.

(2) The People's Chamber takes its decisions by a majority of votes. Laws changing the constitution require the agreement of at least two thirds of the elected deputies.

[. . .]

Article 65

(1) The deputies of the parties and mass organizations represented in the People's Chamber, the committees of the People's Chamber, the Council of State, the Council of Ministers and the Confederation of Free German Trade Unions have the right to put forward bills.

(2) In preparation for meetings of the People's Chamber, the Council of State deals with bills and checks their constitutionality.

(3) The committees of the People's Chamber discuss the bills and present their views to the plenary session of the People's Chamber. They are assisted in their activity by the Council of State.

(4) Drafts of laws of fundamental importance are put to the population for discussion before being decided. The results of the people's discussions are to be evaluated in the final version.

[. . .]

Chapter 2   The Council of State

Article 66

(1) As an organ of the People's Chamber, the Council of State carries out between meetings of the People's Chamber all the basic tasks arising from the laws and resolutions of the People's Chamber. It is responsible to the People's Chamber for its activity.

(2) The chairman of the Council of State represents the German Democratic Republic in international law. The Council of State decides on the conclusion of state treaties of the German Democratic Republic. They are ratified by the chairman of the Council of State. The Council of State terminates state treaties.

Article 67

(1) The Council of State consists of the chairman, his deputies, the members and the secretary.

(2) The chairman, the deputy chairmen, the members and the secretary of the Council of State are elected for a period of four years by the People's Chamber at its first meeting after an election.

[. . .]

Article 70

(1) The Council of State deals with bills for the People's Chamber and has them discussed by the committees of the People's Chamber.

[. . .]

Article 73

(1) The Council of State takes basic decisions on questions of defence and the country's security. It organizes national defence with the aid of the National Defence Council.

(2) The Council of State appoints the members of the National Defence Council. The National Defence Council is responsible for its activities to the People's Chamber and the Council of State.

Article 74

On behalf of the People's Chamber the Council of State carries out the permanent supervision of constitutionality and legality of the activity of the Supreme Court and the Public Prosecutor General.

[. . .]

Chapter 3   The Council of Ministers

Article 78

(1) On behalf of the People's Chamber, the Council of Ministers organizes the implementation of the political, economic, cultural and social objectives of the socialist state, and the defence objectives allocated to it. It is a body which works collectively.

(2) The Council of Ministers works out scientifically based economic forecasts, organizes the shaping of the economic system of socialism and guides the planned development of the national economy.

Article 79

(1) The Council of Ministers works on the basis of the laws and resolutions of the People's Chamber and the decrees and resolutions of the Council of State. Within the framework of the laws and decrees it issues ordinances and passes resolutions.

(2) The Council of Ministers guides, co-ordinates and controls the activities of the ministries, the other central state bodies and the regional councils in accordance with the findings of organizational science.

(3) The Council of Ministers decides on the conclusion and termination of international treaties, which are concluded in its name.

Article 80

(1) The chairman of the Council of Ministers is proposed to the People's Chamber by the chairman of the Council of Ministers and is commissioned by the People's Chamber to form the Council of Ministers.

[. . .]

Chapter 4   The local elected assemblies and their subsidiary bodies

Article 81

(1) The local elected assemblies are the organs of state power elected by the enfranchised citizens in the regions, districts, city districts, towns, communities and groups of communities.

(2) The local elected assemblies make decisions on their own responsibility on the basis of law on all matters affecting their territory and its citizens. They organize citizens' participation in shaping political, economic, cultural and social life, and work together with the social organizations of the working people.[6]

[. . .]

Article 82

(1) The local elected assemblies pass resolutions which are binding on their subsidiary bodies and institutions and on the elected assemblies, communities and citizens in their territory. These resolutions must be made public.

(2) The local elected assemblies have their own income and control its expenditure.

Article 83

(1) To look after its responsibilities each local elected assembly elects its council and its commissions. The members of the council shall wherever possible be deputies. Non-deputies may be appointed as members of the commissions.

(2) The council ensures the implementation of the assembly's activities and organizes the guidance of social developments in its area of responsibility. It is responsible to the assembly for all its activities and accountable to the next superior council. The council carries out its work collectively.

(3) The commissions organize citizens' informed participation in preparing and implementing the assembly's resolutions. They supervise the implementation of the laws, decrees and ordinances and the resolutions of the assembly by the council and its specialist bodies.

[. . .]

Section IV   Socialist legality and administration of justice art. 86–106.

Section V   Final Regulations art. 107–108.

(*Die Verfassung der DDR*, Berlin 1968)

D31 From the amendments to the Constitution, 7 October 1974:

Article 1

(old version)
The German Democratic Republic is a socialist state of the German nation. It is the political organization of working people in town and country who are together realizing socialism under the leadership of the working class and its Marxist-Leninist party.

(new version)
The German Democratic Republic is a socialist state of workers and farmers. It is the political organization of working people in town and country under the leadership of the working class and its Marxist-Leninist party.

Article 6

(old version)
(1) In keeping with the interests of the German people and the international obligations of all Germans, the German Democratic Republic has eradicated German militarism and Nazism on its territory and conducts a foreign policy which serves peace and socialism, international understanding and security.

(new version)
(1) In keeping with the interests of the German people and international obligations, the German Democratic Republic has eradicated German militarism and Nazism on its territory. It conducts a foreign policy which serves socialism and peace, international understanding and security.

(old version)
(2) In accordance with the principles of socialist internationalism, the German Democratic Republic maintains and develops all-round co-operation and friendship with the Union of Soviet Socialist Republics and the other socialist states.

(new version)
(2) The German Democratic Republic is allied with the Union of Soviet Socialist Republics for ever and irrevocably. This close fraternal alliance guarantees the people of the German Democratic Republic further progress along the path of socialism and of peace. The German Democratic Republic is indivisibly a part of the community of socialist states. It contributes to strengthening it in accordance with the principles of socialist internationalism and maintains and develops friendship, all-round co-operation, and mutual support with all states of the socialist community.[7]

(old version)
(3) The German Democratic Republic supports the striving of the

nations for freedom and independence and maintains co-operation with all states on a basis of equality and mutual respect.

(new version)

(3) The German Democratic Republic supports in their struggle for social progress the states and peoples who are fighting against imperialism and its colonial regime for national freedom and independence. The German Democratic Republic stands for the realization of the principles of peaceful co-existence of states with different social orders and maintains co-operation with all states on a basis of equality and mutual respect.

(old version)

(4) The German Democratic Republic is working for a system of collective security in Europe and a stable peace order in the world. It supports general disarmament.

(new version)

(4) The German Democratic Republic supports security and co-operation in Europe, a stable peace order in the world, and general disarmament.

Article 8

(old version)

(1) The generally recognized rules of international law serving peace and peaceful co-operation between the nations are binding on the state authority and on every citizen. The German Democratic Republic will never undertake a war of aggression or employ its armed forces against the freedom of another nation.

(new version)

(1) The generally recognized rules of international law serving peace and peaceful co-operation between the nations are binding on the state authority and on every citizen.

(old version)

(2) The creation and maintenance of normal relations and the co-operation of the two German states on the basis of equality are the national concern of the German Democratic Republic. In addition the German Democratic Republic and its citizens aspire to the surmounting of the division forced on the German nation by imperialism, the step-by-step rapprochement of the two German states and their ultimate union on the basis of democracy and socialism.

(new version)

(2) The German Democratic Republic will never undertake a war of aggression or employ its armed forces against the freedom of another nation.

(Amendments from: *Die Verfassung der DDR*, Berlin 1974, pp. 9 ff.)

D32 Law on Elections to the Representative Assemblies of the German Democratic Republic, Election Law of 24 June 1976:

I. Election principles

§ 1(1) The citizens of the German Democratic Republic elect their assemblies in realization of the fundamental right to participation in decision-making and development. Indispensable socialist election principles in this context are the conduct of the elections by democratically-formed electoral commissions, popular discussion on the basic questions of policy, and testing of candidates by the voters . . .

(3) The deputies carry out their responsible tasks in the interests and for the good of the working people of the German Democratic Republic. They maintain close relations with their electors and work collectives and co-operate with the committees of the National Front of the German Democratic Republic and with societal organizations, in particular with the trade unions in the enterprises. They are required to account regularly to their electors for the activity of their representative body and their own work, and to ensure conscientious treatment is given to the proposals, comments, and criticisms citizens make. Any deputy can be recalled by the voters for gross neglect of duty.

§ 2(1) The People's Chamber and the elected assemblies in the regions, districts, cities, city districts and communities are elected by the citizens in free, general, equal and secret elections for a period of five years.

(2) All citizens entitled to vote have equal rights to vote and to stand for election . . .

§ 3(1) All citizens of the German Democratic Republic having completed their 18th year on the day of election are entitled to vote in the elections to the People's Chamber . . .

§ 4 Any citizen of the German Democratic Republic having completed his 18th year on the date of election may be elected to the People's Chamber and to the local representative assemblies . . .

§ 6(1) Elections to the People's Chamber and to the local representative assemblies are called by the Council of State. The elections are called at least 60 days before the date of the elections.

(2) New elections for the People's Chamber and the local representative assemblies take place not later than 60 days after the expiry of the previous term of election . . .

§ 18(1) The deputies to the People's Chamber and the local representative assemblies are elected in electoral constituencies.

(2) Giving consideration to population figures, the Council of State

determines the electoral constituencies and the number of deputies to be elected in each constituency for the elections to the People's Chamber.

(3) Giving consideration to population figures, the local representative assemblies determine the electoral constituencies and the number of deputies to be elected in each constituency for the elections to the local representative assemblies.

§ 9(1) Those candidates who obtain more than half of the valid votes are elected.

(2) If the number of candidates obtaining more than half the valid votes is greater than the number of seats in the particular constituency, then the sequence of candidates on the election proposal determines the allocation of deputies' seats and the successor candidates . . .

II. Electoral commissions (§§ 10–14)

III. Election proposals and presentation of candidates

§ 15(1) The Electoral Commission of the Republic and the electoral commissions of the regions, districts, cities, city districts, and communities call for election proposals in a public announcement at latest 40 days before the date of election.

(2) Election proposals must be handed in to the electoral commission responsible for the election of the relevant representative assembly at latest 30 days before the date of election . . .

§ 16(1) Candidates for election to the People's Chamber, to the regional parliaments, district parliaments, municipal assemblies, city district assemblies and community representative bodies are nominated by the democratic parties and mass organizations. The democratic parties and mass organizations have the right to unify their proposals in the joint election proposal of the National Front of the German Democratic Republic.

(2) The number of candidates nominated for any constituency may be greater than the number of seats to be filled.

§ 17 The candidates to be nominated by the democratic parties and mass organizations should first be examined and proposed by the collectives in which they work . . .

§ 20(1) Candidates are required to present themselves to the voters in their constituency and to answer their questions.

(2) Voters have the right to request that candidates be removed from the voting proposal.

§ 21(1) If voters submit a request to have a candidate removed from the voting proposal, the National Council or the appropriate committee of the National Front of the German Democratic Republic is required to reach a decision together with the democratic parties and mass organizations as to whether the candidature should be upheld or withdrawn.

IV.   Voting wards

§ 22(1) Voting takes place in wards. The wards are formed by the city, city district, and community councils.

(2) A ward shall not include more than 1500 qualified voters, but may not be so small that the secrecy of the ballot is endangered . . .

V.   Voters' rolls (§§ 24–28)

VI.   Voting slips and polling stations (§§ 29–32)

VII.   Casting the vote (§§ 33–36)

VIII.   Election results and validity of the election

§ 37(1) The counting of the votes takes place at the polling station. It is open to the public and is carried out by the election supervisors.

(2) Once the ballot boxes have been opened the voting slips shall be counted. The number of votes cast is determined from the voters' roll and the voting slips present . . .

§ 42 If in a constituency the number of candidates achieving the required majority of votes is fewer than the number of seats to be filled, a further election shall be held within 90 days. . .

IX.   Beginning and end of the deputies' duties

§ 47(1) The deputies' duties begin on their election and end on the day of the election of the subsequent representative assembly.

(2) During the lifetime of the assembly a deputy's mandate expires on death, on loss of eligibility for election, on cancellation of the mandate, or on recall. In cases of death or loss of eligibility for election, the representative assembly pronounces the expiry of the mandate . . .

(4) If a deputy is in gross neglect of the trust placed in him by the working people, the voters and their collectives or the parties and mass organizations in consultation with the National Council or the relevant committee of the National Front of the German Democratic Republic may call for his recall. The representative assembly decides on the recall of a deputy . . .

(6) If a deputy's mandate expires, his place is taken by a successor candidate. The succession of a successor candidate is agreed by the representative assembly in consultation with the parties and mass organizations and the National Council or the relevant committee of the National Front of the German Democratic Republic.

X. Final requirements (§§ 48–49)

(*Gesetzblatt der Deutschen Demokratischen Republik* I, 1976, pp. 3 ff.)

D33 From the Constitution of the Socialist Unity Party of Germany, Berlin 1976:

Preamble

I. Party members, their duties and rights

(1) It is a great honour to be a member of the Socialist Unity Party of Germany. Membership of the Socialist Unity Party of Germany imposes great obligations on every communist. Any working person who accepts the party's programme and statute, who participates actively in building the advanced socialist society in the German Democratic Republic, who is active in a party organization, who submits himself to the party's resolutions and carries them out, and who regularly pays the prescribed contributions, may be a member of the Socialist Unity Party of Germany.

(2) The party member is required:

(a) always to preserve the unity and purity of the party as the principal precondition of its power and strength and to protect it in every way; to take part in the life of the party and to attend members' meetings regularly;

(b) to be active in realizing party resolutions, to strengthen the German Democratic Republic constantly in all respects, to work for a high development rate of socialist production, an increase in effectivity, scientific and technical progress, and the growth of productivity; to demonstrate an exemplary socialist attitude to work, to show the way forward, to be at the forefront in disseminating progressive experience in production, to show respect and consideration for other colleagues at work, and to carry out social duties in an exemplary way;

(c) to work constantly to consolidate solidarity with the masses, to explain to them the meaning of the party's policies and resolutions, to convince them of the correctness of the party's policies, to win them over to work for their implementation, and to learn from the masses. Every party member reacts without delay to their wishes and their needs, to suggestions and criticisms, and plays a part in bringing about necessary changes . . .

(d) to work constantly at raising his political consciousness and at the study of Marxism-Leninism, and to disseminate the Marxist-Leninist world view; to keep to the norms of socialist morality and ethics and to place the interests of society above personal interests . . .

(g) to carry out his work in the state and economic bodies and in the mass organizations according to party resolutions in the interest of working people, to uphold party and state discipline which is binding upon all party members to an equal extent. Anyone contravening party and state discipline is to be called to account irrespective of merit or position . . .

(j) to keep party and state secrets, to practice political vigilance in all matters and to be constantly aware that the vigilance of party members is necessary in all areas and in all situations.

Betrayal of party and state secrets is a crime against the party, the socialist state, and the working class. It is incompatible with membership of the party;

(k) everywhere and in every position to carry out party directions on the correct selection and promotion of party workers according to their political and professional suitability, to practice the necessary vigilance, to combat unfeeling and bureaucratic attitudes in working with people . . .

(3) The party member has the right:

(a) to participate, within his party organization, at party meetings and in the party press, in the discussion of all questions of party policy and the party's practical work, to put forward proposals, to express his opinion freely, until the organization has passed its resolution;

(b) to criticize, at party meetings, at plenary sessions of the party management bodies, and at party conferences and party congresses, the activities of the members and officers of the party, irrespective of their position. Party members who suppress criticism or consciously permit the suppression of criticism are to be called to account;

(c) to participate in the election of party bodies and himself to be elected;

(d) to demand to be present when his behaviour and activity is being considered by the party organization or where decisions concerning him personally are being taken;

(e) to direct questions on any matter to any higher body of the party as far as the Central Committee and to demand an answer to his submission which deals with the matter in detail.

(4) The acceptance of party members is on an individual basis. Conscious, active workers, co-operative farmers, members of the intelligentsia, office workers, and other working people who are sincerely devoted to socialism, and whose period of candidateship has expired, are accepted into membership of the party.

(5) Party members and candidates are required to inform their base organization of any proposed change in their place of work. . .

(6) Party membership is ended by

(a) resignation

(b) deletion

(c) expulsion

(d) death . . .

(8) Anyone who offends against the unity and purity of the party, who does not carry out its decisions, does not respect internal party democracy, contravenes party or state discipline or misuses his membership and the functions bestowed on him, or conducts himself in his public or private life in a manner unworthy of a party member shall be called to account by the base organization or a higher party body. Depending on the nature of the offence, the following party punishments may be decided on:

(a) reprimand

(b) severe reprimand

(c) expulsion from the party. Reprimands, severe reprimands, and expulsions from the party are entered in the registry documents . . .

(9) Expulsion from the party is the most severe party punishment. When deciding on an expulsion from the party the greatest care must be taken and a thorough scrutiny of the accusations made against the party member must be guaranteed.

Expulsion from the party is valid only if two-thirds of party members present at the members' meeting vote for it and if the decision is confirmed by the district leadership . . .

II.   Candidates for the party

(18) A candidature period is laid down for acceptance into the party, so that during this period candidates may become thoroughly familiar with the party programme and statute, prove themselves in their activities at work and in society, and so prepare themselves for party membership . . .

(19) . . . Anyone having completed his eighteenth year may become a candidate.

(20) The candidature period is one year in all cases. The Central Committee has the right to make exceptions in particular cases.

(21) The candidates have the same rights and duties as the members, with the exception of the right to be elected to leading party bodies and as delegates to conferences and party congresses. They attend party meetings in an advisory capacity . . .

III.   Party structure and internal party democracy

(23) The organizational structure of the party is based on the principle of democratic centralism. This principle means:

(a) that all party bodies from the lowest to the highest are democratically elected;

(b) that the elected party bodies are required to give regular reports on their activities to the organizations which elected them;

(c) that all decisions of higher party bodies are binding on the subordinate bodies, that strict party discipline is to be observed, and that the minority and the individual subject themselves in a disciplined manner to the decisions of the majority.

(24) The supreme principle in the work of the leading party bodies is that of collectivity. All leading bodies have to discuss and agree collectively the problems facing the party, the tasks and the planning of work. The principle of collectivity includes the personal responsibility of the individual. The cult of the person and the associated offence against internal party democracy are irreconcileable with the Leninist norms of party life and cannot be tolerated in the party.

(25) The party is structured on the territorial and production principle . . .

(31) Internal party democracy is the basis for the development of criticism and self-criticism, for the consolidation of party discipline, which is a conscious and voluntary discipline, and for the healthy development and continuous strengthening of the party.

(32) Every party organization, every member, every candidate protects the party against influences and elements inimical to it and against factionalism, and stands up for the unity and purity of the party on the basis of Marxism-Leninism. Party members have the duty to guard against internal party democracy being exploited by the enemies of the working class to distort the party line, to impose the will of an unimportant minority on the majority of the party, or to destroy the unity of the party and make attempts to split it by the formation of factional groupings.

(33) Internal party democracy safeguards the free and objective discussion of questions of party policy in all party organizations. Discussions on controversial or insufficiently clear questions are possible in the framework of individual organizations or of the party as a whole. A discussion within the party as a whole is required:

(a) if the Central Committee considers it necessary to discuss this or that question of policy with the whole party;

(b) if the necessity is recognized by several party organizations of the districts and regions;

(c) if there is no sufficiently firm majority within the Central Committee on important questions of party policy.

IV. The supreme party bodies

(34) The supreme body is the party congress. Ordinary party congresses are normally held once every five years.

On its own initiative or at the request of more than a third of party members, the Central Committee may call extraordinary party congresses at two months' notice . . .

(38) The party congress

(a) receives the reports from the Central Committee, the Review Commission, and other central bodies, and passes resolutions on them;

(b) decides on the programme and the statute of the party and determines the party's general line and its tactics;

(c) elects the Central Committee in accordance with the number of members and candidates to be determined by the party congress.

Only those who have been members of the party for at least six years may be elected as members or candidates of the Central Committee. (Exceptions require the special approval of the party congress) . . .

(d) The Central Committee carries out the decisions of the party congress, is the supreme body of the party in the period between party congresses, and is in charge of all its activities. It represents the party in dealings with other parties and organizations.

The Central Committee sends representatives of the party to the principal management bodies of the state apparatus and of the economy, and confirms its candidates for the People's Chamber.

The Central Committee guides the work of the elected central state and social assemblies and organizations through the party groups present in them.

(40) The Central Committee holds a plenary session at least once every six months. Candidates to the Central Committee attend the plenary sessions in an advisory capacity.

In exceptional cases, depending on the nature of the questions to be dealt with, the Central Committee can call other leading functionaries to its plenary sessions for consultation. . .

(42) The Central Committee elects:

the Politburo for political guidance of the work of the Central Committee between plenary sessions;

the Secretariat to supervise ongoing business, particularly to implement and control party decisions and to select cadres;

the General Secretary of the Central Committee . . .

(44) The Central Committee appoints the Central Party Control Commission and decides on its composition.

The Central Party Control Commission has the following tasks:

(a) It protects the unity and purity of the party and combats inimical influences and any factional activity. It concerns itself with members and candidates who falsify and distort party policy with opportunistic and revisionistic views or by dogmatic attitudes . . .

(47) The Central Committee has the right to call party conferences between the party congresses. The party conference deals with urgent questions of the party's policy and tactics and makes decisions on these matters. It may recall members and candidates of the Central Committee and the Central Review Commission who have not fulfilled their duties and make up the number of members from the ranks of the candidates or elect

candidates to the Central Committee and the Central Review Commission . . .

V. *The regional, municipal, district, and municipal district organizations of the party 49–55*

VI. *The base organizations of the party*

(56) The party's foundation is its base organizations. They are formed in the enterprises in industry, construction, transport and communications, agriculture, forestry, food production, and commerce, in government and scientific institutions, in residential districts in town and country, and in the armed forces, if at least three party members are present.

The formation of base organizations of the party shall be confirmed by the district committee or the corresponding political section.

The highest body of the base organization is the members' meeting, which shall be held at least once a month. The members' meeting is quorate if more than half the members organized in the base organization are present. To deal with ongoing business it elects the base organization committee, generally for the period of one year . . .

(57) The party organizations in the production, commercial, transport and communications enterprises, in the agricultural co-operatives, state farms, co-operative plant production sections and other co-operative institutions, in craft co-operatives and in drafting and construction offices, in scientific research institutes, educational and cultural institutions, and medical institutes, and in other institutions and organizations have the right to supervise the activities of the management of the institutions, to fulfil their responsibility for the political guidance of social development in their area.

The party organizations in the ministries, the other central and local state bodies and institutions have the right to supervise the activity of the apparatus in realizing the decisions of party and government and in upholding the norms of socialist law . . .

VII. *The local organizations of the party 64*

VIII. *Party and Free German Youth Movement*

(65) The Free German Youth Movement, the socialist youth organization in the German Democratic Republic, is the active helper and fighting reserve of the party . . .

(66) The Free German Youth Movement recognizes the leading role of the party of the working class . . .

IX. Party organizations in the National People's Army, the Border Troops, the German People's Police and on the railways

(68) Party organizations in the National People's Army, the Border Troops, the German People's Police and on the railways operate according to special instructions confirmed by the Central Committee. Their political sections and party committees are required to maintain close contacts with the local party committees.

X. Party Groups in the elected bodies of the state and of the mass organizations

(69) Party groups are organized in all congresses, consultant bodies, and in the elected bodies of the state and of the mass organizations, where there are at least three party members. The tasks of these party groups consist in strengthening the all-round influence of the party, representing its policies to non-party members, consolidating party and state discipline, carrying on the struggle against bureaucratism and ensuring the implementation of party and government directives. For ongoing business the group elects a secretary . . .

XI. The Review Commissions 71

XII. The financial resources of the party 72–75

(*Statut der Sozialistischen Einheitspartei Deutschlands*, Berlin 1976)

D34 Law on the local elected assemblies and their organs in the German Democratic Republic, 12 July 1973:

Preamble
Chapter I — Principles

§ 1(1) The local elected assemblies are the organs of the socialist state power of the workers and farmers in the regions, districts, cities, city districts, and communities of the German Democratic Republic. The local elected assemblies are elected by the citizens qualified to vote. Under the leadership of the party of the working class and on the basis of the laws and other legal prescriptions they realize the state policies of the Workers' and Farmers' Power of the German Democratic Republic within their territories in close co-operation with the working people and the social organizations . . .

*Chapter II — Tasks and method of operation of the local elected
assemblies, their councils, commissions and deputies*

§ 5 Working principles of the local elected assemblies

(1) The local elected assemblies as working corporations, in their congresses, their councils, their commissions, through the work of the deputies in the enterprises, combines, co-operatives and institutions and in the residential districts, realize the unity of decision-making, implementation and supervision . . .

(2) The superior bodies have to ensure that audited and mutually compatible plan figures and other essential documentation are submitted to the local elected assemblies in good time and in full.

(5) The subordinate elected assemblies are to be involved in working out decisions which affect the material, cultural, and social needs of the citizens of their territory.

§ 6 Calling and conducting of conferences

(1) The local elected assemblies are required to hold regular congresses. The regional congresses are held at least every quarter, the other local elected assemblies at least once every two months . . .

§ 8 Position of the local councils

(1) The councils are responsible and accountable to their elected assembly and the superior council for their activities . . .

Working principles of the local councils

§ 10(1) The local councils are led by the chair. The chair of the council is responsible for ensuring that the decisions of the party of the working class, the laws of the People's Chamber and the decrees and resolutions of the Council of Ministers and the decisions of the superior elected assemblies and their councils are evaluated and form a basis for the whole work done . . .

§ 12(1) The council forms specialist bodies to fulfil its tasks. It determines the tasks of the specialist bodies and supervises their activity. The specialist bodies are conducted on the principle of individual leadership and collective consultation on the basic questions of the matter at issue . . .

(3) The specialist bodies are subordinate to their council and the relevant specialist body of the superior council, and/or to the relevant ministry or another state authority . . .

Formation and position of the commissions

§ 14(1) The local elected assemblies form permanent commissions to carry out their tasks for the duration of their elected period, and temporary commissions to deal with tasks of limited duration (called commissions in the following). The commissions are responsible and accountable to the assemblies.

(2) The members of the commissions are deputies and successor candidates elected by the assembly and citizens appointed by the assembly. The appointed members have the same rights and duties in the commission as

the deputies and successor candidates. In the commissions of the regional congresses at least two-thirds, and in those of the district conferences at least one half, of the members must be deputies and successor candidates. In the commissions of the cities and communities the proportion of deputies and successor candidates may be lower.

(3) The chair of the commission is a deputy. He is elected by the assembly.

(4) The citizens appointed to the commissions are to be freed from their employment to carry out the tasks connected with this. Their wages or salaries continue to be paid. No reduction in income may result.

(5) The commissions may form working groups to carry out tasks. The working group is led by a member of the commission.

Chapter III — Tasks, rights and duties of the Regional Congress and its organs, §§ 20–34

Chapter IV — Tasks, rights and duties of the elected assemblies and their organs in municipal and rural districts, §§ 35–53

Chapter V — Tasks, rights and duties of the elected assemblies and their organs in the cities and communities, §§ 54–71

Chapter VI — Changes in territorial organization, § 72

Chapter VII — Final regulations, §§ 73–74

(Gesetzblatt der Deutschen Demokratischen Republik I, 1973, p. 313)

D35 From an article on the SED and the Bloc parties, January 1974:

In the GDR the existing party alliance under the SED's leadership is characterized by all the parties' unreserved agreement in building the advanced socialist society.

Two "key questions" which one of the parties puts to all its members as a basic requirement are characteristic for the attitude of all four non-communist parties — CDU, LDPD, NDPD, DBD — to the working class and its Marxist-Leninist vanguard and to world socialism. One asks for full recognition of the claim to leadership of the working class and the SED, and the other for a decisive declaration of support for the Soviet Union as the leading power in the socialist world system . . .

The parties linked in friendship to the SED have their firm place in socialist society. They give important assistance for the whole of society when they contribute within their own circles to the formation of socialist state and property consciousness, to the further development of socialist relations of production, to the firm anchoring of the GDR in the socialist world system. The SED's work to serve the whole people is made easier if basic questions of the construction of socialism are clarified by these parties from the viewpoint of the SED's allies and with an exact knowledge of their mentality. And there is no doubt that such a factor considerably aids the development of all allied forces. We do not see the political activity of the other four parties merely in the context of alliance in the socio-economic field. For instance in the effectiveness of the CDU's work we respect the increasing readiness of citizens of the Christian faith to become active together with Marxists in support of socialism in the GDR and all over the world . . .

The central policy laid down by the 8th Party Congress of the SED can only be achieved by common efforts. It fully reflects the increased demands being made on the broad alliance in the GDR that in future too the valuable comments, suggestions and initiatives made by the friendly parties will be counted as part of the treasury of sensible socialist action aimed at implementing the economic policies conceived by the SED and realized by the masses, and that this proven co-operation will be purposefully encouraged.

The development of the working class and its allies continues in large part in the realization of the demands of the economy. Co-operation with the other parties therefore also always serves this important stage in the process of rapprochement in the historically long path to the classless society. Here explicit reference must be made to the great involvement of the allied parties in the transformation of the private capitalist and part nationally owned enterprises which still existed in the GDR until 1972. As a result of the long-term political and ideological work of the SED and all the other parties it was possible to create more than 10,000 new state-owned enterprises in a short time by voluntary agreements, without social conflicts arising. However this does not fully meet the requirements. The allied parties still have the long-term responsibility of giving political and ideological assistance to their members who are the managers of the new state-owned enterprises, so that they can cope with the new problems. This cannot be done solely by the SED and the trade unions within the enterprises, particularly as the level of organization of the workers employed there first has to be raised considerably. Additionally the CDU, the LDPD and the NDPD have very great problems to solve in supporting the existing craft co-operatives, in obtaining new members for them and in the mobilization of all individually employed trades- and craftspeople. Their activity makes it considerably easier for the SED to open up all the reserves of these areas of the economy. It is also self-evident that a party as firmly based in rural districts as the DBD sees its most important task in mobilizing its members to increased activity in developing co-operative relations, in the intensification of agricultural production processes, in the increase of market production, and in the improvement of village life generally.

The SED's policy of alliance with the other parties in the GDR includes the ideological and cultural field too. The ideology of Marxism-Leninism which it upholds has become the ruling one in the GDR. The principles of socialist morality developed by the working class are prevailing in confrontation with outdated attitudes and behavioural patterns which are foreign to socialism, and determine the communal existence of all people united in broad alliance to the extent that they are constantly realized consciously. This is an extremely important area where the parties friendly to the SED are encouraging the success of socialist ideology and helping science and culture to become the common property of the people. Particularly in the sections of society with which they are involved there is still a need to eliminate remnants of bourgeois ideology, elitist attitudes, and false views of history.

(R. Stöckigt: "Die Zusammenarbeit der SED mit den anderen Parteien in der Nationalen Front", in: *Deutsche Aussenpolitik*, vol. 14.1, Berlin 1974, pp. 78 ff.)

D36 Greetings from the Central Committee of the SED to the 12th Party Congress of the Democratic Farmers' Party of Germany, April 1987:

Dear Friends,

The Central Committee of the Socialist Unity Party of Germany conveys cordial greetings to the delegates and guests of the 12th party congress of the Democratic Farmers' Party of Germany (DBD) and to all members of your party, and wishes you a successful conference.

The firm friendly relations which have been developing between the SED and the DBD for nearly 40 years have proved themselves in every stage of our society's progress. In its close association with the party of the working class and with all the parties and mass organizations united in the National Front, your party is contributing significantly to the further development of the advanced socialist society in the GDR. The Democratic Farmers' Party of Germany has always set itself the single aim of helping to consolidate the alliance between the working class and the class of co-operative farmers as the stable political basis of our socialist state, and playing its part in strengthening socialism and securing peace for the welfare of our population

We see the DBD's dedicated and creative activity in preparing for and in evaluating the 11th Party Congress of the SED as evidence of genuine trust and as an expression of responsible comradely co-operation. The members of your party are playing their part in putting its resolutions into practice successfully, particularly in socialist agriculture, forestry, and foodstuffs production. We know that in the DBD we have a reliable ally at our side for the realization of our agricultural policy, and we shall always rely on your active support in dealing with the economic, social, and cultural questions relating to the countryside. For this the committee and all the members have our thanks and recognition.

Dear Friends,

Our efforts are aimed above all at preserving peace. We know how serious, complicated and tense the international situation is, but we also know the realistic possibilities of preventing a nuclear catastrophe and opening up peaceful perspectives for humankind. We give our full and wholehearted support to the far-reaching proposals on disarmament in both the nuclear and conventional spheres which have been made by the Soviet Union and the countries of the Warsaw Pact.

The DBD declares its unanimous support for the continuation of our policy of dialogue and co-operation in order to reach agreements which will lead to equal security for all. The farmer should be able to sow in peace and harvest in peace. For this, the strength of socialism is of decisive importance.

Accordingly the members of the DBD also regard their place of work as a part of the struggle for peace. Together we shall do everything to ensure that war shall never again arise from German territory, but peace instead.

In accordance with its long-standing traditions, the DBD declares its support for the firm fraternal alliance with the Soviet Union and the other countries of the socialist community. Its members take the 70th anniversary of the Great Socialist October Revolution as an opportunity to contribute to the strengthening of this friendship and co-operation.

We have noted with satisfaction that the DBD is fully aware of the increased demands arising from the new period in the further development of the advanced socialist society in the GDR. It has declared the economic and social policy of the SED as its major campaign area and is undertaking a variety of initiatives to realize our economic strategy in agriculture.

The many contributions made by the members of your party to the discussion of the draft resolutions of the 13th Farmers' Congress of the GDR have shown a sense of responsibility and strong confidence in the agricultural policy of the SED. We are convinced that the members of the DBD will continue in the future to ensure the stability of the general intensification in agriculture, to consolidate further the agricultural co-operatives and the state arable and livestock farms, to strengthen their co-operation with each other, and to achieve stable yields from the land and high productivity in livestock. To meet the demands of the times, we must develop agriculture into a branch of the applied sciences and apply key technologies effectively.

The DBD is making an independent contribution to the increasing development of the village as a centre of agricultural production and of farming life. Through their participation in the local representative bodies and in the committees of the National Front, its members are working actively for a broader development of socialist democracy, and of citizens' action groups in the competition under the slogan "Join in to make our towns and communities more beautiful". They attach importance to up-holding farming traditions such as farming people's pride in themselves, their hard work, and their way of life, and also to participating in the intellectual and cultural life of the village.

In our socialist society the class of co-operative farmers has clear and secure prospects in its alliance with the working class. Together, we will continue to improve people's working and living conditions and make life increasingly rich and attractive.

With full confidence in the vitality of our alliance and the new impulses and initiatives your 12th Party Congress will give rise to, we wish all members of your party success in their work, health and personal welfare. With socialist greetings,
Central Committee of the Socialist Unity Party of Germany
E. Honecker
General Secretary

(*Neues Deutschland* vol. 42 no. 99 of 28 April 1987)

D37 Message of greeting from the Central Committee of the SED to the 13th Party Congress of the National Democratic Party of Germany, May 1987:

Dear Friends,

The Central Committee of the SED conveys cordial, friendly greetings to the delegates and guests of the 13th party congress of the National Demo-cratic Party of Germany.

The Socialist Unity Party of Germany knows that in the National Democratic Party of Germany it has at its side a responsible and energetic comrade-in-arms in the further development of the advanced socialist society and in the struggle for peace. As a party with close friendly ties to the SED, you have from the start taken an indispensable and distinctive place in the political organization of our country. The members of the NDPD are working energetically with all the social forces united in the Democratic Bloc of Parties and mass organizations and in the National Front to further economic, social, intellectual and cultural development in the GDR and to continue to improve our life in peace, democracy and human dignity.

We greatly appreciate it that the National Democratic Party of Germany has adopted the aims of the 11th Party Congress of the SED for individual active social involvement, and that these decisions are being supported and put into practice by the achievements and attitudes of its members in the workplace and in social life. The results thus achieved are an expression of the shared campaign of the National Democratic Party of Germany and the Socialist Unity Party of Germany. The Central Committee of the SED expresses warmest thanks to you for this committed activity.

Our co-operation will continue to be governed unshakeably by the principle that all citizens regardless of social origin, ideological or religious conviction have the widest opportunities of participation in working, in planning, and in governing. In this joint constructive activity, the alliance between the working class and the other classes and social groups and the political-moral unity of our population will continue to consolidate itself further.

The National Democratic Party of Germany devotes itself with all its strength to the most important concern of our time, the preservation and safeguarding of peace. Evidence of this is provided by the readiness of the members of the NDPD, both in word and in deed, to regard their workplace as a place of struggle for peace. In so doing they act in accordance with their commitment, based on historical experience, to do everything so that war may never again come from German territory, but peace instead.

The Soviet Union's programme to free our earth of all nuclear weapons by the year 2000 has the support of us all. Mikhail Gorbachov's initiative on the immediate conclusion of a separate treaty for the removal of intermediate range missiles in Europe offers a historic opportunity as the first important step towards nuclear disarmament. We join in welcoming the USSR's proposals for negotiations on the reduction and subsequent removal of missiles with a range of 500 to 1000 kilometres stationed in Europe, and also on the banning of chemical weapons. The initiatives by the GDR and the CSSR on the creation of a chemical weapon free zone and a nuclear weapon free corridor in central Europe could make substantial contributions to the creation of a climate in which negotiations on the removal of all nuclear weapons in Europe as well as on conventional disarmament will be carried on successfully.

Dear Friends,

The National Democratic Party of Germany is making significant achievements on our proven path of a united economic and social policy. In political-ideological work it is justifiedly concentrating on the share of its own members in the realization of economic strategy with the year 2000 in view and on the intellectual requirements for the extensive application of key technologies. The result of this is your party's contribution to the increase in economic output in the GDR.

Through its socially determined political activity, the NDPD contributes significantly to ensuring that the craftspeople and tradespeople who are members of or sympathetic to your party meet people's expectations of effective repair, distributive, and service sectors. In the "Planning Initiative" movement led by your party, craftspeople and tradespeople are striving successfully to meet society's requirements and to support local government demands in the regions.

The strengthening and further development of our socialist homeland, the protection and defence of the GDR, and firm friendship with the Soviet Union have always been a particular concern of the NDPD. With the progressive development of socialist national consciousness you are creating the conditions for every member of your party to play an active part in dealing with the matters that concern society. The participation of thousands of members of the NDPD in the elected assemblies, the committees and working parties of the National Front of the GDR, in the mass organizations and on other social bodies is further evidence of the variety and effectiveness of socialist democracy. The community improvement campaign "Join in to make our towns and communities more beautiful!" is an area in which they have been extremely active.

The Central Committee of the SED is convinced that the 13th Party Congress of the NDPD will give your party new impetus for the general strengthening of socialism in the GDR and for the campaign for peace. We wish all members of the National Democratic Party of Germany creativity, health, and personal welfare for their responsible activity.

With socialist greetings,
Central Committee of the Socialist Unity Party of Germany
Erich Honecker
General Secretary

(*Neues Deutschland* vol. 42 no. 106 of 7 May 1987)

D38 Message of greeting from the National Democratic Party of Germany to the Central Committee of the SED, May 1987:

Dear friend Erich Honecker,

The delegates to the 13th party congress of the National Democratic Party of Germany have assembled as is customary in Leipzig to discuss and pass resolutions on the role of our party in the struggles of today. At the beginning of our congress we convey to you and to all members of the Central Committee of the Socialist Unity Party of Germany our cordial greetings.

We regard our 13th party conference as being determined by the requirements of the qualitatively new stage in the formation of the advanced socialist society in our German Democratic Republic which was ushered in with the 11th Party Congress of the Socialist Unity Party of Germany. In our party congress we are setting out to meet the demands which will take us on to the year 2000 and which will fulfil the meaning of socialism more fully with every step forward that society takes.

The clear statement of social policy put forward by the 11th Party Congress of the Socialist Unity Party of Germany, namely that everything is to be done for the benefit of the people and for peace, provides a content and a target for our co-operation. It strengthens the political and moral unity of our population at a time when socialism is employing its potential for peace and progress in an even more co-ordinated manner in a world-wide initiative.

There is great confidence in our country's alliance policy. It has proved itself nationally and internationally, and it has a visible influence on political stability, economic vigour, and the high standard of intellectual and cultural life. The unity of economic and social policy provides us with a challenging field of activity in which to put into practice our party's share of social responsibility. In all areas, members of our party are involved in securing a high rate of economic growth and developing modern forces of production to this end, and in helping to apply to this all available intellectual and material potential. We are playing our part in consistently improving the guarantee of personal security and welfare for all the people of this country, since the extent and quality of the repair, service, and distributive sector available to people makes a direct contribution to this. The planning initiative which 25,000 members of our party involved in trades, crafts, and distribution have been involved in for many years now will be given new impetus by our party congress.

In our political and ideological activity we give energetic support to the constant improvement of all aspects of life in the regions in accordance with the wishes and needs of the population. We attach increasing weight to our members' active involvement in and further development of the intellectual and cultural life of our Republic, which is rich in ideas and characterized by the ideals of our society.

In our participation in the National Front, the elected assemblies, in the machinery of state, taking up the wide range of involvement and develop-mental activity offered to our party, we do our best to assist and further socialist democracy, with its richly developed formal structure, in the German Democratic Republic.

Today, as never before, it is being demonstrated that socialism is the mainstay for the preservation and consolidation of peace, which is threatened by the confrontational policies of the most aggressive imperialist circles. The essential unity of socialism and peace is one more manifestation of the profound humanism of our social order, which has succeeded in preventing a new worldwide conflagration on our planet for well over 40 years. Socialism's peace offensive, its programme aiming for a nuclear-free world, all the initiatives in this area undertaken by socialism have given a powerful impetus worldwide to a new stage of the struggle for peace.

Humankind is clearly presented with the prospect of rejecting the life-endangering arms race in favour of peaceful competition, of international co-operation for mutual benefit. Our country's campaign to set up a coalition of forces for peace, reason and realism, the SED's initiatives on disarmament and your own productive involvement for these aims, dear friend Erich Honecker, have met with respect and have been influential throughout the world.

The members of the National Democratic Party of Germany are most profoundly in agreement with and committed to socialism's efforts for peace. Accordingly the military defence of peace and socialism is an absolute requirement for them and for all social groups in our country. The consolidation of the fraternal alliance with the Soviet Union and the other states of our community is an essential part of our programme, and is inextricably involved in the fulfilment of our patriotic duty.

Now, as we are about to begin our discussions, we declare that we stand solidly by our word which we gave to the 11th Party Congress of the Socialist Unity Party of Germany.

The Socialist Unity Party of Germany can count on the National Democratic Party of Germany and its members in the realization of socialist policies leading up to the year 2000. We shall always stand side by side with the communists of our country — and this in all situations and under all conditions.

The delegates of the 13th party congress of the National Democratic Party of Germany
Leipzig, 7 May 1987

(*Neues Deutschland* vol. 42 no. 107 of 8 May 1987)

D39 Report on Erich Honecker's meeting with leaders of the other political parties and the National Front, November 1987:

Berlin (ADN): On Monday, the General Secretary of the Central Committee of the Socialist Unity Party of Germany, Erich Honecker, received the chairman of the Democratic Farmer's Party of Germany, Dr. Günther Maleuda, the chairman of the Christian Democratic Union of Germany, Gerald Götting, the chairman of the Liberal Democratic Party of Germany, Professor Dr Manfred Gerlach, the chairman of the National Democratic Party of Germany, Professor Heinrich Homann, and the president of the national council of the National Front of the GDR, Professor Lothar Kolditz, for an exchange of views on current questions of internal and foreign policies. The talks took place in the context of common action for the further realization of the decisions of the 11th Party Congress of the SED and for the policies for the welfare of the people and for peace which are backed by all the parties and mass organizations in the Democratic Bloc and in the National Front.

[. . .]

In the German Democratic Republic, Erich Honecker continued, the fulfilment of the tasks we are faced with has become the cause of all classes and sections of the population. The party congresses of the parties linked to the SED by ties of friendship, which took place this year after the 11th Party Congress of the SED, were impressive in their assessments and in their positive outlook and also testified to the total unanimity of views on questions of internal and foreign policy. The statements made at these congresses that our comradely co-operation in the Democratic Bloc and in the National Front is and will remain an indispensable driving force in the further development of the advanced socialist society can only be emphasized. The SED knows that in the DBD, the CDU, the LDPD, and the NDPD it has on its side tried and tested comrades-in-arms who are firmly determined to pursue the course of a united economic and social policy first promoted by the 8th Party Congress of the SED 16 years ago and to achieve further new successes to improve everyday life and the welfare of our citizens. The activity of all parties and mass organizations in the socialist German Democratic Republic is determined by the requirement to be there for the population and for its interests.

(*Neues Deutschland* vol. 42 no. 270 of 17 November 1987)

D 40　Organizational structure of the SED

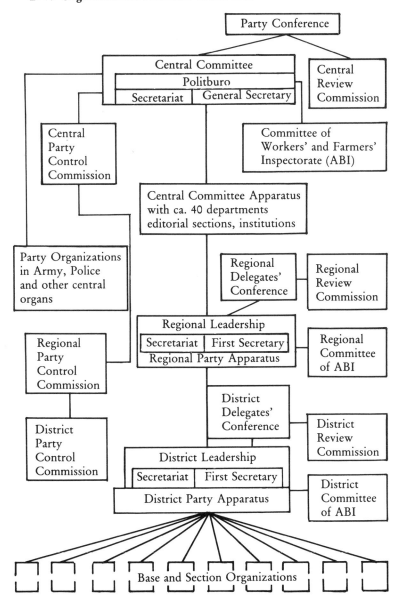

D41 From the Programme of the Socialist Unity Party of Germany, 1976:

The Socialist Unity Party of Germany is the politically conscious and organized vanguard of the working class and the working people in the socialist German Democratic Republic. The tasks and aims which it pursues are those of the revolutionary working-class movement as formulated by Marx, Engels and Lenin. In its activities it is unswervingly guided by the idea of doing everything for the good of the people, for the interests of the working class and all other working people. It considers its task to be the continued building of an advanced socialist society. Its ultimate goal is the construction of a communist society.

The Socialist Unity Party of Germany emerged from the struggle which the revolutionary German working-class movement had carried on for more than a hundred years against feudal reaction and capitalist exploitation, against imperialism and militarism, fascism and imperialist war. It embodies the revolutionary traditions of the Communist League and of revolutionary German social democracy. It continues the work of the Communist Party of Germany and fulfils the legacy of the anti-fascist resistance. It is the heir to all that was progressive in the history of the German people.

The Socialist Unity Party of Germany is a contingent of the international communist movement. It is firmly committed to proletarian internationalism. It is fraternally allied with the Communist Party of the Soviet Union, the most tried and tested Communist Party, the first to lead the working class to power in alliance with the peasantry in the Great October Socialist Revolution. Led by the Party of Lenin, the Soviet people has created an advanced socialist society and is now successfully forging ahead along the road to communism. The Soviet Union and its glorious army contributed decisively to the crushing defeat of German fascism, and thus to the liberation of the German people from fascist servitude, thereby paving the way for its advance towards democracy and progress.

The merger in April 1946 of the Communist Party of Germany and the Social Democratic Party of Germany to form the Socialist Unity Party of Germany (SED) is of historic importance. The founding of the Socialist Unity Party of Germany showed that the cardinal lesson from the history of the German working-class movement had been well and truly learned: the working class can only fulfil its historic mission if it overcomes the division caused within its ranks by imperialism and opportunism, if it establishes unity on a revolutionary basis and if it is led by a purposeful and closely knit Marxist-Leninist Party, which is experienced in struggle and firmly attached to the mass of the people.

Led by the Socialist Unity Party of Germany, the working class and the peasantry in the German Democratic Republic put an end once and for all to the rule of the German bourgeoisie and Junkers which had unleashed two world wars in this century. An alliance of all democratic forces was forged on the basis of revolutionary working-class unity. An anti-fascist and democratic revolution was carried out and the socialist revolution led to victory in a continuous revolutionary process and in fierce struggle against imperialist reaction and its henchmen.

Under the leadership of the Socialist Unity Party of Germany, the German Democratic Republic saw a fundamental change of direction in the history of the German people, a change towards socialism. In the shape of the German Democratic Republic the working class, allied with the peasantry and the other working people, established and consolidated its political power, creating a socialist workers' and farmers' state as a form of the dictatorship of the proletariat. On the basis of the teachings of Marxism-Leninism, relations of ownership of the principal means of production were changed along revolutionary lines, and a firm political and economic foundation was laid for the solution of the social, cultural and ideological tasks facing socialist society. A secure way of life, a steady increase in living standards for all working people and the emergence of a new kind of political awareness – these are striking results of socialist construction. A socialist nation began to emerge in the German Democratic Republic during the process of socialist transformation.

The victorious socialist revolution that has taken place in the German Democratic Republic must be seen in the context of the world revolutionary process. An essential feature of the formation of the world socialist system, it was directly linked to the construction of an advanced socialist society in the Soviet Union and to the socialist revolutions taking place in other countries.

In its long-term aims and in its practical work the Socialist Unity Party of Germany is guided by the universally applicable laws of socialist revolution and of socialist construction, as confirmed by the world revolutionary process, and applies these laws creatively to the concrete historical conditions prevailing in the German Democratic Republic.

In socialism, political power is exercised by the working class. Led by its Marxist-Leninist Party, the working class pursues the interests of the people, in alliance with the class of co-operative farmers, intellectuals and professional people and the other working people.

Socialism rests on the social ownership of the means of production in both its forms: public property owned by the whole of society and co-operatively owned property. In a planned socialist economy, the means of production are used to ensure a steady increase in national wealth in the best interests of the working class and of all other working people. Science and technology are developed and applied for the common good.

In socialism, production relations and all social relations are characterized by conscious and friendly co-operation and mutual aid. This is the foundation for the political and moral unity of the people, for the full development of the initiative and activity of all working people.

Socialism frees the working people from exploitation and oppression. It needs and staunchly defends peace. It gives all members of society every opportunity to develop the fullest reach of their creative powers, to acquire a high standard of education, to make active use of their democratic rights and freedoms for the advancement of socialist society and to realize all the potentialities of their personality. Socialism satisfies the vital needs of the working people to an ever larger extent. It is a fundamental tenet of socialism that everyone contributes according to his ability and receives according to his work. Socialism holds out to all people the prospect of a life that is fulfilled and of a future that is bright.

The dominant ideology in socialist society is Marxism-Leninism, the scientific world outlook of the working class. Socialist patriotism and proletarian internationalism are more and more determining people's actions. As the socialist nation grows to full maturity it draws ever nearer to the other nations of the socialist community.

The Socialist Unity Party of Germany draws on the experience gained by the Communist Party of the Soviet Union and the other fraternal parties in the establishment of a new society. Imperishable friendship and cooperation with the Communist Party of the Soviet Union and with the Soviet people was, is and remains the chief source of strength and the basis for the development of the socialist German Democratic Republic.

It is thanks to the great achievements of the working class and the other working people that the foundations of socialism were laid in the German Democratic Republic, that socialist relations of production were carried to victory and the organization of an advanced socialist society was undertaken. The 8th Congress of the Socialist Unity Party of Germany set out and explained the tasks to be accomplished in building an advanced socialist society. Basing itself on the historic achievements scored by the working class and all other working people under the leadership of the Socialist Unity Party of Germany and taking account of the new social requirements that have arisen, the Socialist Unity Party of Germany makes it its aim for the coming period to forge ahead with the building of an advanced socialist society in the German Democratic Republic, thereby creating essential conditions for the gradual transition to communism.

(*Programme of the Socialist Unity Party of Germany*, Dresden 1976, pp. 5–9)

D42 The construction of an advanced socialist society in the German Democratic Republic, 1976:

The Socialist Unity Party of Germany sets itself the aim of continuing the construction of an advanced socialist society in the German Democratic Republic, thereby creating fundamental conditions for the gradual transition to communism.

The establishment of an advanced socialist society is a historic process marked by far-reaching political, economic, social, intellectual and cultural changes.

The establishment of an advanced socialist society makes it necessary for all advantages and motive forces, all facets and spheres of social life to be developed on planned lines at high levels. This includes the productive forces and the relations of production, social and political relations, science and education, socialist ideology and culture, the totality of working and living conditions as well as national defence. An advanced society presupposes that socialist relations of production prevail completely.

To build an advanced socialist society means — to create all the material, socio-economic, political and ideological conditions required for pursuing at a progressively higher level the primary object of socialism, which is to do everything for the good of the people, for the interests of the working class, co-operative farmers, intellectuals and professional people and the rest of the population. In accordance with the fundamental economic law of socialism, the central policy in the construction of an advanced socialist society consists in raising the cultural and living standards of the people on the basis of a rapid pace of development of socialist production, increased efficiency, scientific and technological advance and growing labour productivity.

To build an advanced socialist society means — to establish an efficient material and technological basis for steady economic growth, high labour productivity and efficiency. The optimum use of productive resources is the chief method of achieving this. It is of crucial importance to combine the achievements of the scientific and technological revolution organically with the advantages of socialism.

To build an advanced socialist society means — to pursue economic and social policies as an integrated whole. The purpose of seeking a rapid growth of production and its efficiency is to improve working and living conditions in a systematic manner. The consistent implementation of the principle that everyone should contribute according to his abilities and receive according to his work is a major impetus behind economic and social progress.

To build an advanced socialist society means — to develop the relations of production more fully as relations based on friendly co-operation and mutual aid among working people and among staffs and to enhance collective attitudes in social relations.

To build an advanced socialist society means — to increase the role of the working class and of its Party as the leading force in society and continuously to strengthen its alliance with the class of co-operative farmers, with intellectuals, professional people and the rest of the working population. This also means systematically to bring all classes and strata of the community closer together on the basis of the Marxist-Leninist world outlook of the working class, socialist production relations, continuous improvements in working and living conditions and the increased application of scientific and technological progress in all fields of social life. This makes it necessary for further steps to be taken to overcome gradually all substantial distinctions between town and country and between mental and physical labour.

To build an advanced socialist society means — to consolidate the socialist administrative and legal system in a comprehensive manner and to give socialist democracy full scope to develop. Wide-ranging social activities by workers, co-operative farmers, intellectuals and other working people, who participate in the management and planning of social development with an acute sense of political responsibility and a high degree of proficiency, are a characteristic feature of advanced socialism.

To build an advanced socialist society means — to enhance the socialist consciousness of the broad mass of people still further, actively to shape their Marxist-Leninist world outlook and communist morality and to overcome egotism, individualism and other manifestations of bourgeois ideology in a determined manner.

To build an advanced socialist society means — to guarantee the effective protection of peace and socialist achievements at all times and to strengthen in all citizens of the GDR the preparedness to defend socialism. Led by the Socialist Unity Party of Germany and closely allied with their class brothers and companions-in-arms in the Soviet army and the armed forces of the other signatory states to the Warsaw Treaty, the National People's Army, the frontier force, the other defence and security forces of the GDR and the workers' militia perform their duties to help safeguard peace in Europe and create favourable conditions for socialist and communist construction.

To build an advanced socialist society means — to keep strengthening and deepening the fraternal alliance with the Soviet Union and the other countries of the socialist community. Advanced socialist society is the joint revolutionary accomplishment of the working class and of all working people in the countries of the socialist community. Socialist economic integration between the member states of the Council for Mutual Economic Assistance provides a firm basis for the socialist nations to achieve ever fuller co-operation and to draw closer and closer together in all fields of social life.

Consequently, to build an advanced socialist society means — to do everything to ensure that relations within society and people's physical and intellectual capacities can develop to the best advantage and to do all that is necessary for people to shape their lives in a meaningful and cultured manner and for the thoughts and actions of working people to be motivated by socialist ideology, by the Marxist-Leninist world outlook of the working class.

[. . .]

The social structure

The socialist mode of production has radically changed the structure of society in the German Democratic Republic. The exploitation of man by man and class contradictions have been done away with once and for all. The determined alliance policy pursued by the Socialist Unity Party of Germany has, on the basis of socialist relations of power and ownership and on the strength of working people's socialist consciousness, given rise to close and lasting relations of friendly and creative co-operation between the working class, the class of co-operative farmers, intellectuals and professional people and the other sections of the working population.

The leading role of the working class and its Marxist-Leninist Party as well as the importance of the trade unions increase in all fields of social endeavour during the construction of an advanced socialist society. The Party will continue to direct its efforts towards strengthening the influence of the working class in all spheres of human activity.

The working class is the principal political and social force in social progress and the numerically strongest class. It holds political power, it is directly linked to socialist public property and it produces the bulk of the material wealth of society at large. Its interests reflect the fundamental interests of the entire people. Its role in social production and its leadership by a Marxist-Leninist Party enable the working class — the most highly organized, most disciplined and most politically conscious class — to lead the way in the struggle of all working people for social advance. It is capable of living up to its historic mission because Marxism-Leninism, the only scientific word outlook, is its guide to action.

The Socialist Unity Party of Germany considers it its task to bring out fully the political awareness and creative energy of the working class. The realization of the leading role of the working class is inseparably bound up with the solution of the political, economic, social, intellectual and cultural tasks arising in the construction of an advanced socialist society.

The main areas in which the working class develops further are the campaign for increased labour productivity and for scientific and technological advance, the socialist emulation and innovation movements and the active participation of workers in management and planning and in the further advancement of socialist democracy. Qualities such as creativity, initiative, fellowship, thirst for knowledge, a sense of social responsibility, mutual aid and a cultured way of life are becoming more and more pronounced in this process.

The Socialist Unity Party of Germany seeks a systematic increase in the level of political and ideological development of the working class and in the political and vocational qualifications of the working people. This will help to overcome the principal distinctions between physical and mental labour step by step. Workers qualified for skilled jobs will make up a growing proportion of the total labour force and more and more workers will benefit from specialized and higher education.

The alliance between the working class and the class of co-operative farmers is the political foundation of socialist society. The Socialist Unity Party of Germany will continue to give much attention to the constant strengthening of this alliance. The tried and tested alliance between the working class and the co-operative farmers will be enhanced by the progressive industrialization of farming and the optimization of socialist production relations in agriculture as well as by the interpenetration of agriculture and the other sectors of the economy involved in food production.

Living conditions in the countryside will become more and more similar to those in urban areas. Great stress will be laid on the continuous improvement of housing conditions in the countryside. Workers and co-operative farmers are working together and for each other. The working class helps the farmers in developing the socialist way of life in the countryside. The co-operative farmers, by their work, raise the cultural and living standards of the entire people and thereby improve their own lives. The co-operative farmers' standard of Marxist-Leninist education and technical qualifications, and the degree of their organization and conscious participation in the constuction of an advanced socialist society will increase.

The intelligentsia, the professional and intellectual section of the population, in alliance with the working class and the class of co-operative farmers, makes a growing contribution to the all-round development of socialist society. The social composition of the intelligentsia is distinguished by the fact that it has its origins primarily in the working class and the class of co-operative farmers. Due to its social background and the nature of its work this section is inseparably linked with all other working people in socialist society. New forms of joint activity have come about among workers and salaried employees, technologists, engineers and economists, co-operative farmers and agronomists as part of the process of intensifying social production. The socialist intelligentsia will contribute significantly to social progress by performing outstanding work in science and technology, education, medicine and culture. The Socialist Unity Party of Germany advocates a systematic development of the conditions necessary for the creative activity of scientists, teachers, medical practitioners, cultural workers and other intellectuals and professional people and a systematic increase in their share of the working population.

Socialist society offers craftsmen and small tradesmen favourable opportunities for using their energies and abilities in the best interests of the community, playing an active part in the construction of the new society and receiving adequate reward for their work. Craftsmen and tradesmen are expected to contribute significantly to the safeguarding and extension of services for the general public.

The various classes and sections of society are drawing closer together in a momentous and prolonged process governed by the objective laws of history. This process will advance owing to the fuller development of socialist relations of production, the advancement of the productive forces in town and country, the enhancement of socialist democracy, the raising of educational standards, the growth of mental labour in the process of production and the further inprovement of working and living conditions.

The closer association of the various classes and sections of society takes place within the framework of leadership by the Party on the basis of the Marxist-Leninist world outlook and the ideals of the working class. It leads to a stronger political and moral unity of the people and goes hand in hand with the development of a socialist way of life.

The Socialist Unity Party of Germany devotes much attention to the promotion of women. In all fields of human endeavour, working women make a tremendous contribution to political, economic, scientific, technological, social, intellectual and cultural progress. The Socialist Unity Party of Germany will make every effort to create everywhere conditions enabling women to make ever fuller use of their equal status in society and allowing for further improvements in women's working and living conditions. The consolidation of women's status in society and the development of their personality require determined efforts to ensure that women can reconcile the demands of their job still more successfully with their duties towards child and family.

The Socialist Unity Party of Germany puts its full faith in young people, devolving upon them heavy responsibilities in the construction of an advanced socialist society and in creating the conditions for the gradual transition to communism. Young people play a major role in the all-round strengthening and protection of the GDR. The Party passes the revolutionary fighting and working experience of the working class on to the rising generation and encourages boys and girls to acquire fundamental Marxist-Leninist knowledge, comprehensive qualifications and professional skill as well as the political and moral stature of revolutionary fighters for communism. It considers it the class duty of all communists to bear particular responsibility for the upbringing and education of young people in the spirit of communism.

The political system of an advanced socialist society

The policy of the Socialist Unity Party of Germany is aimed at the continued all-round strengthening of the socialist workers' and farmers' state as a form of the dictatorship of the proletariat representing the interests of the whole people of the GDR. It is the chief instrument of the working people, led by the working class, in the construction of an advanced socialist society and along the road to communism. The Leninist principle of democratic centralism is the proven foundation for the structure and activity of all organs of socialist state power and their co-operation.

The socialist state directs the planned development of society's productive forces, and promotes scientific and technological progress and a steady increase in labour productivity. The state develops the socialist relations of production, friendly co-operation, mutual aid and socialist team-work among working people and it raises their educational and cultural standards and their socialist sense of responsibility. The tasks of the state in the domain of social policy will steadily grow in importance.

The state organizes national defence and is responsible for seeing that the socialist system and the right of its people to live in peace are reliably protected. It safeguards public and private property and the rights and freedoms of its citizens.

It is one function of the various organs of the state to promote and implement fraternal co-operation with the Union of Soviet Socialist Republics and the other states and peoples of the socialist community in all fields of activity on the basis of bilateral and multilateral treaties, and to strengthen the GDR as an inseparable part of the socialist community as well as to preserve the sovereignty of the GDR and to repulse any attempt by imperialist states to encroach upon this sovereignty.

The main path of development for the socialist state will be to bring out and maximize all the advantages of socialist democracy. Citizens' multifaceted participation in the running of public and economic affairs is increasingly becoming the dominant feature of life in socialism. The socialist state guarantees all citizens their political freedoms and social rights: the right to work, recreation, free education and health protection, provision for the elderly, the sick and the disabled, equal rights for all citizens irrespective of race, nationality, world outlook, religious convictions and social status. It guarantees equal status for men and women in all areas of political, economic and cultural life.

The Socialist Unity Party of Germany encourages working people's preparedness to contribute to the fulfilment of the tasks facing the state and society and to accept their fair share of responsibility. The authorities are obliged to take due account of citizens' initiatives and proposals in carrying out their tasks.

The SED is guided by the idea that the role of the popular representative bodies as the elected organs of government will increase in importance. Their work is characterized by the ever wider and increasingly expert participation of working people, and collectives thereof, in the management and planning of economic, social and cultural development, in the preparation, enforcement and supervision of laws and government decisions. The authority of members of Parliament and other elected assemblies is to be constantly enhanced.

The SED favours measures to bring central and local government to a higher level of efficiency to cope with the growing tasks arising in the construction of an advanced socialist society. This makes it necessary for the various organs of government to adopt a scientific, rational style of work, to maintain close ties with the people and to deal with problems as they arise, and it requires a streamlining of the administrative process. All organs of the state bear a large measure of responsibility for establishing ever closer relations of confidence between citizens and their socialist state. The SED deems it necessary to take an uncompromising stand against examples of bureaucratic and unfeeling behaviour. Strict accountability and control by the public are essential ingredients of socialism. The Worker's and Farmers' Inspectorate has a major role to play in this respect.

In conformity with the principles of democratic centralism evolved by Lenin, central management and planning of social processes will be focused more and more on expertly deciding fundamental questions. The responsibility and initiative of local authorities, enterprises, co-operatives and institutions in carrying out administrative tasks will be encouraged. Co-operation among local authorities, towns, villages and associations thereof, and between these and enterprises, social organizations, and National Front committees will open up substantial reserves to be used for the good of the working people.

The systematic development of the socialist legal system to reflect the degree of maturity of socialist society and the upholding of legal protection and justice are an integral part of the policy pursued by the Socialist Unity Party of Germany. Socialist law is an expression of working-class power. It serves to further the interests of working people, to protect the socialist system, civil freedoms and human dignity. The establishment of optimum rules of law, especially in the economic sector and in the relationship between the countries fraternally allied in the socialist community, will assume great importance.

It is a major task of the authorities, social organizations and every single citizen to encourage people to observe the socialist rules of law of their own free will, to protect socialist property, including from damage, loss and fire, and to experience discipline and a high degree of vigilance. The strict enforcement of socialist legality requires that violations of the law be punished appropriately.

The work of the judiciary and the security organs will be linked still more closely with public activities to enforce socialist legality and to ensure order and security; and the rights of social courts — arbitration and disputes commissions dealing with minor civil cases — will be expanded.

The social organizations of working people play a great role in the implementation of socialist democracy. The Socialist Unity Party of Germany will support the trade unions, the Free German Youth, the Women's Democratic Federation, the Gymnastics and Sports Federation of the GDR, the League of Culture and all other working people's organizations in the fulfilment of their specific tasks.

The trade unions are the most comprehensive form of class organization of the working class. They are schools of socialism and socialist economic management. Being representatives of working people's interests, they bear a large share of responsibility for the all-round strengthening of the socialist system and the stable development of the socialist economy.

Socialist democracy in the sphere of material production will continue to grow in importance. The responsibilities of the trade unions increase simultaneously with the role of collectives in socialist enterprises. In the socialist emulation campaign, the trade unions mobilize the workers for the attainment of ambitious economic goals. Through their activities, they encourage a socialist attitude to work. Persistent efforts to keep improving working and living conditions figure prominently in the work of trade unions. The unions play a major part in forming and carrying out the social policy of our Party.

The Free German Youth is the socialist youth organization of the German Democratic Republic. The Socialist Unity Party of Germany supports the Free German Youth as the active helper and reserve force of the Party. It considers it the primary task of the socialist youth organization to mould class-conscious fighters for social advance and to see to it that all young people make use of the opportunities given them to organize their work, study and leisure, indeed their whole life, in a meaningful way and that they become the architects and staunch defenders of socialism and communism.

Long-standing co-operation with the allied parties and mass organizations united in the Democratic Bloc and in the National Front of the German Democratic Republic is one of the principles of the alliance policy pursued by the Socialist Unity Party of Germany in building up an advanced socialist society. The National Front, being a socialist movement of the people, contributes significantly to bringing the various classes and sections of the community closer together on the basis of the world outlook and ideals of the working class. It develops close relations between people in urban and rural communities. Its political work at grass roots level is important for the continuous development of socialist democracy, for the systematic improvement of working and living conditions, for the beautification of towns and villages and for a many-faceted intellectual and cultural life.

The Party is the leading force in the construction of an advanced socialist society and in the transition to communism

The Socialist Unity Party of Germany is the Marxist-Leninist Party of the working class and of all working people in the socialist German Democratic Republic. It is the leading force in the construction of an advanced socialist society. The further enhancement of its leading role in all spheres of social life is essential for paving the way for the gradual transition to the construction of a communist society. To serve the well-being and happiness of the people, to lead the way with unfaltering step and to set an example to the millions building the new society — this is what the struggles and lives of communists is all about.

The Party's task is to provide political leadership in the social development of the German Democratic Republic on the basis of scientific strategy and tactics. As the tasks involved in the management and planning of social processes in all their forms and aspects become ever wider in scope and increasingly complex, political leadership of society by the Marxist-Leninist Party assumes a proportionately greater importance. It is the overriding factor in the successful shaping of a society bearing the mark of the victorious, revolutionary working class. The working class is only capable of accomplishing its revolutionary and creative historic mission if the Party, as its politically conscious and organized vanguard and chief class organization, lives up to its responsibilities in providing leadership.

Marxism-Leninism in its entirety is the theoretical foundation for all the Party's activities. Only on the basis of this universally valid scientific doctrine and its creative development is it possible to carry the revolutionary struggle for the interests of the working class and all working people to victory. Marxism-Leninism is the most reliable guide in the building of an advanced socialist society and in the transition to communism.

The Socialist Unity Party of Germany provides the conscious and systematic activity of the working people with both direction and purpose; it enhances and strengthens socialist class consciousness, and it arouses and stimulates the creative initiative of the people in shaping a socialist society and way of life. The central idea of the political and ideological work of the Socialist Unity Party of Germany is to arm the working class and all working people with the revolutionary ideas of Marxism-Leninism, to explain to them the policies of the Party, to develop their socialist thought, feeling and action, to mobilize them into action and to enable them to resist all influences of imperialist and bourgeois ideology. Each and every member of the Socialist Unity Party of Germany must be an active fighter on the ideological front.

Wherever a communist works and lives he will disseminate and champion Marxism-Leninism as a guide to conscious action for the interests of the working class and all other working people, and he will demonstrate the superiority of socialism, its values and achievements.

The further enhancement of socialist patriotism and proletarian internationalism is among the foremost political and ideological tasks of the Socialist Unity Party of Germany. Socialist patriotism is heightened by the pride people take in their revolutionary traditions and by their awareness that they have achieved great things and opened up new horizons in the construction of the socialist German Democratic Republic. Socialist civic awareness — and with it pride about what has been accomplished — will have to be linked even more firmly with the internationalist awareness that the further strengthening of our Republic adds to the strength of the socialist community and the entire world revolutionary movement. Conversely, the all-round strengthening of the socialist community is essential for the German Democratic Republic to forge further ahead.

Wherever a communist works and lives he will work in an exemplary manner for his socialist homeland, which is an integral part of the family of nations gathered around the Soviet Union, and he will implant the ideas of socialist patriotism and proletarian internationalism in the hearts and minds of the people.

The aim of the Party's political and ideological work is to channel the energy, initiative and creativity of working people towards the attainment of the objectives set out in this Programme, especially to promote and constantly raise socialist working morale. This is of fundamental importance for the accomplishment of the economic and overall social tasks envisaged and for the development of a socialist personality. Political and ideological work will have to lay greater emphasis on the educational impact of collective work so that the characteristic features of socialist personalities may develop to the best advantage.

Wherever a communist works and lives he will be firmly committed to the Party's central policy of improving working and living conditions and he will, in an active and exemplary way, encourage creative initiative, conscientious work and a concern for the preservation of public property as well as all socialist patterns of thought and behaviour.

A major object of political and ideological work is to refute, forcibly and conclusively, imperialist ideology and policy in all its manifestations. The Socialist Unity Party of Germany will defend Marxism-Leninism against any attack. Historical experience shows that only the realization of the teachings of Marx, Engels and Lenin, only socialism, can solve the problems facing humankind. Through its ideological work the Party heightens class vigilance towards any hostile machinations.

Wherever a communist works and lives he will loyally stand by the revolutionary working class and the ideals of communism, and he will resolutely expose the inhuman and reactionary nature of imperialism and unceasingly struggle against its ideology.

Special demands will be made on the press, radio and television. They will cope successfully with their growing tasks if they wield the truth as a sharp weapon and spell out what is right, using clear language and compelling arguments. The socialist mass media will see their influence increase further; what they have to say owes its impact to the correctness of our theory and policy which finds its practical confirmation in real life, in the experience of the people.

The Party will thoroughly and systematically arm all its members with the scientific doctrine of Marxism-Leninism, its proven and superior intellectual weapon. Central to all forms of its educational work will be profound study of the works of Marx, Engels and Lenin, of Party decisions, and of documents of the world communist movement, especially of the decisions and experiences of the Communist Party of the Soviet Union. The unity of theory and practice will be consistently ensured in the education and further training of cadres. The first essential will be to develop the capacity of all members to produce arguments that are cogent and backed up with facts, and to defend the class position of the working class in a militant way.

As a voluntary association of communist fighters for a common cause who actively and selflessly work for the implementation of Party decisions, the Party will continue to strengthen political, ideological and organizational unity and cohesion within its ranks. Underlying the structure of the Party, its inner life and the methods of its work is the principle of democratic centralism. Strict application of this well-established principle, which is inseparably linked with consistent adherence to the Leninist standards of Party life, is a cardinal principle for a Marxist-Leninist Party. It guarantees that all communists are united in will and in action.

Collective decision-making and individual responsibilty, confidence and mutual help, criticism and self-criticism are characteristic features of Party life, which moulds the character of a communist, demanding and promoting all his abilities and talents enabling him to exercise his duties and his rights. An atmosphere of communist solidarity is evolving on this basis.

The relations of confidence which the Socialist Unity Party of Germany maintains with the working class, the co-operative farmers, intellectuals and professional people and the rest of the working population are the most important foundation for its successful activity. Teaching the working people while at the same time learning from them, the Party is leading the way, relying on the creative energies of the people.

Collective decision-making is the paramount principle underlying the activity of Party committees. It draws on a wealth of experience and multiplies the strength of the community. At the same time, it is proving to be the safest means against complacency, bureaucratic attitudes, disregard of criticism, and subjectivism.

It is chiefly through the activities of its branches, through the day-to-day work of every comrade that the Party brings its guiding and organizational influence to bear on all areas of social development. For every member and candidate member the branch is his political home in which he is deeply rooted, which is a source of decisive stimulation for his life, work and struggle, and in which he feels at ease and gains ever new strength thanks to the truly communist atmosphere of commitment and confidence prevailing there. The branches provide a direct link between the Party and all working people. It is their activity above all that adds to the strength and influence of the Party.

The work of Party collectives and of each of their members in administrative departments and economic bodies, in enterprises and institutions is gaining in importance. Their purposeful and persistent political and ideological work on the basis of Party decisions is the clue to further advance in all spheres of social life. Party members play an active role in the trade unions which provide the working class with much of its leverage in the economy and society.

It largely depends on the persuasiveness, mobilizing force and exemplary work of the communists active in the Confederation of Free German Trade Unions, in the Free German Youth, in the Women's Democratic Federation of Germany, in the Gymnastics and Sports Federation of the GDR, in the German-Soviet Friendship Society, in all other social organizations and in the committees of the National Front in which way these bodies fulfil their responsible tasks in building an advanced socialist society.

As the politically conscious and organized vanguard of the working class in the German Democratic Republic, the Socialist Unity Party of Germany has developed into a strong, large and militant Marxist-Leninist Party during the successful construction of socialism. It will continue to draw class-conscious workers into its ranks, because only a Party deeply rooted in its class is capable of enabling the revolutionary working class to fulfil its historic mission as the architect of a new society.

The Socialist Unity Party of Germany is a wing and integral part of the international communist and working-class movement, a Party pledged to proletarian internationalism. In keeping with the international character of the historic mission of the working class it makes its own contribution to the advance of the world revolutionary process, carrying out its international class duty.

The Socialist Unity Party of Germany considers that the attitude to the Communist Party of the Soviet Union and to the Union of Soviet Socialist Republics continues to be the telling indicator of fidelity to Marxism-Leninism, to the revolutionary cause of the working class and its historic mission.

The Socialist Unity Party of Germany systematically develops and expands its fraternal and intimate relations of friendship with all communist and workers' Parties in the countries of the socialist community. As socialism gathers more and more strength, their closer co-operation in all areas of political, theoretical, ideological and organizational activity assumes still greater importance, because it is socialism that gives the decisive impetus to the irresistible world revolutionary process.

The Socialist Unity Party of Germany will consolidate and expand its fraternal and friendly relations with the communist and workers' Parties in the capitalist countries. Its constant preoccupation is to complete its tasks in the anti-imperialist struggle and in the campaign for peace and security through internationalist co-operation and to promote the exchange of experience and views between all revolutionary forces.

The Socialist Unity Party of Germany will develop and expand its fraternal relations with the communist and workers' Parties of Asia, Africa and Latin America. It will work to develop and expand its friendly co-operation with the revolutionary-democratic and anti-imperialist parties and movements of the peoples in these regions. It will continue to extend fraternal solidarity to all peoples fighting for their freedom and for independence and social advance.

In all its activities the Socialist Unity Party of Germany will strictly honour its internationalist obligations. It will make an active and systematic contribution to strengthening the unity and cohesion of the world communist movement on the basis of Marxism-Leninism and proletarian internationalism. It will contribute to uniting the powerful forces of the world socialist system, of the revolutionary working-class movement in the capitalist countries and of the national liberation movement in the fight against imperialism, the mortal enemy of the peoples, and in the struggle for social progress on all continents and in all countries.

In the interests of joint action against imperialism and for a durable and stable peace, in the interests of common struggle, especially against the forces bent on sabotaging the policy of peace, the Socialist Unity Party of Germany seeks co-operation with all democratic organizations and movements. It supports joint initiatives with socialist and social-democratic parties to meet the peoples' vital interest in security and peaceful co-operation in Europe and in the world at large, and to meet urgent demands of working people in the present and in the future.

The Socialist Unity Party of Germany is unwavering in its belief that the just cause of the international working class will emerge victorious on a worldwide scale.

Communism is our aim

In the German Democratic Republic, the working people are building an advanced socialist society under the leadership of the Socialist Unity Party of Germany. The accomplishment of this task is a historic step along the road to communism, which coincides with communist construction in the Union of Soviet Socialist Republics and the development of socialism in the other countries of the socialist community.

Marxism-Leninism provides a scientific definition of the second phase of communism, which is being confirmed by the universally valid experience of socialist and communist construction in the USSR and in the other socialist countries.

Communism is a classless society in which all means of production are socially owned, in which there are no social distinctions and in which all members of the community develop their mental and physical capacities to the full and use them for the greater good of the community.

Communism is a society in which the productive forces, the source of all social wealth, are developed on planned lines on the basis of steady advances in science and technology in order to be used with maximum efficiency for the well-being of the people.

Communism is a society which will enable people, on the strength of their scientific world outlook and their spiritual potentialities, to develop the productive forces, the relations of production and intellectual and cultural life in a planned way and to master nature and their own social development to an ever greater extent.

Communism is a society of universally educated human beings who display a high degree of political awareness, who administer public affairs consciously and rationally and who ensure maximum efficiency of production and services.

Communism is a society in which work for the common good is the prime necessity of life, a society in which all working men and women avail themselves of their abilities to secure the greatest benefits for the people.

Communism is a society in which everyone will contribute according to his ability and receive according to his needs.

Essential for the realization of the communist principle of distribution is very high productivity of social labour as brought forth by the creative efforts of working people in communist society and by the effective use of the material and technological foundations of communism.

The material and spiritual requirements of man will develop steadily in correlation with material resources; and individual abilities, demands and inclinations will be marked by great diversity and scope. Their development and satisfaction presupposes a rapid increase in production and an acute sense of responsibility towards future generations in the management of the natural environment.

As science, technology and culture advance, man's spiritual requirements grow. Differences in demands, intellectual capacities and activities give rise to a great variety of material and spiritual requirements. Communism encourages the gifts and abilities of all members of society.

Three tasks inseparably linked with each other will have to be achieved in building communism:

First, to lay the material and technological foundations of communism.

Second, to establish communist relations of production and a communist character of labour.

Third, to develop communist social relations and to mould the new man distinctive of communist society.

Communism is a society that gives everyone full opportunity to perform creative work and to lead a cultured and meaningful life. The establishment of an advanced socialist society opens the way to laying the material and technological foundations of communism, transforming socialist social relations into communist social relations and developing communist consciousness. The pace at which the construction of an advanced socialist society and the transition to communist construction are accomplished depends on the work, the political consciousness, the creative initiative and the organized action of millions of working people in town and country.

The progressive, gradual transition to communism, and the emergence of a classless society take place along planned lines and on a scientific basis, full play being given to the initiative and creativity of all people under the leadership and guidance of the Marxist-Leninist Party.

The establishment of communism will be the crowning achievement of the historic struggle waged by the international working class against exploitation, oppression and war, and for peace, democracy and social advance.

The peoples will build socialism and communism, led by the Marxist-Leninist Parties whose role in the life of society is growing continuously. The countries of the socialist community will draw closer together to reach a qualitatively new level of association on the basis of a high degree of socialist economic integration and multifarious forms of co-operation in all areas of social life.

The process of convergence between socialist nations will make further headway owing to their economic, political and intellectual interests and to their friendship and all-round co-operation.

Communism is the bright future of mankind. In communism, all exploitation and oppression will have been abolished and man will have been rid of the scourge of war. Communism will be a world of peace, work, freedom, equality and brotherhood. In communism, all peoples of the world, all human beings will be able to realize their potentialities to the full.

It is for this noble aim that the Socialist Unity Party of Germany is fighting.

(Source as above)

D43 Political parties and political representation, from "The German Democratic Republic", the official handbook produced by the foreign Press Agency, Panorama DDR, 1986:

The GDR is a democratic state. Its Constitution, elected assemblies and authoritative bodies represent the unity of all political and social forces of the people gathered under the leadership of the working class and its party, the Socialist Unity Party of Germany (SED). The alliance of all classes and strata and the socialist ownership of the means of production are fundamentals of socialist society.

The proven co-operation between the SED and the other political parties and mass organizations is marked by strict respect for the complete political and organizational independence of all elements of the political system in the GDR.

Comprehensive political, economic, social and cultural rights guaranteed by the law make sure that all citizens have the chance to play an active part in the preparation, implementation and control of government decisions.

Basic rights and duties

The Constitution of the GDR guarantees all citizens the basic right to live in peace and to participate in formulating the country's political and economic strategies and shaping its social and cultural life.

The right to participation in public affairs is solidly ensured. All government authorities are elected in a democratic process. The public takes an active part in their work, and the people are involved in the management of society, in planning and developing social life.

Every citizen has the same rights and duties, irrespective of nationality, race, philosophy, religious confession, social background and position in society. Upon completion of their 18th year of life every citizen of the GDR has the right to vote and is eligible for all people's assemblies.

The right to work is guaranteed under the Constitution and the Labour Code and practised in everyday life. Socialist ownership of the means of production and state planning and management are the reasons why full employment and job security are ensured in the GDR. All citizens can rest assured in the knowledge that they will receive sound training followed by a job. The right to equal pay for equal work applies to both men and women, adults and youths.

The right to education ensures that a high level of education is imparted to all young people regardless of the social status of their parents, and that everybody has access to the highest education institutions. The integrated socialist education system offers everyone equal opportunities. All young people have the right and the duty to learn a trade or profession.

The right to freedom of expression is guaranteed. Every citizen can, in compliance with the principles of the constitution, freely and publicly express their opinion without prejudice to their person or status. The freedom of the press, radio and television is firmly protected. The law forbids any manifestation of militarist and revanchist propaganda. Expressions of hatred of any particular faith, race or nation will be regarded as criminal acts and punished accordingly.

The right to freedom of conscience and belief means that every citizen is able to profess their religious faith and to worship. The churches and other religious communities function in compliance with the relevant legal stipulations.

Equal rights for women are assured in all spheres of life. State authorities are obliged to treat women as citizens with equal rights and to promote women in society. Socialist society has created all the necessary political and economic conditions for implementing this basic human right. There is not one single democratic institution in the GDR where women are not duly represented and do highly appreciated work. Economic independence of women is guaranteed by the right to work.

Young people's rights, in particular the right to work and leisure, to equal political involvement, to education, to joy and happiness as well as the realization of these rights offer the young every opportunity to help advance the socialist development of the GDR. Responsibility and confidence is placed in young people in all areas of development.

The legal system

The legal system in the GDR serves to implement the interests of the working people, uphold legality and protect the freedom and dignity of the citizens. It ensures that laws and regulations are strictly adhered to. Legal security is an essential feature of the socialist state. It guarantees equality before the law. Legality is guaranteed by including the citizens in the administration of the law and in the mechanism to monitor adherence to the law.

The administration of justice is ensured through the Supreme Court, the county and district courts and the lay courts. The People's Chamber of the GDR lays down the guidelines for the work of the Supreme Court and the Prosecutor General.

Lay courts are an integral part of the socialist legal system. As a form of democratic involvement in the administration of justice they operate as grievance commissions at enterprise level and as arbitration commissions in residential areas in the towns, communities and in the production co-operatives, dealing with cases of industrial law, minor civil matters and other petty legal disputes.

The Department of Public Prosecutions is entrusted with the task to protect the public against criminal offenders. It is headed by the Prosecutor General and sees to the strict observance of law.

The German People's Police is under the jurisdiction of the Ministry of the Interior. The police have the responsibility of maintaining public order and security as well as guaranteeing a peaceful life for each and everyone. Their most important task is to prevent and ward off threats to life and limb. They lead the fight against crime and other breaches of the law. In their work they can rely on the support of many voluntary helpers who, above all, work in road safety committees and voluntary fire brigades.

Political parties and mass organizations

In the GDR there is no social class or stratum which lives from the exploitation of another. Instead, everyone has the same interest in seeing that state and society develop for the good of all citizens and that everyone, according to performance, can enjoy the fruits of society's successes. Through their specific capabilities, traditions and attitudes all classes and strata make their contribution to society.

In the same way as the GDR is the result of the combined efforts of the leading working class, the co-operative farmers, the intelligentsia and other working people, the political system is characterized by trusting and comradely co-operation between the parties and mass organizations.

The following parties and mass organizations have their own representatives in the people's assemblies at all levels:

The Socialist Unity Party of Germany (SED)

As the party of the working class the SED is the leading party in the GDR. In Marxism-Leninism it has at its disposal a theory of society and its development which is scientifically based and has shown its practical worth. It translates into reality the tasks and goals which Marx, Engels and Lenin identified as the mission of the working class in building a socialist society in the interests of all working people. The SED, which was founded in the spring of 1946 and was the result of the merger of the two German workers' parties — the Communist Party of Germany (KPD) and the Social Democratic Party of Germany (SPD) — is continuing to uphold all the revolutionary traditions of the German workers' movement. It unites in its ranks more than two million of the most progressive members from the working class, co-operative farmers, the intelligentsia and other working people. The highest party organ is the Party Congress which takes place every five years. There the general direction and the principles of the policy of the SED are decided on and the Central Committee is elected which will lead the party between congresses.

The Democratic Farmers' Party of Germany (DBD)

The DBD was founded on 29 April 1948 as a democratic party for working farmers. Its main concern is that each of its members should make their own contribution to strengthening socialism and peace. The DBD makes an important contribution to strengthening the alliance between the working class and the co-operative farmers, to introducing new scientific and technological findings in agriculture, increasing the efficiency of agricultural production and promoting socialist development in the villages. The DBD has approximately 110,000 members.

The Christian Democratic Union of Germany (CDU)

The CDU unites people who, motivated by Christian faith and traditions, are committed to peace, human dignity and social justice and actively build socialism. It acts to get social concerns of people of Christian faith considered in government policy and promotes co-operation between Christians and Marxists on a basis of equal rights and duties. The CDU was founded on 26 June 1945 and has approximately 132,000 members.

The Liberal Democratic Party of Germany (LDPD)

The LDPD is predominantly a party of craftsmen, retailers and intellectuals. Its political motivations are rooted in the struggles of progressive bourgeois democrats who fought in the interest of the people against militarism and fascism. Under the party's statutes, the members are called upon to take an active part in implementing the GDR's peace policy and continuing its course of translating economic progress into social benefit. The LDPD was founded on 5 July 1945 and has approximately 96,000 members.

The National Democratic Party of Germany (NDPD)

The NDPD is mainly composed of members of the former middle classes. It greatly helped to overcome nationalistic thinking. Its members are private and co-operative craftsmen, tradespeople, intellectuals and cultural workers. The main thrust of the party's political work is to strengthen socialist state consciousness. The NDPD bears a great deal of responsibility for the political and moral as well as the socio-economic development of these sectors of the population it represents. The party was founded on 25 May 1948 and has more than 100,000 members.

The Confederation of Free German Trade Unions (FDGB)

The FDGB is the unified, free and independent trade union organization and is the largest mass and class organization of the workers, embracing 16 industrial and other unions with a total membership of more than 9 million. This is over 97 per cent of all working people, excluding the members of co-operatives.

At the national and local level the trade unions play an equal and constructive role in the management of the state and the economy. All laws which concern the working and living conditions of the working people must be discussed with the FDGB and require union consent. The unions have an important say in the planning of the economy ranging from the discussion of yearly plans for each enterprise to the adoption of the national economic plan.

The FDGB was founded on 15 June 1945. Since 1 January 1949 it has been a member of the World Federation of Trade Unions.

The Free German Youth (FDJ)

The FDJ has approximately 2.3 million members. On a voluntary basis more than three quarters of all young people aged between 14 and 25 have decided to join this organization. The FDJ is the uniform and independent political youth organization in the GDR. The junior wing of the FDJ is the Ernst Thälmann Pioneer Organization for boys and girls of six to 14 years of age.

The FDJ has particularly close relations to the Socialist Unity Party of Germany and is the party's active helper and reserve force amongst the young.

The FDJ was founded on 7 March 1946. Since 1948 it has been a member of the World Federation of Democratic Youth and since 1950 a member of the International Union of Students.

The Women's Democratic Federation of Germany (DFD)

The DFD is the unified, democratic mass movement for women. It has set itself the task of winning over women from all groups of the population to the idea of active involvement in society and is particularly active in residential areas and at grassroots level. It offers women a wide range of educational opportunities and social involvement and helps to make the equal rights of women in society, as guaranteed in the constitution, a reality.

The DFD was founded on 8 March 1947. 1.5 million women from all sectors of society form the membership. Since 1948 the DFD has been a member of the Womens' International Democratic Federation (WIDF).

The League of Culture of the GDR (KB)

The members of this the largest cultural organization in the GDR take a keen interest, in their more than 10,000 interest groups, in all aspects of cultural life in towns and villages. They devote a great deal of attention to the work environment and the promotion of knowledge, science and technology. They encourage the upholding of, and the familiarization with, the cultural heritage, the spreading of art and literature and varied cultural and creative activities of the citizens.

The League of Culture was founded on 3 July 1945 and has more than 265,000 members, with more than 20 per cent of its members being under 30 years of age.

The Mutual Farmers' Aid Association (VdgB)

The VdgB is a mass organization made up of co-operative farmers and gardeners. Its 570,000 members help boost agricultural production through institutions aimed at reducing the strain of work and increasing productivity.

The VdgB helps co-operative farms and small-scale producers through its facilities, hire centres and DIY-workshops.

The National Front

The National Front was born in 1949, the foundation year of the GDR, giving the new state a wide foundation in all classes and strata and among all democratic and patriotic forces in the country. Nowadays it is the GDR's socialist popular movement which unites the political parties, mass organizations and individual citizens. The National Front organizes and supervises all public elections in the GDR. It has taken it upon itself to make people aware of their civic responsibility, to co-operate closely with the people's assemblies, the enterprises and other institutions and to develop a rich intellectual and cultural life in the towns and communities. It encourages socialist civic consciousness and citizens' initiatives.

Hundreds of thousands of people are taking part, for example, in community improvement campaigns offering their help to implement the country's housing programme. They participate in laying out children's playgrounds, building indoor swimming pools and sprucing up residential areas. In the neighbourhoods they assist elderly people and maintain parks and green spaces, sports grounds and cultural establishments.

The Democratic Bloc is the core of the National Front and an umbrella organization uniting all political parties as well as the Confederation of Free German Trade Unions, the Free German Youth, the Women's Democratic Federation of Germany, the League of Culture and the Mutual Farmers' Aid Association. It is a forum to discuss all fundamental issues of the GDR's domestic and foreign policies, ensuring united action of the members of all political parties and mass organizations. All decisions must be taken by consensus and the office of chairman rotates on a regular basis.

The people's assemblies

The elected people's assemblies are the basis of the system of state authorities. They constitute all government departments. All people's assemblies are elected for a period of five years in free, general, equal elections by secret ballot.

The elected representatives are accountable to the electorate. They must report on their activities and include the electors in the preparation, implementation and monitoring of governmental decisions. Work methods include regular political surgeries in enterprises and their constituency. An elected representative who grossly neglects his duties can, in accordance with the procedures laid down in the law, be recalled by the electorate.

The elected representatives in the German Democratic Republic are not full-time politicians but continue with their respective occupations. If necessary for the exercise of their duties as an elected representative, they are exempted from work and continue to receive full pay.

Every people's assembly establishes its committees or commissions. Besides the elected members, these bodies include also citizens with specialist knowledge in certain spheres. The committees and commissions are entrusted with the task to prepare drafts and resolutions, to consult and to monitor the implementation of resolutions adopted.

The People's Chamber is the GDR's supreme representative body. It is the sole constitutional and legislative authority of the country and nobody may curtail its rights. The members of the People's Chamber enjoy personal immunity. The work of the People's Chamber is guided by a presidium whose President is Horst Sindermann, a member of the Politburo of the SED Central Committee.

The People's Chamber takes fundamental decisions concerning the structure and activities of the central government bodies. It elects the chairmen and members of the Council of State and the Council of Ministers, the Chairman of the National Defence Council, the President and the judges of the Supreme Court as well as the Prosecutor General.

The People's Chamber defines the guidelines of the country's foreign policy. It approves or terminates international treaties and is authorized to decide on a state of defence. It can decide to hold plebiscites.

The members of the People's Chamber for the 1986–90 legislative period were elected on 8 June 1986 by 12,392,094 citizens which means that they received 99.94 per cent of the votes cast. Turnout at the election was 99.74 per cent of the electorate.

The Council of State is a body elected by, and responsible to, the People's Chamber. The Chairman of the Council of State is Erich Honecker, General Secretary of the Central Committee of the SED. The Council of State represents the GDR under international law. It is vested with the right to ratify or denounce international treaties. It takes fundamental decisions on matters relating to the defence and security of the country. The Council of State issues the writ for elections to the People's Chamber and the local assemblies and ensures that these elections are prepared and held in a democratic manner. It also exercises the right of amnesty and pardon.

The Council of Ministers is the government of the GDR. An organ of the People's Chamber, it is responsible for translating the state's political strategy into practical measures in the fields of foreign policy, economy, welfare, culture and defence. It is vested with the task of organizing the integrated management of economic processes which are of decisive importance for the country's economy as a whole.

The Council of Ministers stipulates the principles underlying the work of the individual ministries and other departments of central government, defines their competences and monitors the discharge of their duties. It co-ordinates the activities of ministries and other state authorities at the national level and their co-operation with local councils.

The ministers are required to explain the laws and resolutions of the Council of Ministers to all local assemblies and their councils as well as the citizens and to discuss with them the tasks to be solved. The Chairman of the Council of Ministers is Willi Stoph, a member of the Politburo of the SED Central Committee.

The local councils are bodies elected by the local assemblies in the counties, districts, towns, boroughs and communities. They are accountable to the respective assemblies and carry out, on their authorization, the political, economic, social and cultural tasks which come under their jurisdiction.

The election of deputies to people's assemblies

The National Front is the political force organizing and supervising the election process. It has been established practice since the GDR was founded for the political parties and mass organizations to put their candidates nominated for the elections to assemblies at all levels onto one common list of candidates to be presented to the electorate by the National Front. Electoral law requires all candidates proposed for election to an assembly to be monitored first of all by their work teams. If prospective candidates fail to get through this preliminary examination their party or organization may not enter them on the list of the National Front. In this way, the working people have a decisive role to play in determining who shall represent their interests in the elected assemblies. After acceptance by their work teams candidates are required to present themselves to the voters in their constituency and answer any questions they may have. In preparation for elections lists of candidates are drawn up to ensure that all people entitled to vote can exercise their right to vote. The constituency represented by an assembly which is to be elected is divided into wards. For every ward an election committee is formed which ensures that voting at the polling station runs smoothly and properly. In all elections the number of nominated candidates exceeds the number of mandates available. On the day of the election every voter has the opportunity to cross out on the joint list of the National Front those candidates in whom he has no confidence. Voters are entitled to go to the polling booth and vote in secret. After the election the votes are counted in public at the polling station. Candidates who receive more than half of the valid votes cast are elected.

The run-up to the election is always used for a broad discussion on the results of the previous legislative period and on future tasks. It is an opportunity for the citizens to familiarize themselves just as thoroughly with developments on the national scale as with projects concerning their town, village or neighbourhood. Here also they have the opportunity to bring their influence to bear on state planning and decision-making through their suggestions, comments and, if necessary, critical remarks.

Millions of GDR citizens are involved in decision-making:

206,000	elected representatives
186,000	citizens co-operate on the standing committees of local people's assemblies
388,000	people sit on National Front committees
359,000	are involved in the administration of justice
610,000	citizens sit on parents' groups and parent-teacher associations at school
300,000	people are members of shop councils

Members of the People's Chamber according to social background
(Learned trade or first occupation)

Workers	271
Co-operative farmers	31
Office workers	69
Members of the intelligentsia	126
Others	3

Proportion of young deputies (between 18 and 25 years) and of female deputies

	Young deputies per cent	Female deputies per cent
People's Chamber	9	32
County assemblies	17	39
District assemblies	22	43
Village assemblies	15	37
Borough assemblies	23	41

Elected trade union representatives

At group level	1,445,000
Shop stewards	336,000
Cultural organizers	324,000
Sports organizers	275,000
Social insurance representatives	322,000
Safety representatives	307,000
Members of sub-branch committees (AGL)	174,000
Members of trade union branch committees at enterprise, firm and school level	353,000

Members of women's commissions	79,000
Members of retired persons' sub-branch committees	30,000
Members of auditing commissions	129,000

(Panorama DDR: *The German Democratic Republic*, Dresden 1986, pp. 57 ff.)

D44 Resolution of the Central Committee of the SED and the Council of Ministers of the GDR on the Workers' and Farmers' Inspectorate of the GDR, 6 August 1974:

I. The principal tasks of the Workers' and Farmers' Inspectorate

(1) The Workers' and Farmers' Inspectorate (ABI) has the task of helping the party of the working class and the government in carrying out supervision of the realization of its decisions and directives in the combines, enterprises, co-operatives and institutions, and in the state authorities and economic management bodies . . .

It is an important task of the Workers' and Farmers' Inspectorate to help the managers of the state authorities and economic bodies in their successful realization of the state plans and tasks, and to disseminate useful experience. In its activity it does not replace the responsibility of the managers of the state authorities and economic bodies, or the state authorities supervising the implementation of decisions and state instructions. The activity of the Workers' and Farmers' Inspectorate is directed towards:

(a) supervising systematically the fulfilment of the state plans and tasks for the all-round strengthening of the Republic and for the improvement of working and living conditions in a planned way,

(b) uncovering national economic reserves in the use of working time, fixed assets, materials, and financial funds and making effective use of these within the plan to raise the effectiveness of societal production,

(c) influencing the increased adoption of scientific work organization in production and administration, encouraging the introduction of new progressive working methods, and supporting socialist group work, socialist competition, and the innovators' movement,

(d) improving the work of the state authorities and economic management bodies, and using its influence to ensure that managers fulfil their supervisory duties and their duty to supply information to the working people and account to them regularly,

(e) considering carefully the comments, suggestions, criticisms, and submissions made by working people and using its influence to ensure that managers deal with these conscientiously and according to the legal requirements in force,

(f) combating energetically all manifestations which contravene social-ist legality or state discipline, wastage and squandering of people's property, bureaucratism and unfeeling behaviour towards human beings. . .

(3) The Workers' and Farmers' Inspectorate is the supervisory body of the party of the working class and of the government in the areas laid down by resolution. The elected assemblies, the parties and social organizations, and the spheres of national defence, security, justice, and foreign affairs are not subject to its supervision . . .

II. The Committee of the Workers' and Farmers' Inspectorate of the GDR and its organs 7–21

III. The rights of the organs of the Workers' and Farmers' Inspectorate

(22) The organs of the ABI have the right to demand spoken or written information and statements, to examine papers and documents, and to demand written materials which are necessary for the implementation of supervision . . .

The organs of the ABI evaluate the outcome of their supervision with those responsible and put forward proposals for the dissemination of useful experience or for the removal of any shortcomings. Where abuses and contraventions of legality are ascertained they have the right to give those responsible instructions on the re-establishment of legality, and to demand that those to blame shall be called to account personally . . .

Those responsible are required to evaluate carefully the proposals of the organs of the ABI and to carry out their instructions, or have them carried out, without delay. They have to inform the organs of the ABI of this.

(23) Additionally the committees of the ABI are entitled to demand that the relevant bodies and institutions apply economic and material sanctions rigorously, that they carry out reviews and in-depth investigations, and that they provide reports without charge.

The chairs of the committees of the ABI can suspend measures and instructions which are in conflict with decisions of the Central Committee of the SED, with laws of the People's Chamber, and with decisions of the Council of Ministers of the GDR, and can demand that they be revoked by the immediately superior managers . . .

(*Gesetzblatt der Deutschen Demokratischen Republik I*, 1974, p. 389)

D45 Visit to the Politburo, 1984:

The section head introduces me and refers to my submission. Erich Honecker looks at me: "Comrade Professor, please give a short explanation of the purpose of the events you are planning." I give my explanation. All eyes are directed at me. No one interrupts me. Then Honecker looks across at Norden and Hager. There is good reason for this. Each of the members of the Politburo is the absolute ruler in his field. None of the other Politburo members will attempt to interfere in the affairs of another. Only the General Secretary is permitted to cross these boundaries. Norden is responsible for propaganda and Hager for science and culture, and so the planned events come into their sphere of responsibility. Therefore they are to speak first. Norden speaks of the importance of Paul Robeson for the GDR and the international working class. Hager nods in agreement. Honecker looks round. Paul Verner asks, "Will the event cost us dollars?" "No!", I reply. Now there are friendly smiles, the atmosphere becomes somewhat less formal. Sindermann wants to know what the state of Robeson's health is, and then Honecker asks me about Robeson's influence on the American public. My answer appears to be satisfactory. Honecker looks at the clock. The time has already been exceeded. Honecker's eyes move round the Politburo members. There is agreement. I notice the section head beside me breathe a sigh of relief. Everything has gone well. The submission is agreed, passed as a resolution of the Politburo, and is thus the highest law in the GDR. As we leave the conference room the wheels of the party apparatus are already beginning to turn, all of the relevant social machinery is being set in motion. The resolution of the Politburo is converted into practice with quite striking perfection. From now on our committee has at its disposal the total resources of the GDR — the whole party and state apparatus, the trade unions, the National Front, the mass media, the education system, the scientific and cultural institutions, generous finances, simply everything this society has to offer. What small and relatively unimportant committee in any part of our earth could even dream of such possibilities? But for our committee it was no dream, but reality. The reality of real socialism! A positive or a negative reality? Imagine if the President of the United States or the Chancellor of the Federal Republic of Germany, together with their cabinets, received the representatives of every little committee in their country to decide whether and how they are to put on certain cultural events. Any modern social system must eventually collapse under such a nonsensical over-centralization — even real socialism! So why then do they practise this nonsensical over-centralization? This over-centralization is nonsensical only from the viewpoint of a rational democratic organization. On the other hand it is completely in tune with the political nature of real socialism, a dictatorship of the party apparatus. It is in a dictatorship's nature that it does not just seek to concentrate all power in its hands but in fact must do so. For without such a concentration the dictatorship stops being a dictatorship, dictatorial bureaucracy would be able to turn into a democratic centralism and real socialism develop into a truly democratic socialism. And that would mean the death of the gods. But gods are immortal! Or are they?[8]

(Franz Loeser: *Die unglaubwürdige Gesellschaft*, Cologne 1984, pp. 53 f.)

Notes

1. Whereas the People's Congress Movement was very much an attempt at mobilizing grass roots opposition to the threat of the division of Germany, the Soviet blockade of West Berlin was a harsh political display of strength against this division in the wake of the separate currency reform in the western zones. It was counterproductive in propaganda terms and misfired badly, especially in its effect on West German attitudes. In Germany it heralded the beginning of Cold War brinkmanship.

2. It is very much a matter of debate whether any of the GDR constitutions ever met or reflected constitutional or political reality. For a discussion of the constitutions cf. Inge Christopher's article in David Childs (ed.), *Honecker's Germany* (London, Allen & Unwin 1985, pp. 15–31). On the concept of a GDR national literature cf. the discussion between Raymond Hargreaves and Andy Hollis in *GDR Monitor* 7 and 8. For an analysis of the issue of national consciousness cf. G.L. Schweigler, *National Consciousness in Divided Germany*, London/Beverly Hills, Sage 1975.

3. Opportunism and revisionism are strong terms of condemnation within the communist movement. They are predominantly levelled at social democrats, but also at dissidents within the communist parties. A 1958 GDR encyclopaedia characterizes opportunism as politics without principles which abandons the revolutionary class struggle for momentary gains. Opportunism and revisionism believe in the gradual reform of capitalism and are therefore anathema to the communist movement. Revisionism (also reformism) claims that Marxism is outdated and must be reformed.

4. A Slavonic minority of over one hundred thousand Sorbs in the Dresden and Cottbus regions receives special consideration politically and culturally.

5. In 1967 29% of all enterprises were privately owned but produced only 2% of national production. These enterprises are almost exclusively owned by tradesmen, small shopkeepers and publicans.

6. Local government is conceived very much as executive arms of the central government. Recent discussions in *Neues Deutschland* seem to hint that more local self-government might be envisaged.

7. It is interesting to note that the GDR constitution lays down constitutionally what the GDR's foreign policy aims are, especially in respect of the Soviet Union and the Third World.

8. Franz Loeser's book in many respects makes embarrassing reading; nevertheless, it is a rare document inasmuch as it provides an individual's insider experience. Cf. 'Biographies' on Loeser.

3 Public Opinion, Mass Organizations and the Organization of the Masses

"The political system of the GDR comprises all government and social forces and is based on democratic participation by the people. It includes the SED, the political parties allied to it and the mass organizations."

The fundamental principle of public and political life in the GDR is the policy of alliance (*Bündnispolitik*). This principle envisages an alliance between the working class and its party and other classes for the purpose of overcoming the division of society into classes. Through such an alliance, under the conditions of socialism, the other classes are given a positive perspective. Such classes and sections of society would include farmers, farm-workers, trades-men, small entrepreneurs, and members of the intelligentsia. Initial instances of the implementation of the policy of alliance were the anti-fascist democratic coalition, the People's Congress Movement, and the formation of the National Front; a subsequent and crucial alliance is that between the working class and the co-operative farmers. The basis of the alliance policy is that with increasing congruence of interests and increasing social homogeneity a new type of society will emerge. This was proclaimed by Walter Ulbricht in 1967, but the party's position was modified in the Honecker era when it was acknowledged that the GDR was not yet a classless society but rather a non-antagonistic class society.[1] The multi-party system, the mass organizations and professional organizations play an important role in the policy of alliance. They are not only "transmission belts" for propaganda but also have a societally integrative function. As well as their role in lobbying, they also have a mobilizing role for the achievement of a permanent revolutionary process. Apart from the professional associations, the most important mass organizations are: the Confederation of Free German Trade Unions (FDGB), the Free German Youth (FDJ), the Women's Democratic Federation of Germany (DFD), the League of Culture, the National Front, the German-Soviet Friendship

Society, the Society for Sport and Technology (GST), and the Mutual Farmers' Aid Association (VdgB). All of these organizations play an important part in the forming of public opinion. Most are seen and see themselves as "schools of socialism". All of them recognize the leading role of the SED, and within the context of alliance policy they can be described only as junior partners.[2]

As specific example: the role, function, and self-image of the trade unions in the GDR, and in particular the relationship between the FDGB and the SED, have been very clearly defined. The FDGB sees itself as an instrument for the realization of the decisions taken by the 11th Party Congress of the SED, and it clearly acknowledges the primacy of the SED. The Free Confederation of German Trade Unions is the largest of the mass organizations, with a membership of 9.5 million. Its function, as defined at its 11th congress, is to make proposals and suggestions which the SED will consider. It views itself quite explicitly as a Marxist-Leninist organization: the FDGB is a trade union movement which meets the criteria laid down by Lenin in *On the Role and Tasks of the Trade Unions under the NEP*. This position has prevailed officially since the 3rd FDGB Congress in 1950, and is acknowledged in the FDGB's official history. At this congress the FDGB committed itself to the GDR, to Marxism-Leninism, the leading role of the SED, friendship with the Soviet Union, democratic centralism, and a planned economy. At this stage the FDGB had already gone well beyond the Directive No. 2 of the Soviet Military Administration of June 1945 and the proclamation which constituted the FDGB's own "birth certificate". By 1948, even before the SED declared itself a party of the new type, the FDGB had acknowledged the primacy of the SED and had *de facto* become a Leninist trade union movement. In 1948 it became part of the anti-fascist democratic bloc as a partner of the SED and relinquished its autonomy. Since that time, the FDGB has made a major contribution to the implementation of the SED's economic and social policy and to the GDR's internal stability. It has been through the FDGB that the SED has established its power base and at the same time projected an image of participatory socialism. However, despite the mass membership of the FDGB and its important role for the SED, successive reports by Walter Ulbricht and Erich Honecker to the SED congresses have devoted very little space to the trade union movement.[3]

The mass organizations have the fundamental task of organizing the masses and forming public opinion. The high level of participation does, however, also mean that the people have to keep themselves informed to be able to participate. In this respect the mass media play a different role from their equivalents in the UK. The ten biggest national dailies are all published by the parties or mass organizations: *Neues Deutschland* is the central organ of the SED; *Neue Zeit* (CDU); *Der Morgen* (LDPD); *Nationalzeitung* (NDPD); *Bauernecho* (DBD); *Tribüne* (FDGB); *Junge Welt* (FDJ); *Deutsches Sportecho* (German Sports and Gymnastics League); and the *Berliner Zeitung* and *BZ am Abend*, which are the responsibility of the Berlin SED. A similar picture obtains for the regional daily and weekly papers. In addition there are SED workplace papers and specialist periodicals. Within the Politburo and the Central Committee Secretariat there are specialist departments dealing with guidelines on press policy. News collection is centralized in the ADN (General German News Agency) and the GDR media are not permitted to obtain news elsewhere. Furthermore, the GDR media can boast an effective self-censorship mechanism at editor level. As for radio and television, which are state run, it must be borne in mind that the population of the GDR has ready access to West German radio and television, and the vast majority avail themselves of the opportunity to watch West German TV programmes. There is no doubt that the SED is aware of the lack of popular appeal of the GDR media, and this awareness has repeatedly figured in its statements.[4]

The churches can be claimed to be the only autonomous mass organizations in the GDR. This position is acknowledged in Article 39 of the constitution. Also acknowledged is the fact that the churches play an important role in the social sphere; they run hospitals, old people's homes, children's homes, and kindergartens. The relationship between the churches and the state has always been an uneasy one, but has stabilized since the 1970s despite the protestant church's involvement with the unofficial peace movement. Since 1971, the protestant church has officially seen itself as a church within socialism; the position of the minority Roman Catholic church can be described as a church co-existing with socialism.

Documents

D46 From Walter Ulbricht's speech on socialism as a socio-economic formation, 12 September 1967:

After careful investigation of the new processes in the development of the forces of production and relationships of production in the German Democratic Republic, and on the basis of the theory of Marxism-Leninism, we formulated at the 7th Party Congress of the SED (17–22.4.1967) the strategic target of forming the advanced social system of socialism and thus perfecting socialism. The setting of this target means a general application of the experiences gained in the fulfilment of the programme agreed by the 6th Party Congress. In doing so our party, in conformity with the spirit of Marxism-Leninism, has productively reinforced the concept of socialism as a new social order.

What is the most important conclusion we have reached in this respect? It is that socialism is not a short transitional phase in the development of society, but rather a relatively independent socio-economic formation in the historical epoch of the transition from capitalism to communism on a world level. It was formerly usual, mainly on the basis of Marx's remarks on the Gotha Programme, to consider socialism to be only a transitional phase in which society has to free itself from the "birthmarks" of capitalism and create the material and intellectual prerequisites for the second phase of communism. Little attention was paid to the fact that socialism develops on its own basis. The burden of the capitalist past made it more difficult to reach this insight. Accordingly the categories of socialist economics which are formally similar to the categories of capitalist economics (money, price, profit, and others) were frequently seen as an unavoidable "evil" whose effectiveness had to be overcome. Of course the construction of socialism includes the struggle against the remnants of capitalism and is linked to the overcoming of the material and intellectual consequences of capitalism. But we see these processes from the positive viewpoint of what is most important, most central and most determining for the new order of society: socialism is being erected in the Workers' and Farmers' State on the foundation of a qualitatively new type of relationships of production.[5]

(W. Ulbricht: "Die Bedeutung des Werkes "Das Kapital" von Karl Marx für die Schaffung des entwickelten sozialen Systems in der DDR", in: *Zum ökonomischen System des Sozialismus in der DDR*, vol. 2, Berlin 1967, pp. 530 f.)

D47 From Walter Ulbricht's definition of the "Socialist Human Community", 22 March 1969:

We know of course that the development of the socialist human community in the period of the transition to a full socialist society is a complicated and complex process in the course of which the remnants of the old in the thought, feelings and actions of human beings have to be overcome by their education and self-education. The socialist human community which we are realizing step by step goes far beyond the old humanist ideal. It does not mean only readiness to help, kindness, fraternity, love for one's fellow men. It includes both the development of individual socialist personalities and the development of the many to a socialist community through the process of working together, learning, participation in planning and management of social development, and particularly also in the work of the National Front and in a varied, full and cultured life.

In the past years many elements of the socialist human community have emerged in the Socialist Work Brigades, the housing communities, and in the development of socialist democracy. The principles of socialist morality exert an increasing influence on the shared lives of the citizens of the German Democratic Republic. The message has spread around the world that the "German Miracle" which has taken place in our Republic is not simply an "Economic Miracle" but above all consists in the great transformation in human beings.

But we are still far from completing our development into a socialist human community. Those who believe it is enough simply to be polite and friendly to their neighbours have an oversimplified view of the matter. The development of the socialist human community is and remains a matter of great interest and concern to us all. It is realized in the work collectives, in the various forms in which citizens participate democratically in the affairs of society, in the schools and not least in the family.

(W. Ulbricht: "Unser guter Weg zur sozialistischen Menschengemein-schaft", in: *Das System der sozialistischen Gesellschafts- und Staatsordnung in der DDR. Dokumente*, Berlin 1969, p. 245)

D48 From Kurt Hager's speech on the advanced socialist society, 14 October 1971:

Marxism-Leninism is the indivisible unity of dialectical and historical materialism, political economy, and scientific communism. The 8th Party Congress called for action against tendencies to set a low value on this unity. For the whole practical activity of the working class, and the strategy and tactics of its revolutionary struggle, are based on this unified theoretical foundation . . .

The process of constant consolidation and further development of the class alliance of the working class with the class of co-operative farmers, the socialist intelligentsia, and other sections of the working population was characterized by the 8th Party Congress as the formation of the political and moral unity of the people. The 8th Party Congress had good reason to abstain from the use of the concept of the human community which was formerly very frequently applied. The concept of the socialist human community indubitably expresses the development of new social and human relationships. However when applied to the present period in the development of the construction of socialism it is not scientifically exact as it obscures the class differences which in fact are still present and over-estimates the state of rapprochement which has in fact been reached between the classes and sections of society.

It obscures the leading role of the working class, the necessity for a firm alliance with the co-operative farmers, the intelligentsia, and the rest of the working population, and the existence of various remnants of capitalism.[6] This concept does not do justice to the complicated, contradictory and prolonged development process of socialist social relationships. As Marx, Engels, and Lenin constantly emphasized, a harmonious society of this kind, in which the birthmarks of capitalism in men's consciousness and behaviour are totally eradicated and the division of society into classes and strata is superseded can only be achieved with the coming of the communist society.

The advanced socialist society was first set up in the Soviet Union. In the course of the 1960s, the comprehensive development of the advanced socialist society was inaugurated in other socialist countries. The present stage of development of the socialist countries is described accurately and uniformly by the Marxist-Leninist theory of the Soviet Union and the other socialist countries as "developed socialist society". We therefore find ourselves in complete accord with the collective conclusions of the CPSU and the other fraternal parties of the socialist countries. This emphasizes anew the universally valid character of Marxist-Leninist theory.

On the other hand we cannot ignore the fact that the description "advanced social system of socialism" in practice often resulted, particularly in the economic sphere, in the disappearance of the clear meaning and content of our policies under a jumble of concepts borrowed from system theory. In many publications the concept of the system was abused. Serious, solid scientific work was often replaced by sonorous jargon. How else can we describe word formations such as "working-class sub-system", "cultural sub-system", "provision sub-system", "complex territorial-provision system", "multidimensional structured societal total subject with the working class as its nucleus and leading power". We must not permit the nature of socialism and the meaning of our activity to be obscured in this way . . .

If in agreement with the classic authorities of Marxism-Leninism, the experiences of the Soviet Union and our own experiences we consider socialism to be a phase of the unified communist social formation, this does not however mean that socialism is merely a short transitional stage. Quite the contrary. Our experiences in constructing socialism have taught us that the creation of a socialist society in accordance with the specific conditions of a particular country can be a long process. Precisely for this reason, the concept of the advanced socialist society is of great importance for scientific communism. It expresses the fact that in this period of the construction of socialism the task is to guarantee a harmonic and optimally proportional development of all areas of society, in which the focus is exclusively the human being and his needs. At the same time it emphasizes that great exertions are required for this task . . .

In the light of these statements on the communist formation of society the thesis that socialism is a relatively independent social formation is not tenable. This thesis obscures the fact that socialism is the first, lower phase of the communist social formation. It further obscures the fact, historically proven by the Soviet Union's example, that on the basis of the development of socialist relationships of production and its material and technical base the advanced socialist society grows gradually into a communist society.

The theory of socialism as a relatively independent social formation therefore cannot be made to conform to the Marxist-Leninist theory of the transition from socialism to communism. Since socialism and communism represent two phases of a unified social formation created by the working class and all working people under the leadership of the party and have a common socio-economic foundation, the transition from the lower to the higher phase can take place only by the gradual formation and development of the seeds of communism, only through the full unfolding of socialism.

(Kurt Hager: *Zur Theorie und Politik des Sozialismus. Reden und Aufsätze.* Berlin 1972, pp. 162 ff.)

D49 From the definition of "revolution" in the Dictionary of Marxist-Leninist Philosophy:

The *socialist revolution* is the greatest and most radical change in human history, as it removes the exploitation of man by man and all forms of oppression, abolishes antagonistic class society and thus initiates the development towards the classless society and to perpetual *peace* (q.v.). It accomplishes the transition to a society without exploitation and oppression in which for the first time human beings form their own history consciously, with insight into society's laws of movement. It affects all aspects of society, draws the broad masses of the people into the movement of history and raises them to a role in the creation of history.

The leading force of the socialist revolution is the working class with its Marxist-Leninist party. On the basis of its objective position in the development of society it has the historic task of overthrowing capitalism and setting up socialism. Under the leadership of its revolutionary fighting party it captures political power in alliance with all working classes and sections of the population, and sets up the *dictatorship of the proletariat* (q.v.), the instrument for the construction of the new society, the most important condition for the victory of the revolution. The capture of political power is not the completion but merely the beginning of the socialist revolution, for its major task is now the economic, political and cultural construction of the socialist society. Socialist ownership of the means of production, the economic basis of the socialist society, can only be achieved with the aid of the dictatorship of the proletariat. Therefore socialist state authority is not merely a means to destroy the old order but above all an instrument to complete the socialist transformation in politics, economics, and culture.

(*Wörterbuch der marxistisch-leninistischen Philosophie*, Berlin 1986, pp. 456 f.)

D50 Letter to Erich Honecker from the Democratic Women's Federation of Germany (DFD) 10 November 1981:

Dear Comrade Erich Honecker,

The office-bearers of the federation committee of the DFD address this letter to you with the particular purpose of expressing the thanks of the women's organization for all the policies again discussed at the 3rd conference of the Central Committee of the SED in the interests of women and families and for their social security which have been reflected in the laws on the national economic plan for 1982 and the Five-Year Plan 1981 to 1985. We think here of the proposed increase in the numbers of creche and kindergarten places, the construction of new schools, gymnasiums and child-care centres. This is all in the interest of women and mothers, who of course want the best for their children.

Great approval was expressed for the new measures in social policy such as the extensive wage increases for sectors in which a large number of women work; the specifications on payment of apprentices and on grants; the extension of credit conditions for young married couples. You may be assured that in particular the increase in child allowance for the third and all subsequent children met with a very warm reception. We should like to thank the party of the working class most cordially for this on behalf of the members of our organization.

Dear Comrade Honecker, we will continue to give our full support to the policies of the party of the working class, which are always directed towards the good of the people and towards peace. Everywhere in the residential areas of towns and cities and in the villages our members are taking part in realizing the decisions of the 10th Party Congress of the SED. This is shown by the achievements realized and the many successful initiatives undertaken by the 17,300 groups of the DFD which have held their annual general meetings in the last few weeks. They took stock of their achievements and decided on new programmes of action. They will make every effort to increase their achievements still further and obtain good results by the 11th Federation Congress (4–5 March 1982).

We are conscious that higher demands are now being made on our organization too, on individual members, groups, and committees. Therefore we intend to make more and more women from all sections of the population familiar with the political and social tasks in our Republic, and involve them more and more in social life and the solution of questions of common concern.

We resolve:

— to develop political mass activity of a kind that helps every woman to make the SED's policies more completely her own concern, so that it becomes her incontrovertible conviction that the stronger our Republic becomes and the stronger our socialist community, the more secure and stable peace becomes;

— to direct our attention to helping in the realization of the great aims in the interest of families, good care and education for our children, the protection of mother and child, and for rest and recreation, to create still better conditions for working mothers so that they may make more extensive use of their skills and abilities and their willingness to play their part may be employed still more effectively;

— to help ensure that as planned the places to be created in creches, nurseries and schools are supplied in good time, additional reserves are made available, and that existing facilities are still better employed;

— to work to make the climate still more favourable for families and children everywhere and to ensure that a rich intellectual and cultural life furthers people's wellbeing;

— to assist in the spread of the socialist principle of economic use of resources, to discover reserves of raw materials and to concern ourselves still more with ensuring that all recycleable waste materials from households are recovered. We want to assist in ensuring order, security, and cleanliness in the residential areas and help to ensure that energy is used economically and that public property is cared for and looked after;

— to encourage still more women to produce and supply additional agricultural produce. Our members in the villages should see it as their obligation to ensure that no square metre of soil remains uncultivated. By collecting kitchen waste in the towns and cities we intend to make larger quantities of feedstuff available for livestock production. We carry out all these activities and achievements as part of the National Front's "Join In" campaign of socialist competition.[7]

(leben und handeln. Funktionärorgan des Demokratischen Frauenbundes Deutschlands. Heft 2, February 1982, pp. 1 f.)

D51 Excerpt from Inge Lange's article "Policies on Women in the 35th Year of our Republic's Existence", January 1984:

At the 10th Party Congress of the SED, the leading bodies of our party, the trade unions and the women's organization, as well as the managing bodies of the state and the economy were set the task "of making good use of these social and individual assets which were created with the establishment of equal rights for women, in order to increase still further the effectiveness of women's will to contribute to the further development of the advanced socialist society." . . .

At present more than 4.7 million women and girls are in employment or at school, college or university. That is half a million more women than in 1970, although in the period since then the female residential population of working age has increased only by just under a quarter of a million. The rate of employment thus rose to 89 per cent at present. Lenin once said that "what has been adopted in culture, in everyday life, in normal practice" can be considered to have been attained. Precisely this applies both quantitatively and qualitatively to women's employment in our country.

This is also made obvious in the level of professional qualification achieved. At present women make up 50 per cent of skilled workers, 11 per cent of master craftsmen, 60 per cent of all technical college graduates and 36 per cent of all university graduates. The number of female production workers with specialist qualifications has more than doubled since 1970, from 28.3 per cent to the present 58.4 per cent. In agriculture 87.7 per cent of women have completed vocational training and 79.2 per cent have a specialist qualification.

The rapid increase in women's qualification also had a positive effect on their representation in positions of responsibility. At present one-third of all management functions overall are carried out by women. In the cultural and social sectors including education and the health service the figure is as high as 56.6 per cent, in commerce, light industry, the service economy, posts and communications around 50 per cent. Furthermore women now make up 38.4 per cent of all elected representatives, 28 per cent of mayors, 32 per cent of heads of schools, and 54 per cent of judges.

It is quite clear that these fundamental changes in the social position of women could only be carried through thanks to the extensive sociopolitical measures initiated by our party. Thus in particular an enormous development in the capacity and the network of pre-school institutions has taken place. By the end of 1983 the number of places in creches has almost doubled since 1970, so that at present 657 of every 1000 children of the relevant age have a place.

As for the kindergarten, the number of places available has in fact more than doubled over the same period, so that our Republic is the only country so far in which all children whose parents wish it can be admitted to these facilities, looked after and prepared for school entry. The same applies to the development of afternoon care centres for pupils in the first four years at school.

Children are the living proof — in the most literal sense — of the correctness of the path adopted by the 8th Party Congress, for since 1975 the number of births has again begun to rise. To make the associated problems clear it should be remembered that in 1963 our Republic reached its highest number of births with 301,400 babies. From this point on the number dropped year after year — although the law on women's right to interruption of pregnancy was not passed until 1972 — and reached its lowest point in 1972, when only 179,172 babies were born. This was no longer enough even to maintain the current level of population. But already in 1977 over 223,000 babies were born, and in 1983 it is anticipated that more than 230,000 children will come into the world.

Bearing in mind August Bebel's statement that instead of excessive nourishment of their feelings and emotions women need "a good helping of keen common sense and exact reasoning . . ., knowledge of the world and of people", our party has always devoted the greatest attention to the involvement of women in political life. This is evident in their conscious and active participation in the all-around strengthening of our Republic, in their committed work in socialist competition and in the innovators' movement, in the initiative to increase the performance of our economy and in the vigour with which women contribute to the securing of peace and to anti-imperialist solidarity.

It is also a great merit of our party that in its work with the masses of women it always links the fundamental political issues most closely with everyday life. In this way in particular it has reached the hearts and minds of women with the result that the vast majority of them make the class-conscious decision to play a full part in helping to realize our good policies. The extent to which our party attracts women can be seen from the fact that 34.4 per cent of the members and candidates of the SED are women — that is 762,000 women. 4.7 million women are members of the FDGB; not only do they make up 52.2 per cent of the total membership, but in practice every second official trade union function is carried out by a woman. 1.4 million are members of the DFD, of whom 73.7 per cent are not members of a political party.

(*Neuer Weg* vol. 39 no. 1 (1984) pp. 3 ff.)

D52 Report by the Committee of the Democratic Women's Federation of Germany, 6 March 1987:

The speaker began by saying that the members of the DFD, women from all classes and sections of society, are participating in many positive ways in the popular movement which the 11th Party Congress of the SED has initiated in our Republic. It is an important obligation for them to devote all their powers to realize the policies of the SED, which are directed to the wellbeing of the people and to peace, and to make their personal contribution towards the further strengthening of our socialist GDR.

Throughout our organization, we have thoroughly evaluated the statement by Erich Honecker which he made to us when he received a delegation of the Federation Committee a few days after the 11th Party Congress. We have further developed our activities in the city residential districts and in the villages and have involved more women than ever in achieving our targets. What we are doing for the Republic in this way also represents our thanks for the great attention our party pays to women and family life, and for the help and support which our organization always receives from the Central Committee of the SED, said Ilse Thiele to rousing applause.

She outlined impressive results achieved by the DFD in the competition for the 12th Federation Conference with the slogan "Everything for the welfare of the people and for peace": more than 21 million working hours for improving the appearance of the residential environment and for looking after playgrounds, parks and gardens; recovery and delivery of 48,320 tonnes of waste paper, textiles and scrap metal; almost 18 million hours of neighbourhood assistance; 795 new guardianship agreements with children's institutions.

In all these activities, the president of the DFD stressed, it is clear that our friends are conscious that they are making a contribution to peace by their work. They have made the slogan "My workplace — my post in the peace struggle" the guideline for their activity in our territory, and here too they are devoting all their powers to the implementation of the decisions of the 11th Party Congress of the SED.

This was confirmed by hundreds of thousands of personal conversations, by over 50,000 women's public meetings, and by 57,360 forums on politics, economics, and society. The groups of the DFD have supported intellectual and cultural life with more than 167,000 meetings on culture and free time, and have brought women more leisure and relaxation.

The members of the DFD have shown great commitment and initiative and have worked tirelessly in women's interests and for the well-being of our citizens, sacrificing so many hours of their own free time for the common good. There was loud and protracted applause as the president warmly thanked all members, all women and the social groups co-operating with the DFD for this important and varied work.

(*Neues Deutschland* Vol. 42 of 6 March 1987)

D53 From the General Directive on the Economic Plan, 5 May 1987:

(6) The managers in the combines, enterprises, co-operatives and institutions, in close co-operation with the committees of the works party organizations, with the trades unions and with the Free German Youth, must explain to the working collectives the analysis of the state objectives for 1988, including the objectives for developments in working and living conditions. They must create all the preconditions for *the workers' creative, democratic participation in drawing up the plan.* Care is to be taken that the workers in every works section and brigade and every work and union collective give their comments on the state requirements in good time in the course of thorough discussion of the plan, and are able to introduce their comments, conclusions and proposals. In this way the principle of "participation in planning, participation in work, participation in government" is fulfilled. The managers of state and industry are required to make comprehensive use of the proposals and comments on the achievement and surpassing of the plan's aims.

Socialist Community Work, the Innovators' Movement, and the Young Innovators' Movement, as effective factors of socialist rationalization, must be oriented towards the most important objectives. The Innovators and Rationalizers, and the works sections of the Chamber for Technology, are to be set concrete scientific-technical and economic tasks and goals.

The Youth Research Collectives of the FDJ are to be actively involved in the preparation of demanding goals and tasks for research and development. They are to be assigned projects from the science and technology plan demanding particularly high levels of performance.

Managers bear the responsibility for ensuring that all proposals, comments and criticisms are taken notice of, investigated, and realized in accordance with social requirements and capabilities. All competitive initiatives and the recommendations put forward in trade union submissions and in FDJ proposals are to be evaluated carefully, used for the achievement of the targets set in the 1987 plan and the accepted commitment to surpass it in terms of actual production, and used as a basis in drawing up the draft 1988 plan and in preparing the Works Collective Contract for 1988.

The Politburo of the Central Committee of the SED, the Council of Ministers of the GDR and the Confederated Committee of the Confederation of Free German Trades Unions are certain that with their proposals in the planning discussion to draw up the national economic plan for 1988 and also with their industriousness, initiative and energy, the working people of the GDR will create the essential preconditions for the full realization of the decisions of the 11th Party Congress of the SED.

That is an important contribution to the consolidation of the international positions of socialism, to detente and disarmament, and to the normalization of the international situation.

(*Neues Deutschland* vol. 42 of 5 May 1987)

D54 From the President's speech at the 11th Congress of the League of Culture, June 1987:

The President of the League of Culture of the GDR, Professor Hans Pischner, began his speech by recalling an entry made by Johannes R. Becher in his diary in 1950 when he was thinking about past and present, about history and culture, about the role of the author. "Peace, peace, peace! How can we do more for it, how can we do everything for it? That is the question, the question for the second half of our century."

The speaker pointed out how up-to-the-minute and farsighted this statement by the League of Culture's founder appeared today, when nothing was closer to the hearts of people in our country and in the whole world than the wish for peace. By bringing forward far-reaching proposals and initiatives, socialism was pressing for the real chance to be seized of banishing war from the lives of humankind and of initiating an era of lasting peace.

It was being realized everywhere more clearly than ever before that the desire for peace called above all for action for peace. The main question before the 11th Congress was how the League of Culture of the GDR might also do everything it possibly could in this direction.

In the GDR, policies for peace and the good of humankind were seen as a requirement imposed by history. It was the result of the proven social strategy of the SED in its development of the advanced socialist society, and of its successful pursuit of its major objective in its union of social and economic policy, that in our country political stability, dynamic growth of the economy and efficient application of science and technology went hand in hand with the increasing affluence of the population, a high educational standard, and a flourishing scientific and cultural life. "The League of Culture of the GDR, its members and officials, feel a great attachment and obligation to these policies", the President declared.

To carry on along this path with continuous new challenges, with the year 2000 in view, as laid down by the 11th Party Congress of the SED, "strengthens confidence and optimism in the future, commitment and creativity, it both demands and encourages everyone's views and contributions, the experiences and suggestions of each individual." That was also reflected in the work of the cultural organization; in its name Professor Pischner thanked the party of the working class for its wise and logically consistent policies, which were directed towards the preservation of peace and the good of the population.

To applause from the delegates he declared, "Here there is a special word of thanks for the General Secretary of the Central Committee of the SED, our friend Erich Honecker, whose great personal commitment for a happy future without wars and for the interests of all working people we can observe almost every day."

[. . .]

In the extensive and democratic discussion on the first day of their congress, the delegates debated the future responsibilities of the League of Culture and its members in the further realization of the resolutions passed by the 11th Party Congress of the SED. In the discussion, a wealth of valuable experience arising out of the work of previous years was presented, and reports were given on future aims and projects.[8]

(*Neues Deutschland* vol. 42 of 12 June 1987)

D55 From the report on the 6th Conference of the FDJ in Neues Deutschland, 3 July 1987:

Good interim report on the FDJ's commission from the 11th Party Conference
3125 industrial robots installed, 8800 flats modernized, best achievement so far on the USSR natural gas pipeline, 237 kilometers of railway network in the GDR electrified, House of Youth as model . . .

[From our reporters Matthias Loke and Wolfgang Schönwald]

Berlin. An interim report on the "FDJ commission from the 11th Party Conference of the SED", evaluating the 4th plenum of the Central Committee of the SED, was made by the 6th conference of the Central Council of the youth organization which began in Berlin on Thursday.

Wilfried Possner, secretary of the Central Council and president of the Ernst Thälmann Pioneer organization, pointed out in the opening report of the two-day discussion that by the end of June FDJ initiatives had led to the installation of 3125 industrial robots, the saving of 67.5 million working hours, and the production of two billion marks in the material and energy economies. Young people had converted or modernized 8800 flats. 360,000 tonnes of scrap metal and 80,000 tonnes of waste paper had been returned for recycling. With these results, 50 per cent of the year's targets had been achieved. These deeds were to be regarded as showing agreement with the SED's policies and as a contribution to the overall strengthening of the GDR and to the securing of peace. The FDJ commission from the 11th Party Congress and the Pioneer commission "Always ready — at our comrades' side!" had proven themselves as a mobilizing programme of action for the younger generation.

The speaker further stated that the organization's commission to support the repair and modernization of power stations is being fulfilled. 840 FDJ delegates are assisting in the high-quality completion of the planned projects. On the Central Youth Project of the natural gas pipeline the young collectives on the building sites in the USSR were recording the best performance so far since the 11th Party Congress of the SED. During the same period 237 kilometers of the Republic's railway network had been electrified, 111 kilometers of which was ahead of schedule.

Wilfried Possner dealt critically with instances where youth clubs of the FDJ had not been completed according to plan, fashion products for young people in some cases were insufficient to meet the demand, and where there had been excessive slowness in putting the results of the "Young Innovators' Movement" into production, particularly in regard to consumer goods. The Central Council called upon the relevant FDJ leaderships to work energetically for the accomplishment of all targets and to report on this to the next conference.

The speaker considered in detail the demands arising in the communist education of the younger generation. The basic concern of the youth organization was and remained the formation of young citizens who in all situations hold firm to their native country and act in a class-conscious way.

(*Neues Deutschland* vol. 42 of 3 July 1987)

D56 On the role of the Free German Youth Movement as a "helper and reserve of the Party", from Erich Honecker's report to the Tenth Party Congress of the SED, 1981:

Comrades,

With joy and satisfaction we see that the young generation has made the Programme of our Party its own. The tasks it was given by the 9th Congress are being fulfilled with revolutionary commitment and civic responsibility. In our society, the Party and the young generation see eye to eye since the socialist objective of peace and welfare for the people corresponds with the ideals of the young, offering them secure prospects for the future. Socialism needs youth, and the young generation needs socialism.

Young workers, engineers and scientists, young co-operative farmers, students and apprentices, school pupils and members of the armed forces contribute to strengthening and protecting our German Democratic Republic and securing peace in the spirit of socialist patriotism and proletarian internationalism. In a class-conscious manner young people in their deeds and plans uphold the revolutionary traditions of the fighters against war and fascism, the pioneers of post-war reconstruction and the initiators of the socialist emulation movement.

The members of the Free German Youth have at all times proved themselves to be loyal heirs to the Communist Manifesto and reliable supporters of the Programme of our Party. The great initiatives undertaken by our socialist youth league ran through the entire history of our State, from the now already legendary building of the Sosa Peace Dam to the building sites of the "FDJ Initiative Berlin", the largest of the projects for which the FDJ has taken on responsibility in recent years. More than 13,000 members of the Free German Youth from different counties came to Berlin and side by side with their Berlin colleagues do exemplary work in further enhancing Berlin's role as the capital of our country.

The excellent results of the activities of both the FDJ and the Pioneer organization in honour of the 10th Congress reaffirm the ties of trust that link the young generation with our Party. Never before was a state on German soil able to look at its young generation with such pride as the German Democratic Republic. Under the leadership of the SED successive generations are growing up whose characteristic features are persevering diligence in learning and studying, creative, honest and disciplined work, readiness and ability to defend their homeland, anti-imperialist solidarity and fraternal alliance with all fighters for social progress. This is an important achievement of our socialist society, an earnest of success on the road to communism.

Youth in the GDR sees its interests represented and its ideals embodied in our workers' and farmers' state. This socialist state has always been and will continue to be a state devoted to its young generation. Again the correctness of our Party's youth policy was proved. We will remain true to our tried and tested principle of placing full confidence in youth as well as entrusting it with high responsibility. In this connection, we devote special attention to working-class youth.

Today there is no sphere in which the Free German Youth is not holding its own. It faces the challenges of the eighties with great motivation, creativity and a sense of responsibility, proving its worth as a reliable helper and loyal reserve of the SED at all fronts of the class struggle. Let us recall the numerous initiatives of the over 38,300 youth brigades and the broad youth movement for the mastery of science and technology. Let us recall the vigilance displayed by FDJ members of the armed forces in defending the achievements of our people. And last but not least let us think of the respect the FDJ has earned in the eyes of democratic world youth for the part it is playing in the World Federation of Democratic Youth and in the International Union of Students, and of the activities of the FDJ Friendship Brigades working on three continents.

The successful building of an advanced socialist society demands the continuation on a higher level of the communist education of youth. The socialist youth organization turns out staunch fighters for the construction of communist society who act in the spirit of Marxism-Leninism and under all conditions contribute to the realization of the SED Programme. In the course of this successful work, a willingness to achieve high standards, an unshakeable class consciousness and revolutionary commitment to the communist cause should be awakened in all young people.

From the rostrum of our Party Congress we call upon the young participants in the building of the advanced socialist society: Master the teachings of Marxism-Leninism and make them your guiding principle in life! Act in accordance with the communist spirit of doing everything for the well-being of the people! Draw new knowledge from the history of the SED and the experiences gained by the older generation in a lifetime of struggle! Strive for an active attitude to life, a socialist class standpoint that can withstand all the tempests of our time! Seize all the opportunities offered by our socialist society to enrich your fund of knowledge, prove your skills and put your talent to the test! Show what you can do in fulfilling the tasks set forth in the SED Programme as ardent and dedicated fighters for our communist ideals!

To stand one's ground as a socialist patriot and proletarian internationalist today means to stand up in any situation in word and deed for the interests of socialism, offering the enemy not the slightest opportunity wherever he may appear.

Being a true socialist patriot and proletarian internationalist today means treasuring, true to the legacy of Ernst Thälmann and Wilhelm Pieck, the alliance with the Soviet Union, forging the friendship between the socialist countries ever closer and displaying anti-imperialist solidarity with the struggle waged by the peoples for the liberation from exploitation and neo-colonialist dependence.

Being a young architect of our communist future means mastering the scientific and technological revolution for the benefit of our society. It is precisely in this field that the younger generation faces challenges which test their knowledge and capabilities, what they intend to achieve and what they are capable of achieving, and which develop to the full their creativity and revolutionary spirit. The youth work teams and youth projects, the movement of the young innovators' exhibitions and the other economic initiatives of the FDJ are proving grounds for the young people and the formation of their communist personality.

To meet the demands of our socialist society, the young person must also develop all his abilities and talents and pursue a wide range of interests. Thus, the developing character of the socialist way of life of youth gains increasing significance. It is correct for the FDJ, representing as it does the interests of youth, together with the FDGB, the DTSB of the GDR, the GST, with the agencies of the state and other public instances, to work actively on the basis of the Youth Act for the provision of good conditions for a rich intellectual and cultural life and a wide scope of activities in the fields of sports, tourism and paramilitary training, whether in the enterprises, co-operative farms and institutions, universities and schools or urban residential areas and local communities. Special attention should be paid to the youth clubs of the FDJ and the facilities for dancing offered to the young people.

We particularly welcome the fact that the FDJ devotes special attention to communist education in the Ernst Thälmann Young Pioneer Organization. Every possible support should be offered to the Pioneer leaders.

Our Party is firmly convinced that it can also rely completely on the Free German Youth in the implementation of the decisions taken at our 10th Congress. As the revolutionary vanguard of the younger generation in the GDR, it has the support of us all in its work of communist education. A Communist can value nothing more dearly than to evoke enthusiasm for our lofty ideals among the young. We expect every comrade, starting with the education of their own children, to give young people the benefit of their own experience and to help to consolidate the revolutionary unity between the generations.

(Erich Honecker: *Report of the Central Committee of the Socialist Unity Party of Germany to the Tenth Congress of the SED*, Dresden 1981, pp. 189 ff.)

D57 From the report by Harry Tisch to the Eleventh Congress of the Confederation of Free German Trade Unions, 23 April 1987:

Dear delegates, dear guests, colleagues,

The 11th Congress of our Confederation of Free German Trade Unions is determined in its objectives by the conditions and demands of the qualitatively new period of the development of the socialist society in our German Democratic Republic. This period was initiated a year ago with the decisions of the 11th Party Congress of the SED.

The main content of the trade union elections in preparation for the present congress lay in focusing all the trade union organizations of our country on the tasks of this new period so that they are completely up to date on their activities. Our elections showed clearly that the development of informed opinion in our organization is taking place in harmony with the interests of working people.

From the public dialogue among millions of working people there arose the instruction to the delegates to the 11th Congress of the FDGB to discuss those issues which will help us to solve the tasks of tomorrow. That is in accordance with the good democratic practices and traditions of the FDGB . . .

Thus, here at the 11th FDGB Congress we can assure the General Secretary of the Central Committee of the SED and Chairman of the Council of State, our comrade and colleague Erich Honecker, that we shall do everything to make our contribution to the realization of the decisions of the 11th Party Congress! (*loud applause*) Trade unionists are concentrating their thoughts, their emotions, and all their actions on this . . .

It is our conviction that the relationship of trust between the party and the trade unions, between the party and the people, which was developed and tempered in the socialist revolution, will continue to prove itself in our common struggle to realize the decisions of the 11th Party Congress.

We shall never let any doubts be cast on this fighting alliance between the party and the trade unions! (*prolonged loud applause*)

(*Neues Deutschland* vol. 42 no. 95 of 23 April 1987)

D58 Report on a discussion between Harry Tisch and leading Gera trade unionists, 22 August 1987:

The tasks of the trade unions in the struggle for peace, detente and disarmament, and the experiences and results achieved in socialist competition, were the major points discussed in a meeting held on Friday in the Thuringian regional capital between Harry Tisch, chairman of the Confederation Committee of the FDGB and member of the Politburo of the Central Committee of the SED, and the secretariat of the Gera regional committee of the FDGB. The chairs of the regional committees of the industry unions and trade unions also took part, as did the chairs of the district committees of the FDGB in the region.

Harry Tisch emphasized that more than ever before it was essential to awaken and encourage creative initiatives and new activities by working people and to make these become obligatory for everyone, so that as demanded by the 11th FDGB Congress an active contribution could be made to the realization of the decisions of the 11th Party Congress of the SED.

At present the most important task was to increase the tempo of development and employment of the key technologies, and to ensure reliably day by day that products planned and accounted for were achieved in full, that production met requirements in quantity, value and quality, and that all contracts entered into were fulfilled in full.

It should also be a matter of trade union concern to ensure an exact process of scrutiny and accountability for all suggestions made by working people concerning improvement in output, improvement of working and living conditions and of intellectual and cultural life. With such treatment the development of the democratic involvement of working people would receive still stronger and more varied impetus.

(*Neues Deutschland* vol. 42 no. 197 of 22–3 August 1987)

D59 From the closing statement by Harry Tisch to the Eleventh Congress of the Confederation of Free German Trade Unions, 25 April 1987:

Dear delegates, dear comrades and friends, dear guests from abroad,

The discussions on the report by the Committee of the Confederation and on the report by the Central Review Commission of the FDGB are completed.

An important part of the work of the Congress has thus been accomplished.

We have discussed together the fundamental questions of our trade union work and our shared voice and shared responsibility in our socialist society, that is, our socialist democracy as a whole.

I should like to express my warmest thanks to all colleagues who have spoken in the discussion . . .

The high point of this conference was the speech by the General Secretary of the Central Committee of the SED and Chairman of the Council of State, our comrade Erich Honecker. (*prolonged loud applause*)

In a manner which moved all delegates deeply, Comrade Honecker traced the wide historical sweep from our trade union beginnings in 1945 through to the present trade union activity of our FDGB as an active participant in shaping the advanced socialist society in the GDR. Yes, we are proud to have realized the fundamental aims of the trade union movement in our socialist country.

On the basis of the clear social strategy of our Marxist-Leninist party the FDGB has made a decisive contribution to the abolition of the exploitation of man by man and the securing of the fundamental rights of working people, in particular the right to work.

Today the work of working people serves solely the welfare of our people and its peaceful present and future.

The remarks of our comrade and friend Erich Honecker have convincingly shown our trade union responsibility to help at all times in guaranteeing the three harmonious aspects of socialist economic policies, social policies, and policies for peace.

We shall see to that with all our trade union strength and perseverance!

The close fighting alliance between the SED and the FDGB will here once again prove itself! (*prolonged loud applause*)

Dear delegates,

In the course of our discussion 47 colleagues spoke.

Our debate reflected the creative climate of our society, in which productive participation in planning, the will to high achievement, and the personal responsibility of the individual and the working collective develop fully in the realization of the decisions of the 11th Party Congress of the SED . . .

Here in our country working people and their unions are, as comrade Erich Honecker said, masters in their own house (*loud applause*), and when at this congress they put forward their proposals for new sociopolitical measures, and the leadership of our party and our state agree to these, then that is clearly a different world; it is our socialist world. (*prolonged loud applause*) . . .

And therefore I am extremely pleased that following on the report, the discussion also clearly oriented itself towards pursuing socialist competition energetically under the proven slogan: "High achievements for the good of the people and for peace — Everything for the realization of the decisions of the 11th Party Congress of the SED!" (*prolonged loud applause*)

After all it is self-evident that if we as a union propose new sociopolitical measures then we must also keep in view a corresponding growth in the economy. For the leadership of our party and state cannot write out any uncovered cheques . . .

(*Neues Deutschland* vol. 45 no. 97 of 25–26 April 1987)

D60 From Lenin's "Role and Function of the Trade Unions under the New Economic Policy", 12 January 1922:

Contact with the masses, i.e., with the overwhelming majority of the workers (and eventually of all the working people) is the most important and fundamental condition for the success of all trade union activity. In all the trade union organizations, from bottom up, groups must be formed of responsible comrades — not all of them must be Communists — with many years of practical experience, who should live right among the workers, study their lives in every detail, be able unerringly, on any question, and at any time, to judge the mood, the real aspirations, needs and thoughts of the masses. They must be able without a shadow of false idealization to define the degree of their class consciousness and the extent to which they are influenced by various prejudices and survivals of the past; and they must be able to win the boundless confidence of the masses by comradeship and concern for their needs. One of the greatest and most serious dangers that confronts the numerically small Communist Party which, as the vanguard of the working class, is guiding a vast country in the process of transition to Socialism (for the time being without the support of the more advanced countries), is divorcement from the masses, the danger that the vanguard may run too far ahead and fail to "straighten out the line," fail to maintain permanent contact with the whole army of labour, i.e., with the overwhelming majority of workers and peasants. Just as the very best factory, with the very best engines and first-class machines, will be forced to remain idle if the transmission belts from the motor to the machines are damaged, so our work of Socialist construction must meet with inevitable disaster if the trade unions — the transmission belts from the Communist Party, to the masses — are badly fitted or function badly. It is not sufficient to explain, to reiterate and corroborate this truth; it must be backed up organizationally by the whole structure of the trade unions and by their everyday activities.

(*The Essentials of Lenin* vol. II, London 1947, p. 766)

D61 From the account of the Third FDGB Congress in the official history of the FDGB, 30 August–3 September 1950:

The 3rd FDGB Congress was an important event in the history of the German working-class movement. For the first time a trade union congress declared its support for the Workers' and Farmers' State, for Marxism-Leninism, for the leading role of the party of the working class, for friendship with the Soviet Union, and for the principles of proletarian internationalism. In doing so, the delegates lived up to their historical responsibility. They declared unanimously that the trade unions would fight for the all-round strengthening of the German Democratic Republic. The congress's decision to use all the power of the trade unions for the fulfilment of the first five-year plan meant its participation in the creation of the foundations of socialism in the GDR.

The delegates fulfilled the legacy of the more than one hundred years of struggle by German trade unionists for the liberation of working people from exploitation and oppression, for social security and for a life in peace and happiness. The 3rd FDGB Congress was a milestone in the development of the trade unions as schools of socialism.

(*Geschichte des Freien Deutschen Gewerkschaftsbundes*, Berlin 1985, pp. 362 f.)

D62 Proclamation of the Founding of New Free Trade Unions, 15 June 1945:

The tyranny of Hitler's fascism has been crushed by the Allied armies. Millions of dead and wounded, ruined cities, destroyed property, widows and orphans are an accusation. Hitler has proved the terrible truth of the boastful statement he made on seizing power: "Give me ten years and you will no longer recognize Germany." Hitler has violated his own nation by his barbarous racial theories and the campaign of destruction against other peoples.

The way to the abyss began even before 1933. The forces of democracy were split and too undecided to offer decisive resistance. The first of May 1933 was the blackest day in the history of the workers' movement. Hitler came to unlimited power. Murder and enslavement within the country was the beginning. He smashed the workers' and employees' trade unions to allow himself to carry out his criminal plans unhindered. From what was seized the fascists formed the *Deutsche Arbeitsfront* (German Work Front), an instrument to enslave the working population and to prepare their war of conquest. It was led by adventurers and those who profiteered from the people's suffering.

Then the war of conquest began, the campaign of destruction against other nations. Armaments industrialists, major landowners and other militarists joined in league with Hitler and his criminal clique and cold-bloodedly sacrificed the German people to their hunger for power. Hitler ordered foreign cities to be "erased": Warsaw, Rotterdam, London and Stalingrad were destroyed. He inflicted the harshest fate on the Slavonic peoples. Workers of both sexes from other nations were enslaved. Wherever the hordes of his SS and Special Units appeared, they brought with them blood and tears, hunger and death. And the German Army was an unresisting tool for Hitler's atrocities.

After the German trade unions were smashed there were men who came together to take an active part in the struggle against Hitler's fascism. Many of them became the victims of the Gestapo executioners. The struggle by the active anti-fascist groups was denied success. Accordingly the Allied armies had to use their forces to carry on the costly struggle to liberate Germany from the rule of the fascist warmongers. It was only with the Red Army's conquest of Berlin that Hitler met his ignominious end. Now we can see for ourselves that the Allied Nations have not prosecuted the war in order to destroy the German people.

After the Red Army's entry into Berlin, a civil administration was set up with the City Commandant's permission, on the basis of the *unity of all anti-fascist democratic forces*. The necessary measures to secure provisions for the population and to re-establish normal life have been initiated. The order of the Supreme Head of the Soviet Military Administration gives workers and employees the right to combine in free trade unions. *This means that the time to re-organize in trade unions, which workers and employees have long awaited, has now come.*

The undersigned have formed a committee for the reconstruction of free, democratic trade unions for Greater Berlin. We are convinced that we express the will of the working population of Berlin when we declare that:

The new, free trade unions should bring together all previous tendencies and act as *a unified group fighting for the total eradication of fascism and for the creation of a new, democratic law for workers and employees.* Their task is primarily to assist in the rebirth of our people and the healing of the wounds which Hitler's infamous war has inflicted on the world. They are to assist in creating a democratic Germany which means to live in peace and freedom with other nations. They intend to assist in regaining the trust of other nations by sincere hard work in reconstruction and reparation for what has been destroyed in other countries.

The committee will draw up the trade union principles and agree them with the International Trade Union Committee. We propose that the workers and employees of Berlin should express their opinions on the following:

First Tasks of the Free Trade Unions:

(1) Determined struggle against the Nazi ideology and the poison of German militarism. Purging of active fascist elements in all positions in the city administration and in the enterprises.

(2) Direction of all efforts to ensure supplies for the population and to rebuild Berlin by hard work. Speediest possible recommissioning of supply enterprises and workshops, energy supply and transport services in Greater Berlin.

(3) Representation of the workers and employees within the framework of the Occupying Authorities' regulations by the conclusion of wage agreements and the organization of industrial health and safety standards and working provisions. Participation in the reconstruction of the economy and of social insurance with guarantees of democratic rights of participation for workers and employees.

(4) Education of the working population in the spirit of anti-fascism, and democratic progress, and education towards the recognition of their social position. Cultivation of solidarity with workers of other countries and consolidation of friendship with other peoples.

Workers and Employees!

The Nazi tyranny is dead! It is now up to us to set to work on the reconstruction, despite all the difficulties. Once more, as after 1918, the fate of our country lies in our hands. This time we must not fail.

Let us show the world that, having learned from the past and conscious of its best trade union traditions, the united working population is of a mind to create an anti-fascist bulwark and that it is determined to turn its full efforts to the creation of a democratic Germany and to peaceful co-operation with other nations.

The Preparatory Trade Union Committee for Greater Berlin

(W. Ulbricht: *Über Gewerkschaften. Aus Reden und Aufsätzen. Band II 1945–1952*, Berlin 1953, pp. 7 ff.)

D63 From Walter Ulbricht's speech at the first trade union conference in Halle/Saale, 29 August 1945:

On the Relationship of the Free Trade Unions to the Two Workers' Parties

Recently some trade union officials have spoken of the "party political neutrality of the trade unions". It is no accident that in the draft statutes prepared by those trade union officials there was no mention of the fight to destroy Nazism. It is a good sign for the anti-fascist vigilance of trade union members that they rejected these attitudes. How can anyone speak of party political neutrality after 12 years of fascist rule during which the poison of fascist ideology penetrated deep into the working class?

It is no accident that bourgeois circles also appear as supporters of "political neutrality", as expressed in the newspaper of the Christian Democratic Union. These circles would like to limit trade union activity to minor day-to-day matters and prevent the power of trade unions being used to obtain and secure workers' rights in the work place, the economy, and the state.

Already in the early years of the German trade union movement representatives of the bourgeoisie made efforts to turn the free trade unions into economic organizations. Thus the present bourgeois parties are merely continuing with their old policy. At the beginning of the century Professor Sombart was one of the best-known proponents of the political neutrality of trade unions. Professor Sombart particularly supported "freeing the trade unions from the tutelage of social democracy". His purpose becomes obvious when the professor writes in his book *Dennoch!* (Nevertheless!) that it is "a question of expediency whether the worker believes he can better achieve his interests through an independent workers' party or through influencing other parties which already exist". So the Social Democrats of the time were a thorn in the flesh of this advocate of bourgeois interests because they made it difficult to influence the workers and therefore also the trade union members in the spirit of a conciliation between labour and capital. For Sombart claims that "capitalism and socialism are not irreconcileable opposites".

Today's propaganda for party political neutrality also only serves the purpose of dividing trade unionists from the most progressive forces of the workers' movement in order to be more easily able to confuse the working population.

The demand for "political neutrality" is the expression of the fear certain circles have of the united strength of the working class. This unity has its basis in the united front of the Communist Party and the Social Democratic Party and in the close and friendly co-operation between the two parties and the free trade unions. This does not in any way mean an equivalence of party and trade unions.

The party is the vanguard. The most progressive, most active, politically best-educated workers and employees belong to it. By contrast the trade union is an organization which is intended to include the whole class, all workers, employees, and technicians, independent of their party political and ideological views.

Therefore anyone who is not an employer can be accepted into the trade union. The close friendly co-operation between the trade unions and the united front of the two workers' parties is in the very best interest of the union members, for while the trade unions can on their own achieve small improvements in the workers' position, a lasting fundamental rise in the standard of living of the working class is only possible by changing the political balance of power within the state. That depends on the proper connection between the economic and the political struggle for the rights of the working class, for the destruction of reaction and for the strengthening of the position of representatives of the working class in the local and state administration bodies and in the economic bodies. Accordingly trade union members have a direct interest in the fusion of SPD and KPD into a united workers' party. This would strengthen the political power of the working class and provide greater development opportunities for the trade union struggle.

In *Wages, Prices and Profit*, Karl Marx, strikingly portrayed the possibility of trade union activity in the following words:

"Trade unions do a good service as rallying points of resistance against the acts of violence of capitalism. They partly fail their purpose whenever they make inappropriate use of their power. They wholly fail their purpose whenever they limit themselves to fighting a running battle against the effects of the existing system instead of attempting at the same time to change it, instead of using their organized strength as a lever for the ultimate liberation of the working class, i.e. for the final abolition of the wage system."

[Marx/Engels, *Ausgewählte Schriften in zwei Bänden*, Dietz Verlag, Berlin 1951, pp. 420 f.]

Applied to us, this means that without the political struggle by the united front of the workers' parties, the essential interests of the working masses cannot be enforced successfully.

Trade union officials who speak of "party political neutrality" also fail to recognize that the situation today is different from what it used to be. The trade unions used to be primarily social democratic trade unions. Today, however, they are united free trade unions. Today there is a united front of the two workers' parties, which has set as its goal the unification of the working class. It is in the interest of the two workers' parties and the whole of the working class that the free trade unions become schools for anti-fascism and class consciousness. That is not possible without a link to the major ideological work of the two workers' parties.

It would be an illusion to believe that the free trade unions can accomplish their tasks without the united front of the workers' parties.

The only trade union officials who are speaking of "party political neutrality" at the moment are those who represent special interests of some kind or another and who are uninterested in or inimical towards the united front.

It is our opinion that the general interest of the working class and the demand for its unification necessitate joint discussion of important issues by the representatives of both parties and the trade unions. This will help to bring about a closer friendly relationship.

(W. Ulbricht: Source as above, pp. 51 ff.)

D64 From Walter Ulbricht's speech to the Second Party Congress of the Socialist Unity Party of Germany, Berlin, 2–4 September 1947:

The Achievements of the Free Trade Unions in the Reconstruction

In the great work of rebuilding, the free trade unions have particularly distinguished themselves. They started from the correct recognition that trade union success is only possible in the long term if the power of monopoly capitalism is removed and the employers' organizations of large-scale capital are no longer permitted. This was in the main achieved in the Soviet Occupation Zone. This can surely be described as the greatest success in the history of the German trade union movement.

Further development in the economy and in the state also offers new tasks for the trade unions. By reaching new wage agreements, fixing better wage conditions in the enterprises, improvement of the supply of provisions for the workers, and by extending social insurance the trade unions are fighting directly for the day-to-day interests of the workers.

However trade union work in the Soviet Occupation Zone can only lead to success if the economic plan is achieved and overachieved and if *labour productivity increases*. Trade union members must be made aware that a real improvement in their position is possible only if the trade unions also help to make the nationally owned enterprises into economically exemplary enterprises, to uncover mistakes and weaknesses by their supervision and so to further the development of industry.

Under the conditions of democratic order in the Soviet Occupation Zone it is possible to harmonize the measures adopted by the economic organs and the interests of the trade union organization. . .

(Source as above, pp. 178 f.)

D65 From Walter Ulbricht's speech to the FDGB Committee Conference, 6–7 July 1948:

[. . .]

Planning of this kind is however only possible with the support of the free trade unions. In the Soviet Occupation Zone the trade unions are one of the leading forces in the state. They have the chance to exert decisive influence on developments in the state and in the economy and on the shaping of working people's living conditions. Our new state order in which the laws are passed by the democratically elected parliaments is based primarily on the mass organizations of the working population. In class terms, the upholder of this state order is the working class in alliance with the working farmers, the progressive intelligentsia and the democratic forces in the middle classes. From an organizational viewpoint the leading force is the party of the working class, the Socialist Unity Party of Germany, which works together with the other democratic parties and the progressive democratic mass organizations, the trade unions, the mutual farmers' aid associations, the FDJ and the DBD . . .

(Source as above, p. 247)

D66 Extract from the Constitution of the FDGB, 1950:

[. . .]

(4) The Free German Trade Unions are a social mass organization which is not party politically bound. They unite on a voluntary basis all workers and employees of all occupations irrespective of nationality, sex, or political or religious conviction. They are founded on the class struggle. Their aim is the socialist order of society. They are schools for democracy and for socialism.

(5) a) The Confederation of Free German Trade Unions (FDGB) regards the Socialist Unity Party as the party of the working class; it is its conscious organized vanguard. It is the originator of the national economic plans which are so important for the German people. The Socialist Unity Party is the champion of the German people in the struggle for peace and for the national unity of Germany.

b) The Free German Trade Unions strengthen and deepen the alliance of the working class with the working farmers.

c) The Confederation of Free German Trade Unions is prepared to work together with all organizations which are active for the establishment of the democratic unity of Germany and the safeguarding of peace . . .

(6) The Free German Trade Unions fight for the all-round strengthening of the German Democratic Republic. They educate their members in democratic state and national consciousness. They work constantly to raise the political consciousness of their members. They play an active part in the elections to the organs of the people's assemblies and send their representatives to these organs.

(7) The Free German Trade Unions develop in their members the feeling of proletarian internationalism. As a member of the World Federation of Trade Unions (WFTU) the Confederation of Free German Trade Unions (FDGB) fights for international unity in the struggle of the working classes and for a lasting peace. They support a continuing consolidation of the German people's friendship with the peoples of the Soviet Union and the People's Democracies. In this way the Free German Trade Unions make a decisive contribution to the world peace bloc which is led by the Soviet Union.

[. . .]

(10) The Free Trade Unions carry on a determined struggle against all manifestations of opportunism, against narrow interpretations of trade unionism, against sectarian and bureaucratic tendencies, as only in this way can the fighting strength and unity of the trade unions be increased and the major social objectives be accomplished. They can carry on this struggle successfully only if criticism and self-criticism as a law of development become an integral part of all trade union work.

(11) The Free Trade Unions support state planning and direction of the economy; they mobilize working people to fulfil the Five-Year Plan, the great plan in the struggle for a peaceful, progressive Germany in which the people's standard of living and their material and cultural situation will attain a hitherto unknown level . . .

(*Protokoll des 3. Kongresses des Freien Deutschen Gewerkschaftbundes*, Berlin 1950, pp. 576 f.)

D67 From Walter Ulbricht's speech at the Second Party Conference of the SED, 9–12 July 1952:

[. . .]

The trade unions are schools for socialism. According to FDGB resolutions it is the task of the trade union organizations to represent the economic interests of the workers, to further their intellectual and cultural development, and to lead socialist competition. It follows that the first task of the trade union leadership in an enterprise is to put through the house agreement. If members of the trade union leadership explain the fundamental importance of the house agreement and the role of the working class to the workers, if they really care about their people, then we will make progress . . .

(W. Ulbricht: *Die gegenwärtige Lage und die neuen Aufgaben der Sozialistischen Einheitspartei Deutschlands*, Berlin 1952, pp. 140 f.)

D68 On the role and duties of the trade unions, from Erich Honecker's report to the Tenth Party Congress of the SED, April 1981:

Comrades,

The FDGB, with its nearly nine million members, is making an important contribution to the shaping of an advanced socialist society and to the all-round strengthening of our socialist state. We should like to use this platform of the 10th Party Congress to convey our most sincere expressions of gratitude to this, the greatest class organization in our country.

The trade unions have always met their obligations as the faithful comrades-in-arms of our Party. On the basis of the Constitution of the GDR and the Labour Code, they have rights which are unique in the history of the German trade union movement. Through the trade unions, which represent the most comprehensive mass organization of the ruling working class and the organization of those who own the means of production, millions of workers are directly involved in the management and planning of social processes. Every day, they help to mould socialist democracy. The trade unions organize socialist competition and, in particular, promote initiatives which aim at a sharp increase in labour productivity and a high degree of efficiency and quality. They steer the creativity of the workers towards accelerating scientific and technological progress.

Their work is characterized by comradely co-operation, mutual assistance, a spirit of innovation and a sense of community, all of which goes towards making the best performances become the social standard. The overall objective is to increase our economic potential and meet the challenges of the eighties.

In accordance with their position in our society, the trade unions place great stress on the careful handling of public property and the country's resources. The thoughts and actions of the workers are being increasingly influenced by two simple truths — that only as much can be consumed as has been produced, and that no one can live at the expense of others. This is crucial if the working and living conditions of the people are to be constantly improved. A wide field of activities has opened up for the trade unions, by means of which they satisfy the growing needs of the workers for a decent standard of intellectual and cultural life, as well as for a rich and fulfilled leisure and recreation. The traditional movement summed up by the motto "Work, learn and live in a socialist way" should be the subject of the attention it deserves in every enterprise.

This shows how comprehensive the trade union representation of interests is in the further development of advanced socialist society. The more actively the trade unions meet the demands made on them, the more their great authority among the people will grow. Our trade unions function as schools of socialism as Lenin intended.

The unions play a great part in spreading Marxism-Leninism among millions of non-party members. They play a major role in promoting the class viewpoint and the anti-imperialist solidarity of the workers and enabling the working class to successfully exercise its leading role in our society. Very successful in this respect are the "Schools of Socialist Labour", in which about three million workers participate.

We have a great feeling of respect for the diligent social work of the many honorary union officials, in particular the shop stewards. Everywhere, and at all times, they are worthy of the full support of our Party organizations. It is a matter of honour for every comrade to be a good trade unionist.

(Erich Honecker: *Report of the Central Committee of the Socialist Unity Party of Germany to the 10th Congress of the SED*, Dresden 1981, pp. 156 ff.)

D69 From the President's report at the Ninth Congress of the Chamber of Technology (KDT), 5 December 1987:

All the activities of the socialist engineers' organization form a part of the great creative initiative of the working people of the GDR to realize the policies for the welfare of the people and the safeguarding of peace which were resolved by the 11th Party Congress of the SED. This was emphasized by the President of the KDT, Professor Dagmar Hülsenberg, who presented the report of the presidium of the Chamber of Technology. In the name of the organization's 290,000 members she declared: Acceptance of responsibility and commitment to safeguarding peace means for us the greatest efforts in science and technology for the all-round strengthening of socialism and the realization of the economic strategy of the SED looking forward to the year 2000.

This clear declaration of political commitment was impressively reflected in the KDT initiative "top performance for key technologies", she said. It was expressed in the 14,700 KDT projects realized in evaluation of the 11th Party Congress of the SED. In the run-up to the present congress the members of the engineers' organization have taken on 17,600 new collective and personal obligations.

(*Neues Deutschland* vol. 42 no. 286, 5–6 December 1987)

D70 Promotion of television and radio in the directives for the Five-Year Plan 1976–1980:

The effect of radio and television is to be raised by programme improvements in order to promote more strongly the development of socialist consciousness and to satisfy better the growing demand for information, education and entertainment. Television for schools is to be expanded. Investment in radio and television is to be concentrated on the further expansion and modernization of studios and the improvement of reception.

(*Directives for the Five-Year Plan for the GDR's national economic development 1976–1980*, Dresden 1976, p. 147)

D71 On increasing the impact of ideological work on the masses, from Erich Honecker's report to the Tenth Congress of the SED, 1981:

Comrades,

Taking pride in the accomplishments of their socialist fatherland, the working people are increasingly being inspired by the ideas of socialism. The policy of giving undivided attention to the masses, which pervades all activities of our Party, and our strict adherence to the principle of maintaining a continuing open dialogue with the working people on all aspects of our domestic and foreign policy have borne rich fruit. The ties between the Party and the people, and the relationship of trust existing between them have become closer still. This can be seen from the wide-ranging activities whereby the working people are demonstrating their commitment to the policy of the Party and successfully putting it into practice.

The readiness of the working people to do their utmost reflects effective political and ideological work, which has gone a long way towards developing a correct approach to the challenges of the day. It becomes clearly apparent here what a tremendous advantage it is for socialism to be able to rely on the conscious and voluntary initiative of the masses, on their active participation in the exercise of power. This is a major reason why, historically speaking, our socialist system is clearly superior to the capitalist system.

The demands being made on the quality and effectiveness of agitation and propaganda keep growing all the time. The emphasis must be on the responsibility of the individual in socialist society, on the concordance of personal and social interests. Everyone, whatever his place in the community, will have to do his fair share to bring out the advantages of socialism ever more fully.

Then there are the new demands being made on the standard of our political and ideological work as a result of the fact that people are becoming more exacting intellectually. We are dealing with knowledgeable, educated citizens who will not put up with clichés and empty slogans. They expect to be fully informed and provided with compelling arguments in order to find their way about politically.

Finally, the aggravation of the international class struggle between socialism and imperialism is a major factor. We are witnessing a continual increase in the ideological aggressiveness of imperialism, in its anti-communist agitation and subversion. This is a long-standing policy that has failed time and again, but one that is dangerous all the same. What we have here is an attempt undertaken by those who find themselves historically on the defensive to stop the unstoppable — the worldwide transition from capitalism to socialism.

It is common knowledge that we are building up our socialist society while being exposed to foreign influences and to constant imperialist attempts at interference. This can only strengthen our resolve to keep demonstrating the superiority of our Marxist-Leninist ideology anew by means of our successful domestic and foreign policy. A perennial requirement for us is to display ideological vigilance, steadfastness and the ability to counter the attempts at manipulation made by the imperialist opinion-makers by projecting our firm class position.

Our mass political work, reflecting the inextricable unity between politics, economics and ideology, is chiefly designed to make the working people acquainted with the economic laws of socialism and the content of our economic strategy with a view to motivating and mobilizing them for a steep increase in economic performance. We will be meeting the demands made on us if all working people look upon scientific and technological progress and its speedy translation into tangible economic and, hence, social results as a matter of vital importance. We are confident that the URANIA society will as it has since the 9th Congress, be making a significant contribution towards this end.

The more widespread and effective application of the best practices in socialist competition constitutes a major source of material and intellectual reserves. Much of the responsibility for systematically organizing this exchange of experiences and clarifying all ideological questions connected with the striving for a high level of performance, for implementing the socialist performance principle, and for constantly enhancing socialist working morale, discipline and order, rests with managers and administrators, from minister to supervisor or foreman, under the leadership of local Party branches and in co-operation with the trade unions.

More than ever it is essential to address every political and social issue in class terms and to grasp the essence of a matter within a given system. The answer to the question *Cui bono?* remains the litmus test for the analysis of any phenomenon, for making correct decisions and for taking correct action in any situation of the class struggle. This goes as much for the tasks arising in the building of socialism as for the struggle against imperialism and its counter-revolutionary machinations.

Historical propaganda, which has experienced a great upsurge in recent years, is of great value for raising the level of socialist awareness. The outline "History of the SED" and other works such as the life of Ernst Thälmann have become immensely popular. Mention should also be made here of such television productions as "Karl Marx: The Young Years", serials devoted to Marx, Engels and Scharnhorst, documentary film entitled "From The Ruins Newly Risen" and other programmes. They enable the citizens of our country, notably the rising generation, to draw important lessons for coping with the revolutionary challenges of our day. This is not least the case because we give an authentic account of historical events.

One task requiring mention in this context is the need to foster new traditions born on our socialist development and related to socialist construction in the GDR. What we must bear in mind here is that with the German Democratic Republic having existed for more than 30 years the majority of our people have had first-hand experience of socialism, but not of capitalism. Born into a new society, these citizens take the advantages and values of socialism so much for granted as a feature of life that the full extent of these advantages can only be appreciated if seen in historical perspective.

Since the primary objective of our political and ideological work is to equip the working class and all other working people better and better for the exercise of power, it is common practice in Party work for communists, wherever they work, to talk to the masses in a climate of trust, explaining Party policy to them and helping them to clarify the questions and problems that are uppermost in their minds. The political dialogue with all citizens is a perennial task. More than before we must draw into that dialogue those people whose attitude towards socialism is not sufficiently consolidated. Their varying degree of political awareness, education and experience must be taken into account. All this makes exacting demands on the Party's 150,000 political education workers.

Comrades,

The mass media are playing an exceedingly important role in our day. They are instruments of ideological struggle in the hands of the workers' and farmers' state and, on the other side, in the hands of the imperialist bourgeoisie.

In the period since the 9th Party Congress, as before, the press, radio and television of the GDR have proved reliable instruments of our socialist system, effective weapons in the struggle against imperialism. They have contributed significantly to providing a political orientation for the working people and satisfying their intellectual and cultural needs. The scope of the media has increased still further. At present, 1,770 newspapers and periodicals with a combined circulation of 40 million copies are published in the GDR. By now 90 per cent of all households in the GDR are furnished with television sets, 17 per cent of them with colour sets. Virtually every family has one or more radios.

The foremost task now before the press, radio and television is to recognize that the active dissemination of our socialist ideology, information on domestic and foreign policy, intellectual and cultural enrichment, and entertainment in the widest sense of the word, form an integrated whole and must be implemented as such. Continuing emphasis will have to be laid on depth of ideological analysis, quickness of response to political developments and mass appeal, a task that must be imaginatively carried forward.

Above all the role of the press, radio and TV demands further expansion as a social forum for the exchange of experience among the working people. This means that the working people gain a hearing for their ideas, initiatives, proposals and critical suggestions and that more work is being done with readers', viewers' and listeners' letters and contributions by workerscorrespondents.

Neues Deutschland, as the organ of the SED Central Committee is faced with the task of continuing its exemplary role. The country newspapers of our Party, with a daily circulation of about five million copies, also bear great responsibility in the work with the masses. As far as the 600-odd works' newsheets are concerned, experience has shown that the better they are utilized by the party committees the better they live up to their social function.

TV programmes having been quite effective during the last few years, the task now is to comply even more with the high standards of a society as developed as ours and the multiple interests and demands of the millions of viewers. This includes doing more for the complementary character of the 1st and 2nd TV channels.

(Erich Honecker: *Report of the Central Committee of the Socialist Unity Party of Germany to the 10th Congress of the SED*, Dresden 1981, pp. 183 ff.)

D72 Churches and other religious communities, from the foreign press agency's official handbook, 1986:

For historical reasons that are due to the work of Luther and the Reformation, the Protestant creed is well and truly dominant in the GDR. About 4,300 pastors do their service in eight Evangelical provincial churches which merged to form the Federation of Evangelical Churches of the GDR in 1969.

The Catholic Church in the GDR breaks down into two Dioceses, three Episcopal Districts and one Apostolic Administration and is headed by the Berlin Bishops Conference, the union of Catholic bishops in the GDR. There are 988 pastoral communities and 1,144 clergy. Moreover there are, mainly in regions with a high percentage of Catholics, men's and women's orders, monasteries, convents and other monastic facilities.

Apart from these, there are 40 other religious communities in the GDR, most of which are affiliated to worldwide organizations. There are eight Jewish communities for citizens following this creed, which are organized in the Union of Jewish Communities in the GDR. To practise their religion they may avail themselves of eight synagogues and houses of prayer which, having been destroyed during the time of fascism, were rebuilt from government funds and consecrated. The same can be said of the 125 Jewish cemeteries, one of the largest of its kind in Europe being the Jewish cemetery in Berlin-Weissensee.

The churches and other religious communities manage and practise their activities in line with the Constitution and other legal stipulations in force in the GDR. Guided by the principle that the state and the church should be separate, the socialist state in its relationship towards the churches is striving for a matter-of-fact atmosphere marked by mutual understanding and complying with the Constitution. Tribute is paid to the commitment shown by the churches to the cause of safeguarding peace and ensuring all people's well-being.

For the care, promotion and rehabilitation of the mentally and physically handicapped as well as for elderly people, the churches run a large number of charitable and welfare facilities. The state assists them by financial allocations and personnel training.

Destroyed during the Second World War, many churches and chapels in the GDR were restored and rebuilt with government assistance. A great number of Protestant and Catholic churches and community centres are set up in new residential areas as part of a special construction scheme.

Church music, Christian literature and art as well as church publications have assumed a substantial scale in the GDR. The Evangelische Verlagsanstalt and the St. Benno-Verlag are publishing houses run by the churches with the largest congregations.

Churches in the GDR are actively involved in alleviating hunger and poverty and helping the victims of natural disasters in the framework of campaigns called Bread for the World and Distress in the World and support the anti-racism programme of the World Council of Churches.

(Panorama DDR: *The German Democratic Republic*, Dresden 1986, p. 69 f.)

D73 From the report on Erich Honecker's talks with church leaders, 6 March 1978:

Erich Honecker acknowledged the engagement for peace which the churches recognize as their role in accordance with the Christian maxims of respect for life and responsibility for one's neighbour. Their work for the maintenance of peace, for *détente* and understanding between nations could only be considered with satisfaction. In particular the great importance of the churches' contribution towards ending the arms race and banning weapons of mass destruction, particularly the neutron bomb, should be emphasized. "For us and assuredly for you too", said the Chairman of the Council of State, "it gives cause for concern that despite the progress in *détente* the arms race is constantly being speeded up by the actions of the imperialists . . ."

The Chairman of the Council of State expressed his appreciation for the humanitarian help given by the churches in the GDR to poor nations and those struggling for their liberation. In this way the noble cause of banishing racism and neo-colonialism from the life of humankind was being assisted. The GDR actively supported the struggle of the nations for freedom, independence, and progress, and for the construction of their new way of life . . .

Calling to mind his statement of 29 October 1976 to the People's Chamber, the Chairman of the Council of State declared that our socialist society offers security and protection to every citizen irrespective of age or sex, ideology or religious confession. It gives citizens clear prospects and the opportunity to help in constructing the future, to develop their abilities, talents, and personalities. As Erich Honecker stressed, the equal rights and equal respect accorded to all citizens and their unrestricted involvement in the development of the advanced socialist society represent a norm which characterizes the relationships between people and is binding on all. Correspondingly the path to a high educational standard and professional training and development stood open to every citizen in the GDR, and particularly to every young person.

On the situation of the churches and of Christians in the GDR, the Chairman of the Council of State declared that together with the clear separation of church and state, the freedom to practise one's religion was guaranteed by the constitution and ensured in practice. "We show a very great deal of understanding in this matter, and we shall hold to that."

The worldwide recognition of the GDR had made it possible for the churches in our country to take an active part on equal terms in the ecumenical movement. Our state valued highly the ecumenical activities of the churches in the GDR for peace, *détente*, and international understanding. Bishop Schönherr, speaking on behalf of the conference of the protestant churches in the GDR, said: "Both sides, starting from their own premises, are concerned with responsibility for the same world and the same human beings. And the situation is that these human beings are always at one and the same time citizens of the state and holders of a basic conviction. Since the individual cannot be divided up, all kinds of meetings like this are not only useful but essential. And I may stress that the Christian does not understand his existence as a citizen as merely a case of respecting the existing laws in a purely formal manner, but that on the basis of his faith he knows himself to share responsibility both for the whole and also for the individual and the individual's relationship to the whole."

Bishop Schönherr described the church in socialism as a church which helps the Christian citizen and the individual congregation to find a way in socialist society with the freedom and responsibility of faith and to endeavour to seek the best for all and for the whole. The church in socialism would be a church which as such, with the same freedom of faith, is ready to make a full and committed contribution wherever human life is upheld and improved in our society, and to help wherever necessary to avert danger to human life . . .

In the course of the talks many detailed issues were discussed and resolved. These included for instance church broadcasts on radio and television, questions of spiritual welfare work in prisons, and old-age pensions for church workers appointed for life. State support was promised for church activities in connection with the Luther anniversary in 1983.

As a conclusion both sides were able to determine with satisfaction that the relationships of the church to the state had been characterized increasingly by objectivity, trust, and frankness in recent years.

(*Konstruktives, freimütiges Gespräch beim Vorsitzenden des Staatsrates*, in: *Neues Deutschland* vol. 35. no. 56 of 7.3.1978)

D74 From an interview with Erich Honecker on Luther and church–state relations in the GDR, 6 October 1983:

Erich Honecker: It is a basic feature of our relationship to our historical inheritance that we take up the work and legacy of all who have contributed to progress and the development of world culture, and cultivate and develop them in accordance with our socialist and humanist ideals. For this reason commemorations of historical anniversaries are high points in the social life of the German Democratic Republic . . .

To think that we are honouring Luther to belittle Müntzer would be misguided. It is important for the historical and traditional consciousness of our people in socialism that Luther and Müntzer are not placed in contrast to each other as opposites irreconcileable right from the start. They have to be treated dialectically as the two great figures of the first German revolution. Luther unleashed a movement which made a Müntzer necessary and possible. In this sense both Luther and Müntzer are an indispensable part of our inheritance and our tradition . . .

Even if the Marxist view of Luther in the GDR has meanwhile developed further, there was no need to correct this basic position. However, GDR historians have devoted intensive study to the whole epoch in which Luther lived and worked. In this process new knowledge and insights on the personality, work, and influence of the reformer were gained . . .

I should like to emphasize again that the freedom of religion and of conscience of the citizens of the GDR is guaranteed in all circumstances. Of course all citizens are equal before the law irrespective of their ideology or religious confession. That is shown not least by the fact that acts against the freedom of belief and of conscience and the freedom of worship are punishable under the criminal law in our country. But certainly our socialist state cannot accept reference to this freedom as an excuse for contraventions of state and legal order; this goes beyond the bounds of the constitution . . .

Indeed, the meeting with church leaders on 6 March 1978 initiated new impulses for the constructive development of the relationships between state and church in the GDR. I share your impression that the co-operation so far between the Martin Luther Committee of the GDR and the Luther Committee of the Evangelical Churches in the GDR represents a confirmation and affirmation of that meeting. And the co-operation of the Luther committees has not only furthered their common plan but has also had a stabilizing effect on state-church relations. I know that the Evangelical Church in the GDR is holding firm to the path of the 6 March 1978. We too shall continue along this path . . .

As I already said, the relationship between state and church should be further developed by open discussion, frank clarification of problems, and readiness to take constructive steps. Anyone familiar with the wide and varied opportunities for church activity in the GDR will be clearly aware of our understanding attitude towards the legitimate interests of the churches . . .

Understanding for church concerns has increased proportionally as the churches have described their position in our society as that of "church in socialism", and acted accordingly. This is one result of the continuous development of state-church relations over many years. You will probably yourself have noticed that the seven church congresses in 1983 and other church events relating to the Luther celebrations were carried out with full church autonomy and with extraordinary support from the state. Here the state side has, to use a current church text, dared much in faith: faith in the present position of church-state relations and faith in the churches.

(*Interview Erich Honeckers mit der BRD-Zeitschrift Lutherische Monatsheft. DDR-Lutherehrung. Manifestation der Humanität und des Friedens,* in: *Neues Deutschland* vol. 38 no. 236 of 6.10.1983)

D75 From the declaration by the leaders of the Evangelical Church in the GDR on the tenth anniversary of the Helsinki Agreement, 1 August 1985:

Trust, dialogue and the renunciation of violence must take the place of suspicion, hostility and the threat of violence in international relations.

The experiences of the past ten years, in which confrontations and tensions have occurred again and again, show that there is no sensible alternative to co-operation between states of differing economic and political systems. Indeed this co-operation is urgently necessary to deal with the constantly growing distress and poverty in the developing countries. The indissoluble connection between peace and justice also calls for the continuation of the efforts for improvement in the humanitarian sphere in accordance with the final document agreed at Helsinki. We ask the governments of the two German states to do everything to fulfil their particular responsibility. The initiatives put forward by political parties against the arms race, e.g. for a chemical weapon-free zone in central Europe, should be considered carefully. But the opportunities for people in the German states to meet each other should also no longer lag behind usual international arrangements.

We ask the Christians in our country to continue to accompany the path of Helsinki with their prayers, their patience, and their impulses for peace. The peace witness of our churches includes the efforts of every individual to dare over and over again to take his own concrete steps to create peace. Peace is the key word for human co-operation. This peace is always concrete and must be upheld every day in our day-to-day lives. We encourage everyone to let their Christian conviction show in, and have its effect on our society. With trust in our Lord's approval we can be allies of hope!

(*Neues Deutschland* vol. 40 no. 178 of 1.8.1985)

D76 From "Theses concerning Martin Luther: the 500th Anniversary of the Reformer's Birth"; the official quincentenary brochure, 1983:[9]

Martin Luther was born on 10 November 1483 and died on 18 February 1546. As one of those who paved the way for the intellectual and political conflicts that surged through Germany and Europe in the age of the decay of feudalism, the rise of urban capitalism and the earliest bourgeois revolutions, he is one of the greatest men in German history and a figure of world stature.

The roots of the German Democratic Republic lie deep in German history. As a German socialist state, it is the product of the age-old struggle for social advance on the part of the progressive forces in the German nation. All this progress, together with all those men and women who brought it about, form an inalienable part of the traditions that have moulded our national identity. As Erich Honecker has put it: "All those who have striven for social and cultural progress have their place in the traditions that we cherish and uphold, irrespective of the social class or group to which they belonged." This is the spirit in which the German Democratic Republic now pays its tribute to Luther's historical achievement and seeks to uphold its progressive values.

[. . .]

The victory of the working class and its allies, together with the establishment and consolidation of socialism, has created in the German Democratic Republic the necessary conditions for a fair and reasoned assessment of the importance of Luther. We pay tribute in our country to all those of earlier generations who in the conditions of their own day and age fought with all their might to lead mankind forward and to enrich our culture. Our assessment is a critical one; we do not ignore the class-bound contradictions of their age, nor do we judge them by unhistorical criteria.

[. . .]

There are a number of museums and memorials to Luther and the Reformation in the German Democratic Republic. These are maintained by the state, which is at pains to preserve the cultural and ethical values associated with the great Reformer and his movement. Like all other religious communities, the various denominations within the Protestant Lutheran tradition are guaranteed extensive freedom of action under the GDR constitution, and Christians work side by side with all the other people in the country for peace, *détente* and disarmament in the face of the profound problems facing mankind at this complex and critical moment in history. And in company with all other Christians, the followers of the

Lutheran tradition are playing their parts in the creation of an advanced socialist society, not least through their selfless work in charitable organizations devoted to the care of the sick, the disabled, the aged and the young. In so doing, they preserve and enrich their own traditions, which have helped to create the cultural and moral climate that has prevailed in Germany and other countries over the past centuries. This is the spirit in which the party and state leadership of the GDR has always been ready to discuss the humanitarian concerns of the Christian Churches and to provide a fertile soil for co-operation.

The progressive achievement of Luther has its firm place in the cultural tradition of the German Democratic Republic. Proof of this, if proof were needed, is to be seen in the fact that a National Luther Committee was formed under the chairmanship of Erich Honecker, General Secretary of the SED Central Committee and Chairman of the GDR Council of State, in order to co-ordinate the 500th anniversary celebrations. Our appreciation of Luther and his work also encompasses the endeavours of all those who, by calling to witness the example set by the great Reformer and his teachings, are carrying on their own struggle for justice, progress and peace in the world.

In the words of Erich Honecker: "May these celebrations serve, in a spirit befitting the universal influence exerted by the Reformation to encourage us in our struggle to preserve peace and to enable the nations of the world to live together in harmony."

(*Theses Concerning Martin Luther 1483–1983: The Luther Quincentenary in the German Democratic Republic*, Dresden 1983, pp. 3, 34–6)

Notes

1. The discussions about whether socialism is an independent (transitional) historical phase or whether it is the first stage of communism must not be seen as a purely theoretical discussion. It is of fundamental importance for the self-perception of the GDR and has fundamental consequences for political decision-making processes. There have been recent indications that the SED leadership might acknowledge that even antagonistic contradictions between classes could exist in socialism. It is worth noting that since Marx the definition of classes themselves has been a major problem.
2. The SED, despite its considerable membership, is still a cadre party. It is not perceived as a mass organization. In fact media reporting talks of the SED and the mass organizations such as the trade union movement. The SED is still perceived as the avantgarde of the working-class movement. It has been subject to a number of "cleansing processes" in which members have been expelled and new ones recruited.
3. The trade union movement, like the SED, is organized on the principle of democratic centralism, i.e. along Leninist lines. Unlike the British trade union

movement (but like the West German trade unions) it is industry-based, i.e. all working people in the same industry belong to the same union nationwide. Unlike the STUC, the TUC, and the West German DGB, the primacy of the central FDGB over the individual industrial unions is paramount.

4. There has also been considerable evidence of *glasnost* (openness) in the media since 1987. It is symptomatic in itself that M. Gorbachev's speeches (on *glasnost* and *perestroika*) are printed in full in *Neues Deutschland*.

5. The discussion on the status of socialism as a separate historical phase has as its most fundamental concept the types of relationship of production. Gorbachev's present drive for *perestroika* is very much based on a re-assessment of this concept of the types of relationship of production; his views have much in common with those propagated by Che Guevara, cf. *Venceremos: The Speeches and Writings of Che Guevara*, ed. John Gerassi, London, Panther 1969, esp. ch. 19, 22, 24, 32.

6. It should be noted here that if a society without class contradictions were achieved, the leading role of the working class party would become anachronistic.

7. The DFD was founded in 1947 on an anti-fascist platform, as a non-party-political organization for the struggle for peace and a democratic Germany.

8. The *Deutscher Kulturbund* was founded in 1945 on an anti-fascist platform, as a non-party-political organization. Its aim was the cultural regeneration of Germany after twelve years of Nazism. The latest (June 1988) official GDR figures (in *GDR Review* 63/88) give a membership of 268,000. The League of Culture comprises 10,895 hobby and interest groups in literature and the arts, monument preservation, local history, science, environmental protection, photography and others. 3452 citizens, nominated by the League of Culture, are members of the People's Chamber, regional, district, and village councils.

9. It is interesting to compare the earlier "official" line on Luther in the *Lexikon A-Z in zwei Bänden*, published in 1958 by Verlag Enzyklopädie Leipzig. Luther is there severely criticized for his stance on the Peasants' Revolt in 1525 and is described as having abandoned the peasants to their fate; he is held to be partly responsible for the defeat of the peasants. In the same encyclopaedia Thomas Müntzer is portrayed as a much more positive revolutionary figure of the Reformation.

4 Economic and Social Policy

In the 1976 programme of the Socialist Unity Party of Germany, chapter II, "The construction of an advanced socialist society in the German Democratic Republic", the following statement is made:

To build an advanced socialist society means to pursue economic and social policies as an integrated whole. The purpose of seeking a rapid growth of production and its efficiency is to improve working and living conditions in a systematic manner. The consistent implementation of the principle that everyone should contribute according to his abilities and receive according to his work is a major impetus behind economic and social progress.

The unity of economic and social policies has been particularly highlighted during the Honecker era, and this emphasis marks a new departure in SED policy.[1] Within the framework of a socialist mode of production where the bulk of the means of production is no longer in private ownership, economic and social developments are centrally planned, and largely also centrally managed, according to the scientific theory of Marxism-Leninism. The Socialist Unity Party is not only the custodian of Marxism-Leninism but also the instigator of economic and social policies. Since the raising of the people's material and cultural level is based on the rapid expansion of socialist production, the main thrust of socialist economic policy is towards the intensification of socialist production by means of increasing efficiency and higher labour productivity. This, however, requires a high level of expertise on the part of the working people. "It is impossible to construct an advanced socialist society without high standards in education, culture and political consciousness of the people, just as an advanced socialist society is not viable without an advanced material and technological basis." Although the GDR now ranks among the world's top ten industrial nations, although it can and does boast considerable achievements in the field of education and culture generally, in social policy towards women and in health, and although it compares favourably with the other socialist countries in terms of housing and standard of living, it still lags

167

behind the top western industrialized nations in the two latter fields.

From the very beginning, education has been one of the cornerstones of economic and social policy and planning. Born out of Marxist-Leninist ideology, German educational tradition, the experience of the collapse of the Third Reich, demographic problems (such as a severe manpower shortage), and the desire for rapid industrialization, the education system of the GDR assumed its final shape with the 1963 Bill and 1965 Law "concerning the integrated socialist education system of the German Democratic Republic". For some time now education in the GDR has been acknowledged as a major achievement, and in view of the aims stipulated there is certainly statistical evidence to support this evaluation. If the concept of an educated and educative nation is measured in terms of regular readership in libraries, book publication figures, visits to concerts and the theatre, participation in amateur dramatics, choirs, etc., then the GDR is a world leader. The fundamental structural principle of the education system is integration. The sequential components of the system are described as integrated, as is the unity of theory and practice within a framework of general education for all. The system also aspires to create a "new man" as a well-rounded personality with an integrated educational background providing a unity between intellectual and scientific education on the one hand and moral and social education on the other.[2] Polytechnic education illustrates the integration of the educational and the vocationally practical. Integration also affects the relationship between school and home, school and the youth organizations, industry and agriculture and educational institutions. Further, integration refers to life-long learning. Everybody is to be educated to the fullest extent of their abilities and their interest, and this requires the integration of general and specialist education. Equal attention is paid to all sectors of education, whether school, pre-school, or tertiary; and in fact education features regularly and prominently in official statements such as the SED party programme or the economic plan. However, criticism can also be heard, for instance on such matters as the authoritarian style of teaching, the treatment of left-handed pupils, and the fact that life-long learning often only means continued learning in one's own vocational area.

A striking example of the attempt to integrate economic and social policy is provided by policies on women.[3] Although it was not a central issue at the 3rd FDGB Congress in 1950, delegates did raise the issue of male prejudice and the need to mobilize women because of the shortages in the workforce. In his report to the 2nd Party Conference of the SED in 1952, Walter Ulbricht for the first time emphasized the integrated nature of economic and social policy in respect of women and demanded an increasing role for women's committees. Although equal pay for equal work had been decreed by one of the first directives of the Soviet Military Administration, it became increasingly clear in the course of the 1950s and 1960s that it was not enough simply to decree equality and legislate accordingly, but that when social practice is lagging behind, special social policy measures have to be adopted. This was not only imperative from the ideological viewpoint but also economically necessary because by the 1970s, women constituted more than half the workforce; in 1977 for example 86 per cent of all women of working age went out to work. The financial aspects of this policy were highlighted by Honecker in his report to the 9th Congress of the SED in May 1976 and acknowledged in the Directives for the Five-Year Plan issued by that congress and also in the 1976 programme of the SED. By 1981, in his report to the 10th Congress, Honecker could reflect with some satisfaction on the measures taken over the last five years. Social policy concerning women still figures, although less prominently, in the Directives issued by the 11th Congress of the SED for the Five-Year Plan 1986–1990 and in the Five-Year Plan Act for 1990. The reports by the Central Statistical Office of the GDR indicate measures taken for the fulfilment of the national economic plans. The social policy measures include health-care facilities, maternity leave, sickness leave (also to care for a sick child), creche and kindergarten facilities, provision of meals at educational institutions and workplaces, and special provision for female students. However, despite the high participation rate of women in higher education, in party work and in the mass organizations, in management positions, and as elected representatives on district councils, regional councils, and in the People's Chamber (30 per cent), women are barely represented in the highest echelons of the SED and the state, and a number of other negative features can be mentioned: sexist jokes can be found in the media, advertizing is also sexist, and women still do the bulk of the housework, with men enjoying more leisure time. There is also a high divorce rate.[4]

Documents

D77 From the Programme of the SED: on the unity of economic and social policies, May 1976:

The unity of economic and social policies

Led by the Socialist Unity Party of Germany, the working class and all other working people in the German Democratic Republic have created an efficient and stable socialist planned economy that is being brought to an increasingly higher level of strength and efficiency. The economic and social policies of the Party are based on the conscious utilization of the objective economic Laws of socialism.

The Socialist Unity Party of Germany will continue to make every effort to ensure that increases in performance and output and the increasingly widespread application of scientific and technological innovations benefit the working class and all other working people, and that cultural and living standards are raised more and more, resulting in the spiritual enrichment of man.

The Socialist Unity Party of Germany considers that a gradual improvement in the living standards of all working people presupposes a high level of performance in socialist production and sustained economic growth. This is achieved by an optimum relationship between accumulation and consumption and by the full exploitation of the GDR's economic potential, including the tapping of reserves throughout the economy, i.e. in all sectors, branches and enterprises.

Increased labour productivity is the main source of economic growth. It brings about a continuous increase in national income as the material basis for the ever better satisfaction of both individual and public needs.

The economic and social policies of the Socialist Unity Party of Germany are a major factor in bringing the various classes and sections of society still closer together, in reducing substantial distinctions between physical and mental labour and bridging the gap between the living conditions in town and country. The application of the principle of reward according to merit is combined with the gradual obliteration of social distinctions.

The housing programme now in progress is the lynchpin of the SED's social policy. Its aim is to solve the housing question by 1990. A long-standing objective of the revolutionary working-class movement will thus be accomplished. The provision of new housing will have a growing effect on the general standard of housing, on meaningful leisure pursuits and human relations. Housing construction goes hand in hand with the provision of efficient transport, catering and welfare services.

Urban and rural development places high demands on architects and those engaged in the building and related industries. Long-term plans will have to combine the modernization and improvement of residential areas, the construction of new dwellings and the preservation and renovation of residential buildings in such a way that the cultural wealth and progressive features which cities and towns have acquired in their structure and appearance during the course of history are preserved as far as possible and that ever more favourable conditions are established for the further evolution of a socialist way of life. Special attention will have to paid to the development of Berlin, the capital of the GDR, as the political, economic, intellectual and cultural metropolis of the GDR.

The Socialist Unity Party of Germany considers that work is the most important sphere of social life. It wants to see the socialist character of work fully brought out in every respect. Working conditions will have to be so organized that they promote job satisfaction, working morale and creativity as well as working people's sense of order, safety and discipline.

Scientific and technological progress must be effected while paying constant attention to, and securing constant improvements in, health protection and safety at work. It is necessary to reduce heavy manual work and work involving health hazards in a systematic way and to design machinery and devise techniques with growing emphasis on safety considerations and ease of operation. Social and health services and cultural amenities in enterprises will be expanded. Priority will be given to improving working and living conditions for shift workers.

In conformity with the development of the national economy, the purpose of the incomes policy pursued is to enable working people to earn more by increasing their output or raising the standard of their work. The share of the national income accruing to the working class will continue to grow to reflect its rising level of performance, role and responsibility.

The principle of reward according to merit — the basic principle of distribution in socialism — will continue to be consistently applied. Working people's pay as their chief source of income will remain the key factor in the advance of their cultural and living standards. An efficiency-orientated wages policy is geared to this objective. It encourages the creative initiative of the working class and all other working people to increase labour productivity and to raise their qualifications, and it furthers the interest of the working population in socialist rationalization, including the use of up-to-date technological norms and standards. The lower ranges of income are to be raised progressively as qualifications and output increase.

Public funds assume growing importance for the development of real income. They will increase at a faster rate than wage and bonus funds and will be chiefly used to develop health and social services, education, culture and sport.

Depending on the growth of labour productivity, the Party is seeking a further differentiated prolongation of annual holiday leave and the gradual introduction of a 40-hour week by shortening daily working hours while retaining the five-day week. Simultaneously, the efficient organization of catering and other services will add to working people's leisure time. Working people's recreational needs will be satisfied to an ever larger extent. This makes it necessary to make available more places in holiday resorts, to raise the standards of recreational and catering facilities there, to promote tourism, and to expand local possibilities for spare-time activities and outdoor recreation. Special attention will be devoted to recreation schemes for families.

The Socialist Unity Party of Germany shows special concern for the promotion of the family, the well-being of mother and child and assistance for large families and young married couples. Financial burdens arising from the birth, care and upbringing of children will, to an increasing extent, be recognized and borne by the whole community. Families with several children will be given further assistance. Opportunities for mothers of small children and those of school age to pursue a job will be improved systematically.

Care when aged, ill or disabled will be systematically improved following on from the growth in the economy.

Cultural, social and medical services for those who retire from employment and for all senior citizens are a major concern of the Socialist Unity Party of Germany. They are constantly being expanded and improved. Living conditions for the retired population will be further improved in a systematic manner. A variety of measures will be taken to enable the elderly to participate more actively in society. The provision of jobs to suit the needs of senior citizens will be stepped up in line with their wishes and abilities. More housing adjusted to the needs of the elderly as well as residential homes for the aged and nursing homes will be provided.

Citizens who are physically or mentally handicapped are to be assisted to take part in the life of society through a complex of rehabilitation measures, through the provision of appropriate education and employment opportunities, and through medical and social care.

The Socialist Unity Party of Germany is concerned to ensure steady improvements in health protection and to create favourable conditions for the findings of modern medical science to be applied and for the quality of medical work to be improved. The number of medical practitioners will be increased and the network of health establishments extended. Their equipment will be systematically modernized and expanded. Patients are free to consult a doctor of their own choosing. All pharmaceutical products and other medical supplies required will have to be made available in continued high quality and sufficient variety. The Red Cross in the GDR will assume growing importance in carrying out health policy.

The SED will encourage environmental protection and planning in the interests of a steady improvement of working and living conditions and of economic efficiency. Industrial enterprises and co-operative and state farms will have to make an especially great contribution towards this objective.

It is imperative on a scientific basis to preserve, and make national use of, nature as the inexhaustible source of human life, health, enjoyment and prosperity so that she may allow future generations to lead a secure and happy life in a communist society. Better conditions for work and leisure pursuits will be created by determined efforts on the part of the community to protect the soil, preserve the purity of the air and water and to reduce noise.

(*Programme of the Socialist Unity Party of Germany*, Dresden 1976, pp. 23 ff.)

D78 From the handbook of the planned socialist economy published by the State Planning Commission of the GDR, 1977:

In 1971, the decisions of the 8th SED Congress provided the basis for the systematic and all-round further development of the planned socialist economy of the GDR. This primarily applies to the central policy task formulated in line with the basic economic law of socialism. This central policy consists in "further raising the standard of living and cultural level of the people on the basis of a high growth rate in socialist production, increasing efficiency, scientific and technological progress and rising labour productivity". The aim of our economic activities and the ways and means for achieving it were thus laid down. Our central policy is an expression of the unity of economic and social welfare policies pursued by the socialist state. This unity of economic and social welfare policies is the guideline governing the further development of socialist society and sets out focal points to be realized by way of managing the national economy on planned lines.

Economic policy covers all measures taken by the socialist state in the economic field which serve the working class under the leadership of its Marxist-Leninist party in implementing its class interests.

Social welfare policy comprises all measures geared to systematically satisfying the material and intellectual needs of the people and to bringing forth the socialist way of life in accordance with the level reached in socialist development. It thus contributes towards drawing the working class and the other classes and strata closer together.

Our country's economic policy creates the conditions necessary for implementing its socialist social welfare policy. This is why economic and social welfare policies form an inseparable unity in socialism.

In accordance with the decisions of the 8th SED Congress, the role and function of the central government bodies were further strengthened under the 1971–1975 Five-Year Plan and closer links established between their work and the nationally owned enterprises, industrial complexes and associations of nationally owned enterprises responsible for their own management and planning activities and for unfolding the sense of creative initiative on the part of working people.

In 1971–72, the existing semi-state and private industrial enterprises were transferred into socialist ownership in that the state purchased the still existing private shares. These enterprises accounted for 11.2 per cent of industrial output at that time.

As a result 100 per cent of the industrial output came from socialist enterprises, including 95 per cent nationally owned and five per cent co-operative in 1974.

[...]

The conditions and basic content of socialist planning in the GDR.

The German Democratic Republic is a socialist industrial country with an intensive agriculture. Its advanced national economy is organized and managed in a scientific manner and on a national scale. The great development potentials of a planned socialist economy are not only theoretically founded but have been proved in practice over a period of 60 years in the Soviet Union and for more than 30 years in the GDR and the other socialist countries.

The character of the planned socialist economy arises from:
the socialist ownership of the means of production, notably of public property (i.e. the socialist property of the state);
the nature of the socialist state, which as the organ of power in the hands of the working class and its allies, represents the decisive instrument with which the working population organizes and develops its public property;
a highly developed material and technological basis which has emerged during the past 30 years along planned lines and which features a high level of socialization of production as well as a working class consciously employing its energy for the benefit of society;
the internationalist nature of socialism and the close union of the socialist countries around the Soviet Union.

The experience gathered by the GDR and the other members of the socialist community prove that planning is feasible and necessary in the construction and further strengthening of socialism. This is the only way of guaranteeing the swift development of the economy, free from crisis and in the interests of all working people.

The public ownership of the means of production is the indispensable economic basis of the socialist state. The state property of the means of production is transformed into socialist property through the socialist character of the state and thus into a genuine basis for planning. Owing to the class content of the bourgeois state, transfers of enterprises to state ownership result in state capitalist property which continues to be managed in the interests of the ruling class and its profit.

Bourgeois theoreticians label the planned socialist economy as useless. They falsify it as a "bureaucratic, centrally administered rigidly controlled economy" and assert that the planned organization of labour in the socialist economy is incompatible with the interests of the working people. They recommend the elimination of central planning and the application of "socialist market economy" patterns. They place their special hopes in the "national patterns of socialism" which are being spread under the banner of the "improvement", the "humanization" and "democratization" of socialism, as a counterpoise to the practical experience gathered with the planned socialist economies of the Soviet Union and the other socialist countries.

Such concepts are pseudo-scientific. They are deliberately designed to slander the planned socialist economy. The bourgeois theoreticians form their judgement superficially from certain real phenomena existing in highly industrialized capitalist countries. These countries have for decades had a system of state monopoly regulation (planification) with the help of which the state exerts its influence on the economy. This state monopoly regulation rules out overall social planning owing to the fact that the bulk of the means of production is private property and because of prevailing power relations. The state monopoly regulation system and the planned socialist economy have nothing in common either with regard to their social aims or the means applied. State monopoly regulation was and continues to be aimed at preserving and augmenting the profits of the capitalist monopolies. The direction by and the influence of the capitalist state on the economy by way of its money and credit policy, its tax policy and similar things represent an abortive attempt to lessen the objective contradictions existing in the capitalist system. They are no means for the mastery of overall national economic processes.

Today, the classical market, price and profit mechanism alone is no longer able to solve the problems in the highly industrialized capitalist countries (for instance, inflationary trends, price increases, partial crises within the general crisis of capitalism). This makes it incumbent on the bourgeois state to interfere in capitalist economic circulation through state monopoly regulation.

Although bourgeois theoreticians today recognize the interference by the state in the economy as an existing fact, they present the state as something neutral standing above the classes. They deny the class question, the ownership relations in the means of production and the social structure of the state.

There undoubtedly exists a well-organized internal system of planning and management within imperialist trusts and even within the framework of multinational corporations. But these are unable to replace overall national economic planning, because the interests of the monopolies are not oriented towards the objective interests of society as a whole, but towards ensuring and augmenting monopoly profit. This is the object of their planning which is in complete contradiction to the interests of the working class and all working people. Social development under capitalism takes place under the conditions of competition, at the cost of the working people and even of smaller entrepreneurs, as is borne out by the growing number of such enterprises going bankrupt.

What is involved in the planned socialist economy is the organization of systematic management of social reproduction for the well-being of working man in an effective, methodologically rational and unbureaucratic manner. Socialist construction does not take place without obstacles or hindrances. Successes can be accompanied by and give rise to difficulties and contradictions which must be overcome. The struggle against the influence of bourgeois ideology, our efforts to educate people to adopt a socialist attitude towards labour and the organization and unfolding of the creative initiative and activity of working people call for a great amount of energy and purposeful action.

The socialist management and planning of the national economy is no task to be fulfilled by planning experts alone, but is an affair of all working people. It is a basic concern of the planned socialist economy to enable people to share in managing and planning the economy ever better. As long as the planned socialist economy has existed, bourgeois theoreticians have tried to label the planning system as an institution relieving the working people of thinking. They hold that a small number of experts who work this system out push working people into a meaningless and spineless mass existence. This is completely incorrect as proved by the practical experience gathered by the socialist countries.

A realistic plan can only be drawn up with the active and conscious co-operation of working people in all phases of its elaboration and execution. Planning and actions of the people form a unity in socialist society, for which reason the plans of the socialist countries are in line with actual, real development conditions. It is only for this reason that the plans of the socialist countries can have binding force on all members of society.

When speaking of the binding character of plans this means that the targets set in them and the resources available form the foundation for all managerial activities at all levels of management. This holds for ministries, economic management bodies, territories, enterprises all the way through to the individual workplace. This is why there exists an inseparable unity between plan elaboration and execution and the control of plan fulfilment in all its sections. Growing quality in planning is therefore necessarily linked with working people's higher level of education, culture and political consciousness in socialist society.

In their socialist economic and social welfare policies, the party of the working class and the socialist state are faithful to the principle of establishing ever closer links between central management and planning by enterprises, co-operative societies and local government departments. This is a reflection of democratic centralism, a fundamental political principle of running and organizing socialist society and its state. It forms a unity of central management along planned lines and the democratic co-operation and self-responsibility of working people. Democratic centralism is incompatible with anarchism which denies the necessity of centralized management. It has nothing in common with bureaucratic centralism which keeps people away from management activities and stifles their sense of initiative.

(Panorama DDR: *The planned socialist economy of the German Democratic Republic*, Dresden 1977, pp. 32 f., 48–51)

D79 From the statement by Willi Stoph, chairman of the Council of Ministers, in support of the Five-Year Plan for the GDR's national economic development 1986–1990 and the 1987 National Economic Plan, November 1986:

Distinguished Members of the House,

The House was presented today with the drafts of the Five-Year Plan Act for the GDR's economic development 1986–1990 and the 1987 National Economic Plan for discussion and adoption. Pursuant to the resolutions adopted by the 11th Congress of the Socialist Unity Party of Germany, the two Bills are geared to the all-out strengthening of the German Democratic Republic and the systematic continuation of our well-established policy; to serve the common good and safeguard peace.

These Bills contain the appropriate tasks in line with the directives issued by the 11th SED Congress. They have been fully endorsed by the SED Central Committee at its 3rd plenary meeting.

In the future, our central policy of translating economic achievements into social benefits will continue to be the pivot of the economic strategy which we have staked out on a long-term basis until the end of this century. This proven policy is a continuous source of fresh impetus and ramarkable initiatives with a view to strengthening our economic potential and improving the working and living conditions of the people. The daily experience that industrious work benefits society as a whole as well as its individual members spurs on the activities and creativity of the working people, mobilizing them to participate in concrete actions to accomplish the tasks before them.

Efforts must be focused on increasing the effectiveness of science and technology

Our efforts will be focused on increasing the effectiveness of science and technology, particularly by widening the applications of high-tech and key technologies, in order to achieve and maintain a high technological level which secures a place for the GDR among the technologically most advanced nations of the world. To achieve this it will be necessary, *inter alia*, to continue our policy of the full-scale intensive development of the economy on a long-term basis and to accelerate the rate of innovation of production.

An integral part of and an indispensable precondition for sustained dynamism in our economic development in the period from 1986–1990 and beyond will be the intensification and perfection of our economic, scientific and technological co-operation with the USSR and the other members of the Council for Mutual Economic Assistance in accordance with the pertinent decisions taken at the highest political level. The relevant tasks stipulated in the present Bills require concentrated efforts to develop highly productive key technologies and use them on a wide scale, achieve high quality standards in manufactured products, accelerate the pace of intensification of the national economies of our countries through co-operation and exploit to this end new forms of co-operation in science, technology, production and foreign trade.

[. . .]

Dynamic economic growth continues

Distinguished Members of the House,

The Bills before you are aimed at continuing the dynamic growth of our national economy. They take into account the increased economic potential, the higher educational levels of the people and the considerable scientific and technological capacities of our country. At the same time, they respond to the needs that derive from the continuation of our combined and mutually complementary economic and social policies.

We plan to increase the produced national income by 4.5 per cent in 1987, and by 25 per cent in the five-year planning period. In other words, we will produce 100 per cent more national income in 1990 than we did in 1975. The new stage of the economic strategy is characterized by an even better utilization of the qualitative factors of economic growth, notably the rapid development and large-scale application of key technologies.

The following figures show this: by 1990 the net output and labour productivity in the economic sectors coming under the industrial ministries will have grown by 50 per cent compared with 1985, the unit input of raw materials and feedstocks important to the economy will decrease annually by an average 4 per cent, prime costs in the industrial sector will be reduced by 2.2 per cent, and unit transport expenditure will go down by 3.2 per cent.

It is planned that no less than 90 per cent of the increase in national income shall come from higher labour productivity whose growth rates must be accelerated further. Productive consumption per unit of national income must be reduced by an average of 2.1 per cent annually. A faster introduction of energy-saving technologies and production methods, which represent the most advanced scientific and technical levels, should reduce energy consumption in the economic sector.

Building on what has been achieved in 1986, it will be necessary to ensure even higher increases in performance levels in the next year: in the industrial sector net production is to grow by 9 per cent and labour productivity by 8.6 per cent; prime costs are to be reduced by 2.3 per cent, and material expenditures are to go down by 2.4 per cent. These goals put high demands on:

the utilization of all increasingly complex and interdependent factors helpful to intensifying economic processes and

research and development to achieve results in science and technology which keep pace with the most advanced international developments and break new ground.

High demands are also placed on:

accelerated product innovation to meet international market conditions and to meet the domestic requirements of private consumers and the economy;

the most effective use of investment funds available and

substantial cuts in material and financial inputs in all spheres and at all levels of the economic reproduction process.

In tackling all these tasks we rely on the high level of qualification, the wealth of experience and the industrious work of the people which, in the final analysis, are the decisive factors for achieving the objectives that we have set for ourselves. It is, therefore, the uppermost duty of everyone holding political or economic responsibility to promote their creativity and initiative. It is fully in line with our successful policy that economic growth results in further improvements in the material and cultural standards of living of the people. In the period 1986–1990 per capita real income will grow on average 4 per cent annually.

[. . .]

Ambitious targets in the consumer sector

In keeping with the resolutions of the 11th Congress of the SED all draft plans set ambitious goals for the manufacture of consumer goods. The production of consumer durables is to go up 31 per cent by 1990 as against 1985. This places both the plants traditionally associated with the production of consumer goods and those chiefly engaged in the manufacture of capital goods under the obligation to redouble their efforts to supply high-quality, sought-after products for domestic and external markets.

The demand for fashionable clothes and high-quality consumer durables must be met better and better by attaining high product innovation rates.

The 1987 National Economic Plan envisages a 6.5 per cent increase in the output of new consumer durables compared with the previous year. Consumer wishes in all their diversity must be taken into account and efforts must be increased to match spare part supplies with the demand.

It is the duty of each producer of consumer durables to see to it that the demand for high quality is fully met. In keeping with this rapidly growing demand the production of such technical goods as colour televisions, radios, refrigerators, freezers, washing machines, sewing machines and motorcycles must be considerably increased.

With a projected 23 per cent growth in the 1986–90 period, light industry is expected to manufacture more ranges of fashionable, easy-to-care clothing. The production of fashionable clothing for young people must be better adjusted to their needs, with 70 per cent of the articles produced being replaced annually. With a view to increasing performance levels in light industry and improving working conditions there we plan to streamline entire plants and production stages.

For regionally administered industry, the Five-Year Plan envisages that the projected 25 per cent growth by 1990 will have to be accomplished by increasing the output of traditional products and establishing new lines of consumer durables. This includes much-sought-after household appliances and gardening implements as well as miscellaneous household goods, spare parts and accessories.

By producing new ranges of toys, sports implements, musical instruments and recreational goods, the combines and plants in this sector will help satisfy diversified consumer needs in the field of leisure activities.

Solving the housing question as a social problem by 1990

Honourable Members of the House,

In accordance with the Bills before you, the workers of the construction industry will again be faced with exacting tasks. In keeping with the resolutions of the Party, the housing question as an issue of social relevance will be resolved in the 1986–90 period. Attaining the ideal of the revolutionary working-class movement is a matter of truly historic significance. At the same time, workers in the construction industry will have to cope fully with the tasks intended to reinforce, rationalize and modernize the material and technological base of the national economy and all other social spheres.

The contribution of the construction industry to the growth of our national income must be increased considerably in the period 1986–90 by raising net output 31 per cent, including a 5.6 per cent rise in 1987, and reducing average annual prime costs by 2.1 per cent. The target is for new investment projects to reduce unit construction costs by 10 per cent and to slash construction time by about 15 per cent by 1990. This requires speeding up scientific and technological progress and the growth of labour productivity still further.

Intensification all the way

Major objectives are
  to raise efficiency during the planning stage;
  to apply modern engineering knowledge with a view to conserving materials and energy;
  to add higher value to indigenous raw materials and to develop highly productive technologies by using microelectronics and robotics.
Building capacity is to be deployed in a concentrated way and construction projects are to be prepared and carried out impeccably everywhere.

The scope and speed of renovation, modernization and repair schemes will be increased further in order to preserve our existing housing stock, which makes up an important proportion of our national wealth. Repair services for residential buildings alone will have to grow by 35.4 per cent by 1990 compared with 1985. This puts greater demands on construction firms administered at the district level, on building departments in industries, on the co-operative and private craft sector, on housing authorities and on building teams in agriculture.

The building materials industry has the task to ensure stable supplies of high-quality building materials from indigenous resources to the economy and the general public.

The Bills start from the premise that performance levels in the transport system must be raised to match the planned growth of production and the projected development of passenger transport. In passenger transport, priority must be given to quality, timekeeping and reliability. This means organizing commuter and school services in such a way that working hours can be fully used and that only a minimum of leisure time needs to be used for transport services.

To improve long-distance services additional express services will be inaugurated between county towns. Microelectronic systems will have to be introduced in order to make it easier for passengers to buy tickets and reserve seats.

[. . .]

On agriculture

Honourable Members of the House,
  In implementing the resolutions of the 11th SED Congress the pace of the development of production, labour productivity and efficiency must be further accelerated in the agricultural, forestry and food sector. This is the foundation for stable, continuous supplies of high-quality foodstuffs for the consumer market and of primary products for industrial processing from our own resources and for the fulfilment of our export obligations.
  Crop production continues to be developed as a major priority. By 1990

an average yield of 5.07 tonnes of grain equivalent per hectare of farmland will have to be attained. It is our prime concern to use the soil, our most important means of production, completely and efficiently and, through co-operation between crops and livestock farms, to raise soil fertility levels constantly. The aim is to achieve a grain output of 11.9 million tonnes by 1990 in order to render grain imports superfluous. Livestock production will have to concentrate on raising yields per animal coupled with further improvements in feed conversion efficiency.

Here the emphasis is on cattle farming, with maximum rough forage rations being given to achieve daily weight gains of at least 700 grammes per animal and an annual milk yield of 4,000 kilogrammes per cow. To raise the output of sheep wool to a projected 8,760 tonnes by 1990 it is necessary to increase stocks to some three million sheep.

The Bills before you start from the premise that better use must be made of the advantages of socialist relations of production in agriculture and all qualitative growth factors. Strengthening co-operative and state farms and co-operation between them are decisive foundations for rapid increases in yields, performance levels and efficiency.

It is essential to forge ahead along the well-tested path of full scale intensive development by applying scientific findings and publicizing the experience of the best farms. More than before emphasis must be laid on doing scientific groundwork, particularly in the field of state-of-the-art technologies, on attaining top performance levels and ensuring short research and lead times. Our agroscientific research potential must be used more effectively.

[. . .]

Housing to be improved for 3.2 million people

The housing programme will continue to be the linchpin of our social policy in this Five-Year Plan period. To this end 1,064,000 dwellings will be built or modernized, providing accommodation for some 3.2 million people. The scope of the programme is highlighted by the fact that in the historically brief span of 20 years, i.e. since the 8th Congress, a total of 3,475,000 dwellings have been newly built or modernized within its framework.

Increasingly, housing construction will move to inner-city areas over the next few years. A harmonious blend of new and old buildings will be more and more characteristic of our towns and villages, making life more pleasant and beautiful.

The construction and modernization of schools, kindergartens, creches, retail outlets, restaurants, service centres, outpatient clinics, sports grounds and youth clubs will be carried out in a planned and purposeful way. Great importance will be attached to the construction of homes for the elderly.

Referring to improvements in housing conditions also means pointing to the great display of initiative by citizens in towns and villages. Just think of the results achieved in the community improvement campaign, in the co-operative housing sector and in the reconstruction campaign run by the FDJ. It remains a major concern of the socialist state to promote all these initiatives.

In accordance with the resolutions adopted by the 11th SED Congress, we continue our incentive wage policy.

The present high level of provision of consumer durables will be maintained and raised further. Taking into account the growing monetary income of the population, the total supply of commodities will have to be increased by 4 per cent annually. In line with demand, the provision of industrial goods will be increased above average by 5.3 per cent. The long-established policy of maintaining stable retail prices for essential commodities will be continued.

All state officials and economic managers must regard continuous supplies of essential commodities, primarily staple foods, children's articles, miscellaneous household goods and spare parts, as a high priority. This involves tapping hidden local resources to ensure stable supplies of fresh produce and seeing to it that the whole range of commodities is available in the shops during opening hours. Combines and enterprises must fulfil their delivery contracts with the distributive sector fully and on schedule so that all ranges of commodities can be offered in the shops as planned.

Using the material and financial resources available, further improvements must be made with regard to the efficiency and attractiveness of the distributive sector. A pleasant atmosphere, the adjustment of shopping hours to the working hours and shift periods of local residents, the shortening of waiting times at supermarket checkout points and the attractive interior design of shops, restaurants and markets do not depend solely on material conditions. They are decisively influenced by the dedication of the sales staff, by their knowledgeable and friendly service as well as by order and cleanliness.

School, kindergarten and canteen meals are to be further improved in terms of quality.

Service sector to grow by 5.1 per cent annually

Measures will be taken to improve repair and other services, notably those for which there is a growing public demand. This requires an average annual increase of 5.1 per cent. Services for the general public are to be considerably improved by creating good conditions at collection points, extending the network of repairs carried out at customers' places and raising quality standards while at the same time cutting waiting times. Co-operative and private craftspeople will continue to enjoy support to extend their services in the interest of the people.

The advantages of the socialist education system are being brought to bear in an increasingly comprehensive fashion for the communist education of the younger generation and their preparation for life and work in our society. In the field of school education, the main task will be to raise the standard of general knowledge yet further. Educational content and quality levels are designed to ensure a solid, high-quality basic education that can be built upon, bearing in mind factors such as economic progress, the challenges of the scientific and technological revolutions, developments in the cultural and other fields of social life, and the resulting demands on the all-round development of the personality and the communist education of young people.

As before, all parents who so wish may send their children to a kindergarten. Efforts must be made to ensure that children may attend such facilities in their immediate neighbourhood.

To ensure a well-balanced influx of newly trained skilled workers in all economic sectors and occupations, a total of 918,000 young people are to be trained in the coming Five-Year Plan period. This will continue to guarantee an apprenticeship for every school-leaver. By 1990 new syllabuses will have to be introduced for all vocational training courses and classrooms for instruction in computer operation will have to be established.

In the higher education system, programmes are to be upgraded so as to combine the acquisition of solid general and specialist knowledge with a thorough political and ideological education based on Marxist-Leninist theory. University teachers have the task of training experts capable of taking a bold, forward-looking and science-based approach to the issues of our day, governed by the needs of social development and willing and able to confront the challenges involved in the mastery of science and technology. The same demands apply to postgraduate courses for employees with university and technical college education.

The ongoing improvements in the field of social and health care are proof of the humanitarian ethic underlying our socialist state. The Bills provide for the expansion of inpatient and outpatient facilities in order to assure all citizens of primary medical care. The attainment of this aim will be facilitated by the creation of another 2,700 medical and dental posts.

Special attention will be devoted to maternal and child care and to care for the elderly. We plan to provide or modernize 45,600 additional places in creches and 18,700 places in old people's and nursing homes.

Child allowances to be substantially raised as of May 1987

As resolved at the 11th SED Congress, government allowances for children will be substantially raised as of 1 May 1987.

The further improvement of material conditions for the arts to flourish is an integral feature of the draft plan. The task is to make more varied and effective use of all suitable facilities to promote manifold cultural and intellectual activities. We expect our artists and cultural workers to help enrich our life with their specific contributions, to portray socialist reality in a convincing manner and to take an active and dedicated stance in the struggles of our time.

It must remain a major concern of society as a whole, all state bodies, factories and institutions, to provide good conditions everywhere for young people to engage in meaningful and varied intellectual and cultural activities, in sports and outdoor recreation on the basis of the decisions adopted at the 12th Congress of the FDJ. The bodies responsible must check on the fulfilment of the plan drawn up by the Council of Ministers as to youth centres and youth research.

[. . .]

New demands on managers

The measure adopted in August 1986 by the Council of Ministers on the further improvement of management, planning and cost accounting open up entirely new possibilities for the combines and their constituent enterprises. They must be used to the full, with a sense of responsibility, to further improve the reproduction process from raw material input to the output of high-value products, including subsupplies. This also refers to high-quality, demand-oriented production of great efficiency to meet industrial, consumer and export needs and to the strict fulfilment of contracts.

The attainment of the targets mapped out in the Bills make high demands on those holding posts of responsibility in state bodies, combines, co-operatives and institutions. Their task is to mobilize their work teams to reach high performance levels and to organize precisely the implementation of the tasks formulated. This requires the provision of optimum conditions at every level so that the plan can be fulfilled every day and every month.

As was convincingly demonstrated at the meeting held recently by the SED Central Committee and the GDR Council of Ministers with the chairmen of district councils and the mayors of cities and boroughs, the local authorities bear a growing measure of responsibility for the implementation of our economic and social policies. They have to ensure full-scale intensive development in the area under their responsibility, tap hidden local reserves to raise performance and efficiency levels and create ever better local conditions for economic reproduction for all combines and enterprises. In doing so, their aim is to achieve gains in efficiency and to improve people's well-being by organizing co-operation among local assemblies, factories and institutions while making use of local resources.

Honourable Members of the House.

With today's adoption of the 1986–90 Five-Year Plan and the 1987

National Economic Plan, the two documents assume legal force. They will then become the foundation for the concerted efforts of all central and local authorities, of all combines, factories and co-operatives, of all scientific and other institutions.

Our aim is to strengthen the GDR and maintain peace

The realism expressed in the plans to be adopted today by the People's Chamber is based on the diligent and creative work and the dedication of the working class, the co-operative farmers, the members of the intelligentsia, millions of working women and men throughout the country. We count on the socialist competition organized by the trade unions and on the manifold initiatives of our young people such as the Young Innovators' Movement and the youth work and research teams. The work of hundreds of thousands of citizens in the Chamber of Technology and other public organizations is of immense value. The tried and tested close co-operation taking place between the allied parties in the Democratic Bloc and between all citizens in the National Front will be developed further on a comradely basis.

Their joint work reflecting the humanitarian ethic of our society helps to strengthen the German Democratic Republic in all areas and to maintain peace. The Bills to be discussed and approved today are designed to accomplish these objectives.

The Council of Ministers calls on all members of the People's Chamber and of the local assemblies to help implement our plans by showing dedication, drawing on their rich experience and forging close ties with all our citizens.

Honourable Members of the House,

I would like to ask you now to approve the Bill on the Five-Year Plan for the GDR's National Economic Development 1986–90 and the Bill on the 1987 National Economic Plan.

(Panorama DDR: *Five-Year-Plan Act: The development of the GDR's national economy in the period 1986–1990*, Dresden 1986, pp. 5–6, 12–13, 24–26, 27, 29 34)

D80 From the GDR Central Statistical Office's report on the fulfilment of the economic plan in the first half of 1987:

During the first half of 1987, the working class, co-operative farmers and the rest of the working population in town and country have compiled an impressive record which will contribute to the successful implementation of the resolutions adopted by the 11th Congress of the Socialist Unity

Party of Germany. With their initiatives under the motto "My place of work is my place in the struggle for peace", they strengthened the position of socialism in the German Democratic Republic and helped safeguard peace. It is thanks to the creative work of its people that the German Democratic Republic has made further headway in building an advanced socialist society. The party, the government and the people are linked with one another by closer bonds than ever before.

Our economic potential has been increased and our dynamic economic growth has continued systematically. Major progress has been recorded in our main field of activities, the policy of turning economic successes into social progress as the centrepiece of our economic strategy. All of this was achieved on the basis of the fundamental orientation provided by the resolutions of the 3rd session of the SED Central Committee and the speech delivered by Comrade Erich Honecker, General Secretary of the SED Central Committee and Chairman of the GDR Council of State, at the conference of first secretaries of the party's district committees.

The Confederation of Free German Trade Unions mobilized the creative potential of working people in socialist competition conducted under the slogan "Outstanding performances for the benefit of the people and in the interests of peace — Let us do our utmost to implement the resolutions of the 11th SED Congress". The 11th Congress of the FDGB provided a major boost. New initiatives were generated within the framework of socialist competition for the further implementation of the 11th SED Congress resolutions. The seminar held by the SED Central Committee with the general managers of industrial combines and the party organizers of the Central Committee ushered in outstanding activities. This is testified to by the pledges made in the names of more than three million people working in combines in industry, construction and the transport and communications sectors to overfulfil plan targets for specific products with a view to attaining significant increases in the final output available for distribution in 1987. Mention should be made, above all, of the 51 Heroes of Socialist Labour who led their work teams to achieve the highest ever daily output, helping to fulfil the 1987 national economic plan and exceeding targets in specific sectors to mark World Peace Day this year.

The 13th Farmers' Congress of the GDR mapped out the long-term course for the continued implementation of the resolutions adopted at the 11th SED Congress in agriculture, forestry and food processing.

The record of economic development must be rated all the more highly as great strain and additional expenditure were caused by extreme weather conditions. The strength of socialist planning, the strength of socialist democracy and the ability of the SED to introduce appropriate measures with sufficient foresight have once again proved their worth in this complicated situation.

The call by Comrade Erich Honecker, General Secretary of the SED Central Committee, to annul the effects of the unusual weather conditions through assistance and solidarity by all social forces, was responded to by millions of working people who achieved outstanding performances at work, also in extra shifts during the week and at weekends. Thanks to people's sense of initiative and commitment, it was possible to make up for the temporary arrears in the course of the first three months of the year. Particularly good performances were shown by those employed in the coal and energy sector and workers in the transport sector, who were helped by members of the National People's Army, the German People's Police and personnel from the Ministry of State Security. It was thus possible to increase the plan surplus in major sectors month by month.

Fuller use was made of the qualitative factors of economic growth. We are successfully working to combine the advantages inherent in socialism more effectively with the achievements of the scientific and technological revolution for the benefit of all. Key technologies were developed and applied at a faster pace. During the first half of 1987, science and technology achieved significant results, thus making a greater contribution to strengthening the GDR's economic potential and its position among the world's leading nations.

The GDR's sustained economic growth rests on a well-functioning system of socialist planning, which has once again proved its efficiency, dynamism and flexibility. Democratic involvement by citizens is an inseparable part of socialist economic planning in keeping with the principle of democratic centralism. The tried and tested principle "Take part in working, planning and government affairs!" is being applied with a great sense of initiative in all sectors of society.

New measures designed to further improve management, planning and cost accounting have been introduced, particularly as regards broader application of the principle that firms and combines in industry and construction should earn the resources needed for intensively extended reproduction through their own operations. As the backbone of the planned socialist economy, the industrial combines are the chief force behind economic growth. They are decisive in increasing the effectiveness of science and technology.

In continued pursuit of the objectives set by the Free German Youth's 11th SED Congress Campaign, young people have made a significant contribution to the positive economic record compiled during the first six months of 1987. The scientific and technological potential of youth, notably that of 5,206 youth research teams and the 45,654 youth teams, is a major contributory factor to the top achievements accomplished during the first half of the year.

In keeping with the true spirit of socialism , increased economic performance is put to the benefit of the people. Material and cultural living standards have been maintained and further raised along planned lines. Economic security and optimism, full employment and prosperity are characteristic features of people's life in the GDR and motivate their actions. Another expression of economic security in the GDR is the major increase in state child allowances, brought into effect on 1 May 1987. The house-building programme, the centrepiece of the GDR's social policy, is continuing at a fast pace. The housing conditions of another 305,000 people were improved during the first half of 1987.

The GDR is implementing the objectives of its economic development in close fraternal co-operation with the Soviet Union. The agreements reached in Berlin between Comrade Erich Honecker and Comrade Mikhail Gorbachev, the general secretaries of the SED Central Committee and the Central Committee of the CPSU, ushered in a new stage of co-operation in accordance with the requirements of full-scale intensive economic development. Major projects for the future are being jointly tackled by the two countries under the Long-Term Programme for the Development of Co-operation between the GDR and the USSR in the Field of Science, Technology and Production in the Period up to the Year 2000. The focus of activities is on close collaboration in developing and applying key technologies and ensuring high scientific and technological standards of production.

In close alliance with the USSR, the GDR contributes its share to enhancing socialist economic integration with all members of the Council for Mutual Economic Assistance (CMEA) in keeping with the Large-Scale Programme for Scientific and Technological Progress of the CMEA Countries in the period up to the year 2000.

The local government authorities have made a more effective contribution to ensuring all-round plan fulfilment in locally administered firms and co-operatives and to providing more favourable conditions for the development of centrally administered combines in their respective regions. Rationalization at regional level was increasingly used as the chief path towards exhausting local resources in the interest of economic growth and for the welfare of the people through their close co-operation with firms and co-operatives. The results attained under the Community Improvement Campaign testify to people's feeling of belonging to their socialist homeland.

The economic requirements of national defence, internal security and public order have been met as an integral part of economic policy in accordance with the demands arising from intensification.

The following are the principal results achieved in implementing the 1987 national economic plan during the first half of the year:

• The national income produced grew by three per cent over the same period last year. This is a great achievement in the face of the extreme weather conditions during the first few months of this year and the resulting considerably higher demands. The increase in national income was exclusively attributable to rises in labour productivity.

Net output in industry rose by 6.4 per cent and labour productivity by 6.8 per cent. The faster pace initiated in 1986 in raising labour productivity, compared to net output, has thus been continued. Industry, with its share of over 80 per cent, accounted for the bulk of the increase in national income. Manufacturing output rose by 4 per cent.

In the construction sector, labour productivity experienced a greater increase, with 4.7 per cent, than net output which went up by 3.8 per cent. Building output rose by 2 per cent.

The agricultural sector topped state plan targets for fatstock, milk and eggs. Supplies of fatstock were 2 per cent above the level of the same period last year. Spring sowing was carried out speedily and in good quality.

• The accelerated production and introduction of key technologies were decisive factors behind the GDR's sustained economic growth.

The micro-electronics sector of the economy has been expanded through the introduction of new integrated circuits. The current range of active micro-electronic units comprises approximately 1,400 basic types.

Output compared with the same period last year rose as follows:

Monolithic integrated circuits	by 44 per cent
Office, personal and desktop computers	by 62 per cent
Memories for computer technology	by 79 per cent
Printers	by 93 per cent
Fibre-optics cables	by 193 per cent
Special-purpose equipment for the manufacture of semiconductor devices	by 82 per cent
Microlithographic devices	by 32 per cent

The stock of CAD/CAM workstations and systems has risen to a total of 31,000. The number of industrial robots in use is now 73,000.

The computing sector has been expanded through the mass production of 16-bit desktop computers and more efficient 8-bit personal computers. The production of efficient 32-bit computers for ambitious CAD projects has been initiated.

In systematic pursuit of their pledge, the workforce of the nationally owned Robotron Elektronik works in Dresden produced 843 16-bit desk-top computers in excess of the plan.

• 198 projects from the state plan for science and technology have been completed with a view to achieving top scientific and technological standards in the application of key technologies.

The economic effect of science and technology has been further enhanced.

During the first six months of 1987, a total of 2,651 new products, processes and technological methods were introduced into production. The quality and efficiency of production has been raised through new products representing a value of 52,000 million marks.

The proportion of top-level achievements in the projects that were introduced into production from the state plan for science and technology reached 90 per cent.

Over 2,600 contracts have so far been concluded between combines in industry and construction, the Academy of Sciences, universities and colleges.

• During the first half of this year, the "Return resources to the state as a contribution to raising national income" initiative was a significant factor in our efforts to reduce productive consumption. Material and financial resources to the tune of 2,300 million marks were saved and a cheque for this sum was remitted to the State Bank.

Prime costs in the sectors coming under the industrial ministries were reduced by 1.3 per cent and in the sectors coming under the Ministry of Construction by 1.2 per cent.

Unit transport expenditure in the national economy dropped by 3 per cent.

• A total of 30,000 million marks was invested in the economy during the first six months of 1987.

The proportion of investments for the rationalization and modernization of fixed assets has increased, accounting for 79 per cent in manufacturing industry.

In-house manufacture of branch-specific equipment for rationalization purposes was 15 per cent higher than in the same period last year in the sectors coming under the industrial ministries.

Major production equipment was in use for 17.3 hours per calendar day on average.

• The material and cultural standards of living were maintained and raised further along planned lines in pursuit of our central policy of turning economic success into social progress.

The housing programme was continued in the first half of 1987, with 101,643 dwellings being completed through new construction or modernization. This is 4,243 dwellings in excess of the planned figure.

Working conditions have improved, among other things, through the new creation or the restructuring of 140,000 workstations, with the latest scientific principles of work organization being applied.

Net monetary income rose by 4 per cent, reflecting the increase in economic performance.

Retail trade turnover grew by 3 per cent over the same period last year. Stable supplies of basic foods were ensured. Firms in all branches of industry made finished products for the consumer market valued at 46,500 million marks in terms of retail prices. This is 3.8 per cent more than in the first half of 1986.

The service and repair work carried out for the general public went up by over 5 per cent.

• During the first six months of 1987, imports and exports had an overall value of 83,000 million marks. The GDR achieved a surplus to the tune of 2,200 million marks in its trade with the socialist and the non-socialist countries. Trade turnover with the USSR, the GDR's main trading partner, accounted for over 39 per cent of overall foreign trade turnover.

• The development of Berlin, capital of the GDR, as the political, economic, scientific, intellectual and cultural centre of the German Democratic Republic has been continued systematically using the strength of the entire republic. Berlin's industrial firms increased their net output by 9.3 per cent on the basis of full-scale intensification. This growth in net output was almost completely attributable to rises in labour productivity.

Berlin's building workers and, together with them, those employed in the construction industry and other sectors of the economy from all countries of the republic, are successfully implementing ambitious projects. The housing conditions of another 31,200 Berliners were improved through the construction and modernization of 11,571 dwellings, including the required communal facilities. Exemplary results have been achieved in rehabilitating entire street blocks, for instance, in Wilhelm-Pieck-Strasse, on Bersarin-Platz, in Frankfurter and Stralauer Allee and in Kietzer Feld in Berlin-Köpenick. Much of the credit for this goes to the 20,000 plus young people involved in the FDJ Berlin Initiative.

The anniversary of Berlin highlights an outstanding event in the life of the German Democratic Republic. The more than 1,200 performances of the festive programme that have taken place to date and the swiftly changing appearance of the capital city show in an impressive manner how vigorously Berlin's role as the political, economic, scientific and cultural centre of our country is being enhanced. Berliners and their guests commemorate the 750th anniversary of the city as a genuine people's festival, a festival of *joie de vivre* and of peace.

(Panorama DDR: *Report by the Central Statistical Office of the GDR on the fulfilment of the National Economic Plan in the first half of 1987*, Documents on the policy of the German Democratic Republic 2/87, Dresden 1987, pp. 3 ff.)

D81 From the speech of the Chairman of the Council of Ministers of the GDR, Willi Stoph, Member of the Politburo of the Central Committee of the SED, to the Fifth Session of the People's Chamber of the GDR, introducing the Bill on the National Economic Plan for 1988, 18 December 1987:

The bill on the National Economic Plan for 1988, which was agreed by the Central Committee of the Socialist Unity Party of Germany at its 5th Session and is now presented for discussion and decision is directed towards the further consistent realization of the resolutions of the 11th Party Congress of the SED. It can be said with full justification that this plan has a key role in the fulfilment of the Five-Year Plan for 1986–1990.

The General Secretary of the Central Committee of the SED and Chairman of the Council of State of the GDR, Erich Honecker, brought out the main emphases for the plan year before us in his closing speech at the 5th Session of the Central Committee. In this he gave a fundamental orientation of decisive importance for the work of the Council of Ministers and its organs, for the local councils and for all combines, enterprises and co-operatives, and for scientific and all other institutions.

The objectives for the year 1988 are informed by the necessity of further increasing performance in all sectors of the national economy and of accelerating the improvement in production efficiency through comprehensive intensification. This is of fundamental importance for the successful continuation of the central policy of integrated social and economic development for the good of our people, the strengthening of socialism and the safeguarding of peace. In this, as before, we rely on the industrious and enterprising work of the millions of working people in town and country, on the creativeness of the scientists, engineers and innovators, and on the committed activity of the managers in the enterprises, the combines, and the organs of the state.

It is in the nature of socialist democracy in the German Democratic Republic to involve the working people and all other citizens actively in the formation of political objectives and in the drawing up and accomplishment of social tasks.

This basic concept also underlay the drawing up of the national economic plan for 1988. With the constructive co-operation of the trade unions, more than 6.2 million working people took part in discussion of the plan and submitted more than 649,000 suggestions for opening up reserves in performance and efficiency, for perfecting management, planning, and economic accounting, as well as for the further improvement of living and working conditions.

The workers, co-operative farmers, members of the intelligentsia, and other working people who spoke and put forward clever thoughts and ideas expressed at the same time their resolve to improve their own performance and so to do all in their power for the fulfilment and wherever possible for the well-directed overachievement of the plan targets. Many combines and enterprises have created an important basis for this by the exemplary all-round fulfilment of the plan by the end of November this year.

Overall it can be stated that in 1987 the growth in the economy of our country was continued successfully in implementation of the economic strategy agreed by the 11th Party Congress.

Up to the end of November the national income in the economy was increased by 4 per cent; industrial goods production in the industry ministries' sector was increased by 3.6 per cent, net production by 6.1 per cent, and labour productivity by 6.5 per cent. Considerable achievements with high economic profitability were attained in important sectors, particularly in the development and practical application of key technologies.

Building production rose by 2.3 per cent. In implementation of the housing construction programme, the centerpiece of the social policy of party and government, 190,240 housing units were built or modernized by the end of November, improving living conditions for a further 571,000 citizens. The co-operative farmers and all working people in the agricultural, forestry, and food production economy have achieved a high and stable performance with high achievements in crop and livestock production and in ensuring the supply of products in day-to-day demand.

(*Neues Deutschland* vol. 42 of 19–20 December 1987)

D82 Law on the integrated socialist education system, 25 February 1965:

Preamble

First Part: Principles and objectives of the integrated socialist education system and social factors in education
§ 1(1) The objective of the integrated socialist education system is a high educational standard for the whole people, the formation and education of all-round and harmoniously developed socialist personalities who consciously shape social life, change nature, and lead a fulfilled, happy life as human beings should.

[. . .]

§ 2(1) With the integrated socialist education system the socialist state guarantees all citizens of the German Democratic Republic equal rights to education.
(2) The basic elements of the integrated socialist education system are:
the institutions of pre-school education,
the ten-class general polytechnic school,
the institutions for vocational training,
the educational establishments leading to university entry,
the engineering and specialist colleges,
the universities and colleges,
the institutions for training and continuing education for working people.
The special schools admit children with physical or mental disabilities.
(3) The integration in the aims and structure of the socialist education system includes differentiation in the later stages of the educational process in accordance with the needs of society and with individual talents.
(4) The socialist education system is so structured that it is possible for

every citizen to proceed to the next highest level, right up to the highest educational institutions, the universities and colleges. The best and most capable are selected for the highest educational institutions. In this consideration is to be taken of the social structure of the population of the German Democratic Republic.

[. . .]

§ 4(1) The socialist education system applies the principle of the integration of education and life, the integration of theory and practice, and the integration of learning and study with practical activity.

(2) By the integration of learning and study with practical activity and the integration of theory and practice in the educational process, it is to be ensured that school students, apprentices, and students are made capable of constructive work, of constant improvement of their knowledge, abilities and skills, of practical application of what they have learned, and of independent research.

(3) The integration of teaching and productive work includes vocational orientation in general school. This is intended to assist in harmonizing the needs of the national economy and the talents and inclinations of the individual.

(4) Young people's activity and responsibility are furthered by participation in social life in the educational establishments, in the national economy, and in the public sphere. In the educational process young people are trained in conscious action for socialism by the accomplishment of concrete tasks.

§ 5(1) In the socialist education system the principle of the integration of education and training applies.

(2) School students, apprentices, and students are to be educated to love the German Democratic Republic and to be proud of the attainments of socialism so that they are prepared to place all their powers at society's disposal, to strengthen and defend the socialist state. They should comprehend the lessons of German history, in particular the history of the German workers' movement. They are to be educated in the spirit of peace and friendship between the nations, socialist patriotism and internationalism.

(3) School students, apprentices, and students are to be educated in the love of work and in respect for work and for working people. They should be prepared to carry out mental and physical labour, to take part in social life, to accept responsibility and to prove themselves at work and in life.

(4) School students, apprentices, and students are to be provided with a thorough knowledge of Marxism-Leninism. They should recognize the laws of development of nature, of society, and of human thought and know how to apply them and acquire firm socialist convictions. In this way they will be made capable of understanding the meaning of life in our times, of thinking, feeling, and acting in a socialist way, and of fighting to overcome

contradictions and difficulties in the tasks facing them.

(5) The education process and the lives of school students, apprentices, and students are to be so organized that they are educated in conscious civil and moral behaviour in the collective and by the collective. They shall learn to understand that helpfulness, friendliness, politeness and obligingness, respect for their parents and all older people, and sincere and honest relationships between the sexes are characteristics of a socialist personality . . .

§ 7(1) In socialist education there is close co-operation between state institutions, social organizations and the family. As centres for education, the institutions of the socialist education system integrate the manifold educational efforts of state and society. They co-ordinate the educational effects of young people's work and social lives, of their cultural and sporting activities.

(2) The teaching staff of all educational establishments bear a great responsibility for the fulfilment of the aims and objectives of the socialist educational system. This demands of them extensive knowledge and skills and exemplary social behaviour.

(3) The socialist enterprises and the agricultural co-operatives have an important educational function. They have to ensure that school students, apprentices and students take part in the life of the enterprise, that they are introduced to modern technology and science and at the same time are involved in the socialist community work of the work brigades and re-search collectives.

(4) In the German Democratic Republic the family has important tasks and a high responsibility in educating children as worthwhile human beings and good citizens. In a socialist state, society's educational aims and parents' interests are in harmony. What all parents want for their children is assured: a peaceful future, secure prospects, and a thorough education which prepares for life. The socialist educational establishments work closely with the parental home and help the family in bringing up the new generation.

(5) Young people in the German Democratic Republic bear a great responsibility for their education. They use their own initiative in taking up the opportunities society offers them for their development to highly educated young socialists. Young people are offered trust and given a great deal of responsibility in learning, in work, and in their free time. Accord-ingly the institutions of the socialist educational system work in close co-operation with the Free German Youth movement and the Ernst Thälmann Pioneer organization, the independent political organizations of the younger generation.

(6) Taking part in Pioneer Clubs, Young Technologists' Clubs and Sections, Young Researchers' Sections, Young Tourists' Sections, student clubs, student theatres, student planning offices, in study and interest groups and in sports associations is an integral part of the socialist educa-tional process. It serves particularly to further special abilities and talents.

Second Part: School Attendance — Freedom from School Fees §§ 8–9

Third Part: Creches and Kindergartens

1st Section: Creches
§ 10(1) Children from their first weeks of life to the completion of their third year, particularly those whose mothers are employed or studying, are cared for and looked after in the creches in close co-operation with the family . . .

2nd Section: Kindergartens
§ 11(1) The kindergartens are places where children come together and enjoy themselves. They admit children from their third year to the beginning of school attendance, particularly those with working or studying mothers . . .

Fourth Part: General Schools

1st Section: Ten-Class General Polytechnical School
§ 13(1) The ten-class general polytechnical school (referred to as general school hereafter) is the basic school type in the integrated socialist education system . . .

§ 17(1) Full-day school is in accordance with the high requirements placed on education and with our young people's need for meaningful leisure-time activities and creative involvement. It should be implemented in a high quality manner for a constantly increasing number of pupils in all schools. School and extra-curricular education should be closely linked . . .

2nd Section: Specialist Schools and Specialist Classes
§ 18(1) Specialist schools are schools providing a general education which serve particular requirements in developing the new generation for the economy, science, sport, and culture. The specialist schools admit pupils with high performance and particular abilities.

(2) Specialist schools and specialist classes oriented towards technology, mathematics, science, languages, art, and sport shall be set up.

3rd Section: Special Schools
§ 19(1) The special schools and other special educational institutions (hereafter referred to as special schools) have to ensure the education and training of all children, young people, and adults with appreciable physical or mental disabilities . . .

5th Section: Educational Establishments leading to University Entry
§ 21(1) All pupils who have completed a general school education and working people with an education of general school standard can obtain university entry qualifications in various ways.

(3) General school leavers can obtain university entry qualifications by

attending the Extended General Polytechnical School (referred to as extended school hereafter) and the university entry classes in the institutions for vocational training. These institutions lead to a university entry qualification in two years and also provide a vocational training at the same time . . .

Fifth Part: Vocational Education Establishments

1st Section: Vocational Training
§ 32(1) In the German Democratic Republic every young person has a right to vocational training.

(2) Vocational training is carried out according to integrated state principles . . .

(3) Vocational training is provided for vocations determined in the systematology of the vocations for which training is required . . .

§ 33(1) Vocational training includes basic and specific vocational expertise and ability and is directed towards the successful practice of the vocation. In general it takes place in two sections, basic vocational training and training in particular skills . . .

2nd Section: Training and Continuing Education for Working People
§ 39(1) The Works Academies carry out the training and continuing education of working people in accordance with the needs of the enterprises and branches of the economy, and ensure a raising of the standard of general education. The Works Academies fulfil their tasks with the assistance of the scientific and technical specialists of the enterprises and the scientific institutes. They co-operate with the other educational institutions and the social organizations.

(2) The educational institutions in agriculture further the vocational training, further education and general education of the rural population, and contribute to raising the standard of intellectual and cultural life in the villages.

(3) The People's Colleges conduct courses for General School and Extended School Leaving Certificates and for certificates in individual subjects, as well as courses on various other subject areas. They take on courses leading to vocational qualifications not covered by other educational institutions.

Sixth Part: Colleges and Universities

1st Section: Engineering and Specialist Colleges
§ 41(1) The engineering and specialist colleges are institutions for advanced specialist training, in which scientific, technical, and economics specialists are trained for industry, agriculture, construction, commerce, transport and communications, education and culture, for the health service and for other sectors of social life . . .

2nd Section: Colleges of Art

§ 50(1) The colleges of art train socialist artists and art workers in close connection with artistic practice. The training conforms to the demands arising from the continuation of the socialist cultural revolution . . .

4th Section: Universities and Colleges

§ 52(1) The universities and colleges of the German Democratic Republic have to train and educate academically highly qualified personalities with a socialist consciousness who are ready and able to take a conscious part in developing the process of propagating the latest scientific findings more intensively in production, culture, and all other sectors of socialist society, and to take on responsible positions . . .

§ 55(1) The integration of teaching and research applies to all work at the universities and colleges . . .

(2) Research in universities and colleges is to be organized in such a way that, on the basis of the plan for the sciences

principal scientific and national economic objectives are attained;

different scientific disciplines work together and mutual socialist co-operation between the universities or colleges and social practice is developed.

(3) The co-operative relationships between the universities and colleges and the Association of Nationally-Owned Enterprises, the appropriate organs of the state and the economy, and the academies are to be directed urgently towards long-term research projects . . .

§ 56(1) Every citizen of the German Democratic Republic with university entry qualifications has the right to apply to study at a university or college.

(2) Admission to study is granted by the universities and colleges on the basis of the state plan and on the principle of performance. Account is to be taken of the social structure of the population. Suitability tests may be carried out.

(3) Correspondence and evening courses of study offer all citizens the opportunity to complete a college or university course without interrupting their occupational activity. Students taking part in correspondence or evening courses have legally determined reductions in their working hours.

§ 59(1) During the course of study, performance tests and examinations are held. They test the knowledge acquired by the student, the standard of scholarly thought, and the ability to apply theoretical knowledge to practical problems.

(2) The course of study is concluded by a state examination. A certificate entitling the holder to the appropriate academic degree or professional description is issued on passing the examination.

§ 60(1) On graduating, students are to be encouraged to take up their activity wherever they best serve the all-round development of the German Democratic Republic with their knowledge and abilities.

(2) The official bodies of the state and the economy are required to prepare for the employment of graduates in such a way that students are assigned their future activity at latest one year before they graduate and after their examinations can take up an activity appropriate to their achievements.

Seventh Part: Cultural Institutions §§ 66–68

Eighth Part: Planning and Management of the Integrated Socialist Education System §§ 69–77

Ninth Part: Responsibility of Society for the Integrated Socialist Education System § 78

Tenth Part: Final Regulations §§ 79–80

(*Gesetzblatt der Deutschen Demokratischen Republik I*, 1965, pp. 83 ff.)

D83 From the Programme of the SED: on the development of education and the communist upbringing of youth, May 1976:

The Socialist Unity Party of Germany will continue to devote much attention to improving the unified socialist education system, in particular to instilling communist ideals in the young generation.

The function of the education system is to bring up and train young people who have the knowledge and skill required for creative thinking and independent action, whose personal beliefs and attitudes reflect their Marxist-Leninist world outlook and who feel, think and act in a spirit of socialist patriotism and proletarian internationalism.

The education system serves to bring up and train harmoniously developed people who make full use of their abilities and talents in the best interests of socialist society and who distinguish themselves by the pleasure they gain from work and their readiness to defend their country, by their team spirit and pursuit of great communist ideals.

The ten-year comprehensive polytechnical school forms the backbone of the socialist education system. It provides all children with a high level of general education. By imparting knowledge in a scientific and practically oriented way from a working-class perspective, it is to give pupils a grasp of the processes of development going on in nature and society and a penetrating understanding of history, especially of revolutionary traditions, as well as of literature and art. The whole of teaching work is to be improved — especially during class contact — to encourage self-reliance in study and creative thought and activity among pupils and to orientate them still better to the practical needs of society. A command of foreign languages, especially Russian, is of special significance.

The further development of the polytechnical nature of our schools and the comprehensive application of the principle of linking teaching with productive work is of decisive importance for a communist upbringing, especially for the development of a communist attitude to work.

The Socialist Unity Party of Germany considers it the educational mission of the socialist school to enable young people to meet the tough challenges of socialist and communist construction. The demands made on political and moral education continue to grow. Through the active involvement of collectives of the socialist youth and children's organizations, it is to work to develop communist beliefs and attitudes and to help young people to find answers to their questions about our time and their purpose in life.

Collaboration between schools, parents, enterprises, the socialist youth organization and the Ernst Thälmann Pioneer Organization in the upbringing of the young generation requires much attention. The Socialist Unity Party of Germany will give every possible support to the valuable educational work performed by parents, teachers, instructors in all educational establishments, Pioneer organizers and activists in the youth organization.

The intensification of production and the development of sciences and technology make heavy demands on education and training. Vocational training is to be improved further. Apprentices are to be equipped with sound and useful knowledge and skills that will enable them to work creatively in their trade through instruction in practice- and job-related theory.

The Socialist Unity Party of Germany is concerned to ensure that all government agencies and public organizations, enterprises and cooperatives fully meet their responsibilities for vocational training and advice for a new generation of highly skilled young workers.

Greater demands will be made on personnel training and adult education. The main objective will be to increase the number of adult persons with the qualifications of a skilled or supervisory worker and the number of technical school and university graduates. It will also become necessary to offer better opportunities for people to improve their general knowledge and to acquire a thorough knowledge of various fields of interest.

The network of universities, colleges and technical schools is to be enlarged further. The Socialist Unity Party of Germany deems it necessary to develop training, education and research as a unity, and to ensure the highest possible standards of quality and efficiency. The study of the fundamentals of Marxism-Leninism is to be systematically improved in accordance with its importance for education and training.

The Party considers that sound elementary training in any subject should go hand in hand with a systematic effort to enable students to assimilate scientific knowledge unassisted and to put theoretical findings to practical use. This presupposes a practice-oriented and creative atmosphere and an intense scientific, intellectual and cultural life in all institutes of higher and technical education.

The Party considers it necessary to develop the material basis of the unified socialist education system on planned lines, especially stressing the need

to improve the equipment of schools and vocational training establishments with modern teaching aids,

rapidly to enlarge the material basis for teaching and research at institutes of higher and technical education, and

to meet public demand for accommodation in creches and kindergartens.

(*Programme of the Socialist Unity Party of Germany*, Dresden 1976, pp. 53 ff.)

D84 From the Five-Year Plan Act 1986–1990, adopted on 27 November 1986: on general and technical education:

(4.) The ongoing construction of an advanced socialist society calls for measures enabling the education system to evolve at a high level and efforts to develop and utilize its advantages in an increasingly comprehensive fashion for the perfection of communist education for the young and their preparation for life and work in our socialist society.

The central task in the field of national education will be to improve socialist general education.

Bearing in mind factors such as economic progress, the challenges of the scientific and technological revolution, developments in the arts and other fields of social life, and the resulting demands on the all-round development of the individual and the communist education of young people, educational content and quality levels are designed to ensure a solid, high-quality basic education that can be built upon.

It is necessary to systematically raise the level of the entire educational process, to improve the quality of subject teaching and further consolidate the polytechnic nature of secondary school education. Therefore, it is necessary to ensure high quality standards in the training of prospective teachers and to make provisions for periodic in-service training of the teaching staff.

All parents who so wish may send their children to a kindergarten where the children are well looked after, educated and prepared for school life. Further improvements will be necessary to ensure that children may attend such facilities in their immediate neighbourhood.

In the period between 1986 and 1990, 10,661 classrooms, 740 school sports halls and facilities for another 105,015 children in kindergartens are to be built.

To ensure a well-balanced influx of newly trained skilled workers in all economic sectors and occupations, a total of 918,000 young people are to be trained, including about 53,000 young people holding a university entrance certificate (Abitur). The competition programme for the enhancement of vocational training is to be improved further and streamlined to match new requirements. It is to be ensured that adequate numbers of young people opt for military careers.

In accordance with the necessity for the GDR to acquire a leading position in science and technology, new syllabuses are to be introduced for all vocational training courses by 1990. Step by step classrooms are to be established in vocational schools for instruction in computer operation.

Measures are to be taken to assist the Free German Youth organization in the execution of the tasks involved in sponsoring and supervising the instruction of apprentices in information technology.

Vocational counselling must attain higher quality standards and become more effective. It must be ensured that all enterprises and institutions stipulate the demand for, and plan the influx of, young skilled workers five years in advance.

The material and physical conditions of vocational training will improve by the addition of 538 instruction rooms, 4,787 places in apprentice hostels and 38 school gymnasiums to be built or modernized.

Combines and enterprises are to organize industrial training schemes for skilled and supervisory workers in such a way that they can cope with sophisticated technologies and production methods sufficiently early. Increasing emphasis must be laid on the acquisition of indispensable additional vocational qualifications. For certain categories of employment, compulsory advanced training courses are to be phased in.

Universities, colleges and technical schools have the task of augmenting education programmes for students so as to combine the acquisition of profound knowledge in line with advanced scientific developments and prospective social demands with a thorough political and ideological education based on Marxist-Leninist theory.

The rapid advances in science and technology and their application in the economy require that universities and technical colleges lay the scientific groundwork for further progress. To this end, systematic efforts are necessary to draft new programmes for the general and advanced training of engineers, economists, technologists and scientists by 1990.

Basic research at institutions of higher and technical education is to be concentrated on the integrated development and full-scale application of key technologies such as micro-electronics, computer-aided construction, design and manufacturing, robotics, flexible automation, materials upgrading and biotechnology.

The ties existing between universities and technical colleges and industrial combines are to be greatly expanded on the basis of appropriate contracts to be concluded. The links to be established should facilitate both the immediate economic and technological needs of combines and long-term basic research.

To an increasing extent, universities and technical colleges will have to organize and offer postgraduate training courses on key technologies.

The physical inventory, specialized laboratories and CAD/CAM centres which have been established, partly with the assistance of industrial combines, are to be employed to even greater economic effect. Additional fieldwork facilities and CAD/CAM centres are to be made operational together with potential customers and used for training purposes.

Investment schemes in establishments of higher and technical education in the period 1986–1990 provide for the construction or refurbishing of 12,765 places in auditoriums, seminar rooms and laboratories and 5,181 places in halls of residence.

(Panorama DDR: *Five-Year Plan Act: the development of the GDR's national economy in the period 1986–1990*, Dresden 1986, pp. 70 ff.)

D85 From the Law on the National Economic Plan for 1988, 19 December 1987:

The socialist education system is to be further developed on a qualitatively higher level in accordance with the demands of the further development of the advanced socialist society.

In general education, the process of perfecting general socialist education is to be continued. The standard of all work in education and the quality of teaching are to be raised and the polytechnic nature of the schools is to be further emphasized.

The following capacities are to be created in general education system by new building and reconstruction:

	1988
teaching rooms	2035
kindergarten places	21,462
school sports halls	145

The training and further education of skilled and master workers in all occupations and areas necessary for the economy is to be guaranteed by the vocational training system. In 1988 175,488 school-leavers, 10,440 of them with university entrance qualifications, are to be accepted for vocational training and trained as qualified skilled workers for branches of the economy in accordance with the aims of the plan. Professional entrants for a military career are to be secured for the armed forces.

The combines and enterprises, with the assistance of the local councils, are to ensure the planned training of new skilled workers, on the basis of accounting decisions and within the given structure.

By means of adult education in particular, working people are to become qualified in a planned manner to meet the new demands of work.

The university and college system has to create the educational lead necessary for accelerated application of science and technology in the national economy. In 1988, the university and college system is to admit
72,680 students to degree and diploma courses,
53,970 of them to direct study courses.

The university and college system also has to direct training and further education towards mastery of the key technologies in particular.

The economy-based relationships of the universities and colleges with the combines are to be comprehensively extended and directed towards the achievement of peak performance. As a contribution to the attainment of these objectives, joint youth research collectives of the FDJ are to be formed to a greater extent.

The following capacities are to be built or reconstructed:

	1988
Seating in lecture, tutorial and study rooms	4900 places
Accomodation in student residences	1850 places

(*Neues Deutschland* vol. 42 no. 298 of 19–20 December 1987)

D86 From Rudolf Bahro's "The Alternative"; an alternative view of education policies, 1977:

At present it is decided through the plan how many people are to be excluded at each step from the higher functional levels of labour. The existing division of labour is programmed into the educational system more rigidly in our society than under capitalism. Teaching syllabuses for the transmission of knowledge according to clearly differentiated functional levels are derived from the existing social structure of the work positions to be filled. In postgraduate training and higher education in general it is almost exclusively the narrow interests of the branch, the enterprise and even the department that dictate. Someone who is a specialist in chemistry can as a rule only become a chemical engineer and nothing else. But in the most developed industrial countries an "oversupply" of academic training becomes unavoidable, once the least concession is made to the flood of young people into the tertiary sector and the "national economic need" for specialists is gauged on the basis of the present functional structure. Symptoms such as college education for already more than half of the age group in North America, the success of the Open University in Britain, the discussions about the abolition of the *numerus clausus* in West Germany, indicate unmistakably that the educational striving of young people is bursting the barriers of the established functional division of labour, and of so-called economic requirements in general. The attempt can of course be made to meet this developmental tendency with reactionary restrictions, and this is precisely the quintessence of the educational policy pursued by such parties as the SED. Its Politburo has shelved a plan for admission quotas in individual specialisms up till 1990. There is scarcely any better way for a political party to indicate its attitude towards the problems of its society's development today than by the general tendency of its education policy.

The present system of general education [. . .] is anti-aesthetic, and so superficially rationalist and scientist that the subjects of German, history, civics, etc. give hardly an inkling of the human condition. It goes without saying that just as at all other times, there are teachers whose personal quality enables them to break through this restriction. But they are cutting against the grain. Knowledge of human affairs that is taught and accepted without aesthetic emotion must be basically untrue, and particularly so for the individuals involved. Aesthetics, as a method of education, means simply the attempt to present all knowledge that man requires in such a way that it appeals to his own self, and receives a subjective meaning for him. There are many things in our own tradition which we could seek to link up with in the interest of a new synthesis. Let us take simply the Soviet experiments of the 1920s, the inheritance of Makarenko, which well deserves reviving, or the practice of the Soviet Ukranian educational romantic Suchomlinsky. All these of course came out of the pre-industrial era. Yet in the present scientific and technical revolution we shall again be able to do something with these stimulating initiatives, once we cease to equate its significance with that of the first industrial revolution.

For the whole of early and middle childhood, up to the onset of puberty, the powers of rational abstraction are not yet so developed that the abstract concept can be the guiding means for organizing one's own experience and establishing its connection with the overall whole. Where our rationalistic concept of education has led to the stunting of emotional motivation and fantasy, where therefore the immediate aesthetic reflection has been abandoned before rational reflection even begins, a gulf is already created which separates one section of children from the creative life, for creativity does not exist without contact at the level of synthesis. The entire educational process must be organized in such a way that the youthful development of all people leads up to the summit of art and philosophy, the emotional and the rational bridges from the subjective microcosm to the totality. If this is a utopia, it is Marx's utopia too.[5]

(Rudolf Bahro: *The Alternative in Eastern Europe*, tr. David Fernbach, NLB 1978)

D87 From a speech made to the Third Congress of the FDGB in 1950:

The Congress chairman now calls on COLLEAGUE FRIEDA BUSCH to speak.

Colleagues,

I should like to speak to one point of the address by our colleague Herbert Warnke, namely: women in the struggle for peace. If I consider our women's work in the enterprises today and cast my mind back over the International Women's Movement, then I can say that since 1945 we have already made great progress. Women have always been in the front line of the trade union and workers' movement. The Soviet Union after the great socialist October Revolution was the first country to bring equal rights for woman after centuries of oppression. The Soviet Union's victory over Hitler's fascism also set a fundamental transformation of woman's role in society in motion for us. Whereas in the period of fascist imperialism woman's role was simply to bear children and she had neither political nor any other rights in society, now as a result of the transformation of society in the German Democratic Republic and with the generous support of the Soviet Union woman has for the first time been granted the right to participate in deciding all issues concerning our society.

It seems necessary to me to show woman's development in society. Now it has to be stated quite clearly that a large proportion of our women are conscious of their great contribution to society. But there are shortcomings partly because of a misguided attitude held by men, some of whom still believed that they would lose some of their authority with equal rights for women. This can be seen particularly in our enterprises where, precisely because of the misguided attitude the men have, we have not yet managed to make women as well qualified politically and vocationally as would be desirable. However, the Five-Year Plan, which takes up the question of women workers to a greater extent, helps particularly those women who do not yet understand the reason for equal rights to see this.

If today, at a period of the highest political tension and a heightened struggle for peace, we address women in particular, this shows that we have learned from the past. The many signatures of women in the petitions to ban atomic weapons, their work in the peace committees and in the National Front prove to us that no wife and mother is prepared to sacrifice either her children or her husband or any other members of her family for imperialistic warmongering. We have learned from the examples given by Soviet women and the heroic women of France against the war preparations of the imperialist forces. We are aware that we can maintain peace if we practice friendship and solidarity with all peace-loving women of the world.

It must therefore be the duty of every peace-loving woman to take her place in the ranks of the Women's Democratic Federation to fight for the maintenance of peace. We will give the best proof of this on 15 October. Only by voting for the candidates of the National Front can we secure peace, for they also represent a vote of confidence for our government and its policies. I would like to call on all female colleagues and all women to join in the struggle for the aims of the National Front and in the struggle to maintain peace. (*applause*)

(*Protokoll des 3. Kongresses des Freien Deutschen Gewerkschaftbundes*, Berlin 1950, pp. 146 ff.)

D88 From the address by the Secretary of the Central Council of the FDJ to the Third Congress of the FDGB 1950:

Colleague Wiesner, Secretary of the Central Council of the FDJ:
    Dear colleagues, in my discussion I should like to report briefly how the FDJ sets about making all the preparations for coming to grips with the great Five-Year Plan, and at the same time make two proposals. In the control figures for the Five-Year Plan it states that the total number of those in employment is to be raised by 890,000. The great need for labour makes it necessary to raise the percentage of working women. The proportion in industry is to be raised from 33.3 per cent to 42 per cent. Colleague Warnke already put forward the objective of obtaining thousands of women in particular in the mobilization of new labour power.

(Source as above, p. 217)

D89 From Walter Ulbricht's report and final address to the Second Party Conference of the SED, 9–12 July 1952:

Work with women

The high objective of constructing socialism can be achieved only if women take an enthusiastic part in the attainment of this objective. (*loud applause*) It is first of all necessary to win for it the girls and women employed in the enterprises, who are a part of the working class. Although women and girls accomplish outstanding achievements in production they are still being inadequately promoted by many of the enterprise, union, and party leaderships. For this reason the Politburo has decided to promote the creation of women's committees in the enterprises. The women's committee is the democratic form of association of the women in an enterprise, including the whole mass of women irrespective of membership of an organization and without any exceptions. Through it women have the opportunity to represent their common interests. The election of women's committees is also necessary in the production co-operatives and in the institutes, in transport and in commerce. *Party leaderships are obliged to support the women's initiatives in every way. (wild applause)*

As for the *work of the Women's Democratic Federation of Germany*, we can state that this organization has done great work in the struggle to maintain peace. It fulfils important tasks in educating women of all confessions and ideologies as conscious and equal citizens of the Republic, who bring up their children in the spirit of peace and progress and who by their active participation in the parents' councils make an important contribution to improving the activities in the general schools. The party leaderships should support the organizations of the DFD with comradely co-operation.

[. . .]

Support for the women's committees

In the discussion several comrades emphasized their experiences with the activities of the women's committees in the enterprises. The promotion of these committees is of great fundamental importance. This question was decided by the Politburo on the basis of the recognition that if the working class plays the leading role, working women must be involved, for after all they are a part of the working class. *(applause)* But many of our comrades in the party, and in particular our trade union officials, are of the opinion that the working class consists only of men. *(laughter, applause)* Let me say quite frankly: what women have reported at some conferences is deeply shaming. We shall have all these cases investigated. We shall now bring before the party-control commission every official and every comrade in trade union leaderships who hinders the work of the women's committees. *(applause)*

Comrades, anyone who knows women knows that many of them have become skilled workers in face of strong resistance. No one helped them. Is it not shaming for us that this happens in our Republic? The question has to be put frankly. At the women's conferences we have seen women who are members of no party, women who have been resettled and have several children, who are activists and better workers than many men. *(applause)* And when these resettlers' wives and agricultural workers' wives start working in the production co-operatives, you will see how well they will work. This means that the comrades must at long last free themselves of this stupid sectarian behaviour towards women workers and put this question frankly in the enterprises. The party leadership has the duty to deal with the question of work among women in the party organization's meeting. If the leading officials do not understand that, then the meeting of party members does. And if there are cases where women have been consciously held back then we shall investigate these and punish the guilty party. Then we shall have a great change in this area in a matter of months, and you will see that things are going forward. (*applause*)

(W. Ulbricht: *Die gegenwärtige Lage und die neuen Aufgaben der Sozialistischen Einheitspartei Deutschlands*, Berlin 1952, pp. 142 f., 164f.)

D90 From Erich Honecker's report to the Ninth Party Congress: on the growing role of the trade unions and the further promotion of women, May 1976:

The working class, as the holder of political power, as the producer of the major proportion of social wealth, is the main social force in our republic. We will spare no pains to enable it to further increase its creative force and influence in all spheres of social life.

The trade unions are playing an outstanding role in this process. Trade-union initiative and activity has increased considerably as a result of the central policy pursued by the SED. The vast potential of the more than eight million members united in the Confederation of Free German Trade Unions has become abundantly clear in their admirable effort to reach the objectives of our economic and social welfare policy. The trade unions have an outstanding record in organizing the socialist emulation campaign. It is through this that the working people directly involve themselves with management and planning and make major contributions to the continuous dynamic development of our economy.

In preparation for the 9th Congress many varied schemes were initiated to intensify social production through new forms and methods. Considerable new reserves were found by the workers making individual pledges to increase labour productivity and raise efficiency and carrying out model shifts. All this helped to make plans more effective and assisted the workers in developing their personalities more fully. Socialist teamwork between workers and members of the intelligentsia to further scientific and technological progress has been stepped up. The trade unions are finding it increasingly easier to link the campaign for high productivity and efficiency to the steady improvement in working and living conditions.

The responsibility of the trade unions is growing because of the emphasis placed upon further promoting the working class and because of the mounting importance which socialist democracy has for material production. We would like to focus the trade unions' attention on continuing to encourage the "Work, learn and live in a socialist way" campaign. This movement links, in an outstanding manner, dedicated striving for higher economic results, and conscientious honest work for the benefit of society — the central idea of a socialist way of living — with a creative acquisition of the world outlook of the working class. This is the way in which work will gradually turn into a deeply felt need for people living in a socialist society.

We are perfectly justified in saying that the trade unions are continually demonstrating that they are both schools of socialism and advocates of the interests of working people. Our Party will spare no efforts to further increase the influence of the trade unions so that they can play their role as true representatives of working people more fully.

Comrades, women and girls have had a great share in the successful development of our society. There are 3.5 million working-class women in our country which is more than half of all workers and salaried employees. Our Party fully acknowledges the work performed by women, and the advancement of women will continue to be a major priority of our Party.

Time has proved that the 8th Congress was correct in deciding that the problems involved in providing women with the ability to make full use of their equal rights should be solved step by step. This is shown by the increasing amount of work done by women for the good of society and by the measures taken to improve their working and living conditions.

Today we are proud to say that women play an invaluable role in all spheres of life. In the younger generation there are hardly any differences in opportunity for the full development of their capabilities and talents. Girls are prepared for life equally well as boys. This is of inestimable value for progress towards a communist future and it represents a great success for our socialist system.

Nevertheless it is quite natural that there are still problems that will continue to deserve our special attention in the future. These are mainly problems related to the better satisfaction of the requirements and needs of working women with children. As can be seen from the Directives for the national economy's development up to 1980, vast monetary funds will be set aside for this purpose. At the same time it is necessary to remove gradually the many small vexations and difficulties of everyday life which often consume a great deal of working mothers' time and cause them no little trouble.

We are of the opinion that as advanced socialist society develops further measures should be taken which would gradually enable working mothers to meet the demands of their work and fulfil their family duties as equal members of society. In this connection, Congress would like to turn to firms and institutions, government departments and social organizations to ask of them that they make every possible effort to give women and families with children any assistance which prevailing local conditions make necessary and which takes into full account the great benefit they bring society.

Without a doubt, the very process of eliminating certain hardships which still affect the lives of women will also be an important contribution to the development of a new socialist way of life. This will encourage people, especially the young, to show attitudes in their private lives which are free from obsolete traditions and habits, and which fully respect the new social status of women in socialism and their great responsibility as mothers.

(Erich Honecker: *Report of the Central Committee to the 9th Congress of the Socialist Unity Party of Germany*, Dresden 1976, pp. 140 ff.)

D91 From the directives for the Five-Year Plan 1976-1980: on social policies in the enterprises:

Social and health services and amenities for intellectual, cultural and sporting activities will have to be expanded for employees in industrial and other enterprises by providing the necessary funds and making all the organizational arrangements required. Special attention will also have to be paid to catering and welfare services for shift workers, women and young people. The measures intended are to be directed towards raising considerably the operating rate of fixed assets by ensuring a substantial increase in multishift working. Working hours and intervals are to be arranged in such a manner that a change-over to shift working is promoted and an effective rhythm of shifts established.

(*Directives for the Five-Year Plan for the GDR's national economic development 1976–1980*, Dresden 1976, p. 129)

D92 From the SED's programme: on the promotion of women, 1976:

The Socialist Unity Party of Germany devotes much attention to the promotion of women. In all fields of human endeavour, working women make a tremendous contribution to political, economic, scientific, technological, social, intellectual and cultural progress. The Socialist Unity Party of Germany will make every effort to create everywhere conditions enabling women to make ever fuller use of their equal status in society and allowing for further improvements in women's working and living conditions. The consolidation of women's status in society and the development of their personality require determined efforts to ensure that women can reconcile the demands of their job still more successfully with their duties towards child and family.[6]

(*Programme of the Socialist Unity Party of Germany*, Dresden 1976, p. 43)

D93 From Erich Honecker's report to the Tenth Party Congress of the SED: the women's policy of the SED, April 1981:

Comrades,

Every day, the women and girls of our country give renewed proof of the high social value of their equality at work, in the family and in educating and looking after children. This is why we are deeply satisfied to note that in the period under review we were once again able to make effective a whole series of measures which considerably improved the working and living conditions of the 4.7 million working, learning or studying women in the GDR and gave special protection to mother and child. As set down in the Party Programme, this allowed the further development of the premises and conditions which we believe to be necessary if women are to live up to their obligations at work and as mothers, as members of socialist society on an equal footing with others.

The truly great advances made regarding the professional work of women and their work in society, their growing share in the responsible functions of the State and the economy, and the continually increasing birth-rate, all bear witness to the fact that in our Republic a high level of equal rights has been achieved as well as the conditions required for their application in everyday life. No one is likely to be more aware of these achievements of socialism than women themselves. This demonstrates their growing efforts to make a larger contribution to society as a whole. And indeed, what the women and girls of today contribute to the social progress of our country is much more than hard work and clever hands. They also contribute professional and political knowledge and skill, courage and faith in their own capabilities and powers.

This is precisely why it is now so important that the leaderships of our Party, the trade unions and the women's organization, but also the leading agencies in the state and the economy, should make good use of the social and individual benefits accruing from equal rights, so as to make women's will to achieve even more effective in the further development of the advanced socialist society. In other words, in the interests of new successes for women too, what has already been achieved must be utilized and developed even more consciously.

(Erich Honecker: *Report of the Central Committee of the Socialist Unity Party of Germany to the 10th Congress of the SED*, Dresden 1981, p. 158 f.)

D94 From the Directives for the Five-Year Plan 1986–1990: on social policy in enterprises:

There is a need to go further towards perfecting social and health care and improving the scope of cultural and intellectual activities in enterprises. In this connection, priority is to be given to improvements in the working and living conditions of shift workers and working mothers.

(*Directives issued by the 11th Congress of the SED for the Five-Year Plan for the GDR's national economic development 1986–1990*, Dresden 1986, pp. 99 f.)

D95 From the Five-Year Plan Act, 1986–1990 adopted on 27 November 1986: on catering and health care:

As regards industrial, kindergarten and school catering services, the task now is to consolidate what has been achieved and to ensure long term improvements in quality standards. Better material conditions must be provided to raise the level of catering and other services for the workforce. Measures will have to be taken to ensure that commuter transport time-tables, the quality of canteen food, supplies of goods and services are better harmonized with the specific requirements of shift work.

Systematic efforts are needed to perfect social and health care and improve the scope of cultural, intellectual and sporting activities of the people working in enterprises, institutions and co-operatives. In this con-nection, priority is to be given to improvements in the working and living conditions of shift workers and working mothers.

(Panorama DDR: *Five-Year Plan Act: The development of the GDR's national economy in the period 1986–1990*, Dresden 1986, p. 68)

D96 From the Central Committee's report to the Eleventh Party Congress of the SED: on education and training, April 1986:

We have established the ten-year general polytechnical school which is closely attuned to practical life, combines learning and productive work and gives all children a sound general education. Compulsory lessons designed to provide a broad basic education backed up by optional lessons to deepen and expand their general education gives our educational system the flexibility it needs to respond promptly to requirements arising from the dynamic development of our society and to provide the educational basis for subsequent vocational training or higher education. This advan-tage of our integrated socialist education system must be further developed and brought more fully to effect..

Acting on the understanding that, for the further construction of an advanced socialist society, it will be imperative to prepare young people in all respects for vocational life in socialist society, efforts in future will also concentrate on providing our schoolchildren with a broad, sound, basic education that can be built upon, on educating them in the spirit of our communist world outlook and morality, and on laying firm foundations for the all-round development of the personality, versatility and creative potential they will need as the future generation of skilled workers, engineers and scientists.

New curricula and textbooks have been introduced since the 10th Party Congress and comprehensive measures are being taken to enable teachers to meet the resultant higher demands. The changes this entails in the content and standards of general education are oriented to foreseeable future perspectives and requirements, but do not affect tried and successful aspects. In deriving conclusions for the education system from the continued construction of an advanced socialist society, including the requirements of the scientific and technological revolution, it is necessary to take into account all the demands arising from the developments that will take place in the production sector, science, socialist democracy, and intellectual and cultural life.

A task that is assuming decisive importance is that of providing the young with sound and reliable fundamental knowledge and skills as a basis for the acquisition of further knowledge, to enable them to acquire knowledge and apply it in practice through their own effort, and to develop their urge to gain further knowledge through personal studies. It is in this context that factors instrumental in raising the quality of educational work are gaining great weight, such as ways of better developing pupils' mental activity and modes of elementary scientific thought and work and their interest in the sciences, in technology and production techniques.

The preparation of school youth for the mastering of the challenges of the scientific and technological revolution is a task to be accomplished in the overall education process. The rapid development of science, technology and production techniques presupposes a better command of fundamental theories, modes of scientific thought and working principles, readily available fundamental knowledge of the basic laws of mathematics, the natural sciences, technology and the social sciences, the ability to learn and work independently and imaginatively. Courses in mathematics, physics, chemistry, biology and the polytechnical subjects are arranged in such a way as to enable the pupils to grasp connections and interrelationships between science, technology, production and society and to understand more fully basic development trends in science and technology and in our economic strategy. In polytechnical instruction, the pupils are now also introduced to the fundamentals of electronics and micro-electronics, information technology and process automation. The aim of this is to give school children a basic knowledge of technical, technological and economic subjects and skills, which also serves as a basis for further developing the content of vocational training.

The opportunities afforded particularly by mathematics, natural science and polytechnical subjects must be fully utilized in order to give the pupils an elementary understanding of informatics and information processing technology. The intrinsic advantages of the polytechnical nature of our schools provides us with excellent opportunities in terms of both material and staff to acquaint pupils with the problems involved in informatics and automation, including computer operation, at shopfloor level, in polytechnical centres and in production facilities themselves, and through co-operation with vocational training establishments and scientific institutions.

The further improvement of the content of social science lessons is and will remain a task of the first priority. Building on the perceptions and experience gained so far with the new teaching materials such as those for civics lessons, teaching in these subjects is to be carried out in such a way that knowledge is imparted in a more concrete and convincing manner, thereby making the lessons more effective in giving pupils a class-based perspective and a sound political and ideological education.

It is against this background that special importance must be attached to history lessons, which are to be improved — and work on the project has already been commenced — with the aim of deepening pupils' knowledge of important historical facts and courses of events, and of the objective interrelationships between them, and imparting a scientifically based view of history, including, particularly, that of the GDR. This has proved to be a very successful approach to the education of young people and is intended to help them understand more fully current and future social developments. The fact that a course giving an introduction to Marxist-Leninist philosophy has been prepared for use within the framework of optional lessons at ten-year schools must be welcomed.

The new programmes for literature lessons and other arts subjects must enhance the effects of an active approach to works of literature and art on the pupil's personality development, their education in communist morality and their conscious awareness of socialist values. We will continue to pay great attention to improving German lessons and lessons in foreign languages, especially Russian.

An important task facing our school and society at large is to educate young people to adopt a healthy way of life and to develop their physical capabilities. To this end, sports lessons and extra-curricular sporting activities are to be made more effective.

It is also imperative to take further steps in the development of optional lessons at our ten-year schools. They present an opportunity to apply a more differentiated approach and to deepen and enlarge upon the general education received by pupils during compulsory lessons. As a result it is possible to take into better account the specific inclinations, interests, talents and gifts that usually appear at this age and to encourage them to the benefit of society.

The preparation of new curricula and textbooks will be continued so that an entirely new curriculum will be available for the ten-year general polytechnical school in 1990. This will ensure high standards of education that can serve as a foundation for further education and will remain valid for several years. Such a process of revising the content of general education involves painstaking work on the part of our teachers, whose aim is to raise the standards of lessons and of educational work in general to a new level.

To encourage the development of the personality, the conditions and opportunities provided by society for meaningful leisure pursuits must be utilized more fully to arouse and satisfy the diverse interests of the pupils, acquaint them thoroughly with new developments, develop their interest in science, art, literature and sport, and encourage gifts and talents.

In view of the fact that the current and future development of our society will call for new standards of behaviour, activity, sense of responsibility, creativity and mutual relations, discipline, reliability and team spirit, the educationalists' attention must be focused on questions concerning the overall behaviour of the young generation such as how to instil in them a spirit of helpfulness, comradeliness, and modesty, and to mould their characters and their feelings. To meet the requirements of current and future conditions of the struggle, it is of the utmost importance to educate our young people in the spirit of the working class, generate and deepen their love and pride of their socialist homeland, educate them along the lines of proletarian internationalism and the unbreakable friendship with the Soviet Union, and inspire them to exercise active solidarity.

Political and moral education justifiably focuses on the development of active personalities whose actions and behaviour are marked by a feeling of responsibility for society as a whole and for themselves. The fact that in our country socialist enterprises in industry, construction and agriculture have to an increasing degree become centres of training and education where the pupils themselves carry out productive work and, through their involvement in the efforts of the working class to achieve high production results, see with their own eyes what depends on honest, conscientious and committed work, is of inestimable value for the success of our education system, which is designed to make work for the benefit of society a natural way of life for young people.

In our educational work, much depends on how all those involved in working with young people succeed in encouraging them and placing demands on them while simultaneously displaying firmness of principle and understanding. It has always been right to assign responsibility to the younger generation, to demand and promote their political activity and to place confidence in them.

The 10th Party Congress called for improvements in the quality and effectiveness of courses preparing young people for university and college studies in view of the increasingly severe demands involved in studies and the subsequent careers of graduates. The measures introduced since then to prepare young people for university entrance after completion of the 10th grade have proved to be successful. It has been possible to meet the required enrolment figures for all important subjects. There is still need, however, to improve standards of instruction in the 11th and 12th grades, and to make study guidance more effective.

The important syllabuses for general education must be carried out to high standards at all schools during the coming decade. This will entail close co-operation between the educational sciences and practice, which in turn will involve studying and analysing more carefully the positive experience, successful teaching methods and imaginative approaches applied by the teachers and to generalize and propagate them more effectively in order to systematically raise the quality of all teachers' educational work.

The qualifications of teachers, and their initial and in-service training have become a matter of key importance. Teacher upgrading courses must be improved and carried out at a high theoretical level and in close relationship with the realities of life, taking advantage of the opportunities available at universities, colleges and technical schools, and other scientific institutions. Upgrading courses are intended to enhance and augment teachers' knowledge and skills systematically, thus helping them to raise their own educational and cultural standards. All this places great demands on teachers' readiness to strive for ever higher qualification levels.

Acting jointly in mutual trust with parents, the school, the Pioneer and youth organization, and the enterprises of our socialist society have already raised generations of young people who, in today's struggles, are carrying on the revolutionary work begun by their mothers and fathers. Qualitatively new social conditions permitting close co-operation between school, parents, enterprises, the Free German Youth with its Ernst Thälmann Pioneer Organization, and other social organizations involved in the education process will arise during the further construction of an advanced socialist society, and these will have to be utilized effectively.

The ambitious task facing kindergarten teachers is to ensure high standards of education at all pre-school facilities so that further strides can be made towards the all-round, healthy development of the children, towards developing their mental ability and moral qualities, towards developing their characters and their relations within groups, and towards preparing them thoroughly for school.

Comrades, the higher standards achieved at secondary schools, the active and optimistic approach of pupils to their future, the need they feel to acquire knowledge and to work have resulted in further improvements in the choice of careers. This is shown by the fact that during the past few years approximately 85 per cent of all school-leavers received an apprenticeship in the trade of their first choice. The advice of parents, many people working at industrial enterprises and in co-operatives, teachers and the staff of career guidance centres helped the young people in making this decision, which is so important for their own lives and for society. We continue to regard the necessity of enabling the up-and-coming generation to opt for new sectors of scientific and technological progress or for traditional trades and occupations on the basis of complete awareness of the implications as something that concerns the whole of society.

In accordance with the task mapped out by the 10th Party Congress for socialist vocational training, an important contribution has been made by that sector to the education of class-conscious skilled socialist workers for all branches of the national economy. More than a million skilled workers and 63,000 supervisors have received thorough training, appropriate to the state of the art in science and technology through the close co-operation of the vocational training establishments and the different enterprises and combines.

At present, more than 85 per cent of the GDR's workforce have completed some form of vocational training. Skilled worker's status has become the basic vocational qualification of the working class, the class of co-operative farmers and the craftsmen. The high standards of initial and advanced training received by our workers and co-operative farmers are reflected in, among other things, the great progress that has been made by our national economy. They also constitute a major factor on which we have based the ambitious targets we have set ourselves in the implementation of our economic strategy.

This development will be systematically continued: by 1990, the proportion of skilled workers, supervisors, university, college and technical school graduates among the GDR's workforce will have risen to approximately 90 per cent. In future, too, all school-leavers will receive an apprenticeship and be assured of thorough vocational training and a secure job upon the completion of training. Our younger generation need not fear being left without an apprenticeship or the threat of dismissal afterwards, nor do they know unemployment. On the contrary, they are assigned challenging tasks in the field of creative labour.

Apprentices respond to these policies of our party with increasingly high standards of performance during both lessons and practical work at vocational school within the framework of socialist competition. The value of the productive work performed by apprentices in industry and agriculture has risen to over five billion marks annually. No less than 95 per cent of all apprentices attain the sound standards of skilled workers by the time they complete their training courses. More than 50 per cent of apprentices pass their skilled workers' examinations with the assessment "good" or better. These results are a credit to their teachers, instructors, and advisers, to the more than 100,000 skilled workers with teaching qualifications, to management staff, and to many work teams.

Under the new Five-Year Plan, a total of 918,000 young people will take up apprenticeships to acquire skilled workers' qualifications, and arrangements are being made for them to be trained for all sectors of the national economy. Skilled workers are held in high regard in our country. To lead young people to love their trade will remain an important task facing all those employed in the vocational training sector.

High levels of vocational training are to be ensured at all combines and their constituent plants to enable the aspiring skilled workers to master the science and technology of the future, to adopt a disciplined and creative approach to occupational work, and to be staunch fighters for socialism ever ready and prepared to defend its achievements. All powers and resources available to combines and the enterprises affiliated to them must be geared to this objective with the indispensible support of the FDJ. In future, too, apprentices must be assigned ambitious tasks at an early stage of their training within the framework of the economic campaigns sponsored by the FDJ. The apprentices of today will be actively involved in determining the face of work and production in the 1990s and into the next century.

In order to adjust the coming generation of skilled workers more fully to future requirements, new syllabuses will gradually be introduced for all skilled trades, beginning in 1986. These new programmes will include micro-electronics, robot technology, automation and information processing in line with future needs. The changes made to the content of the theoretical and practical side of vocational training will first become apparent in trades which are particularly important in connection with the scientific and technological revolution. At the beginning of the new training period, the Fundamentals of Automation will be introduced as a new subject for all apprentices.

The higher demands to be made on apprentices' knowledge, skills and attitudes have been taken into account in the new syllabuses. Greater attention will be devoted to making apprentices aware of the need for an imaginative approach, high quality levels, the sparing use of resources, and shift work. Particularly gifted and talented apprentices are to receive special encouragement and be systematically assigned to work in the most up-to-date production departments or delegated to study at higher education institutions.

Teachers and instructors are to be prepared carefully and well in advance for the use of the new curricula. All enterprises are required to ensure that the productive work foreseen for their apprentices is appropriate to the trades concerned and that modern equipment is used. Apprentices should be trained and employed in youth teams to a greater extent than in the past.

In vocational training, instruction in all subjects must be improved and made more effective. Apprentices are to be enabled to handle modern computers and information processing technology in real time during their training and to take part in automated design and production preparation operations. It is therefore necessary for combines and their constituent plants to gradually establish computer laboratories at vocational schools so that by 1990 a large number of vocational schools will have such facilities available. Such laboratories should also be used for upgrading the qualifications of other working people and for interest groups in the field of science and technology.

(Report of the Central Committee of the Socialist Unity Party of Germany to the 11th Congress of the SED, Rapporteur: Erich Honecker, Dresden 1986, pp. 72 ff.)

D97 From the report by Erich Honecker to the Eleventh Party Congress of the SED in April 1986: women in employment:

Our party's unerring policy of creating an environment in which women can fully exercise their equal rights has yielded satisfying results. This is evident from the tremendous progress in the social status of women in all important respects. For instance, the number of women currently employed, receiving training or enrolled at institutions of higher learning rose to a total of 4.9 million, which is 91.3 per cent of the GDR's female population of working age. No less than 81.5 per cent of all working women hold a university or college degree or have learned a skilled trade. A particularly commendable fact is that 40 per cent of all those participating in upgrading courses to qualify for the management of new technologies are women. The proportion of women in responsible government functions and managerial positions has risen to more than 34 per cent.

Thanks to the dynamic efforts of all social forces, notably the trade unions, the Women's Democratic Federation of Germany, the Free German Youth organization, government authorities and managerial bodies, it has been possible to create opportunities for women to better harmonize employment, social commitment and maternal duties, which generally benefits family life. At their workplaces and in society at large, the female population of our country is making a major contribution as working women and mothers to the enrichment of society, and this deserves great praise. At the same time they can rest assured that in the future our party will continue to work for their specific concerns and to encourage the development of their capabilities and courage to break new ground.

(Source as above, pp. 92f.)

D98 From the Central Statistical Office's report for the first half of 1987: improvements in provision for children:

The number of births in the first half of 1987 rose compared with the same period last year, the figure being 114,941. Increases in monthly child

allowances
    for the first child from 20 to 50 marks,
    for the second child from 20 to 100 marks,
    for the third and any further child from 100 to 150 marks,
became effective on 1 May 1987 in keeping with the resolutions of the 11th
SED Congress. This is another significant measure to enhance the economic security and comforts of families with children. The yearly cost of
such measures is approximately 2,000 million marks.

[. . .]

To improve material conditions in the education sector, another 624
classrooms, 39 school sports halls, 216 places in boarding schools and
kindergartens offering 7,135 places were newly built or modernized. All
children in the eligible age groups whose parents so wished were able to
attend a kindergarten or an after-school centre.

[. . .]

The network of health facilities was expanded according to plan. Consultation hours in the early morning, in the evening and on Saturdays were
extended considerably to make it possible for many working people to see
the doctor of their choice outside their own working hours. The focus of
attention was on attaining tangible improvements in the system of family
doctors in cities and industrial conurbations.

[. . .]

Special attention was devoted to health and social care for working mothers
and their children. The post-natal advice system has seen further progress.
A total of 2,491 creche places were newly built or modernized during the
first six months of 1987.

(Panorama DDR: *Report by the Central Statistical Office of the GDR on
the fulfilment of the National Economic Plan in the first half of 1987*,
Dresden 1987, p. 37)

D99 Law on the participation of young people in shaping the advanced socialist society, and on their all-round promotion in the German Democratic Republic, 1974:

Youth Law of the GDR, 28 January 1974

In the German Democratic Republic the fundamental aims and interests of society, state, and young people are in agreement. Under the Socialist Unity Party of Germany's leadership the working class, all other working people, and young people have created the Workers' and Farmers' State. Together they are shaping the German Democratic Republic, their socialist fatherland.

The socialist order of society, in which exploitation and oppression of human beings is abolished for ever, guarantees young people their decisive rights. The basic rights of the young generation proclaimed by the FDJ in 1946 — political rights, the right to work and leisure, the right to education, and the right to pleasure and happiness — have long been law and social practice in the German Democratic Republic.

The revolutionary tasks facing today's young people are to help shape the developed socialist society in the German Democratic Republic and to participate in firm fraternal alliance with the Soviet Union in the all-round integration of the socialist community of states. This is their fundamental right and their fundamental duty . . .

I. The development of young people to socialist personalities

§1(1) The primary task in the development of the advanced socialist society is to educate all young people to be citizens who are truly devoted to the ideas of socialism, who think and act as patriots and internationalists, and strengthen socialism and protect it reliably against all enemies. Young people themselves bear great responsibility for their development as socialist personalities . . .

§3(1) Young people have the task of participating actively in the development of the advanced socialist society and of increasing their ability to participate in political and social life. Officials of the state, managers of the economy, teachers and educators render young people capable of carrying out their civic rights and duties. They involve them in their work, in accordance with the principles of socialist democracy . . .

II. Promoting the initiative of young working people

§8(1) The continued development of the advanced socialist society demands that young working people — together with all working people — take part in raising the material and cultural standard of living of the people. Young workers, co-operative farmers, members of the intelligentsia, employees, members of production co-operatives and apprentices direct their initiative towards ensuring a high rate of development of socialist production, raising of efficiency, scientific and technical progress, and the growth of labour productivity. By industrious work, high vocational ability and constant improvement of their qualifications they increase the social wealth of the people and at the same time serve their own development . . .

§11 To promote and recognize young people's national economic initiatives, a "Young Socialists' Account" is to be set up. The account consists of financial resources which have been built up by young people either in addition to the plan or through special youth initiatives. These resources will be applied in accordance with Free German Youth proposals, primarily to support political, cultural, sports, tourist and other initiatives by young people, and also to extend the material conditions for youth work in line with the plan.

§12(1) Young working people take an active part in the movement for socialist working, learning, and living. Managers and management bodies in all work collectives promote young working people's efforts towards socialist teamwork. In accordance with the plan they improve the conditions for young people to participate in the various forms of socialist teamwork and so ensure close, comradely co-operation between older and younger working people.

(2) Managers and management bodies take long-term steps to create the preconditions for the formation of work brigades made up of young people and the allocation of particular projects to young people. The leaderships of the Free German Youth and the Confederation of Free German Trade Unions have the right to put forward proposals for the formation and development of youth brigades and youth projects . . .

§14(1) Young people's participation in the Young Innovators' Movement (MMM) is to be promoted by officials of the state and the economy. Managers and management bodies set young people objectives from the Five-Year and One-Year Plans, particularly from the scientific and technological plans, and allocate experienced skilled workers, engineers and scientists to support them.

III. Promoting the initiative of young people in schools and colleges

§19 Education of young people in school
   (1) the all-round socialist education of young people in school is the common cause of the school, the parents, the Free German Youth movement, the Ernst Thälmann Pioneer organization, and all working people. Close co-operation between school and enterprise should be guaranteed.
   (2) The directors and teachers' collectives in the schools secure the all-round development of pupils' personalities by provision of a sound

general education and by a highly effective socialist education. They ensure a high standard of academic teaching which is committed and closely linked to real life, together with rich and interesting extracurricular activities . . .

§21 Education of apprentices

(1) Official government and economic bodies, managers and managements ensure that apprentices are trained as class-conscious socialist skilled workers who are conscious of their responsibility for the further development of socialism. Managers and managing bodies, particularly managers of the vocational training institutions, co-operate closely with the Free German Youth movement, the Confederation of Free German Trade Unions and other social organizations in the training of apprentices. They guarantee the fulfilment of the state educational plans . . .

§22 Education of students

(1) Study at a university or college is a high social commendation and a personal obligation for each student to the working class and the socialist state.

(2) Admission to study is granted on the necessary academic and social performance, in accordance with the needs of the socialist society and in consideration of the social structure of the population. The leaderships of the Free German Youth movement are entitled to take part in decisions on admission to study . . .

IV. Young people's right and honourable duty to protect socialism

§24 The defence of the socialist fatherland and the community of socialist states is the right and honourable duty of all young people. Young people have the task of gaining education in defence policy, pre-military knowledge and skills, and of serving in the National People's Army and the other national defence forces. This honourable service is highly respected by the socialist society . . .

V. The development of culture in the lives of young people

§27 Culture and art enrich the lives of young people in the developed socialist society, are an indispensible part of their activity, and contribute to the all-round formation of the personality. It is the interest and the task of young people to shape their lives in a cultural way, to make meaningful use of their leisure time, to be active culturally or artistically and to participate creatively in the development of culture and art . . .

§29(1) Youth clubs are to be created and further developed to promote the varied interests and activities of young people towards socialist leisure activities. The existing FDJ groups in youth clubs are to be supported in their activity . . .

VI.   The development of physical education and sport for young people
§§ 34-38

VII.   Organization of working and living conditions for young people §§
39-44

VIII.   Organization of holidays and tourism for young people §§
45–50

IX.   The management of the state objectives of socialist youth policy

§51 In the socialist society the state objectives of socialist youth policy are an element of state management and planning.

§52(1) The Council of Ministers, by commission of the People's Chamber and in implementation of the decisions of the party of the working class, lays down the state objectives for realizing socialist youth policy. It guarantees that the demands of socialist youth policy are taken into consideration in state management and planning, and with the help of its subsidiary bodies oversees their integrated implementation . . . The Office for Youth Issues as an official body responsible to the Council of Ministers ensures supervision of the implementation of the state objectives of socialist youth policy.

(2) The Central Council of the Free German Youth has the right to submit proposals on resolutions and decrees on socialist youth policy to the Council of Ministers. It is entitled to put forward proposals to the Council of Ministers for the appointment of the director of the Office for Youth Issues.

(3) Youth research is to be developed in a planned way to work out a scientific basis for socialist youth policy. The Office for Youth Issues of the Council of Ministers of the German Democratic Republic is the body controlling scientific research on youth in the German Democratic Republic . . .

X.   Final regulations

§57(1) Young citizens within the meaning of this law are all citizens of the German Democratic Republic up to completion of their 25th year.

(*Gesetzblatt der Deutschen Demokratischen Republik I*, 1974, pp. 45 ff.)

D100 From the Labour Code of the GDR of 16 June 1977:

The Labour Code is the fundamental source from which socialist labour law derives. It reflects the great achievements accomplished by the working class and guarantees a high level of legal security. It lays down rights and duties applicable to all working people and enterprises. The constitutionally guaranteed rights of the trade unions, as the all-embracing class organization of the working class, to represent the interests of working people in state, economy and society have been further elaborated in the Labour Code.

[. . .]

Promotion and protection of women, youth and certain groups of persons

Section 3

The socialist state shall ensure that conditions are created everywhere which enable women to live up increasingly better to their equal status at work and in vocational education and to reconcile even more successfully their occupational activities with the duties they have to fulfil as mothers and within the family. The labour law shall contribute to the planned improvement of working and living conditions for women. It shall ensure that women receive special treatment and protection upon taking up and during employment and that they are granted material support during motherhood.   .

[. . .]

Section 30

The women's promotion plan

(1) Measures geared towards the promotion of women's creative abilities in the labour process, their political and technical training and further qualification, their systematic preparation for managerial functions and the improvement of their working and living conditions shall be laid down in the women's promotion plan.

(2) The women's promotion plan shall be concluded between works managers and enterprise trade union committees and form part and parcel of enterprise collective agreements.

(3) Together with the enterprise trade union committees, works managers shall ensure that women are involved in drafting the women's promotion plan. Reports shall be given to women on the fulfilment of the women's promotion plan.

Section 148

(1) Women shall be granted special consideration for training and further education. Priority shall be given to the systematic training of female production workers to become skilled workers. A greater number of women shall be qualified for holding managerial functions. The relevant measures shall be laid down in the women's promotion plan.

[. . .]

Section 185

(1) Fully employed women having a household of their own shall be given an additional monthly day off if
    (a) they are married,
    (b) children up to the age of 18 belong to their household,
    (c) family members in need of nursing belong to their household, provided that this need has been certified by a doctor,
    (d) they are 40 years of age or over.

[. . .]

(4) An additional day off per month shall also be granted
    (a) to fully employed single fathers with children of up to 18 when this is necessary for them to look after the child or children respectively,
    (b) to fully employed men in the event that their wives are certified ill by a doctor and that the day off is necessary for the fulfilment of household work.

[. . .]

(5) Standard wages shall be paid for the additional monthly day off . . .

Section 186

(1) Working people shall be released from work in the event that their children are certified ill by a doctor or that they have to consult a doctor with their children. The same shall apply when they personally have to look after their children during temporary quarantine in creches or kindergartens.
(2) Single working people released from work for the purpose of caring for their sick children shall be supported by social security. They shall receive 90 per cent of their net monthly earnings for up to two working days.
(3) In the event that single working people have to stay away from work for more than two days, social security shall grant financial support equivalent

to the sick pay working people are entitled to as from the seventh week of their own illness.

[. . .]

Section 210

Special protection of working women and young people

(1) The health and working capacity of women and young people under 18 years of age shall be under special protection.
(2) Working conditions shall be in keeping with the physical and psychological characteristics of women and with young people's physical development.

[. . .]

(4) Women and young people shall not be assigned physically heavy labour and work detrimental to their health.

Care for the children of enterprises personnel and socialist education of young people of school age.

Section 233

(1) Enterprises shall systematically create and maintain children's facilities in co-operation with local authorities and their councils. They shall help working people find places in creches and kindergartens for their children.
(2) Enterprises shall support working people in the care of sick children in co-operation with the health service.

Section 234

(1) Enterprises shall be required to take up any opportunity for providing the children of their personnel with recreational holidays in camps run by them or other forms of holiday organization.
(2) Cultural, youth and sports facilities of enterprises shall be open free of charge to schoolchildren for extra-curricular activities and leisure pursuits.

Special rights of working women and mothers
Section 240
Basic principle

(1) Enterprises shall be required to systematically improve working and living conditions and thus to offer working women with children ever

better opportunities for harmonizing their occupational activities and development with their tasks as mothers and within the family.

[...]

Section 241
Training and further education

(1) Special measures shall be laid down in regulations for women with children of up to 16 in their household to promote and support them in training and further education.
(2) Enterprises shall be required to grant women with children of up to 16 years in their household every possible assistance in their training and further education ... In the event of rationalization schemes and structural changes, enterprises shall create the conditions necessary to ensure that the required qualification of women is carried out as far as possible during working hours.

Special protection of working women in the interests of motherhood.
Section 242

(1) Expectant and nursing mothers as well as mothers with children of up to one year of age shall not be assigned work listed in specific regulations.
(2) Expectant and nursing mothers as well as mothers with children of up to one year of age shall not be required to do work detrimental to the health of women or children according to the opinion of the works doctor or the doctor of the pre-natal advice centre.
(3) In cases where Sections 242 (1) and (2) apply, enterprises shall assign working women to another reasonable job. They shall be paid at least their former average wage.

Section 243

(1) Night work and overtime shall be forbidden for expectant and nursing mothers.
(2) Women with children of pre-school age in their households may refuse to work over-time or on the the night shift.

Section 244

(1) Women shall be granted maternity leave for a duration of six weeks before delivery and twenty weeks after childbirth. In the event of more than one baby being born and in the event of a complicated delivery maternity leave after childbirth shall be twenty-two weeks.
(2) If the delivery takes place prematurely, maternity leave after childbirth

shall be prolonged by the time the leave before delivery was shortened. In the event of a belated delivery maternity leave before childbirth shall be prolonged to the day of delivery.

(3) If a child is still in the clinic six weeks after its birth or if he or she has to undergo hospital treatment at a later date, but before the end of post-delivery maternity leave mothers shall have the right to interrupt their leave and take the remainder when the child is released from hospital. The latest date for starting the remaining leave shall be a year after the date of interruption.

(4) For the duration of maternity leave before and after childbirth women shall receive grants equivalent to their net average earnings from social security.

Section 245

(1) Women shall be granted their annual holidays before or immediately after maternity leave on request.

[. . .]

Release from work after maternity leave
Section 246

(1) Mothers who so wish shall be released from work following their maternity leave up to the first birthday of the child.

(2) If no place in a creche can be found for a child, mothers shall be entitled to release from work until a creche place can be provided, but no longer than up to the end of the childs' third year of age.

(3) The provisions of Section 246 (1) and (2) shall also apply to other working people when they look after and bring up a child in place of the mother.

(4) In certain circumstances, mothers shall receive monthly social security benefits during the time they are released from work in accordance with legal regulations. Otherwise, they shall be released from work without earnings-related payment being granted.

Section 247

(1) During release from work in terms of Section 246, women shall have the right to social care by their enterprise. Enterprises shall be required to create the conditions enabling women to attend training and further education courses during the time of their leave. Affiliation to the enterprise shall not be considered interrupted on account of this release from work.

(2) After the end of the leave, enterprises shall be required to employ the women concerned in keeping with the provisions contained in their con-

tract. If women apply for resumption of work before the envisaged date, enterprises shall have to ensure their further employment within two weeks in accordance with the provisions of the employment contract.

Section 248
Release from work for visiting pre- and post-natal advice centres

(1) Women shall be released from work in keeping with regulations when
(a) they have to go a pre-natal advice centre,
(b) they have to visit a post-natal advice centre with their babies and this is impossible outside working hours.
(2) An earnings-related benefits shall be paid for this time.

Section 249
Nursing breaks

Nursing mothers shall be granted two nursing breaks of 45 minutes each a day upon presentation of a relevant certificate.These breaks may be had coherently at the beginning or at the end of the working day. Mothers shall receive an earnings-related payment for this time.

Section 250

Expectant mothers and mothers shall be covered by special protection against dismissal . . .

Section 251
Special benefits for single fathers

The provisions concerning working hours and holidays valid for fully employed mothers shall also apply to fully employed single fathers when this is necessary in the interest of child care. This question shall be decided by works managers with agreement of the competent enterprise trade union committee.

(Panorama DDR: *100 years of August Bebel's "Women and socialism": Women in the GDR*, Dresden 1978 pp.122 ff.)

D101 From the decree on the promotion of women students with a child and expectant mothers studying at colleges and technical schools of 10 May 1972:

Section 2

Women students with a child, and expectant mothers attending study courses shall be granted special support. It shall be ensured on principle that the study courses need not be interrupted or prolonged.

Section 3

(1) The heads of colleges or technical schools shall provide in the annual economic plans of their institutions for the creation of appropriate working and living conditions for women students with a child or student married couples with a child in accordance with existing possibilities. This shall particularly apply to housing and study conditions, the accommodation and care of children and service centres.

(2) Specific stipulations concerning regular health care for women students with a child shall be laid down in the section of the institutions' annual national economic plan devoted to working and living conditions.

(3)The heads of colleges and technical schools shall be required to ensure that the necessary material conditions for the special care of women students with a child are created and conclude agreements with the local government authorities on the provision of places in creches and kindergartens in keeping with regulations.

[. . . .]

Section 5

(1) The heads of departments in colleges and technical schools shall be required, if this is requested by women students with children or expectant mothers, to conclude a promotion agreement.

(2) These promotion agreements shall contain:

measures designed to make up for the study time lost as a result of unavoidable failures to take part in lectures and practical periods,

measures concerning the necessary postponement of examinations and the preparation for examinations,

measures designed to ensure the application of legal regulations for the protection of mother and child.

(3) The individual study and work conditions and the situation of the family shall be taken into account when promotion agreements are drawn up.

(4) Promotion agreements shall be concluded with the competent FDJ and trade union committees co-operating.

(Source as above, pp. 137 f.)

D102 From the regulation on apprenticeship of 15 December 1977:

Section 9
Promotion of mothers in vocational training

(1) Expectant mothers or mothers undergoing vocational training shall be given specific support by enterprises with a view to enabling them to complete their apprenticeship and pass their skilled worker's examination. Working together with the relevant FDJ and trade union committees enterprises shall be required to lay down the necessary measures. Parts of practical training which are not permitted to be carried out by an expectant mother or cannot be undertaken because of a medical certificate may be made up after the maternity leave. Other sections of the training may be undertaken first instead.

(2) In order to protect the health of mothers and to ensure the care of the children, apprentices shall not attend practical and theoretical training during the legally fixed maternity leave. The training can be continued 10 weeks after childbirth at the earliest at the request of mothers if personal conditions allow them to do so and if it is reasonable from a medical point of view.

(3) In order to ensure a successful completion of vocational training, the apprenticeship contracts of apprentices who had to interrupt their vocational training shall be extended by the required time.

(Source as above, p. 138)

D103 From the foreign press agency's official handbook "The German Democratic Republic": on social policies for the promotion of families and working women, 1986:

The state bestows extensive care upon working women and families. Over 90 per cent of women of working age have a job. Their qualification receives special attention. There exist women's promotion schemes at all enterprises. Women form the bulk of the workforce in the trade, health and service sectors, in kindergartens and creches, and in the education system. As far as material production is concerned the women working there (40 per cent of the total workforce) cope perfectly well with the transition from traditional manufacturing techniques to state-of-the art technology. In the GDR there is absolute protection against dismissal during pregnancy.

Women are granted 26 weeks' maternity leave while receiving their full net average wage. In connection with childbirth women receive an allowance to the tune of 1,000 marks. When the first child is born working women are entitled to statutory paid leave for up to one year to look after their infant at home. For the third and every further child they are granted child-care leave of up to 18 months. That means full exemption from work with 70 to 90 per cent of their net earnings. Their job is reserved for them whatever. Mothers working a full working day who have two or more children up to the age of 16 work just 40 hours a week without any wage reductions. All working mothers with two children are able to take paid leave to care for their sick children.

The basic holiday for mothers working full time with several children is between 20 and 23 working days. If their work in shifts they receive up to 10 additional days.

Women working full time with a household of their own are granted one paid day off per month to do work around the house, providing they are either married, have children younger than 18 living in their household or have dependents in need of attention.

Of no little importance in ensuring women the opportunity to take advantage of their right to work is the fact that all children between the ages of three and six can be provided with a place in a kindergarten and that for 73 per cent of all children up to the age of three a place in a creche is available. All expenses involved are paid by the state, except for a token financial contribution parents have to pay for food.

The encouragement given to families is a major social aspect serving the interests of working women. Young married couples (age limit 30 years) are granted interest-free loans to the tune of 7,000 marks, which are repayable within 11 years. When the first child is born, 1,000 marks are waived, another 1,500 marks on the birth of the second and a further 2,500 marks upon the birth of the third child.

Families with severely handicapped children are given special assistance in addition to medical care. The mothers of such children are able to work reduced hours while being paid their full wages; they receive extra holidays and a financial allowance in the case of the child falling ill.

Families with three or more children are given preferential treatment by allocating them larger homes with all the mod cons. Between 1976 and 1985 70,000 large families moved into a newly built flat or an owner-occupied house. In addition, such families receive rent allowances, they can take advantage of free laundering services and state allowances for the purchase of clothes and furniture, as well as package tours to holiday resorts free of charge or at reduced prices. They are sent on courses of spa treatment, pay lower prices for tickets at all cultural facilities and receive school meals and milk free of charge.

As of 1 May 1987, family allowances will be increased substantially: for the first child they will be raised from 20 marks to 50 marks per month, for the second child from 20 to 100 marks, and for the third and all further children from 100 to 150 marks.

(Panorama DDR: *The German Democratic Republic*, Dresden 1986, pp. 159 ff.)

D104 From Erich Honecker's address during consultations between the Secretariat of the Central Committee of the SED and the First Secretaries of the District Party Organizations, 12 February 1988:

Of course we are following the developments in the Soviet Union and the other socialist countries most attentively. At present they are characterized by a great variety of reviews and changes taking the most varied forms. These concern the acceleration of social and economic developments and the further raising of the standard of living, and so also concern the question of making socialism more attractive and appealing in its peaceful competition with the capitalist system. We have been working together with the other socialist countries for decades to open up more effectively the inherent potential of socialism. We exchange our experiences and learn from each other. The developmental processes which have been initiated in the socialist states will improve conditions for more effective mutual co-operation. The GDR supports the efforts of its brother states to increase their economic strength and supports the further intensification of co-operation at a higher standard. We too receive the same support in our further development of the advanced socialist society in the GDR.

All the past experience of the socialist states has shown that the construction of socialism is a constant process of searching creatively for the best ways of meeting new requirements and solving new problems. Naturally, it is important that each country reacts promptly and flexibly to the new challenges in accordance with concrete national and international circumstances. In the case of the GDR, the formulation of our strategic programme for the further development of the advanced socialist society has never at any time been regarded as completed. Rather we proceed on the assumption that, as stated in the programme of the SED, this is a process of deep-reaching political, social, intellectual and cultural transformations. This demands that, in order to carry forward continuously our sociopolitical programme with its central theme of the unity of economic and social policies, new answers appropriate to our national circumstances must constantly be found to the questions that life raises. It is self-evident that in this we give consideration to the experiences of the other socialist countries in their socialist construction, and utilize this experiences too. However that is very far from meaning that we simply copy them. That would be harmful.

(E. Honecker: *Mit dem Volk und für das Volk realisieren wir die Generallinie unserer Partei zum Wohle der Menschen*, Berlin 1988)

Notes

1. The interrelationship between economic and social policies has been a major issue in the countries of "real existing socialism" and has at times been a matter of considerable debate. It is of crucial importance in the context of a planned economy and has occasionally given rise to erratic pronouncements: during the fifties W. Ulbricht predicted that by the early 1960s the GDR would have overtaken the FRG in its standard of living, and N. Krushchev went on record predicting that by 1980 all basic commodities would be free in the Soviet Union. M. Gorbachev's drive for *perestroika* is based on a new interpretation of the relationship between economic and social policies.
2. It is fair to claim that education has always held a fundamental position in Marxist-Leninist ideology, and seems to have a higher status in the GDR than in most western countries.
3. Marx, Engels and Lenin continually stressed the special role of women in society. In 1868 Marx wrote to Ludwig Kugelmann: "Social progress can be measured exactly in terms of the social position of the fair sex (the plain ones included)."
4. It is difficult to interpret the high divorce rate (in 1975 2.5 per 1000 of population). Divorce is certainly easy to obtain; in fact women are in the majority of those bringing divorce petitions. This indicates a high degree of independence on the part of women, and GDR sources connect this with the social provision made for single-parent families. On the other hand the figures point to considerable strain within families, possibly due to the "double shift" women are involved in as workers and housewives.
5. Bahro's critique is mirrored in a considerable number of literary works written in the GDR.
6. This statement does at least implicitly acknowledge the "double shift" problem experienced by women.

5 The Judiciary, Security and Defence

The German legal tradition conceives that law and justice can only be achieved within and under the protection of the state. A *Rechts-staat*, i.e. a state based on the rule of law, is necessary to protect individual citizens against the arbitrary use of power. Within the context of a democratic state, this requires the separation of powers between the legislature, the executive, and the judiciary. The Federal Republic of Germany sees itself as such a *Rechtsstaat*.[1] In the Federal Republic the judiciary, and in particular the Federal Constitutional Court, has played an important role in controlling both legislative bodies and governmental activity. By contrast, such separation of powers does not exist in the German Democratic Republic. GDR publications are quite specific about the function of the law and the judiciary. They are to serve the development of socialist relations between citizens, to uphold socialist legality and to protect and enhance the workers' and farmers' state. The Supreme Court itself controls the work of all other courts, and is accountable to the People's Chamber, or if the latter is in recess to the Council of State. The People's Chamber appoints the judges to the Supreme Court. In fact, all chief justices, judges, lay justices and members of lay courts are elected either by the People's Chamber, the regional or district councils, or directly elected by the public, and they are accountable to those who elected them and may be removed by these bodies. It is interesting to note that the vast majority of public prosecutors are members of the Socialist Unity Party. On the other hand, the constitution states categorically that all judges are independent and subject only to the law. Yet according to the SED party programme, socialist law is an expression of working-class power, and article 94 of the constitution stipulates that only persons loyally devoted to the people and their socialist state may be judges; also, according to the constitution the Marxist-Leninist party is the leading and guiding force in socialist society.

There is undoubtedly a continuous drive to involve as many people as possible in the legal process. The new civil code of 1976 had been a matter of widespread public debate which resulted in over 4000 submissions being made to the People's Chamber. Apart from the social courts there are road safety committees, safety inspectors, etc. operating on a voluntary basis. Citizens are strongly encouraged to participate in crime prevention and crime reporting. According to GDR statistics, crime figures have decreased considerably since 1950. Much is made in GDR publications of the rehabilitationary character of the legal processes, yet when court proceedings are reported in the media it is at times difficult for the outsider to detect much of an attempt at re-education or rehabilitation.[2]

Anyone visiting the GDR from the UK (or even more so from the Scandinavian countries) will be struck by the high numbers of uniforms on the streets in towns and cities. Apart from the members of the armed forces, these are worn by the People's Police. This high uniformed police presence would appear to indicate an acute internal and external security awareness. If GDR crime statistics are taken as valid, it could be argued that the GDR police forces are primarily involved in a system of preventative law enforcement, rather than actual law enforcement and detection of crime. At present the uniformed police presence is no longer paralleled by prominent official statements on the subject; in his report to the 11th Congress of the SED in April 1986, Erich Honecker devoted a mere six lines to matters of law and public order. In Walter Ulbricht's report to the 3rd party conference of the SED in 1952 law and public order issues figured far more prominently.[3]

The German People's Police consists of the uniformed branch, the traffic police, the CID, the transport police, and the passport and immigration department. The police authority is the Minister of the Interior. The People's Police has very similar remits to that of western democracies, but it is also responsible for the training of factory militia units. These *Kampfgruppen*, which are recruited at factory and plant level, originally had the function of protecting factories, industrial plant, and other workplaces. In recent years their function has been that of a territorial army or home guard; this force of 400,000 men is virtually an SED army. The People's Police has a strength of 73,000, not including the transport police of 8000 men and 15,000 police officers who are specifically responsible for the constant protection of factories, public offices, etc. These figures themselves represent a police density which is much higher than in the Federal Republic and twice that of the UK. A further important aspect of the People's Police is that it is quite openly presented not only as a means of guaranteeing and enforcing "public order and security" but also as a means for the construction of socialism.

A further important agency responsible for internal security is the Ministry for State Security, or State Security Service of the GDR (*Stasi* or *SD*). The Ministry for State Security encompasses the functions of a secret political police, the office of an investigation bureau with executive powers for political crimes, and of information gathering and surveillance. It was established by law in 1950. Its present head is Erich Mielke (appointed 1957), who is also a member of the People's Chamber, an *ex officio* member of the Council of Ministers, a member of the Central Committe of the SED since 1950, a full member of the Politburo since 1976, and an army general since 1980. The Ministry of State Security probably employs in excess of 20,000 officers who enjoy military rank, and is reportedly supported by between 60,000 and 80,000 informants. Because of the nature of its work, details of its work are very limited and at best sporadic. On the other hand, its public existence as a ministry with all its offices at regional, district, and enterprise level ensures that all GDR citizens know about it and its remits and functions. On the occasion of Mielke's 80th birthday the SED official newspaper *Neues Deutschland* carried a four-page congratulatory letter by the Central Committee outlining Mielke's functions. The only function omitted was that of espionage, which for example in the 1970s resulted in the resignation of Willy Brandt as chancellor of the Federal Republic because an SD spy, Günter Guillaume, had worked in his chancellery.[4]

A very high profile is accorded to external security matters. The National People's Army (*NVA*) was founded on 1 March 1956 and is totally integrated into the Warsaw Pact. Conscription has been in force in the GDR since 1962. According to the Constitution and the SED programme the People's Army is a socialist army whose task it is to defend the GDR's achievements against external aggression and to strengthen the Warsaw Pact. The armed services recognize the leadership of the SED and acknowledge and encourage the SED's growing role in their ranks. An integral part of training in the People's Army is devoted to Marxism-Leninism and political education. The SED has its own party organizations within the armed services, as does the FDJ. Virtually all officers are members of the SED. GDR publications intended for circulation in Western countries are quite open about the socialist character of the NVA.

In his report to the 5th meeting of the Central Committee of the SED, Werner Felfe, speaking on behalf of the Politburo, emphasized the importance of national defence and the GDR's specific position as a front-line state. Felfe projected an image of the GDR where virtually every GDR citizen has been mobilized for the defence of the country. In that sense the GDR's defence capability in human terms is therefore much greater than the approximately 170,000 presently serving in the National People's Army.

Documents

D105 From the official handbook "The German Democratic Republic": on the administration of justice, 1984:

The functions of the judicial system in the GDR are to uphold socialist legality and to protect and enhance the workers' and farmers' state. It safeguards freedom and a life in peace, the rights and the dignity of man.

The law courts in the GDR — the Supreme Court, the county and district courts — form part of the integrated judicial system. The Supreme Court is the highest organ of justice. It is answerable to the People's Chamber or, when the latter is in recess, to the Council of State.

For many years now, experienced workers, co-operative farmers and other working people of both sexes have sat on the bench as lay judges on a par with professional judges. They are involved in the assessment of legal proceedings, the collective reform of offenders and in supporting the activities of lay courts.

Lay courts work in the form of **grievance commissions** at enterprise level and **arbitration commissions** in residential areas. The former deal chiefly with labour disputes, but also — just like the latter — with petty offences and minor civil matters.

The **Department of Public Prosecutions** is headed by the Prosecutor General and ensures strict observance and correct application of the law in order to protect the socialist society and the state as well as the rights of citizens.

The **German People's Police** works to protect socialist society and the state, the peaceful life and creative activities of the people and to uphold public order and safety. The German People's Police is charged with preventing and eliminating threats to the life and health of the people and to socialist and personal property. In fulfilling its tasks, it is able to rely on the co-operation of tens of thousands of voluntary helpers, the members of the voluntary fire brigades, road safety committees and other groups who undertake unpaid work to maintain order and security.

(Panorama DDR: *The German Democratic Republic*, Dresden 1984, p. 68)

D106 From the foreign press agency's booklet on the GDR legal system, 1978:

1. A new society requires new law

A new Civil Code, adopted by the People's Chamber (Parliament) after years of preparatory work, came into effect in the GDR on January 1, 1976. It superseded the **Bürgerliches Gesetzbuch** dating from 1896 which had until then remained partly in force.

The enactment of a new body of civil law, one of the major objectives set by the 8th Congress of the Socialist Unity Party of Germany (SED) in June 1971, marked the end of a process through which the entire system of law inherited from the past has been replaced by a new one. New laws have now been passed to cover all areas of human activity to suit the conditions and requirements of socialist construction. They include the Labour Code, the Family Code, the Socialist Education Act, the Youth Act, the Local Government Act and the Penal Code.

The radical transformation of society effected on the territory of the GDR since 1945 necessitated this remoulding of the legal system. The whole of national life was reorganized on anti-fascist, democratic and, subsequently, socialist lines, giving rise to a social system differing fundamentally from all previous systems. The regeneration of all forms of existence of human society in socialism makes it possible and, indeed, mandatory to create qualitatively new law, socialist law.

The class nature of the law
Law and justice are not immutable. At every stage of development, human society produces a particular kind of law and legal concepts determined by the interests of the ruling class.

The GDR is well on its way to a fully-fledged socialist society. Socialism has been put on a firm footing with industry and agriculture operating under socialist conditions. The commanding heights of the economy — industrial enterprises, mines, banks and transport services — are in the hands of the whole people. The farmers have voluntarily pooled their land in co-operatives to introduce socialist methods of production. Most of the craftsmen have also joined together in socialist co-operatives. A socialist planned economy has been organized on the basis of social ownership of the means of production.

At the present stage, working people's efforts are directed towards developing an advanced socialist society more fully, thereby laying the foundations for the gradual transition to communism. The activity of the state and of society at large is geared to the implementation of the central policy outlined in the Programme of the SED. Its main idea is to secure further increases in the material living standards and cultural level of the people by ensuring a high rate of growth of socialist production, increased efficiency, scientific and technological progress and growing labour productivity. People in the GDR feel in increasingly concrete terms that the fruits of their labour accrue to themselves and that it pays to pull one's weight for the good of the community. The identity of individual and social interests proves to be the mainspring of human activity in a socialist society.

In the course of the revolutionary changes that have taken place in the GDR law and justice has acquired a completely new content and function. The working people, who exercise all state power, make and administer their own law. Their legal system serves the interests of the working people, it helps to safeguard their achievements and to encourage progress in all fields of social endeavor.

A major function of socialist law is to provide a framework for the management and planning of the economy and other areas of national life, for the organization and management of affairs in enterprises and administrative departments and for labour relations. The object in mind is to ensure that the people use their common property to the best advantage, that the principle of reward according to merit is fully applied in practice and that the unity between economic and social policies is guaranteed. Socialist law encourages citizens to participate in public and economic affairs, in education and cultural development on the broadest possible scale.

The leading role of the working-class party

A new, socialist type of law does not come into being spontaneously, just as the socialist State does not emerge and develop by itself. The Marxist-Leninist party is the leading and guiding force in socialist society. Its guiding hand is also felt in the development of the socialist legal system and in the administration of justice.

The Marxist-Leninist party and its top bodies are not administrative power centres as anti-communist propaganda tries to convince people. The party of the working class and its Central Committee carry great authority. This is not authority exercised by an oligarchy remote from the people. Rather, this authority rests on the ideological and organizational unity of the party as an alliance of people who share the same beliefs and display a high measure of discipline in carrying out party decisions adopted in accordance with democratic rules. The party carries great authority because its scientifically substantiated policy meets objective requirements and reflects the interests of all working people, because the party maintains the closest possible ties with workers in town and country and because its members everywhere are known for their devotion to the needs of the working population, to the cause of socialism.

The party of the working class does not make the law, but it issues guidelines for the overall development of society, including the legal system. The Programme of the SED, adopted by the 9th Congress in May 1976, includes a chapter devoted to the question of making the legal system still more effective. The party sees to it that laws are drafted which take account of current and future conditions of development, that citizens take part in the law-making process and that their experience is duly taken into consideration.

In its entire ideological work it lays much stress on bringing about voluntary respect for the law. Party members are expected to set an example to others in upholding legality and promoting a general sense of responsibility for preventing violations of the law and maintaining public order, discipline and security.

[. . .]

To strengthen the socialist legal system — an important task for the party of the working class.

The systematic development of the socialist legal system to reflect the degree of maturity of socialist society and the upholding of legal protection and justice are an integral part of the policy pursued by the SED. Socialist law is an expression of working class power. It serves to further the interests of working people, to protect the socialist system, civil freedoms and human dignity. The establishment of optimum rules of law, especially in the economic sector and in the relationship between the countries fraternally allied in the socialist community will assume great importance.

It is a major task of the authorities, social organizations and every single citizen to encourage people to observe the socialist rules of law of their own free will, to protect socialist property, including from damage, loss and fire, and to exercise discipline and a high degree of vigilance. The strict enforcement of socialist legality requires that violations of the law must be punished appropriately.

The work of the judiciary and the security organs will be linked still more closely with public activities to enforce socialist legality and to ensure order and security, and the rights of social courts will be expanded.

(From the Programme of the Socialist Unity Party of
Germany, adopted at the 9th Congress in May 1976)

Freedom and human dignity are guaranteed
(From the Constitution of the GDR)

Article 19

(1) The German Democratic Republic guarantees to all citizens the exercise of their rights and participation in guiding social development. It guarantees socialist legality and legal security.

(2) Respect for and protection of the dignity and freedom of the individual are mandatory for all state organs, all social forces and each individual citizen.

The construction and tasks of justice

Article 90

(1) The administration of justice serves socialist legality and helps protect and develop the German Democratic Republic, its state and its social system. It protects freedom, a life of peace and human rights and dignity.

(2) It is the joint concern of socialist society, its state and all citizens to combat and prevent crime and other violations of the law.

(3) Citizens' participation in the administration of justice is guaranteed. Details are laid down by law.

Article 91

The generally accepted standards of international law relating to the punishment of war crimes and crimes against peace and humanity are directly valid law. Crimes of this sort do not fall under the statute of limitations.

Article 92

Jurisdiction in the German Democratic Republic is exercised by the Supreme Court, the county courts, the district courts and the social courts, within the framework of the tasks assigned them by law. In military matters jurisdiction is exercised by the Supreme Court, military tribunals and military courts.

Article 93

(1) The Supreme Court is the highest organ of jurisdiction.

(2) The Supreme Court directs the jurisdiction of the courts on the basis of the Constitution, the laws and other statutory regulations of the German Democratic Republic. It ensures the uniform application of the law by all courts.

(3) The Supreme Court is responsible to the People's Chamber and, between its sessions, to the Council of State.

Article 94

(1) Only persons loyally devoted to the people and their socialist state, and endowed with a high measure of knowledge, experience, human maturity and character may be judges.

(2) The democratic election of all judges, lay justices and members of social courts guarantees that justice will be administered by men and women from all classes and sections of the people.

Article 95
All judges, lay justices and members of social courts are elected either by Parliament and local government bodies or directly by the citizens. They are accountable to their electors for their work. They may be recalled by their electors if they violate the Constitution or the law, or commit a serious breach of their duties.

Article 96
(1) Judges, lay justices and members of social courts are independent in their administration of justice. They are bound only by the Constitution, the laws and other statutory regulations of the German Democratic Republic.
(2) Lay justices exercise their function as judges to the full extent and have the same voting rights as professional judges.

Article 97
In order to safeguard the socialist state and social system and the rights of citizens, the Prosecutions Branch supervises the strict adherence to socialist legality on the basis of laws and other statutory regulations. It protects citizens from violations of the law. The Prosecutions Branch directs the struggle against crime and ensures that persons who have committed crimes are brought to justice.

Article 98
(1) The Prosecutions Branch is headed by the Director of Public Prosecutions.
(2) The district and county public prosecutors and the military prosecutors are subordinate to the Director of Public Prosecutions.
(3) Prosecutors are appointed and recalled by the Director of Public Prosecutions, are responsible to him and are bound by his instructions.
(4) The Director of Public Prosecutions is responsible to the People's Chamber and, between its sessions, to the Council of State.

Social courts — a form of direct participation in the administration of justice.
(From the Social Courts Act of 11 June 1968)
Section 1
(1) Social courts are elected bodies to promote self-discipline and responsibility on the part of people. They are a firm integral part of the social legal system and socialist democracy. They make an important contribution to fighting and preventing breaches of the law and settling legal disputes.
(2) The social courts represent a method by which GDR citizens exercise their right to participate in the administration of justice.

Section 2
(1) Disputes and arbitration commissions, as social courts, exercise juris-

diction according to the tasks defined for them by law.

(2) The members of the social courts are independent in their administration of justice. They are bound only by the Constitution, laws and other statutory regulations of the German Democratic Republic.

Section 3

The activities of the social courts serve to safeguard the socialist legality system, and make an especial contribution to:

the safeguarding of citizens' rights and legally protected interests,

the formation of socialist attitudes by individual citizens to one another and to their state,

supporting the trade unions in exercising their constitutional right to participation in decision making at work,

encouraging people's creative potential and improving social relations at the place of work and in residential areas.

Civil law serving the people

(From the GDR Civil Code of 19 June 1975)

Section 1

(1) Further increasing the material and cultural living standards of the people and their development into fully moulded socialist personalities are fundamental tasks of socialist society. These tasks are also served by civil law in the German Democratic Republic.

(2) GDR civil law further develops the basic rights and duties of GDR citizens as laid down in the Constitution. It regulates relations between individual citizens and their places of work and one another which are to contribute toward satisfying their material and cultural needs. It protects public property, the individual and the personal property of individual citizens.

Section 7

Every citizen shall have the right to respect for his personality, especially his honour and standing, his name, his image, his copyrights, and other similarly protected rights to carry out creative activity. By the same token, the individual citizen shall be bound to respect the personalities of other citizens and their rights.

Section 33

(1) All citizens shall have the right to protection against anyone who unlawfully damages their property or adversely affects its use.

Section 94

(1) The socialist state guarantees each citizen and his family the right to accommodation. State housing policy consists in building new housing, modernization, extension and alteration of housing stock, the maintenance and rational use thereof and the fair allocation of living space.

Section 96

In order to guarantee the citizen's basic right to accommodation and to ensure that living space is allocated fairly, all housing shall be controlled by the government with the participation of citizens' committees formed at work and in neighbourhoods. Control is carried out according to the applicable regulations.

Section 120

(1) Every tenant shall have the right to protection against eviction. Tenancy can only be terminated against the tenant's will in the cases stipulated in this act if the landlord succeeds in an application to a court.

Section 148

(1) On purchase of any goods a guarantee must be provided by the vendor. This shall guarantee that the goods adhere to the government quality and safety regulations and that they are serviceable and in proper condition, and that they are fit for the purpose confirmed by the manufacture or the purpose for which they are bought. It shall also guarantee that the goods keep these qualities during the guarantee period providing they are used correctly.

(2) The guarantee covers qualities which are either guaranteed by the vendor or manufacturer, and qualities which are necessary for the particular use agreed upon for the article.

(3) Guarantees and guarantee periods cannot be nullified or limited by contracts.

Basic principles of criminal law
(From the GDR Penal Code of 12 January 1968)

Section 4

The dignity of man, his freedom and his rights are protected by the Penal Laws of the socialist state.

Respect for human dignity, which socialist society also practises towards the offender, is an inalienable precept in the application of criminal law by state and society and in the execution of any sentence passed.

A person may only be prosecuted and brought to justice in strict accordance with the law. An action can only be prosecuted if, at the time of its committal, it was a crime according to the law, if the accused acted culpably and if guilt can be proven beyond any shadow of a doubt. Laws with retroactive effect and the analogous use of criminal laws to the disadvantage of the accused are not permitted.

The rights of the individual, privacy of mail and telecommunication, and inviolability of the home are guaranteed. These rights can only be limited to the extent that the law allows and when absolutely unavoidable. Arrest and detention can only be carried out in accordance with the law.

No one may be regarded as guilty of a crime until his guilt has been proven beyond any doubt in legal proceedings carried out by a court or social judicial body and conviction has been legally pronounced.

The right to defence is guaranteed.

Penalties within the meaning of this Code may only be pronounced by a court. No one may be deprived of his legal judge. Special courts are not permitted.

[. . .]

Can crime rates be reduced?

The GDR has proven that a socialist society can provide all the necessary conditions for success in the fight against crime.

In the past years it has proved possible to reduce considerably the number of crimes. In fact, even in the very early years after liberation from fascism it was possible to greatly limit the number of crimes committed. This was not simply due to the solving of problems caused by the war, as in the following years further decreases were achieved even if, from time to time, setbacks were suffered.

Since 1950, the total number of criminal offences has decreased by more than two thirds. Until 1950, the average annual total of criminal offences committed in the GDR was registered as approximately 470,000. For the period from 1970 to 1975 it was approximately 125,000. This is only a small fraction of the crime rates found in capitalist countries. The worst forms of serious crime have been eradicated in the GDR. Crimes such as banknote forgery, white slavery, bank robbery, drugs offences and kidnapping have not been seen in the GDR for a long time. In the GDR there is no "underworld", no organized or professional crime, no gangsters. Of the total number of punishable offences committed, only 4.5 per cent are true crimes and of the rest many are only minor offences which can be handled by social courts.

This proves that industrialization, urbanization, technological progress and increased consumption do not necessarily lead to a rise in the crime rate. The GDR is one of the leading industrialized countries and yet its steady economic growth and increase in living standards do not result in a rise in the number of punishable offences. On the contrary, these factors are making it easier to prevent crime instead.

What is expected of socialist criminal law?

The social conditions created by socialism must thus be systematically used to their fullest extent in order to achieve further progress in reducing crime. The legal basis for this in the GDR is the 1968 Penal Code. Large sections of the population had an important say in the formulation of this code and when it was drafted in 1967 it enjoyed wide public discussion. This resulted in 8,141 suggestions from some 500,000 citizens on how the code could be improved. These suggestions were given the fullest possible consideration.

Socialist criminal law is not merely intended to justly punish offenders but is mainly concerned with the prevention of crime. The code contains exact stipulations on what actions are considered as punishable offences (e.g., theft, fraud, assault and battery, etc.) and what penalties may be imposed.

The Penal Code expressly turns to all citizens, government and social bodies and work-teams requiring that they be alert to any activities hostile toward socialism and a life of peace in the GDR and to all forms of illegality and irresponsibility. It calls on everyone to take an active part in preventing and detecting crime, removing the causes for it and bringing the guilty persons to justice. Government and public institutions and organizations should co-operate closely with the population to ensure that within their individual fields of responsibility crimes are prevented by scientific man-agement and education. It is the duty of all judicial authorities to use their experience to help firms, social organizations and the people themselves in the prevention of crime and the social rehabilitation of criminals.

Socialist criminal law protects peace, the most valuable human asset, and the socialist state, where freedom and respect for human dignity is guaran-teed. It protects the national economy and public property, as these are the things which enable man to transform his creative powers into peaceful work for the benefit of society and for the benefit of himself. On this basis, socialist criminal law guarantees the protection of every individual citizen, his life, his health, his dignity and his rights.

[. . .]

Punishment is not revenge
Respect for human dignity, which socialist society also practises toward the offender, is a vital part of the administration of justice and the execution of the sentence. In prosecution proceedings the rights of the citizen are only allowed to be limited as much as is legally permissible and absolutely necessary. Revenge is not taken on the wrongdoer, the State takes no retaliatory measures. The reformatory nature of the GDR's criminal law makes it impossible that sentencing should have as its aim the physical or mental suffering of the offender, or his degradation and humiliation. The only point to imposing a penalty is to reform the wrongdoer so that he can once again become a useful and disciplined member of society. This gives the whole concept of punishment a qualitatively new content and morally and humanly justifies the idea of force contained in imposing a penalty as it helps the criminal find a new place in society.

[. . .]

The humanist aims of sentencing are complemented by the great variety of ways in which punishment can be served. For many years, primary import-ance has not been given to imprisonment. In order to re-educate an offender it is by no means always necessary to impose a term of imprisonment. The very classification of punishable offences take account of this. On the whole, indictable offences may be punished with sentences of two or more years imprisonment. Summary or lesser offences are generally handled in a way which involves no imprisonment or criminal proceedings before a social court; more serious misdemeanours may be punished by imprisonment, but never for a term of more than two years.

[...]

The maximum term of imprisonment (except of course life imprisonment) is 15 years, the minimum six months, in exceptional cases three months. This is the result of previous experience which has shown that a short period of imprisonment in terms of days or a few weeks does not usually have any educational effect. Petty offences are not required to be dealt with by imprisonment in the GDR.

An exception is constituted by disciplinary detention of between one to six weeks for hooliganism or crimes of a vandalous nature. Section 41 of the Penal Code states that such terms are to be imposed "when this is necessary in order to promptly and emphatically discipline the culprit." During this period the prisoners carry out some form of socially useful work.

Lastly there is "Arbeitserziehung" which is a specific form of imprisonment for people who criminally endanger public order through asocial behaviour. It is designed to accustom people who stubbornly avoid work to regular disciplined work. The maximum sentence for this is two years, for second and subsequent offences five years.

People can only be sentenced to "Arbeitserziehung" by a court of law and only if the person in question really stubbornly refuses to do any form of work; it is not used for mere cases of lack of discipline at work. This punishment is reserved exclusively for asocial behaviour which has taken on a criminal nature.

Penal servitude, which was still in existence before the introduction of the new Penal Code, was abolished because it was felt that this form of punishment represented such a blow to a person's self-respect that it contradicted the aim of rehabilitating the offender and made it harder for him to adjust and find a new place in society.

(Panorama DDR: *Law and justice in a socialist society: The legal system of the German Democratic Republic*, Dresden 1978, pp. 8 ff., 54 ff., 62 ff., 37, 38 f., 42, 43 f.).

D107 Report on the plenary meeting of the Supreme Court of the GDR, 16 December 1987:

On Wednesday, the plenary meeting of the Supreme Court of the GDR discussed questions concerning the further consolidation of socialist legality in criminal proceedings.

In the report on the discussion it was emphasized that in socialist criminal proceedings the rights of the citizens are strictly upheld in accordance with legality, equality, and humanity.

The President of the Supreme Court of the GDR, Dr. Günter Sarge, praised the part played by the courts in strengthening citizens' trust in their security within the law and in encouraging their readiness to help the authorities in the maintenance of order and security.

The courts were placed under an obligation to continue to raise the quality and social effectiveness of criminal proceedings.

(*Neues Deutschland* vol. 42 no. 296 of 17 December 1987)

D108 Court report from Neues Deutschland, 23 December 1987:

Severe sentences for hooligans
Principal defendant receives four-year prison sentence

The sentence passed by the Central Berlin Municipal Court on 3 December 1987 on four hooligans who had taken part in serious disturbances in front of and in the Zion Church on 17 October 1987 was on Tuesday altered as a result of an appeal by the Public Prosecutor.

The Berlin City Court bases its judgment on the fact that the defendants had formed a mob and had carried out their violent acts in an organized, brutal and ruthless manner. They had shouted fascist and terrorist slogans which had given rise to fear and anxiety among the audience of a concert in the Zion Church. Order and security in the areas had been disturbed considerably.

The judgment makes it clear that excesses like this one, in which skinheads from West Berlin were involved, will not be tolerated. The constitution and law of our state demand that firm action be taken against all manifestations of a fascist or racist nature and that the security of our citizens be guaranteed at all times and in all places. Accordingly, the City Court acceded to the Public Prosecutor's application and sentenced the defendants to severe jail sentences in line with the extent of their participation: Ronny B. to four years, Torsten B. to two years and six months, Sven E. to one year eight months and Frank B. to one year six months imprisonment.[5]

(*Neues Deutschland* vol. 42 no. 301 of 23 December 1987)

D109 From Werner Felfe's address to the Fifth Meeting of the Central Committee of the SED, 16 December 1987:

In August the Politburo received a report from the Public Prosecutor General of the GDR and from the Ministry of the Interior on the Law on the Enforcement of Custodial Sentences. The penal system has its firm place in the totality of society's efforts to restrain criminality. In accordance with our constitution, the individual human being is at the centre of all the efforts of the socialist state. Our society respects the human dignity of every individual, even if he has been sentenced to imprisonment. The humanist nature of our policies determines the way in which prison sentences are enforced. The law at present in force has proved itself in practice. Members of the penal services carry out their duties in a responsible manner, in close co-operation with society, and are guided in their work by the incontrovertible principles of legality, justice, and equality before the law.

The enemies of socialism make great efforts to penetrate our society with anti-socialist ideologies. In order to divert attention from the symptoms of increasing brutality and violence and the revival of fascist attitudes and excesses in the Federal Republic of Germany and West Berlin, they try to manipulate individuals and groups in the GDR into acts of hooliganism, sometimes involving slogans from the Nazi period, against the socialist state and its citizens.

In our workers' and farmers' state, which is realizing the legacy of the anti-fascist resistance, there is no place for plans and machinations of this kind. Firm action is taken against them in accordance with legal requirements.

(*Neues Deutschland* vol. 42 no. 296 of 17 December 1987)

D110 From the Central Committee's report to the Eleventh Party Congress of the SED, April 1986:

The judicial authorities are making substantial contributions towards strengthening socialist legality. Administering justice with a profound sense of responsibility on the principle that all people are equal in the eyes of the law, they are adding to the public's confidence in the legal system as a characteristic feature of our socialist society.

(*Report of the Central Committee of the Socialist Unity Party of Germany to the 11th Congress of the SED*, Rapporteur: Erich Honecker, Dresden 1986, p. 91.

D111 From the preamble to the decree by the Council of Ministers on the People's Police, 9 December 1964:

The German People's Police . . .shall guarantee public order and security in the comprehensive construction of socialism in the German Democratic Republic, reinforce socialist law, and further the progress of society by foresight and prevention of crime.

(*Gesetzblatt der Deutschen Demokratischen Republik I* 1965, p. 65)

D112 From the Central Committee of the SED's congratulations to Erich Mielke, December 1987:

Dear Comrade Erich Mielke,
   The Central Committee of the Socialist Unity Party of Germany offers you wholehearted congratulations on your 80th birthday. We join our best wishes with thanks for the indefatigable work you do on behalf of the working class and for the benefit of our people. We have a high regard for the outstanding part you have played in strengthening, consolidating and defending our German Democratic Republic.

[. . .]

The formation in 1950 of the Ministry for State Security and its development are inextricably linked to your activities. As a leading official, and as Minister for State Security for more than three decades, you have made an outstanding contribution to the strengthening and all-round protection of the workers' and farmers' power in the German Democratic Republic. Under your leadership the Ministry for State Security has proved its worth as a dependable organ of the socialist state at all periods in our republic's history. For this you deserve the highest esteem from our party and the working people of our country.
   It is fundamentally linked to your own personal commitment to our party's policies that the Ministry for State Security enjoys the trust of our people and is respected and supported by them. In this respect we also acknowledge your activities as a deputy to the People's Chamber and as a member of the Council of Ministers of the GDR. You have always devoted your attention and active support to a stable state security, discipline and order.
   Like you, we are pleased that the German Democratic Republic, as a loyal ally of the Soviet Union and firmly anchored in the socialist family of nations, always lives up to its responsibilities in the struggle for peace and the strengthening of socialism. The alliance between the state security

bodies of the GDR and the Soviet Union and the further development of co-operation with the security bodies of the other fraternal countries commands your particular attention.

(*Neues Deutschland* vol. 42 no. 304 of 28 December 1987)

D113 From Deputy Prime Minister Willi Stoph's declaration on the law setting up the National People's Army, 18 January 1956:

As you know, the Law Supplementing the Constitution of the German Democratic Republic was passed by the People's Chamber on 26 September 1955. The working people have expressed their approval of the supplementation of the constitution in innumerable rallies and statements. They recognize that service in defence of our country and its achievements is an honourable national duty for citizens of the German Democratic Republic. The construction of socialism, the further increase in industrial and agricultural production, and the constant increase in the cultural and social standard of our population can be guaranteed for the long term only if the state organizes the necessary protection.

The working people of the German Democratic Republic call for the creation of a National People's Army to protect the only sovereign, democratic, peace-loving German state, which is closely and indissolubly linked to the great bloc for peace by the Warsaw Treaty on Friendship, Co-operation and Mutual Support and also by the State Treaty between the German Democratic Republic and the Union of Soviet Socialist Republics.

The creation of a well-trained National People's Army with modern equipment in the German Democratic Republic is thus fully in accord with the interests of the working population and is an essential undertaking. No responsible democrat and patriot will close his eyes to developments in West Germany; the conclusion that must be drawn from these is that the German Democratic Republic must take all measures to ensure that the imperialists and militarists are kept in check and all their experiments are frustrated. (*applause*)

Until now only police forces have existed in the German Democratic Republic. These include the branches of the People's Police quartered in barracks. However, it is now time to create a National People's Army in our Republic in accordance with the elementary right of every independent sovereign state. The National People's Army will consist of land, air, and sea forces necessary for the defence of the German Democratic Republic . . .

In contrast to the West German mercenary units, which wear American uniforms, our National People's Army will wear German uniforms which conform to the national traditions of our people. There are important progressive traditions in our people's military history, and these also find their expression in military uniform. However, German imperialism and fascism sacrificed the uniform as a symbol of military and patriotic honour, so that the uniform became the embodiment of lack of freedom, oppression, terror, the epitome of militarism.

In the National People's Army, our uniform will take on a truly patriotic meaning as an expression of our readiness to defend our democratic attainments with determination. It is intended that equipping our People's Army with a uniform in line with the national tradition of the German people in its colour, its cut and the way it is worn shall make manifest social progress in our state and emphasize that what is coming into being is a new army of the German people and its working class, free of any aggressive aims.

The National People's Army will be equipped with modern technology and arms, and trained by the most modern methods on the basis of progressive military science.

Service in the National People's Army is an honourable service for the German people and for our state of workers and farmers. Supported by the love of our workers and farmers and the intelligentsia, our National People's Army will be ready and able to safeguard peace, to protect the Republic, and to fulfil honourably the German Democratic Republic's obligations towards the other states participating in the treaty.

(*Stenographische Berichte Volkskammer, 2. Wahlperiode, 10. Sitzung*, pp. 301 ff.)

D114 Law on the Creation of the National People's Army and of the Ministry for National Defence, 18 January 1956:

It is the basic duty of our democratic, sovereign, peace-loving state to protect the workers' and farmers' power and the achievements of working people and to safeguard their peaceful work. The re-establishment of aggressive militarism in West Germany and the creation of the West German mercenary army is a constant threat to the German people and all the peoples of Europe.

To increase the defensive capacity and security of our German Democratic Republic, the People's Chamber passes the following law on the basis of Articles 5 and 112 of the Constitution of the German Democratic Republic:

§1(1) A "National People's Army" is to be formed.

(2) The "National People's Army" consists of land, air, and sea forces necessary for the defence of the German Democratic Republic. The numerical strength of these forces is limited in accordance with the tasks

of protecting the territory of the German Democratic Republic and defending its borders and airspace.

§2(1) A "Ministry for National Defence" is to be formed.

(2) The "Ministry for National Defence" organizes and controls the National People's Army (land, air, and sea forces) on the basis and in implementation of the laws, decrees and resolutions of the People's Chamber and the Council of Ministers of the German Democratic Republic.

(3) The duties of the "Ministry for National Defence" are determined by the Council of Ministers.

§3 This law comes into force with its proclamation.

(*Gesetzblatt der Deutschen Demokratischen Republik I*, 1956, p. 81.)

D115 From the Law on General Compulsory Military Service, 24 January 1962:

§1 General compulsory military service

(1) In accordance with the will and determination of the citizens of the German Democratic Republic to defend our socialist country, general compulsory military service is introduced for the fulfilment of the honourable national duty of protecting our fatherland and the achievements of our working people.

(2) The right to serve voluntarily in the National People's Army is unaffected. The provisions of this law apply as appropriate except where legal requirements provide for a different treatment.

§2 Matters covered by general compulsory military service

General compulsory military service includes the obligation:

    a) to present oneself to be registered,

    b) to appear for interview and medical examination,

    c) to carry out both active military service and reservist military service in the National People's Army,

    d) to inform the authorities of any change in personal circumstances.

§3 Citizens subject to compulsory military service

(1) Military service is compulsory for male citizens of the German Democratic Republic aged between 18 and 50. For officers it ends with the completion of the 60th year.

(2) If the country is placed on a defence footing, all male citizens of the German Democratic Republic aged between 18 and 60 are subject to compulsory military service.

(3) Stateless persons domiciled in the German Democratic Republic may be conscripted for compulsory military service by order of the National Defence Council of the German Democratic Republic.

(*Gesetzblatt der Deutschen Demokratischen Republik I*, 1962, pp. 2 ff.)

D116 From an article in Neues Deutschland by Colonel H. Herbel, 3 February 1962:

In order to maintain peace and the life of the nation, the GDR as the German state which stands for peace and the nation must be protected militarily. Anyone threatening this state is an enemy of peace and of the nation. If this enemy shoots at us, then we must and will shoot back.

We repeat: the enemy are the West German armaments multi-millionaires, the enemy is Lübke who is so eager to shoot, Strauss the NATO war planner, Hitler's generals like Heusinger, Foertsch and their like, who dream of "wiping out" our peaceful German state with atomic weapons.

But all those who obey the order to take criminal action against peace and the nation also become the enemy. People such as Lübke, Strauss and Heusinger cannot and do not wish to carry out their plans with their own hands any more than Kaiser Wilhelm, Noske or Hitler could or wished to. Like the latter group, they again want to employ the people's hands. So they lie to the people and stir them up with propaganda, draft them into their mercenary army and drill them for war. But for the workers, farmers and employees and all ordinary people in West Germany that would be a war fought on behalf of their own enemies and against their own brothers, against their own state, the state which — whether or not they realize it — is looking after their interests.

The deep tragedy of the situation in West Germany is that our own actual brothers could be among those who are to be inflamed against us. But would this mean that our enemy's cause would then stop being our enemy's cause, the cause of people like Lübke, Strauss, Heusinger? Would it cease to be NATO's anti-German campaign? Would the shots fired at us no longer be shots? Breaking the peace no longer breaking the peace? Murder no longer murder? Are we to let them shoot and raze and burn as the Heusingers' armies have always razed and burned? Against their own people? Are we to let them kindle and spread the fire of a war in which they would inevitably themselves perish when it became a world holocaust?

What a good German must do

Many will say, "My brother, my brother-in-law, my nephew in West Germany or even in the West German army won't do anything like that. He doesn't want to shoot at us. He is not for nuclear war, he is against it. He is not a Heusinger, he is good, peace-loving German."

We have no doubt that this is how he sees himself. But we also state quite clearly that the only good, peace-loving Germans in West Germany today are those who take an active stance against the preparations for war and the Bonn policy of making Germans shoot at Germans. Anyone who goes along with people like Lübke and Strauss and falls for the revanchist propaganda of the so-called refugee organizations is not acting like a good German; but nor is anyone who watches the unthinkable being prepared and merely shrugs his shoulders.[6]

(*Neues Deutschland* vol. 17 no. 34 of 3 February 1962)

D117 From the Constitution of the German Democratic Republic, 8 April 1968:

Article 7

(1) The state authorities guarantee the inviolability of the territory of the German Democratic Republic including its airspace and territorial waters and protection and exploitation of the continental shelf.

(2) The German Democratic Republic organizes the defence of the country and the protection of the socialist order and the peaceful life of citizens. The National People's Army and the other national defence forces protect the socialist achievements of the people against all external attacks. The National People's Army carries on a close military co-operation with the armies of the Soviet Union and other socialist states in the interests of preserving peace and security.

(*Die Verfassung der Deutschen Demokratischen Republik*, Berlin 1968)

D118 From the Programme of the SED: on national defence, May 1976:

Together with the fraternal parties, the Socialist Unity Party of Germany will contribute to strengthening and reinforcing the Warsaw Treaty organization as the main area for the co-ordination of the socialist community's security policy and the military policy. The relations of unbreakable friendship and solidarity existing between the fraternal parties in the socialist countries will be cultivated and unceasingly developed as a vital condition for a co-ordinated foreign policy and for the collective organization of the military protection of the socialist community.

[. . .]

The protection of socialism and peace

The effective protection of socialism and peace requires a co-ordinated foreign policy among the socialist states and concerted action by all forces for peace in the struggle against imperialism. Peaceful co-existence of states with differing social systems can only be secured by struggling against the aggressive forces of imperialism, which remain dangerous and influential.

The arms race kindled by the ruling imperialist forces poses a constant threat to world peace. It engulfs huge amounts of money, that might well be used for the benefit of the peoples.

The maintenance of peace and security requires that defence prepared-ness, including on the part of the German Democratic Republic, be further strengthened. The Socialist Unity Party of Germany will continue to contribute to the solution of this task in firm alliance with the USSR and other socialist countries, maintaining unwavering comradeship-in-arms with the Soviet army and the armed forces of the other fraternal countries.

The safeguarding of peace, of the socialist homeland and its gains, and the defence of the German Democratic Republic is the right and moral obliga-tion of each and every citizen of the GDR. The Party, the state and all social organizations will pay steady and close attention to promoting the pre-paredness and capability of all citizens to protect socialism by military means. The military protection of socialism is ensured by military service in the National People's Army, the frontier force or other armed services, by socialist premilitary training, especially of the younger generation, by education into revolutionary vigilance in the spirit of loyalty to the socialist homeland, the German Democratic Republic, by the continuous strength-ening of the workers' militia, by the work of the Society for Sport and Technology, by the extension of civil defence and the fulfilment of all other defence tasks.

The National People's Army, the frontier force of the GDR, the organs of the Ministry of the Interior and of the Ministry of State Security, the civil defence forces and the workers' militia are under the obligation to maintain at any time and under all conditions a high degree of fighting strength, defence capability and morale in order to protect socialism and peace and guarantee the territorial integrity, inviolability of the frontiers and state security of the German Democratic Republic. Bringing national defence constantly up to date requires a high standard of Marxist-Leninist edu-cation and military training for all those serving in the National People's Army and other armed formations. Proletarian internationalism and so-cialist patriotism, friendship with the Soviet Union, military pro-ficiency and iron discipline, love of the working people and devotion to the ideals of communism — those are the most valuable qualities of the defenders of peace, socialism and communism.

The armed services derive their strength from the leadership provided by the Marxist-Leninist Party, hence the growing role of the Party organiza-tions in all sectors of socialist national defence. The leading role of the Party and the unceasing strengthening of the ties linking the National People's Army and the other armed formations with the working class and all other working people are the guarantee for the accomplishment of all the tasks involved in the protection of peace and socialism.

(*Programme of the Socialist Unity Party of Germany*, Dresden 1976, pp. 65 f., 68 ff.)

D119 From the official handbook "The German Democratic Republic": on the National People's Army, 1984:

The National People's Army (NVA) is the military instrument in the hands of the workers' and farmers' state. Its political mission is determined by the interests and objectives of the working class and the vital interests of the entire population.

The tasks of the NVA are clearly defined in the Constitution, Article 7 of which reads: "The National People's Army and the other national defence bodies protect the socialist achievements of the people against all external attacks. In the interests of the preservation of peace and the security of the socialist state, the National People's Army cultivates close comradeship-in-arms with the armies of the Soviet Union and other socialist states."

The highest command posts in the armed forces are held by tried and tested anti-fascists who have proven their devotion to the cause of the working class and the working people in the struggle against fascism and militarism and who have stood the test in the transformation of society and the construction of socialism. They have substantially influenced the emergence of a new generation of officers acting in keeping with the tradition of the peoples' anti-fascist and revolutionary struggle.

Basic military service lasts 18 months during which period the soldiers of the National People's Army maintain close links with their employers and their jobs are retained for them. Similarly, their civil rights and duties, for instance their right to vote and to be elected and party affiliation, continue to be effective.

(Panorama DDR: *The German Democratic Republic*, Dresden 1984, p. 69)

D120 From Werner Felfe's report on behalf of the Politburo to the Fifth Meeting of the Central Committee of the SED, 16 December 1987:

The extent of our defence efforts is determined by the level of the threat from NATO, as Comrade Erich Honecker stated at the reception for graduates of the military academies held in the Council of State on 26

October. The immediate occasion for this statement was the assessment of the military activities of the NATO states, including their manoeuvres in autumn of this year. NATO was testing the offensive capabilities of their troops in central Europe in particular, on the borders of the GDR and Czechoslovakia and on the Baltic. Aspects of the immediate preparations for war, surprise attacks initiating a war, battlefield operations using traditional, chemical and nuclear weapons, and strikes deep into the hinterland of Warsaw Treaty states were rehearsed. Offensive groupings totalling more than 500,000 men were concentrated on West European territory, with the main concentration in the Federal Republic of Germany.

The National People's Army and the security bodies are able and willing to defend peace in the front line of the community of socialist states. In line with the defensive character of the military doctrine of the member states of the Warsaw Treaty, members of the army, border guards and civilian personnel contribute with great commitment to maintain an approximate military strategic balance at all times as a decisive factor in preventing war. The members of the forces controlled by the Ministry of the Interior and the Ministry for State Security, the Civil Defence and the GDR Customs Administration have been equally dependable in guaranteeing the security of our state and public order, in fulfilment of the class commission from the 11th Party Congress.

Continued far-reaching efforts by society are necessary to maintain the necessary defensive capability at all times. These include ensuring the supply of materials and manpower for national defence and the activities of all armed units, and also socialist military training of the population and pre-military training for young people in the Society for Sports and Technical Pursuits.

(*Neues Deutschland* vol. 42 no. 296 of 17 December 1987)

D121 Report on the verification agreement 23 December 1987:

An agreement has been reached between the governments of the German Democratic Republic and the United States of America on carrying out inspections on the territory of the GDR provided for in the Soviet-American treaty on the destruction of intermediate and short-range missiles. Kurt Nier, the representative of the Minister for Foreign Affairs of the GDR, and Francis Joseph Meehan, the US Ambassador to the GDR, exchanged the relevant notes on Wednesday.

In his discussion with the ambassador, Kurt Nier indicated that with the conclusion of the trilateral agreement with the USSR and the CSSR on 11 December together with the agreement with the USA, the GDR for its part had fulfilled important requirements for a rapid implementation of the intermediate-range missile treaty.

On the basis of the agreement between the GDR and the USA, American inspectors and their teams are granted the right of access to the territory of the German Democratic Republic to carry out the inspection functions laid down. The agreement between the GDR and the USA comes into force simultaneously with the Soviet-American treaty.

(*Neues Deutschland* vol. 42 no. 302 of 24 December 1987)

Notes

1. Whereas the Basic Law in the Federal Republic of Germany is very much in the tradition of eighteenth-century constitutional thinkers such as Montesquieu, this is not the case in the GDR. This is especially true of the separation of powers and the constitutional independence of the administration of justice.
2. In this context it is worth noting that the death penalty was abolished in 1987.
3. On the other hand, there is now much more crime reporting in the GDR press than there was up to the early 1980s.
4. Since Brandt's resignation there have been a number of other cases where GDR spies were discovered in the top echelons of the West German civil service and government departments.
5. An interesting account of the administration of justice in the case of hooliganism is provided for the earlier period by Manfred Bieler in his novel *Maria Morzeck oder das Kaninchen bin ich* (1966), which was not permitted to appear in the GDR. During 1987 and 1988 there has been increasing reporting of hooliganism in the GDR press, with particular reference to meetings at the Brandenburg Gate when rock groups have given open-air concerts on the West Berlin side.
6. Heinrich Lübke was President of the Federal Republic of Germany from 1959–1969. Because of his Nazi past and his unequivocal support for the refugee organizations he was constantly attacked by the GDR. Franz Josef Strauss, Bavarian Prime Minister until his death in 1988, but at that time West Germany's Minister of Defence, was the target of GDR propaganda warfare as a symbol of the West's policy of strength.

6 Foreign Relations

Until well into the 1960s the GDR lived in virtual diplomatic purdah, having been recognized only by the Soviet Union, Bulgaria, Poland, Czechoslovakia, Hungary, Romania, China, North Korea, Albania, Vietnam, Mongolia, Yugoslavia, and Cuba. In 1969 and 1970 there followed a number of other, predominantly Arab countries. The reason behind this lack of international recognition was primarily the Federal Republic's implementation of the so-called "Hallstein Doctrine" of 1956. Within the context of WillyBrandt's *Ostpolitik* this situation changed dramatically in the early 1970s. This "Policy towards the East" not only entailed the conclusion of treaties between the Federal Republic and a number of European socialist states who had recognized the GDR earlier, but it also led to a "normalization" between the FRG and the GDR in the form of the Basic Treaty between the two countries. Consequently, apart from a spate of recognitions of the GDR (131 by 1980) and its admission to international organizations such as the United Nations, the GDR itself had to tackle a number of issues such as the determination of its nationhood and question of citizenship.

Whereas because of its model character for a united Germany the 1949 constitution of the GDR had stated that Germany was an indivisible republic and that there was only one German citizenship, the 1968 constitution had attempted to define a different concept of nationhood and national consciousness by distinguishing the GDR as a "socialist state of the German nation". Adherence to the concept of German nationhood was abandoned in the 1974 amendments to the constitution where the GDR is defined as a "socialist state of workers and farmers", i.e. a political organization under the leadership of the working class and its Marxist-Leninist party. In 1967 the GDR had already provided an unambiguous definition of citizenship which *inter alia* makes it possible to deprive a person of his or her citizenship. More recent aspects of the GDR's policy towards the Federal Republic include Honecker's Gera speech of October 1980 and the "policy of reason". It remains to be seen in how far Honecker's visit to the Federal Republic in

1987 will mark the beginning of a new era, and in how far the "policy of reason" will be a meaningful and fruitful development from the policy of peaceful coexistence as exemplified in the SED party programme of 1976. On the occasion of the 5th meeting of the Central Committee of the SED in December 1987, its secretary Werner Felfe certainly saw it as a successful aspect of the "policy of reason and realism". Key words in Felfe's report were "co-operation" and "dialogue". These concepts of co-operation and dialogue are not restricted to contacts at official governmental level but extend also to contacts with socialist and social democratic parties abroad. Apart from the question of private visits between the two countries, the most important issue is that of trade relations. It is in this respect that the GDR would seem to welcome the concept of a "special relationship" between itself and the FRG, a concept otherwise rejected. Because of the special trade treaties between the two countries, the GDR continues to profit indirectly from EEC treaties since these allow the FRG to classify its own trade with the GDR as domestic trade. GDR goods are thus not subject to the EEC's external tariff and control regulations and can enter the Common Market without restrictions. This special relationship is of considerable importance for GDR exports and "dumping policies".[1]

In terms of foreign trade relationships the German Democratic Republic is in a unique situation inasmuch as it is a "junior domestic partner" in the EEC and an important partner in the highly inte-grated Council for Mutual Economic Assistance (RGW or COME-CON). The GDR's foreign trade target is to conduct two thirds of its trade with the COMECON countries. Apart from military and trade integration, the GDR is manifestly integrated politically too into the "eastern bloc". Article 6 of the constitution lays down the special relationship between the USSR and the GDR, while the SED party programme states categorically that "the all-round strength-ening of the socialist community gathered around the Soviet Union is the foremost foreign policy objective of the Socialist Unity Party".

Whereas the author(s) of the article on foreign policy in the authoritative West German *DDR-Handbuch* (1985) stated quite categorically that a thoroughgoing improvement of relations be-tween China and the GDR could not be expected for the time being, this situation has in the meantime changed dramatically. For two years now *Neues Deutschland* has been carrying articles on a new relationship between the two countries, including Honecker's visit to China. Most recently, in the Politburo's report of December 1987 Werner Felfe devotes considerable space to these new developments. However he fails to mention the development of more cordial relationships between the GDR and Albania, as also reported in *Neues Deutschland* from time to time over the last 18 months. These developments indicate that the GDR is at times moving ahead of its senior partner, the USSR, in foreign policy matters. As regards the countries of the Third World, the GDR has always pursued a vigorous foreign policy, at times independent of the USSR, at times taking the place of the USSR in terms of military or economic involvement. It is of particular interest to note the GDR's military and economic presence in a number of African states, and its policy initiatives in Asia, where the GDR declares itself in favour of a neutral Kampuchea. Undoubtedly the GDR is now a well-respected state in Asia and Africa, a respect not limited to socialist states but also shared by such countries as India and Zambia.[2]

Documents

D122 Bundestag Declaration, 28 June 1956: The Hallstein Doctrine:

. . . The recognition of the German Democratic Republic would mean international recognition of the partition of Germany in two States. Reunification would then no longer present itself as the elimination of a temporary disturbance in the organism of our all-German State: it would change into the infinitely more difficult task of uniting two separate States. The history of the unification of Germany in the 19th century illustrates what that can mean. Were the Federal Republic to take the lead in recognition, she would herself contribute to a state of affairs in which Europe and the world would lose consciousness of the anomaly of the present situation and become resigned to it. She would relieve the Four Powers of their responsibility for the re-establishment of the national unity of Germany, a responsibility which they — including the Soviet Union — have so far always recognized. Instead, she would accord to Pieck, Grotewohl and Ulbricht the right of vetoing any reunification. Furthermore, the recognition of the "German Democratic Republic" would mean that the Federal Republic would relinquish its claim to be the spokesman of the entire German people, a claim established in our constitution and which no Federal Government can ignore.

The Federal Government cannot refrain from making it clear once again that it will feel compelled in future to regard the establishing of diplomatic relations with the so-called German Democratic Republic by third States with which the Federal Republic remains diplomatic relations, as an unfriendly act calculated to intensify and aggravate the partition of Germany. The Federal Government would in such a case have to re-consider its relations to the State in question.

The question has been variously discussed in recent times as to whether or not it is useful and possible to establish relations with Germany's eastern neighbours. The Federal Government has examined this problem in all its detail and has come to the conclusion that, under present circumstances, diplomatic relations cannot be established with those countries. That does not mean that the Federal Government is not interested in the establishment of normal relations with the countries in question.

[...]

(H.Siegler: *The Reunification and Security of Germany*, Bonn 1957, pp. 141-2; repr. from *Politics and Government in the Federal Republic of Germany: Basic Documents*, ed. C.C. Schweitzer et al., Leamington Spa 1984, pp. 298f.)

D123a Treaty on the Basis of Relations Between the Federal Republic of Germany and the German Democratic Republic, 21 December 1972:

The High Contracting Parties,
   In consideration of their responsibility for the preservation of peace,
   Anxious to contribute to *détente* and security in Europe,
   Conscious that the inviolability of frontiers and respect for the territorial integrity and sovereignty of all States in Europe within their present frontiers are a fundamental condition for peace,
   Recognizing that therefore the two German States are to refrain from the threat or use of force in their relations,
   Proceeding from the historical facts and without prejudice to the differing views of the Federal Republic of Germany and the German Democratic Republic on questions of principle, including the national question,
   Desiring to create the conditions for co-operation between the Federal Republic of Germany and the German Democratic Republic for the benefit of the people in the two German States,
   Have agreed as follows:

Article 1
The Federal Republic of Germany and the German Democratic Republic shall develop normal good neighbourly relations with each other on the

basis of equal rights.

[. . .]

Article 3
In accordance with the United Nations Charter, the Federal Republic of Germany and the German Democratic Republic shall settle their disputes exclusively by peaceful means and refrain from the threat or use of force.

They reaffirm the inviolability now and in the future of the border existing between them and undertake fully to respect their territorial integrity.

Article 4
The Federal Republic of Germany and the German Democratic Republic proceed on the assumption that neither of the two States can represent the other internationally or act in its name.

[. . .]

Article 7
The Federal Republic of Germany and the German Democratic Republic state their readiness to regulate practical and humanitarian questions in the process of the normalization of their relations. They will conclude agreements with a view to developing and promoting co-operation in the fields of economics, science and technology, traffic, judicial relations, posts and telecommunications, health, culture, sport, environmental protection, and in other fields, on the basis of the present Treaty and for their mutual benefit. The details have been agreed in the Supplementary Protocol.

Article 8
The Federal Republic of Germany and the German Democratic Republic will exchange permanent missions. They will be established at the respective seat of government.

Practical questions relating to the establishment of the missions will be dealt with separately.

Article 9
The Federal Republic of Germany and the German Democratic Republic are agreed that the present Treaty does not affect the bilateral and multilateral international treaties and agreements previously concluded by them or concerning them.

(Documentation relating to the Federal Government's policy of détente, Press Information Office, Bonn, 1978, pp. 178ff. *Official translation*; repr. from *Politics and Government* . . ., pp. 382 ff).

D123b Letter from the Government of the Federal Republic of Germany to the Government of the German Democratic Republic on German Unity, 21 December 1972:

In connection with the signing today of the Treaty on the Basis of Relations between the Federal Republic of Germany and the German Democratic Republic, the Government of the Federal Republic of Germany has the honour to state that this Treaty does not conflict with the political aim of the Federal Republic of Germany to work for a state of peace in Europe in which the German nation will regain its unity through free self-determination.

(Documentation on détente, repr. from above, p. 384)

D123c Supplementary Protocol to the Treaty on the Basis of Relations between the Federal Republic of Germany and the German Democratic Republic:

I

Re Article 3
The Federal Republic of Germany and the German Democratic Republic have agreed to form a Commission composed of representatives of the Governments of the two States. They will review and, where necessary, renew or supplement the marking of the border existing between the two States and draw up the necessary documentation on the course of the border. In the same way, the Commission will contribute to regulating other problems connected with the course of the border, e.g., water management, energy supply and the prevention of damage

[. . .]

II

Re Article 7
(1) Trade between the Federal Republic of Germany and the German Democratic Republic shall be developed on the basis of the existing agreements.

The Federal Republic of Germany and the German Democratic Republic will conclude long-term agreements with a view to promoting a continuous development on economic relations, adapting outmoded arrangements, and improving the structure of trade.

(2) The Federal Republic of Germany and the German Democratic

Republic state their intention to develop co-operation in the fields of science and technology for their mutual benefit and to conclude the necessary treaties for this purpose.

[. . .]

(4) The Federal Republic of Germany and the German Democratic Republic state their readiness to regulate by treaty their judicial relations as simply and expediently as possible in the interests of those seeking justice, especially in the fields of civil and criminal law.

(5) The Federal Republic of Germany and the German Democratic Republic agree to conclude an agreement on posts and telecommunications on the basis of the Constitution of the Universal Postal Union and the International Telecomunication Convention. They will notify such agreement to the Universal Postal Union (UPU) and the International Telecommunication Union (ITU).

The existing agreements and the procedures beneficial to both sides will be taken over in that agreement.

(6) The Federal Republic of Germany and the German Democratic Republic state their interest in co-operation in the field of health. They agree that the relevant treaty shall also regulate the exchange of medicaments and, as far as possible, the treatment of patients in special clinics and sanatoria.

(7) The Federal Republic of Germany and the German Democratic Republic intend to develop cultural co-operation. To this end they will enter into negotiations on the conclusion of intergovernmental agreements. . . .

(Documentation on détente, repr. from above, pp. 384–5)

D123d Statements on Record

The Federal Republic of Germany states on record:
"Questions of nationality have not been regulated by the Treaty".
The German Democratic Republic states on record:
"The German Democratic Republic proceeds from the assumption that the Treaty will facilitate a regulation of questions of nationality".

(Documentation on détente, repr. from above, p. 385)

D124 Declaration of the Governments of the United States, France, the USSR and Great Britain, 8 June 1973:

The Governments of the United States of America, the French Republic, the Union of Soviet Socialist Republics and the United Kingdom of Great Britain and Northern Ireland, having been represented by their Ambassadors, who held a series of meetings in the building formerly occupied by the Allied Control Council, are in agreement that they will support the applications for membership in the United Nations when submitted by the Federal Republic of Germany and the German Democratic Republic, and affirm in this connection that this membership shall in no way affect the rights and responsibilities of the Four Powers and the corresponding related quadripartite agreements, decisions, and practices.

(*The Federal Republic of Germany, Member of the United Nations*, 3rd edn Bonn 1977, p. 170; repr. from *Politics and Government . . .*, p. 309)

D125a–c The German Nation—as set out in the Constitution of the German Democratic Republic:

D125a Art. 1 of the Constitution of 1949:

Germany is an indivisible democratic republic, composed of German states (Länder).

The republic determines all matters which are essential for the existence and development of the German people as a whole; all other matters are to be determined independently by the states. The decisions of the republic are in principle to be carried out by the states.

There is only one German citizenship.

(S. Mampel: *Die Verfassung der sowjetisch besetzten Zone*, Frankfurt 1965, p. 37; repr. from *Politics and Government . . .*, p. 378)

D125b Amendment to the Constitution, 1968:

Because of our responsibility to point the way to the entire German nation to a future of peace and socialism . . . the people of the GDR . . . have given themselves this socialist constitution:

Article 1
The German Democratic Republic is a socialist state of the German nation.

It is the political organization of the working people in the city and the country, who together bring socialism into reality under the leadership of the working class and its Marxist-Leninist Party.

(Friedrich-Ebert-Stiftung (ed.): *Honeckers Verfassung*, Bonn 1981, pp. 49f.; repr. from *Politics and Government . . .*, p. 378)

D125c Amendment to the Constitution, 1974:

In continuation of the revolutionary traditions of the German working class, . . . the people of the German Democratic Republic have given themselves this socialist constitution:

Article 1
The German Democratic Republic is a socialist state of the worker and the farmer. It is the political organization of the working people in the city and the country under the leadership of the working class and its Marxist-Leninist Party.

(*Honeckers Verfassung*, pp. 49f.; repr. from above, pp. 378–9)

D126a The Law on Citizenship (Gesetz über die Staatsbürgerschaft der Deutschen Demokratischen Republik, Staatsbürgerschaftsgesetz), 20 February 1967:

The citizenship of the German Democratic Republic came into existence, in accordance with international law, upon establishment of the German Democratic Republic. It is an expression of the German Democratic Republic's sovereignty and contributes to the further strengthening of all socialist countries.

The citizenship of the German Democratic Republic is membership of its residents in the first peace-loving, democratic and socialist German State, in which the working class exercises political power in alliance with the farmers' co-operative class, the socialist intelligentsia and other labouring people.

§ 1

A citizen of the German Democratic Republic is one who:
  a) was a German national at the time of the establishment of the GDR, had his place of official or permanent residence in the German Demo-

cratic Republic and has not lost his German Democratic Republic citizenship since then;

b) was a German national at the time of the establishment of the GDR, had his official or permanent residence outside the German Democratic Republic, has obtained no other citizenship thereafter and, corresponding to his declaration of intent is enrolled, through registration at one of the authorized German Democratic Republic's agencies, as a citizen of the German Democratic Republic;

c) obtained the citizenship of the German Democratic Republic, according to valid regulations, and has not lost it since.

§ 2

(1) The citizenship of the German Democratic Republic guarantees that the citizens of the German Democratic Republic can avail themselves of their constitutional rights; and demands from them the implementation of their constitutional duties [Pflichten].

(2) The German Democratic Republic affords its citizens protection and supports them in the assertion of their rights outside the German Democratic Republic.

§ 3

(1) According to generally accepted international law, citizens of the German Democratic Republic can claim no rights or duties of another citizenship in relation to the German Democratic Republic.

(2) A citizen of the German Democratic Republic who intends to acquire citizenship from another country, requires the assent of the authorized central agencies of the German Democratic Republic. . . .

§ 4

The citizenship of the German Democratic Republic is obtained through:
a) descent;
b) birth within the territory of the German Democratic Republic;
c) naturalization.

[. . .]

§ 10

(1) With the permission of the responsible agency of the German Democratic Republic, a citizen can on application be released from the status conferred on him by his citizenship of the German Democratic Republic if he has, or desires to take, residence outside

the German Democratic Republic, holds or intends to apply for another citizenship, and if no compelling reason exists to prevent his relinquishing his citizenship of the German Democratic Republic.

(2) The release from the citizenship of the German Democratic Republic will be acknowledged in an official document.

[...]

§ 13

Citizens who have official or permanent residence outside the German Democratic Republic can be deprived of their citizenship for serious violation of civil duties.

(*Gesetzblatt der DDR*, I, No. 2, 23 February 1967; repr. from *Politics and Government* . . ., pp. 379–80)

D126b Additional Law on Questions of Citizenship (. . .Zur Regelung von Fragen der Staatsbürgerschaft), 16 October 1972:

§ 1

(1) Citizens of the German Democratic Republic who, in violation of the laws of the Worker and Peasant State [Arbeiter-und Bavernstaat] left the German Democratic Republic before 1 January 1972, and who have not taken up residence in the German Democratic Republic again, lose their citizenship of the German Democratic Republic with the coming into force of this Law.

(2) Descendants of persons referred to in (1) lose their citizenship of the German Democratic Republic with the coming into force of this Law in so far as they have their residence outside the German Democratic Republic without the authorization of governmental agencies of the German Democratic Republic.

§ 2

Persons referred to in §(1) will not be liable to criminal prosecution for leaving the German Democratic Republic without authorization.

(*Gesetzblatt der DDR*, I, No. 18, 17 October 1972; repr. from *Politics and Government* . . ., pp. 381)

D127 Speech by Erich Honecker, General Secretary of the SED and Chairman of the Council of State (Staatstratsvorsitzender), on "Topical Questions of the Domestic and Foreign Policy of the GDR", at Gera, 13 October 1980:

The German Democratic Republic strives for good neighbourly relations with the Federal Republic of Germany and, just as in our policy towards other Western states, we pursue here, too, a policy of peaceful coexistence. On this basis we have done much in the past to smooth the path for progress in the relations between the German Democratic Republic and the Federal Republic of Germany. It was possible to negotiate numerous treaties and agreements which function fairly well. The results thereof were important prerequisites for a mutually advantageous co-operation based on equal rights.

Obviously it cannot be overlooked that many problems between the German Democratic Republic and the Federal Republic of Germany continue to exist and that we still have a long way to go before complete normality is attained. The main reasons for this are the Federal Republic of Germany's continued attempts, when dealing with the GDR, to disregard decisive principles of the sovereignty of our state, thereby violating the Basic Treaty [*Grundlagenvertrag*]. In this relationship, however, it is only possible to take a step forward when the existence of two sovereign states, which are independent of one another and which have different forms of society, is unconditionally accepted. Every effort to revise the European postwar arrangement must put a strain on the normalization of the relations between the two German states; indeed it puts them in doubt.

The Federal Republic of Germany prevents solutions

It is absolutely vital that the principle of non-interference is accepted without limitation by both sides in the bilateral relations as well as in the relationship to third states. The Basic Treaty obliges its members to do this, of course. In particular, disregard of the principle of non-interference which was, after all, also signed by the Federal Republic of Germany in Helsinki, is in no way compatible with more normal relations. More extensive solutions of various kinds which would be of advantage to the people of the Federal Republic of Germany and the German Democratic Republic are still being heavily obstructed by the Federal Republic of Germany. We have often pressed to have the obstructions removed, but have received no co-operation. This is true above all of the recognition of the citizenship of the German Democratic Republic. As the Federal Republic of Germany adheres to ideas which are not in accordance with international law and as they refuse to respect the citizenship of the German Democratic Republic, the jurisdiction of our state is being denied. But it is certainly a fact that there are two sovereign German states independent of one another. There are, and this is also a fact, citizens of the socialist German Democratic Republic and citizens of the capitalist Federal Republic of Germany.

We consider it necessary for the FRG to accept reality at last, something it will not be able to avoid in the long run, in any case. This would make it easier to settle the most urgent practical questions in tourist travel, in legal aid and in various other fields. The so-called 'Registration Centre' [Zentrale Erfassungsstelle] at Salzgitter should have been dissolved long ago. An end must be put to the issuing of temporary passports for GDR citizens when staying in the Federal Republic, as well as to the issuing of FRG passports for GDR citizens by FRG embassies in third countries.

We also consider it time to exchange ambassadors as is usual in the relations between two sovereign states independent of one another, i.e. to transform the offices of the permanent representatives of the GDR and the FRG into what conforms with international law — into embassies. This would be a visible step towards a normalization of the relations between the two German states.

Of great importance is the situation at the border of the two states, which is also the dividing line between the Warsaw Pact States and NATO. The common Border Commission of the two German states has achieved positive results and important agreements have been arrived at. It would serve the interests of peace and good neighbourly relations, if the border line along the river Elbe could be determined according to international law, an agreement which has so far failed due to the unacceptable positions adopted by the Federal Republic. . . .

(*Neues Deutschland* 14 October 1980; repr. from *Politics and Government. . .*, pp. 388–90)

D128 From the toast by Erich Honecker at a dinner in the "Redoute", Bonn, with Federal Chancellor Helmut Kohl in September 1987:

Federal Chancellor,
Ladies and gentlemen,
Friends and comrades,

I thank you, Federal Chancellor, for the invitation to visit the Federal Republic of Germany and for the warm welcome we have been given. The talks we have started are confirmation of the positive impact of our direct contacts on the development of the relations between the two German states. It is not by chance that great international attention is being paid to these relations. In view of the situation of the German Democratic Republic and of the Federal Republic of Germany in the centre of Europe and of the lessons of history, the importance of their relations goes far beyond their frontiers.

We are aware that the development of our relations, of the relations between the German Democratic Republic and the Federal Republic of Germany, is marked by the realities of the present world, and those realities say that socialism and capitalism cannot be combined just as it is impossible to combine fire and water.

All this notwithstanding, we believe that it is incumbent on the two German states, which are firmly entrenched in the most powerful military coalitions of our epoch, to make an especially active contribution to peace, disarmament and détente. Despite all our differences in the assessment of current political questions, we are agreed that there would neither be winners nor losers in a nuclear war. In our Joint Declaration of 12 March 1985 we state, and we have stressed this here again, that everything should be done to ensure that never again war, but only peace emanates from German soil.

[. . .]

In the face of the sustained complicated international situation, the German Democratic Republic is endeavouring to make common sense and goodwill prevail in international politics, to replace confrontation with co-operation and to build more confidence in international relations. The point is to return to the way of détente which led to good results for nations and for people in the seventies, not least for the two German states and their citizens.

(Panorama DDR: *A success for the politics of common sense and realism: Official visit by Erich Honecker . . . to the Federal Republic of Germany from 7 to 11 September 1987*, Dresden 1987, pp. 9ff.)

D129 Joint Communiqué on the official visit of the General Secretary of the Central Committee of the Socialist Unity Party of Germany and Chairman of the Council State of the German Democratic Republic, Erich Honecker, to the Federal Republic of Germany from 7 to 11 September 1987:

At the invitation of the Federal Chancellor of the Federal Republic of Germany, Helmut Kohl, the General Secretary of the Central Committee of the Socialist Unity Party of Germany and Chairman of the Council of State of the German Democratic Republic, Erich Honecker, is paying an official visit to the Federal Republic of Germany from 7 to 11 September 1987.

General Secretary Honecker and Federal Chancellor Kohl held talks in Bonn on 7 and 8 September 1987. General Secretary Honecker was also received by Federal President Richard von Weizsäcker and had talks with other public figures.

Following the talks in Bonn, General Secretary Honecker will visit North Rhine-Westphalia (Cologne, Düsseldorf, Wuppertal, Essen), Saarland (Saarbrücken, Neunkirchen), Rhineland-Palatinate (Trier) and Bavaria (Munich, Dachau).

During the visit, the following agreements and accords were signed:

Agreement between the Government of the German Democratic Republic and the Government of the Federal Republic of Germany on the Further Development of Relations in the Field of Environmental Protection,

Agreement between the Government of the German Democratic Republic and the Government of the Federal Republic of Germany on the Exchange of Information and Experience in the Field of Radiation Protection,

Agreement between the Government of the German Democratic Republic and the Government of the Federal Republic of Germany on Co-operation in the Fields of Science and Technology.

In a businesslike and open atmosphere, the General Secretary of the Central Committee of the Socialist Unity Party of Germany and Chairman of the Council of State of the German Democratic Republic and the Federal Chancellor of the Federal Republic of Germany held an extensive exchange of views on the present state of affairs in the relations between the German Democratic Republic and the Federal Republic of Germany and possibilities for developing them in the future as well as on current issues in international relations.

Participants in the talks were on the part of the German Democratic Republic

Dr Günter Mittag, Member of the Politburo and Secretary of the Central Committee of the Socialist Unity Party of Germany, Deputy Chairman of the Council of State of the German Democratic Republic,

Oskar Fisher, Member of the Central Committee of the Socialist Unity Party of Germany, Minister of Foreign Affairs,

Dr Gerhard Beil, Member of the Central Committee of the Socialist Unity Party of Germany, Minister of Foreign Trade, and other political figures.

On the part of the Federal Republic of Germany

Federal Minister Dr Martin Bangemann,

Federal Minister Dr Dorothee Wilms,

Federal Minister Dr Wolfgang Schäuble, and other political figures.

General Secretary Honecker and Federal Chancellor Kohl were agreed on the need for both the German Democratic Republic and the Federal Republic of Germany to make particular efforts for a peaceful living together in Europe to meet the responsibility arising from their common history. Never again must war emanate from German soil, only peace.

They emphasized that the relations between the two states must remain a stabilizing factor for constructive East-West relations. It should generate positive impulses for peaceful co-operation and dialogue in Europe and beyond.

General Secretary Honecker and Federal Chancellor Kohl commended the development of relations between the two states since the conclusion of the Treaty on the Bases of Relations between the German Democratic Republic and the Federal Republic of Germany on 21 December 1972. They stressed that the Treaty, together with the accords and regulations agreed so far, constitutes the basis and framework of the relations between the two states. They reaffirmed their Joint Declaration of 12 March 1985.

Mindful of existing realities and notwithstanding the differences in their views on fundamental issues, including the national question, the two sides intend to develop normal and good neighbourly relations on the basis of equality in accordance with the Basic Treaty and to make wider use of the opportunities the Treaty provides.

The two sides agreed to preserve and develop what has been achieved so far, acting on the principle that either state respects the independence and autonomy of the other state with regard to its internal and external affairs. Desire for understanding and realism should be the guideline for constructive co-operation between the two states with the aim of achieving practical results.

The two sides commended the continuing favourable influence of the Quadripartite Agreement of 3 September 1971 on the situation in Central Europe and East-West relations and reiterated the need for its strict observance and full implementation.

General Secretary Honecker and Federal Chancellor Kohl discussed at length questions regarding travel and visits, including travel in urgent family matters. They praised the progress made in this field and reaffirmed the intention of working towards further improvements and easements in the interests of the people.

They welcomed the agreement reached between the Ministries of Transport of the two states on fare reductions for private travel between the two countries and on transit routes between the Federal Republic of Germany and Berlin (West) on the lines operated by the Deutsche Reichsbahn and the Deutsche Bundesbahn.

They also discussed conditions for the expansion of tourism and agreed to create the prerequisites for a gradual development of tourism. They reaffirmed the intention to promote and expand youth tourist exchanges to facilitate meetings of young people from both sides.

They welcomed the conclusion of twinning agreements between towns in the German Democratic Republic and the Federal Republic of Germany considering them an important measure to facilitate people-to-people contacts, including cultural events, and thus developing peaceful good-neighbourly relations between the two states. They will continue to lend their support to such efforts.

They underlined their willingness to further promote exchanges in the field of sport. For this purpose, the opportunities arising from the town twinning agreements shall also be used.

General Secretary Honecker and Federal Chancellor Kohl discussed humanitarian issues including questions of family reunification and remedying of hardship cases. They commended positive results and agreed to continue appropriate efforts in a constructive spirit.

The two sides praised the work of the border commission and declared their intention to complete, in accordance with the Government Protocol of 29 November 1978, the tasks of the border commission which are still pending.

General Secretary Honecker and Federal Chancellor Kohl underlined the great importance they attach to questions concerning the protection of man's natural environment. They assessed the conclusion of the Agreement on the Further Development of Relations in the Field of Environmental Protection as a manifestation of the desire for intensified co-operation in this area.

The two sides agreed to expeditiously continue the ongoing negotiations on a reduction of the salt load of the river Werra and the disposal of potash mine effluents with a view to bringing them to a positive and well-balanced conclusion as soon as possible.

There was agreement on the initiation of talks on measures for the protection of the river Elbe.

The two sides commended the conclusion of the Agreement on the Exchange of Information and Experience in the Field of Radiation Protection as an important step towards extending mutual relations.

They welcomed the conclusion of the Agreement on Co-operation in the Fields of Science and Technology and are agreed on intensifying, on its basis, and for their mutual benefits, relations through contacts between scientists and research institutions in line with co-ordinated projects.

General Secretary Honecker and Federal Chancellor Kohl underlined the great importance of comprehensive and factual information by the press, radio and television for the further development of good neighbourly relations. The two sides accordingly render maximum assistance to journalists in the execution of their duties.

General Secretary Honecker and Federal Chancellor Kohl commended the Cultural Agreement of 6 May 1986 which facilitates the development of cultural relations, and has resulted in a visible increase in cultural exchanges. They emphasized the intention to systematically continue co-operation on the basis of the agreement and widen its scope to include new fields. Work to co-ordinate projects for the period 1988-89 has essentially been completed.

The two sides commended the fact that exchanges of valuable archives, thanks to accords on the return of cultural assets that had been moved from their original places because of the war, have almost been completed. By the end of this year, an agreed regulation will have been reached on the return of paintings that had been put into safe keeping.

Exchanges of experience and co-operation are to be continued and intensified in the fields of health care, agriculture, housing construction and urban development.

The two sides came out in favour of continuing efforts to reach agreements on regulating judicial relations. In the interests of clients, legal matters should be regulated in the easiest and most expedient way possible.

The two sides discussed questions concerning non-commercial payments and will continue their efforts to reduce restrictive regulations and introduce legislation to improve the disposition of property in the interests of the people in the two states.

General Secretary Honecker and Federal Chancellor Kohl stated with satisfaction that economic relations between the two states have been marked by a generally positive development in recent years. They consider trade exchanges as an important element stabilizing overall relations, and declared their interest in a continuous development of economic co-operation on the basis of equality and mutual advantage, also involving small-and medium-sized firms. They reiterated their resolve to further improve the structure of trade and to encourage exchanges of capital goods, notably in the fields of general engineering, electrical engineering, power engineering and environmental protection technologies. The two sides emphasized the importance of co-operation on third markets.

They reaffirmed their intention to continue the regular contacts in the fields of trade and economy.

With a view to continuously expanding economic co-operation on the basis of equality and mutual advantage, it was agreed to initiate talks on the establishment of a joint commission to promote the development of economic relations on the basis of the existing agreements and arrangements.

With a view to further improving communication links, including from and to Berlin (West), the two sides agreed to work for mutually advantageous regulations and agreements notably in the field of rail travel and to enter into talks with the aim of markedly reducing travelling time and shortening the intervals between trains.

They stated their shared intention to further improve, within the limits of technological and economic possibilities, postal services and telecommunications, including from and to Berlin (West), on the basis of the existing post and telecommunications agreement.

The two sides welcomed the talks on the purchase and supply of electric power which are presently being conducted on a commercial basis between energy supply firms in the German Democratic Republic and in the Federal Republic of Germany with the inclusion of Berlin (West). They expect these talks to produce relevant long-term contracts.

General Secretary Honecker and Federal Chancellor Kohl discussed issues concerning international developments. Mindful of the fact that the two states have different social systems and are affiliated to different alliances, they explained their views on the present situation in, and the prospects of, East-West relations.

They declared their willingness to promote, within the framework of their respective alliances, a policy aimed at reducing tensions and safe-guarding peace and encourage the continuation of dialogue and long-term co-operation.

In a joint effort to utilize every opportunity of conducting an increasingly wide and constructive dialogue on matters of concern for the people both in East and West, and guided by the conviction that long-term, stable and durable conditions of peace in Europe cannot be created by exclusively military means, the two sides attach particular significance to the CSCE process. In this context, well-balanced and tangible progress in all fields defined in the Helsinki Final Act is an important yardstick for measuring willingness to work for *détente* and to facilitate the resolution of security issues through confidence building. Both sides spoke out for putting all the principles and stipulations of the Helsinki Final Act and the Madrid Concluding Document into full effect for the benefit of the people and for the good of co-operation between states.

General Secretary Honecker and Federal Chancellor Kohl had, in this connection, a frank exchange of views on the implementation of all human rights.

Both sides stated their intention to join efforts with the other participating countries to bring about substantial results at the Vienna CSCE follow-up conference.

They emphasized the great importance that must be attached, within the framework of the East-West dialogue, to the results of negotiations on effective measures of arms control and disarmament in all fields. Based on the principle of equality and parity, such results must establish a stable equilibrium of forces at the lowest possible level and reduce existing imbalances. They must allow for effective verification.

In this sense, the two sides will work for progress and results through their involvement in the ongoing negotiations and conferences in Geneva and Vienna and bring their constructive influence to bear on the bilateral negotiations between the Soviet Union and the United States.

Both sides stressed the particular importance of an agreement on intermediate-range systems and declared that the worldwide elimination of Soviet and US intermediate-range missiles with a range of over 500 kms would essentially enhance stability and security in Europe and Asia.

They shared the conviction that the conclusion of a relevant agreement will produce positive effects both on other areas of arms control and disarmament and on East-West relations in general. This chance must be seized.

Federal Chancellor Kohl explained the agreed concept of the Atlantic alliance according to which Soviet and US land-based nuclear missile systems with a shorter range must be brought down to lower and equal ceilings in connection with the establishment of a conventional balance and the worldwide elimination of chemical weapons.

General Secretary Honecker directed attention to the proposals submitted by the states parties to the Warsaw Treaty on the reduction of tactical nuclear weapons in conjunction with the armed forces and conventional armaments in Europe.

General Secretary Honecker and Federal Chancellor Kohl voiced their support for the objectives of the Geneva talks which were jointly defined by the Soviet Union and the USA on 8 January 1985, namely to prevent an arms race in outer space and to stop it on earth, to limit and reduce nuclear weapons, and to strengthen strategic stability.

Both sides advocate a 50 per cent reduction in strategic offensive weapons. They point to the importance of the ABM treaty.

Both sides voiced their support for a reliably verifiable nuclear test-ban treaty to be concluded within the framework of the Geneva Conference on Disarmament at the earliest possible time. They deem it possible to gradually approach this goal in the current contacts between the Soviet Union and the USA.

Both sides reiterated their obligations that derive for them from the Treaty on the Non-Proliferation of Nuclear Weapons and stated their interest in strengthening the regime of non-proliferation together with other countries.

General Secretary Honecker and Federal Chancellor Kohl shared the view that progress in the field of nuclear disarmament adds to the urgency of conventional disarmament in order to improve security and stability in Europe from the Atlantic Ocean to the Urals. They underlined the importance of pertinent negotiations and agreed to make every possible effort with a view to establishing, as soon as possible, a substantive mandate at the Vienna talks between the 23 member states of the Warsaw Treaty and the North Atlantic Alliance.

Both sides commended the results of the Stockholm Conference on Confidence- and Security-Building Measures and Disarmament in Europe as an important step towards creating more confidence and predictability in the military field. They stressed the necessity of implementing the Stockholm document in letter and spirit, and will back negotiations on additional confidence- and security-building measures.

General Secretary Honecker and Federal Chancellor Kohl reiterated their determination to contribute to a successful conclusion of the Vienna Talks on the Mutual Reduction of Armed Forces and Armaments and Associated Measures in Central Europe.

Both sides will make resolute efforts for the early conclusion of a treaty on a universal and reliably verifiable ban on the development, manufacture, storage and use of chemical weapons.

They explained their differing views on regional agreements in the field of nuclear and chemical weapons.

They appreciated the fact that the consultations between their government representatives for disarmament have become an integral element of their political dialogue and came out in favour of a continuation of these consultations.

Both sides agreed to continue their efforts to strengthen the United Nations as the universal forum for the peaceful conduct of international relations, the solution of urgent international political, economic, social and humanitarian problems and the promotion of the dialogue on issues of arms limitation and disarmament.

They praised the non-aligned movement as an important factor for international stability.

General Secretary Honecker and Federal Chancellor Kohl characterized their exchange of views as necessary and beneficial for the further development of relations. They advocated continued and intensified contacts at high political and other levels.

The General Secretary of the Central Committee of the Socialist Unity Party of Germany and Chairman of the Council of State of the German Democratic Republic invited the Federal Chancellor of the Federal Republic of Germany for a return visit. The invitation was accepted with thanks. Dates and details will be agreed upon later.

(Source as above, pp. 48 ff.)

D130 From the Programme of the SED: on relations with the Federal Republic of Germany, May 1976:

The Socialist Unity Party of Germany is in favour of developing relations between the socialist German Democratic Republic and the capitalist Federal Republic of Germany, as relations between sovereign states with differing social systems, on the basis of the principles of peaceful coexistence and the rules of international law. Given the basic contradictions between the nature of the social systems in the German Democratic Republic and the Federal Republic of Germany, only a policy based on respect for each other's sovereignty can be conducive to the further normalization of relations and peaceful coexistence of the two states, and to businesslike, equal and mutually beneficial co-operation in the interest of peace.

(*Programme of the Socialist Unity Party of Germany*, Dresden 1976, p. 67)

D131 From the Politburo's report to the Fifth Meeting of the Central Committee: on co-operation with socialist and social democratic parties, 16 December 1987:

Comrades,

The political dialogue with socialist and social democratic parties in the interests of safeguarding peace has an important place in the international work of the SED. Thus in the past weeks a number of further political discussions and contacts took place between the General Secretary of the Central Committee of the SED, comrade Erich Honecker, and other members of the Politburo and leading members of the SPD. In particular, Erich Honecker's meeting in Berlin with the Chief Minister of the Saarland, Oskar Lafontaine, the President of the Senate of Hamburg, Klaus von Dohnányi, and the Mayor of Bremen, Klaus Wedemeier, and his discussions with Dieter Spoerl, member of the SPD parliamentary party in the West German parliament and top candidate in the Baden-Württemberg state elections in spring 1988, with Bjorn Engholm, the leader of the SPD in the Schleswig-Holstein state parliament, and with Gerhard Schröder, the leader of the SPD in the Lower Saxony state parliament, were able to deal with questions of interest to both sides and helped reinforce relations between the SED and the SPD.

The agreement concluded with the SPD party leadership that the SED and SPD working parties on disarmament issues should continue their activity is an important one. Here common proposals on how a non-aggression capability can be achieved are to become the central issue. The SED's working party is led by comrade Hermann Axen.

The common document on "Ideological Struggle and Mutual Security" produced in August by the Academy for Social Sciences of the Central Committee of the SED and the SPD's Commission on Fundamental Values is of historic importance. With this document, an agreement was reached between German communists and social democrats creating for the first time in nearly 70 years a common platform for both parties to co-operate on decisive questions of our time. Starting from the conclusion that humankind must now either survive together or perish together, the focus for co-operation between the two parties is their responsibility in the struggle for peace and common security. The document does not disguise ideological oppositions, nor does it give space to ideological coexistence. There is no convergence between the two social systems.

However, in the conditions of the nuclear age communists and social democrats must make approaches to each other as never before and carry on their ideological disputes in such a way that they assist the common striving for peace. This document will form the long-term basis for the activity of both our parties on questions of peace and security, the peaceful competition of the two systems and their shared responsibility for finding solutions to other global problems facing humankind. It also places high demands on the ideological work of our party organizations.

The document has met with great and increasing international approval.

The meetings which comrade Erich Honecker had during his state visit to Belgium with the leader of the Flemish Socialist Party, Karel van Miert, and the Francophone Socialist Party, Guy Spitaels, were on exactly the same lines.

Other members of the Politburo met leading representatives of the Socialist Party of France and the Norwegian Workers' Party.

Delegations from our party took part in a bilateral colloquium of the Vandervelde Institute of the Flemish Socialist Party, the 86th annual conference of the British Labour Party, and the 39th congress of the Socialist Party of Uruguay. An official delegation from the Panhellenic Socialist Movement of Greece (PASOK) visited the GDR for several days at the SED's invitation.

(*Neues Deutschland* vol. 42 no. 296 of 17 December, 1987)

D132 The West German Undersecretary of State for Foreign Affairs (Staatssekretär) Walter Hallstein, speaking in the Bundestag on the special trade relationship between the two German states, 21 March 1957:

Hallstein emphasized that the federal government had, when signing the Treaties of Rome (EEC and Euratom), made clear that a reunited Germany would be free to decide on its own accession to the treaties and he went on to say in this connection:" . . . we have taken special care to safeguard the position of Berlin and the whole process of the "intra-German trade" [Interzonenhandel] . . . we are very much interested in not only preserving this instrument of intra-German trade, but in actually developing it further. For this reason the treaty on the Common Market *expressis verbis* contains the provision — I quote — "that the execution of the community treaty will entail neither any change in regard to the regulations for the intra-German trade as of now nor any change in the actual conduct of this same trade. It is, therefore, absolutely clear that the present state of affairs by which the intra-German trade is a purely domestic one will remain intact; the demarcation line with the Eastern Zone [Zonengrenze, frontier with the German Democratic Republic] will continue not to be a customs frontier. The federal government retains its full freedom of action in regard to this intra-German trade".

(Auswärtiges Amt (ed.): *Die aussenpolitik der Bundesrepublik Deutschland*, Bonn 1972, pp. 354f.; repr. from *Politics and Government. . .*, ed. C.C.Schweitzer et al., Leamington Spa 1984, pp. 391 f.)

D133 From the Directives for the Five-Year Plan 1981–1985 issued by the Tenth Party Congress of the SED, April 1981:

Socialist economic integration and foreign trade

In accordance with the resolutions adopted at the economic summit of the CMEA member countries, efforts will be made to intensify socialist economic integration, enhance scientific and technological co-operation with the USSR and the other fraternal socialist countries and strengthen the unity and cohesion of the socialist community. With the implementation of the Long-term Programme for Scientific and Technological Progress by CMEA Member Countries up to the Year 2000, contractual co-operation is to be concentrated on the speedy development and broad application of key technologies in the national economy. Within a very short period of time, outstanding performances must be achieved and brought to the stage of practical application in economic areas of key importance. The advantages of the international division of labour among the socialist countries must be exploited to the full in the GDR to further boost efficiency, increase economic potential, rapidly raise labour productivity and facilitate the efficient use and conservation of all kinds of resources.

A matter of prime importance to the GDR's continuing socio-economic development is the comprehensive intensification of economic, scientific and technological co-operation with the USSR on the basis of the Long-term Programme for the Development of Co-operation between the GDR and the USSR in the Fields of Science, Technology and Production in the Period until the Year 2000.

In drafting the annual national economic plan, both the results flowing from the co-ordination of all the socialist countries' economic plans and the long-term trade agreements for the period 1986–90 will serve as a basis.

It must be guaranteed that contractual undertakings on scientific and technological excellence and concerning quantity, quality and supply deadlines are adhered to.

The agreements concluded are to facilitate effective types of specialization and co-operation, the intensified expansion of mutual trade, and steps towards active participation in new integration schemes with a high economic yield.

In the course of further expanding specialization and co-operation in the manufacturing industry, particularly in mechanical engineering, electrical engineering and electronics, priority must be given to the co-ordinated development and manufacture of new products, machines, equipment and instrument systems with high-added value in order to keep pace with scientific and technological progress. The international division of labour must respond with greater agility to the fundamentally new processes we are witnessing in the fields of science, technology and production, and must be organized in a way which allows for immediate and flexible answers to changing demand.

Through enhanced foreign trade relations with the USSR and the other socialist states, the GDR must be enabled to conduct about two thirds of its foreign trade with these countries.

Mutual exchanges of goods must increasingly include state-of-the-art products incorporating raw materials and feedstocks with a higher added-value content. This primarily concerns key technologies such as microelectronics, robotics, automation technology, data and information processing and biotechnology.

With a view to ensuring long-term supplies of raw materials, the GDR will, in accordance with relevant agreements, continue to participate in investment projects in the USSR.

Emphasis is to be laid on the manufacture and export of sophisticated and highly productive machinery and equipment for the extraction and transport of raw materials and fuels and for the modernization and reconstruction of important branches of the USSR economy, notably the food and consumer goods industries.

On the basis of the resolutions adopted at the economic summit of the CMEA member countries, which envisage the intensification of socialist economic integration, and in pursuance of the agreed programmes for co-operation in the fields of science, technology and production until the year 2000, commodity exchange with the other socialist countries will be systematically expanded.

The stable political and economic relations with the USSR and the other CMEA countries provide a firm platform from which also to expand economic and trade relations with non-socialist countries on the basis of equality and mutual advantage. In turn, this will contribute towards strengthening the material basis required for the continuation of a policy of peace and international détente.

Accelerated export growth must be used to expand the GDR's scope for action in trade policy and reinforce its economic and political invulnerability.

In line with the GDR's industrial potential and its position among the world's leading countries, export growth must increasingly be brought about through sales of products from the metal-working industry. It will be necessary to make available high-return, marketable products, respond without delay to the wishes of customers and adapt more fully to the demands made by foreign markets on the export of capital goods.

With a view to ensuring reliable and expanding market positions for the GDR, it is necessary, on account of the rapidly changing demand on international markets, to bring about a decisive acceleration in scientific and technological operations and the practical application of their results, which presupposes an integrated approach to research, development, production and marketing.

Intensifying economic, scientific and technological co-operation with developing countries on the basis of equality and mutual advantage must yield economic benefits for the GDR while effectively supporting the countries concerned in building their national economies.

This will mean taking into account new development trends in these countries, e.g. the development of natural resources, power generation, development of the agricultural sector and infrastructure, and reconstruction of the manufacturing plant, and developing appropriate forms of economic relations such as industrial co-operation, kit production, and consulting and engineering services.

From the platform of solid relations of political, economic, scientific and technological co-operation with the USSR and the other socialist countries, the GDR will endeavour to expand commodity exchange with industrialized capitalist countries unimpeded by political leverage and on the basis of equality and mutual benefit.

(*Directives for the Five-Year Plan for the GDR's national economic development 1981–1985, issued by the 10th Congress of the Socialist Unity Party of Germany*, Dresden 1981, pp. 121ff.)

D134 From the Constitution of the German Democratic Republic, 8 April 1968:

Article 6

(1) In keeping with the interests of the German people and the international obligation of all Germans, the German Democratic Republic has eradicated German militarism and Nazism on its territory and conducts a foreign policy serving peace and socialism, international understanding and security.

(2) In accordance with the principles of socialist internationalism, the German Democratic Republic cultivates and develops all-round co-operation and friendship with the Union of Soviet Socialist Republics and the other socialist states.

(3) The German Democratic Republic supports the strivings of the nations for freedom and independence and maintains co-operation with all states on a basis of equality and mutual respect.

(4) The German Democratic Republic is working for a system of collective security in Europe and a stable peace order in the world. It supports general disarmament.

(5) Militaristic and revanchist propaganda in any form, incitement to war and expression of religious, racial or national hatred will be punished as crimes.

(*Die Verfassung der Deutschen Demokratischen Republik*, Berlin 1968)

D135 From the Programme of the SED: on foreign policy, May 1976:

The content, objectives and tasks of the foreign policy advocated by the Socialist Unity Party of Germany are
— to establish, together with the Soviet Union and the other socialist countries, the most favourable international conditions for socialist and communist construction,
— to strengthen the unity, cohesion and all-round co-operation of the socialist countries, and to promote friendship between them and their closer association,
— to support the struggle of the working class and its communist and workers' parties in the capitalist countries and to continue to strengthen relations with these parties,
— to extend solidarity and support to movements for social and national liberation throughout the world and to co-operate closely with the newly independent countries,
— to gain acceptance for the policy of peaceful coexistence in relations with capitalist countries,
— to give a firm rebuff to the aggressive forces of imperialism, to save mankind from another world war and to secure lasting peace.

The strengthening of the socialist community

In its entire foreign policy the Socialist Unity Party of Germany is guided by the historically established truth that the vital interests of the German Democratic Republic, as a socialist workers' and farmers' state, coincide with the interests of the Soviet Union and the socialist community. It considers that the German Democratic Republic can only accomplish its historic tasks by co-operation with the Soviet Union and the other fraternal socialist countries.

The all-round strengthening of the socialist community gathered around the Soviet Union is the foremost foreign policy objective of the Socialist Unity Party of Germany. It considers it its most important task to develop the fraternal relations existing between the GDR and the USSR in all fields of life as reflected by the Treaty of Friendship, Co-operation and Mutual Assistance signed on 7 October 1975, which forms a stable and lasting basis for these relations. Concurrently, the Party seeks to expand and deepen fraternal co-operation with all other countries belonging to the socialist community.

The relations between socialist countries are marked by proletarian internationalism and by the effective linking of common and national interests. These relations represent a qualitatively new type of relationship between states. They rest on socio-economic, political and ideological affinities and on the objective laws governing the development and convergence of socialist nations.

The socialist community sets an example for a future world community of free and equal peoples. New patterns of political, economic, scientific, technological and ideological relations will gain momentum in co-operation between the socialist countries.

(*Programme of the Socialist Unity Party of Germany*, Dresden 1976, pp. 64 f.)

D136 From the Politburo report by Werner Felfe to the Fifth meeting of the Central Committee of the SED: co-operation with other socialist countries, December 1987:

In the period covered by this report we have also made progress in the further development of relations with the other socialist countries. We have been and remain concerned to reinforce co-operation between the socialist countries while recognizing the multiformity of their development and their responsibility for the destiny of their own people, showing respect for the achievement of friends and allies, and increasing mutual trust and common advantage. In this we are guided by our efforts to demonstrate the advantages of socialism ever more clearly through our further successful progress in shaping the advanced socialist society in our own country and through close co-operation between fraternal countries. This was also the aim of the resolution on the "Reforming of multilateral co-operation and socialist economic integration and of the activities of COMECON" adopted by the 43rd extraordinary meeting of COMECON in Moscow on 13 and 14 October.

At their meeting in September, comrades Erich Honecker and Wojciech Jaruzelski reached positive conclusions on the co-operation between the GDR and the People's Republic of Poland and between the SED and the Polish United Workers' Party in the last two years. This has been given further specific encouragement. Our party takes the position that the firm unshakeable friendship and co-operation between the GDR and the People's Republic of Poland is of extraordinary importance for the cause of socialism and peace. The peace border along the Oder and Neisse continues to be a border which unites our peoples rather than dividing them. This is also the effect of the agreement reached at the meeting for a common project to bring the young people of our countries closer together.

During the official friendly visit of the party and state delegation to the People's Republic of Bulgaria, comrades Erich Honecker and Todor Shivkov signed the programme on the extension and intensification of economic, scientific and technical co-operation between the GDR and the People's Republic of Bulgaria up to the year 2000. They set out their intention to take a qualitatively new step in finding common solutions to the problems arising.

The official friendly visit of comrade Erich Honecker to the Socialist Republic of Romania made an important contribution to bilateral co-operation. In the talks with comrade Nicolae Ceausescu both sides spoke of the high standard of development of long-term, mutually beneficial co-operation. Numerous agreements on its intensification were reached. The exchange of views and experiences between the SED and the RCP on questions of the construction of socialism will be further extended.

In the meetings which comrade Erich Honecker had in Berlin with the Chairman of the Federal Executive Council of the Socialist Federal Republic of Yugoslavia, Branko Mikulic, both sides expressed their satisfaction over the long and stable relations between the two parties, states and peoples.

Relations between the SED and the Communist Party of China and between the GDR and the People's Republic of China have developed in a gratifying way. This is emphasized by the importance of the measures agreed by both sides to extend them further in accordance with the agreements reached by comrades Erich Honecker and Zhao Zhiyang in Berlin. The exchange of delegations and of experiences between the SED and the CP of China was comprehensive. Its focus was on the exchange of information and experiences on topics such as propaganda work, the management of a socialist economy, the socialist state and the socialist legal system, the organizational work of the two parties.

The consultation mechanism on foreign policy issues, which recently reached a high point with the official visit of comrade Oskar Fischer to the People's Republic of China, was further extended. Contacts were extended between the supreme elected assemblies, ministries, the trade unions, the women's and young people's organizations and other social organizations.

Both sides considered economic, scientific and technical relations to be of great importance; concrete agreements were reached on bilateral co-operation in the areas of construction, electrical power supply, agriculture, foodstuffs, and forestry.

Lively exchanges are continuing in the fields of culture and sport. The president of the German Sports and Gymnastics Union of the GDR, comrade Manfred Ewald, attended the most recent National Sports Festival of the People's Republic of China. Guest performances by Chinese artistes and groups formed a successful part of the Berlin Festival. The citizens of our country were able to see evidence of the People's Republic of China's cultivation of its national cultural traditions in such things as the important exhibition of terracotta figures of warriors and horses from the Qin dynasty.

In July comrade Erich Honecker met comrade Feng Wenbin, member of the Central Advisory Commission of the Central Committee of the Communist Party of China, and comrade Zhu Min, the daughter of the legendary Marshal Zhu De of the Chinese People's Liberation Army. Both took part in the festivities for the 750th anniversary of Berlin.

In October comrade Erich Honecker received Carlos Rafael Rodriguez, member of the Politburo of the Central Committee of the Communist Party of Cuba, representative and chairman of the Cuban Council of State and Council of Ministers, who was in Berlin for the meeting of the Joint Committee for Economic, Scientific and Technical Co-operation. In the talks the high level of comradely and fraternal relations between the GDR and the Republic of Cuba was recognized.

The official friendly visit which comrade Willi Stoph made to the Mongolian People's Republic assisted the further successful development of the close and varied relations between the GDR and the Mongolian People's Republic, which have already achieved a high level. Both sides discussed specific measures to realize the agreements made at the highest level, particularly to implement the long-term programme of development of scientific and technical co-operation between the GDR and the MPR up to the year 2000.

(*Neues Deutschland* vol. 42 no. 296 of 17 December 1987)

D137 From the Politburo report by Werner Felfe to the Fifth Meeting of the Central Committee of the SED: co-operation with countries in Asia, Africa and Latin America, December 1987:

It is notable that since the summit meeting of the Non-Aligned Countries in Harare in 1986 the states of Asia, Africa and Latin America have taken an even more committed stance for the prevention of nuclear war and for the elimination of regional trouble spots and conflicts.

The escalating conflict in the Persian Gulf is increasingly dangerous to world peace. The GDR supports Security Resolution 598 as a basis for the peaceful settlement of the conflict between Iran and Iraq. Acts of military force by other states and unilateral sanctions increase tensions and emotions. We support the USSR's proposal to withdraw all foreign warships from the Gulf region and to replace them with UNO forces.

The GDR reaffirms its positive attitude to the proposal for an international Near East Peace Conference in which the PLO is an equal participant.

In his friendly talks with the Foreign Minister of the Democratic Republic of Afghanistan, Abdul Wakil, in mid-November Erich Honecker welcomed the process of national reconciliation in Afghanistan initiated by the Democratic People's Party of Afghanistan as an important contribution to the consolidation of peace in Asia.

The steps taken by the People's Republic of Kampuchea towards national reconciliation and the creation of a neutral, free, independent and non-aligned Kampuchea also have our full support.

Southern Africa remains a dangerous crisis centre in the world. The apartheid regime is the prime hindrance to a peaceful and beneficial development in southern Africa, and this gives rise to great danger to security and world peace. The GDR and the SED will continue to stand firm in solidarity on the side of the peoples of Mozambique, Angola, and the other front-line states, of the ANC and of SWAPO.

Comrade Erich Honecker confirmed to the Defence Minister of the People's Republic of Mozambique, General Chipande, that the GDR sympathetically supports the struggle by Mozambique, the other front-line states who are increasingly united, and the national liberation movements of South Africa and Namibia against apartheid and in defence against the policies of destabilization and aggression carried on by South Africa and its imperialist allies.

The GDR attributes great importance to the states and peoples of Latin America who are attempting to achieve independence and democracy. During his meeting in Moscow with the President of Nicaragua, Daniel Ortega, comrade Erich Honecker praised the self-sacrificing struggle by the Nicaraguan people under the leadership of the FSLN in defence of its revolutionary achievements. He emphasized Nicaragua's important part in bringing about the Guatemala peace agreement which represents a constructive step towards the peaceful settlement of conflict in Central America and so towards the safeguarding of world peace.

(Source as above)

D138 From the official handbook "The German Democratic Republic": on friendship and co-operation with nations in Asia, Africa and Latin America, 1986:

The GDR shows its solidarity with the liberated countries in Asia, Africa and Latin America. It supports their struggle for peace, political and economic independence and social progress, and against imperialist policies of threat, pressure and interference, colonialism, neo-colonialism and racism. True to its foreign policy goals the GDR has always supported the peoples fighting for national and social liberation, and it will continue to do so in the future. The GDR acts on the notion that common efforts for international peace and disarmament help create more favourable conditions for the development of the countries in Asia, Africa and Latin America.

If peace is to be maintained it is more urgent than ever before to defuse sources of conflict and tension everywhere in the world by way of negotiations involving all parties concerned and taking account of their legitimate interests. The GDR continues to assist the people of Nicaragua and endorses the search for a peaceful and just solution to the conflicts in Central America. It demands that the policy of apartheid be ended in southern Africa, support of the racist regime be discontinued and national independence be granted to Namibia. In view of the volatile situation in the Middle East the GDR emphatically calls for the complete withdrawal of Israeli forces from all Arab territories occupied since 1967, the implementation of the legitimate rights of the Palestinian people including their right to self-determination and the establishment of an independent state of their own, and the implementation of the right of all states in the region to independent existence and development. The convening of an international Middle East peace conference under the auspices of the United Nations and with the participation of all parties concerned, including the PLO as the sole legitimate representative of the Palestinian people, would be an appropriate step to bring just and stable peace to the Middle East.

The GDR commends the increased role played by the non-aligned countries in international affairs and combines efforts with them in the struggle to eliminate the danger of war, promote peace, disarmament and development and solve international economic and financial problems. It supports the non-aligned movement's endeavours to establish a new international economic order and resolve international monetary and credit issues in order to enable the non-aligned countries to participate in international co-operation on an equal footing and free from imperialist pressure.

Particularly close ties have been established with the countries opting for socialism, e.g. Angola, Mozambique and Ethiopia. The treaties on friendship and co-operation signed with them provide a solid basis for mutually advantageous relations in the economic, trade, scientific and cultural fields, the training of national cadres and the assignment of experts. Beneficial co-operation also marks the relations with other countries which seek to consolidate their political and economic sovereignty. Almost 400 treaties and contracts were signed with these countries which provide a reliable framework for calculable, long-term and stable co-operation in all spheres.

An important facet of the GDR's foreign policy is the political and economic assistance it renders in the spirit of internationalism to socialist and socialism-oriented countries and national liberation movements in Asia, Africa and Latin America, above all by shipping urgently needed commodities, including food, medical supplies and clothing as well as equipment and teaching aids to help eradicate illiteracy and train national cadres. To this end considerable funds are made available from private solidarity donations organized above all by the Confederation of Free German Trade Unions and the GDR's Solidarity Committee.

(Panorama DDR: *The German Democratic Republic*, Dresden 1986, pp. 86 ff.)

D139 The GDR and Albania agree to exchange ambassadors, 11 December 1987:

In an exchange of aides-memoires, the governments of the German Democratic Republic and the Socialist People's Republic of Albania agreed on Thursday to re-elevate diplomatic relations between the two states to ambassadorial level and to exchange ambassadors.

(*Neues Deutschland* vol. 42 no. 291 of 11 December 1987)

D140 Albanian delegation's visit to Minister for Health, 16 December 1987:

A delegation from the Albanian Ministry of Health held discussions with the Minister for Health Matters in the GDR, Professor Ludwig Mecklinger, in Berlin on Tuesday. Professor Mecklinger stated that the results achieved so far in co-operation on health matters were an important step in the development of closer relationships between the two states and peoples. The leader of the Albanian delegation, Dr Gjergji Minga, announced his country's interest in continuing and extending existing agreements between the health ministries of the two countries. The participants in the discussion exchanged information on important decisions and objectives in the sphere of social policy.

(*Neues Deutschland* vol. 42 no. 295 of 16 December 1987)

Notes

1. Cf. the study by the Economist Intelligence Unit, "East Germany", in *EIU Regional Review. Eastern Europe and the USSR 1986* (London 1986), pp 55–64, but also W.F. Stolper, *Germany between East and West*, National Planning Association, Washington 1960.
2. The GDR plays a particularly significant role in countries like Angola, Ethiopia, and the Congo. It must also be noted that the GDR pursues a very active cultural foreign policy through its various propaganda publications and through the various friendship societies.

7 Literature and Culture

The Anglo-Saxon world, including literary critics and teachers of literature and the arts, would be amazed and probably aggrieved if prime ministers and party leaders were to become involved in matters literary and pronounce on literature and art. Yet on the continent of Europe this is by no means unusual and has been part of public life for at least 150 years. Also, most members of the public in Anglo-Saxon countries, and especially literary critics and teachers of literature and the arts, would feel distinctly alienated if writers, artists, and for that matter intellectuals were to become involved in and pronounce on matters perceived as political. In the Anglo-Saxon world it is generally accepted and expected that a demarcation line exists with arts and culture on one side and politics on the other. Clearly this does not mean that no exceptions exist and that the Anglo-Saxon countries have a literary history which is apolitical. Yet the role of writers and intellectuals in countries like France and Germany has been distinctly different since at least the earlier part of the nineteenth century. It is difficult to imagine a Sartre, a Grass, or a Böll in the Anglo-Saxon context. Yet the role of the writer and intellectual is a central issue of European politics and culture, where they play a political and public role, often regarding themselves as the conscience and consciousness of a nation. Writers in particular have seen themselves and have been seen as instrumental in shaping the conscience and consciousness of their people. In how far such a view constitutes a gross exaggeration of the educative influence a writer can have on the mind of the individual and the value system of a people is another matter. It is noteworthy that one basic question which has been raised in connection with the Third Reich by German intellectuals themselves asks how it was possible that the self-styled "nation of poets and thinkers" gave birth to and succumbed to one of the most murderous and genocidal regimes in human history.[1]

Within the value concepts of Marxism writers, artists, intellectuals, art and culture have always occupied a high position.[2] Marxist writers and politicians have always underlined the formative power of literature and art, either in terms of its contribution to creating and raising socialist consciousness or in terms of its potential subversive influence. Stalin's definition of the writer as the engineer of the soul is often quoted in this context. In the GDR, the role of artists, art and culture was seen well into the 1960s predominantly in terms of its contribution to raising socialist consciousness. Specifically, this applied to problems of considerable societal importance, e.g. (1) how can the minds of young people in particular be cleansed of the corrupting influence of Nazi ideology, (2) how can the level of socialist consciousness be raised to achieve increased productivity, and (3) how can western influences be counteracted.

Art and culture play a central part in the broad aim of the creation of the new man under socialism. Art and culture are to be an integral part of the all-round socialist personality, and the socialist nation is also to be a "cultural nation" (*Kulturnation*). This raises the question of accessibility, both in terms of making art and culture available to the people but also in terms of works of art and literature themselves facilitating ease of approach thematically and formally. The classic document in this respect is still Lenin's 1905 essay on party organization and party literature. The most extreme attempt to date in the GDR to overcome the gap between art and life, the artist and society, and to make culture all-pervasive was the proclamation of the cultural revolution of the late 1950s and its practical implementation in the Bitterfeld Path (*Bitterfelder Weg*). Although the Bitterfeld Path itself acknowledged the poor quality of artistic output in the GDR and saw itself also as a means of raising quality, the partial failure of the Bitterfeld Path highlighted the problem of trying to plan art and culture at this level. Especially from the 1960s onwards there has been continuous debate on issues of quality, choice of theme, and formal and stylistic expression; in particular the degree of control and the requirement for self-censorship has been almost continuously debated. The beginning of the Honecker era saw a period of relaxation of control, but the line became stricter again in the second half of the 1970s and in the early 1980s. There are some signs of a more liberal approach at the time of writing: for example, whereas Christa Wolf's *Frankfurt Lectures*, published together with her novel *Kassandra* in 1983, had passages criticizing both sides in the arms race removed, her most recent book *Störfall* ("Breakdown": 1987), which deals with the effects of the Chernobyl nuclear disaster, was not only relatively widely available in the GDR but was also read by her on GDR television.

At the 10th Writer's Congress in November 1987 concern was expressed on censorship and also on issues such as the environment and the quality of life in socialism. There was also mention of developments in the USSR, which the GDR intelligentsia are watching with cautious optimism. While the statement adopted by the Writers' Congress is unremarkable, it is a new departure for *Neues Deutschland* to report "one vote against and five abstentions".

Since the 1960s the themes of art and literature in the GDR have moved away from the Bitterfeld Path to a greater or lesser extent; in art and in literature the thematic emphasis is now on the individual and individual problems in the setting of the socialist society. Thus the 10th Art Exhibition of the German Democratic Republic still features factory scenes and group portraits of workers, but these are the minority. Individual portraits in a wide variety of styles dominate. This exhibition also illustrates the workings of the GDR's cultural policies. Attendances are high because visits are organized by the enterprises, agricultural co-operatives and institutions, usually in working time; but the claim of high accessibility and involvement is supported by the degree to which the visitors to the exhibition discuss the exhibits among themselves.

The constitution of the GDR lays down in Article 18 the fundamental relevance of culture as a part of political and social life. The SED party programme of 1976 gives an unequivocal and practical commitment to the promotion of socialist culture. For the last two decades, cultural policy has been part of social policy and as such part of the unity of economic and social policy proclaimed by Honecker in the early 1970s. This is evidenced by the fact that cultural policy figures inherently in the five-year plans and the reports and directives issued by the SED.

Documents

D141 From Anna Seghers's speech on "Literature's share in forming the consciousness of the people", given at the Fourth Writers' Congress in 1956:

. . . For in our state the construction of socialism and the transformation of our society is being carried out for the first time on German soil, in the face of difficulties and hindrances. The books we must speak about are a part of the forces working on people's consciousness in this process, particularly in this part of our divided country . . .

When I returned from emigration I travelled from the West right across Germany. The cities were in ruins, and internally the people were in ruins too. At that time Germany was a "unity" of ruins, despair, and hunger. But there were also people who were not numbed with distress, who were beginning to ask the questions which were on everyone's mind: What has happened? What made it happen? — That gave rise to the next question: What must happen to prevent this horror ever returning?

That was the moment when German writers had to come on the scene to account for the situation as clearly and audibly as possible. They had to use the medium of their profession to help bring people to understand the situation they had brought on themselves and to awake in them the strength for a different life, a new, peaceful life.

So began the work of education in the east of Germany.

(Anna Seghers: *Über Kunstwerk und Wirklichkeit*, Berlin 1970, pp. 91 f.)

D142 From the speech by Wilhelm Pieck at the first cultural conference of the KPD, 3–5 February 1946:

We must create preconditions and guarantees to ensure that the elevated ideas of the best minds of our people, the ideas we encounter again in the greatest minds of all people and all times, the ideas of genuine, deeply felt, militant humanity and true freedom and democracy, the ideas of international understanding and social progress, do now really become the dominant powers in our cultural life and at the same time become living forces forming and directing our whole political and social life.

(W. Pieck: *Um die Erneuerung der deutschen Kultur*, typescript in the Wilhelm Pieck archive of the Institut für Marxismus-Leninismus, Berlin)

D143 From the proclamation founding the "League of Culture for the Democratic Renewal of Germany", 4 July 1945:

In the face of these facts, which are so deeply shameful for our fatherland and for our culture, it has to be recognized that the German intelligentsia who should have given leadership to our people failed the test of history when the destruction of Germany could have been averted and the war could have been prevented or at least ended sooner. We have to account to ourselves for the fact that the defencelessness of the German intellect against reactionary forces had its beginnings a long time ago, before Hitler; in the barbaric re-evaluation of all values, in the destruction of realism and common sense, and in the separation of the German intellectual from all public and social matters.

We must confess that the great humanist legacy of German Classicism was also no longer sufficiently alive in the German intelligentsia to give them the unshakeable strength to resist the Nazi regime. While outstanding individuals demonstrated their steadfastness and strength of resistance, the intelligentsia in general submitted to seduction and terror.

It is necessary to recognize this, however bitter it may be, to enable a new German intelligentsia to be formed which feels a vocation to go on ahead and guide the German people on new paths. A fundamental change is necessary so that Germany may rise again. This resurrection of Germany can only take place under the banner of truth, under the banner of a liberal democratic spirit. We must restore truth to a place of honour in order to regain our national honour. We recognize Germany's war guilt. We have unspeakable things to compensate for. We declare ourselves for compensation.

The "League of Culture for the Democratic Renewal of Germany" sets itself the task which today is one of the greatest national tasks of the intelligentsia — to unite all German men and women whose sincere and unshakeable will it is to contribute with all their strength to the intellectual and cultural renewal of Germany. In this time of severe distress in the history of Germany, the best Germans from all occupations and levels of society must be gathered together to create a movement for German renewal with the will to eliminate the remnants of fascism and reaction in all areas of life and knowledge and so to build a new, honest and decent life in the sphere of intellectual culture. It would be disastrous for our fatherland's fate and would bar Germany's way forward into the future if we did not retrospectively uncover and overcome all the errors and weaknesses which made Nazi rule possible and evoked the greatest tragedy of our nation.

The end of military action means the continuation of the struggle against Nazism and reaction and the intensification of this struggle with intellectual means. The total political and military defeat of Hitler's rule was necessary to give us full opportunity to inflict fatal wounds on Nazism in another area — where its false doctrines have taken root in the thoughts and feelings of the German people. It is a mistake to assume that with the military and political collapse of Hitler's rule the Nazi ideology will simply disappear of its own accord . . .

The "League of Culture for the Democratic Renewal of Germany" considers itself to be an instrument to awaken truly liberal feeling and thought, an instrument to awaken the conscience of the nation. In the name of Germany we demand that the causes underlying the greatest defeat in our history should be made totally clear. We demand that the war criminals should be called to account and sentenced as enemies of Germany, traitors to their fatherland and corrupters of the people, and that this should also apply to those who are to be accused of ideological drum-beating and leadership in war criminality. We demand a fundamental change of direction in all areas of life and knowledge. We strive for a new, liberal, democratic ideology. We demand that our German people be educated in the spirit of truth, in the spirit of a militant democratism. This is a work of national liberation and reconstruction of the most extensive kind in the moral and ideological sphere.

The German people must be freed from all the reactionary refuse of its history, which has concentrated itself most ignominiously in Hitler's rule, and the German people must be provided with all the positive elements from its own history and the history of other peoples which are capable of keeping our people viable as such and preserving it once and for all from new imperialist adventures, so that it may be offered the possibility of being readmitted to the community of nations. In this sense the "League of Culture for the Democratic Renewal of Germany" feels its vocation as an intellectual authority placing advice and assistance at the disposal of a Germany arising anew. We shall make the most urgent efforts to have relations with the cultural forces of other nations renewed in consequence of our liberal achievements. We wish to make the German people acquainted with the cultural attainments of all nations, including in particular those of the Soviet Union.

(*Manifest und Ansprachen. Gründungskundgebung des Kulturbundes zur demokratischen Erneuerung Deutschlands am 4. July 1945*, Berlin 1945, pp. 5 ff.)

D144 From Walter Ulbricht's speech at the "Working Meeting of Party Writers and Artists" in September 1948:

Why can a writer not take as his theme how the struggle to build up a factory was carried on! It is after all a very interesting theme to show how the employer and some other people were dispatched, how the struggle for reconstruction was carried on at the expense of enormous effort, what human stories revealed themselves in the process, how engineers who were not initially in favour of the new order gradually began to become involved . . . The depiction of this struggle in a factory and the characterization of those involved is surely a theme that ought to be treated . . .

The Two-Year Plan is not a purely economic matter but a matter of implementing far-reaching changes in society and acquiring a new progressive culture in connection with the struggle for the Two-Year Plan. What is most important is to change people.

(W. Ulbricht: *Zur Geschichte der deutschen Arbeiterbewegung*, Berlin 1960, p. 310)

D145 Cultural tasks under the Two-Year Plan, from the First Party Conference of the SED, 25–28 January 1949:

The progressive elements of our people expect writers and artists to produce creative depictions of the life of working people and their striving for a higher order of society. By working together in this way that great mass initiative will be developed which alone can ensure the achievement and overachievement of the Two-Year Plan ...

The cultural task of educating people to a new understanding of society and a new attitude to work can only be achieved if all writers and artists devote all their energy and enthusiasm to this work ...

The contribution writers and artists make to the Two-Year Plan is their development of a realistic art and their efforts to achieve the highest artistic performance in their sphere.

(*Dokumente der SED. Beschlüsse und Erklärungen*, ed. Central Committee of the SED, Berlin 1951 ff.)

D146 Prime Minister Otto Grotewohl on the relation between politics and art, August 1951:

Literature and fine art are subordinated to politics, but it is clear that they exert a strong influence on politics. The idea of art must follow the line of the political struggle ... Whatever is proved to be right in politics is unconditionally right in art too.

(*Gedichte von drüben*, ed. L. von Balluseck and K.H. Brokerhoff, Godesberg 1963, p. 6)

D147 From the Central Committee of the SED's resolution on writers and authors adopted at the 25th Plenum, 27 October 1955:

The creative activity of our writers and artists still in no way corresponds to the great mission which art can and must fulfil in raising consciousness and consolidating morality in a workers' and farmers' state under the conditions of the construction of socialism. The fact that they are not keeping up with what is necessary for society has been repeatedly criticized and has now become a serious issue in view of the increasing requirements to create a socialist consciousness for millions . . .

Writers and artists . . . must be the educators of the masses under the guidance of the party and must inspire them to higher performance in all areas of social life by the works they create on the basis of Socialist Realism. More than hitherto literature and art must give form to the great conflicts that our people experience in the development of socialist consciousness in the struggle with bourgeois and petty-bourgeois views and habits, and show how these conflicts are overcome. They must take up the varied nature of the problems presented by life in general and the struggle of the National Front of democratic Germany in particular.

(*Dokumente der SED. Beschlüsse und Erklärungen*, ed. Central Committee of the SED, Berlin 1951 ff.)

D148 Alexander Abusch on the role of writers and artists (1957):

Socialist Realism has long become a part of revolutionary tradition, of the revolutionary achievement of our literature and art. However, traditions and achievements can only be preserved if they are further developed into something new and higher. At present, this consists in writers and artists employing the best creative methods of our age to create great works of socialist art which help to change people's consciousness in the spirit of socialism. This is no small task; it does not mean providing illustrations for the Party's daily resolutions. It is the greatest task the writer and the artist have ever been set in the history of our people and of humankind, for it is active participation through their artistic activity in the most profound revolution in people's thought and feelings, in their morality, in their souls; the socialist revolution.

(A. Abusch: "Sozialistischer Realismus und Dekadenz" (1957), in: *Huma nismus und Realismus in der Literatur*, Berlin 1972, p. 155)

D149 From Walter Ulbricht's address to the Fifth Party Congress of the SED, 10–16 July 1958:

In the context of the appearance of the various revisionist groups, some comrades attacked what they saw as dogmatism in the party leadership.

They demanded that all flowers should be allowed to bloom. In our country innumerable flowers bloom, and new kinds will always develop. But we cannot tolerate the harmful weeds which come over from the capitalist West. We did not permit the weeds of the counter-revolution to spread, rather we eradicated them. However we did not fight against the yellow blooms of revisionism with administrative methods but first fought ideologically so that the whole party could recognize where bourgeois ideology had made its entrance and could take up the ideological and political struggle openly.

(*Zur sozialistischen Kulturrevolution*, vol. 1, ed. M. Lange, Berlin 1960, pp. 162 f.)

D150 From the resolutions of the Fifth Party Congress of the SED, 10–16 July 1958:

The socialist cultural revolution is a necessary part of the whole socialist transformation in which cultural mass work is linked closely with political mass work, with socialist education and all measures to increase socialist production and productivity. It is now of prime importance to overcome the separation still existing between life and art, the estrangement between artists and the people.

(*Zur sozialistischen Kulturrevolution*, vol. 2, ed. M. Lange, Berlin 1960, p. 413)

D151 From V.I. Lenin, "On Party Organization and Party Literature", 13 November 1905:

What is this principle of party literature? It is not simply that for the socialist proletariat, literature cannot be a means of enriching individuals or groups: it cannot, in fact, be an individual undertaking, independent of the common cause of the proletariat. Down with non-partisan writers! Down with literary supermen! Literature must become *part* of the common cause of the proletariat, "a cog and a screw" of one single great Social-Democratic mechanism set in motion by the entire politically conscious vanguard of the entire working class. Literature must become a component of organized, planned and integrated Social-Democratic Party work.

"All comparisons are lame," says a German proverb. So is my comparison of literature with a cog, of a living movement with a mechanism. And I daresay there will ever be hysterical intellectuals to raise a howl about such a comparison, which degrades, deadens, "bureaucratises" the free battle of ideas, freedom of criticism, freedom of literary creation, etc., etc. Such outcries, in point of fact, would be nothing more than an expression of bourgeois-intellectual individualism. There is no question that literature is least of all subject to mechanical adjustment or levelling, to the rule of the majority over the minority. There is no question, either, that in this field greater scope must undoubtedly be allowed for personal initiative, individual inclination, thought and fantasy, form and content. All this is undeniable; but all this simply shows that the literary side of the proletarian party cause cannot be mechanically identified with its other sides. This, however, does not in the least refute the proposition, alien and strange to the bourgeoisie and bourgeois democracy, that literature must by all means and necessarily become an element of Social-Democratic Party work, inseparably bound up with the other elements. Newspapers must become the organs of the various party organizations, and their writers must by all means become members of these organizations. Publishing and distributing centres, bookshops and reading-rooms, libraries and similar establishments — must all be under party control. The organized socialist proletariat must keep an eye on all this work, supervise it in its entirety, and, from beginning to end, without any exception, infuse into it the life-stream of the living proletarian cause, thereby cutting the ground from under the old, semi-Oblomov, semi-shopkeeper Russian principle: the writer does the writing, the reader does the reading.

(V.I. Lenin: *Selected Works*, London 1971, pp. 149 f.)

D152 From Walter Ulbricht's closing speech at the Authors' Conference of the Mitteldeutscher Verlag Halle/Saale held in the Palace of Culture of the Bitterfeld Electrochemical Combine, 24 April 1959:

On the basis of the decisions of the 5th Party Conference we must state that the discussions represent an important contribution towards the development of a further blossoming of socialist culture in the German Democratic Republic. The new feature is that instead of a small circle of writers and authors trying to discuss and solve these tasks by themselves everything is being done to develop all the talents and potential present in the population in order *to give socialist culture a very broad base.*

Young writers are to be developed from the working class, the ranks of the workers, correspondents, etc. They are to be given every opportunity to develop their talents. We must at the same time implement practical measures *to enable the workers to storm the heights of culture.*

The task is to create the new socialist national culture on the foundation of the construction of socialism and to use it in the struggle to overcome the remnants of capitalist ideology, of capitalist and bourgeois habits. The task is at the same time to carry on the struggle with artistic means against imperialist and fascist ideology and bourgeois decadence which exert their influence from the West.

Our literature, our art, the fine arts in general must be given a new socialist content and must be made accessible to the whole people. In the context of the great social transformation which has taken place on our territory in the last 14 years, the creative activity of the working people here in the heart of Europe proved what great capacities and what strength are present in the people to develop the new socialist order of society, the socialist economy, and the new socialist culture.

What is the task our writers have been assigned by history?

Their task is to give artistic form to what is new in life, in people's social relationships, in their struggle for the construction of socialism and the socialist reorganization of all aspects of life, so that they inspire people by their artistic achievements and so help to speed up and advance the tempo of development. Working people expect writers to make their great contribution to socialist reorganization in the German Democratic Republic. The major forms of popular education — books, television, film, radio, the press — offer the writer the most varied opportunities to develop his talents.

What do we hope to achieve?

We want to help the working class, the ruling class which exercises political power in alliance with the intelligentsia, working farmers and other sections of the working population, to *storm the heights of culture. With the help of writers and artists and talented working people, we want to shape the culture of the new Germany, that culture which in its form is national and in its content is a socialist culture.*

The working class, which at present is carrying out the socialist reconstruction of our industry together with the engineers, technicians, scientists, and other sections of the working population, can achieve this great objective only with a high level of technical knowledge and a high standard of general education.

What are the important issues in cultural policy at present?

We must make the best works of our classical authors and anti-fascists and progressive literature widely accessible to the people. But at the same time we must develop a new socialist content in literature and art, and make the new socialist way of life the subject of new plays, films, television programmes, etc. This demands *a new quality in writers' activity. This demands that they are so closely linked to current life that they are able to give realistic form to this new socialist life.*

Without underestimating literary works dealing with historical themes or having the struggle against fascism as their subject, I should like to concentrate in my remarks on this new element. Of course many writers still have many interesting themes from their own lives to deal with. However this need not prevent them from standing in the midst of this new life and helping to shape it.

At the same time we want to present the treasures of German and of human culture to the working class and the farmers. We must start from the realization that a large proportion of working people never had the chance to enjoy the great works of our major artists, for instance to listen to Beethoven's Ninth Symphony.

The time has come for us to explain great works of German literature in the clubs and houses of culture and on the radio to give working people the opportunity to become familiar with a play before they see it in the theatre, or to publish appropriate reference works, which are almost totally lacking at the moment. Is it not necessary to develop all working people's understanding for these things in order to make life more attractive and more interesting? It is also necessary to develop the less serious arts, light entertainment. For a long time we had great difficulties since most of what we used was taken over from the West and was more or less well or badly copied.

In the context of developing socialist culture *our own light entertainment culture must be created.* Our writers and composers face a great task in this sphere.

The writer and the problems of life today

There has long been a discussion among writers whether the writer is in a position to deal directly with the problems of life at present. I believe I had the first discussion on this point as early as 1948. That is a long discussion. At the moment no one is talking about it; but many people are not writing either.

At all periods in the history of humankind, writers and poets have been the proponents and harbingers of the new. There is no great work of art which does not in some sense have as its content what is new and progressive.

In the period of the decline of feudalism and the beginning of the capitalist era, at the time of the rise of the bourgeoisie, it was the great bourgeois writers who created humanistic works and carried on the struggle against feudalism. We all know our classic authors and know what an impression and what a deep influence these works still have on the German people today.

Not one of the great figures of literature or the fine arts would have been able to write his works without a deep knowledge of the subject to be treated. Goethe's "Faust" and Schiller's plays make clear in their content the poets' close relationship to their own time and attest to the profound historical knowledge possessed by the two greatest figures of our classical literature.

Is it not today more essential than ever that writers are in the front ranks of those proclaiming the new aspects of society and leading the struggle against what is old, outdated, rotten and decadent? New social relations between people have developed in our Republic. But where is there a depiction of this development in an artistic form to compare with the ones the classic authors of the bourgeoisie produced on the development of their class in the struggle against the feudal order of society? You may perhaps say that such demands are too high. But great works of art can only be created when there is a broad development of culture as a whole. Therefore I wish on principle to say the following about this issue:

We are of the opinion that no one can better give form to the problems of the present than the writer or working person who experiences this new life, the reorganization of this life, and who helps in the struggle for this reorganization. He can do this much better than someone who looks back in ten years' time and writes about all the developments that took place in 1959.(*applause*)

We are of the opinion that *the writer's task at present* is precisely to give form to the new elements in the present socialist reorganization, in the development of all aspects of economic and cultural life, new human relationships, the new social life. But what does that mean? *That means that writers and artists themselves participate in the construction of socialism: for the writer who himself is active and working at the focal points in the development of our new life is best able to recognize and understand the new, to track it down and present it creatively.*

By giving artistic form to what is new in the development of the socialist society, the writer inspires people to achieve important tasks. He makes them conscious of the new and contributes to higher performance and also to the acceleration of developments.

But the writer or the artist must prepare himself for his task. High artistic achievements, high achievements of any kind are not easy to attain.

The central issue of the discussion in the Writers' Association is: how should writers and artists work and participate in the life of the people and the construction of socialism in order to get to know people in their work and in the development of their thoughts? It is only on this basis that writers can properly recognize and give form to what is new in human relationships, the developing conflicts between old habits and outside influences and the new forms of life.

At present the position is that a number of writers are taking part in the life of working people and experiencing for themselves what is new in people's development. To the extent that the writer himself is filled with the new pulsating life of the construction of socialism, his own capability of giving artistic form to this life will grow . . .

Unless it storms the heights of culture, the working class will have difficulty in fulfilling its great tasks to lead socialism to victory. For this reason we set the objective of radical socialist change in the sphere of ideology and culture at the 5th Party Conference in the context of the great objectives of the socialist reconstruction of industry, the development of chemistry, and the struggle to set the world standard in science and technology. We must get away from the old situation, and also from the old views of many workers who say, "Planning and managing the economy and so on, that'll all be done by them at the top; and as for cultural policies, they'll be set by them at the top." Absolutely not! We are not in a position to solve a single, basic problem unless we solve it shoulder to shoulder with you, the workers in the factories, the intelligentsia, the writers.

Take part in planning, in working, in governing! That is no mere slogan; it is a very real and in fact a difficult task, because it demands great specialist knowledge, great knowledge of the management of the workers' and farmers' state authority, and a high standard of education for the working class and all working people. Without that it is impossible!

That means that all of us — from worker to minister — must learn more, a great deal more. This ideological transformation and development forward will go faster if the writers and artists help us, and slower if they do not help us.

Let me say quite frankly that it is going too slowly. The activists, the members of the socialist work brigades are going faster than some of our writers and artists. But no one can claim that the workers have a higher level of education than the writers and artists or that these lack the necessary knowledge.

I want therefore to emphasize that we place the writers' tasks in the framework of the socialist transformation, in the framework of accomplishing our central economic aim of achieving the lead over West Germany in consumption per head of population and in the struggle to set the world standard in science and technology. Obviously we need this increased rate of ideological and cultural development in the German Democratic Republic not only to make life more pleasant for working people and because socialism can only triumph in this way, but also *because in the next few years we must prove our absolute superiority over West Germany in all areas of culture. This applies to all branches of the arts* . . .

Remarks on the work of the Writers' Association

The Fourth German Writers' Congress set our writers, poets, and artists the task of creating the new socialist national literature, which is national in form and socialist in content. What basis is there in the German Democratic

Republic for a socialist national literature?

The basis for the new socialist national literature is the new relations of production in industry and agriculture, and the existence of the Workers' and Farmers' power. On this basis, conditions have been created for the development of new human relationships and true humanity; these make possible great achievements for our writers and artists.

The people, liberated from capitalist exploitation and oppression, are shaping a higher culture, a socialist culture which at the same time contains a systematic development of the best humanistic ideas and traditions of our people. Our Seven-Year Plan is not merely a plan to develop production and the supply of consumer goods. It is at the same time a plan to develop the new socialist way of life. And artistic achievement is not merely a means to help achieve the objectives but an integral part of the whole plan which will lead to the triumph of socialism.

At the time of the 4th Writers' Congress the question was: can writers give artistic form to the national problems of the present socialist reconstruction? This question has still not been fully answered. The discussions at the time were not taken to a conclusion. The discussions were abstract and did not start from the stage of development already reached. They neglected to clarify what had already been achieved. The central issue — that the construction of socialism is above all the task of educating people — was not recognized. And some writers also took a stand against socialist realism. A discussion was held under the influence of Lukács which only held back development.

But in his letter of 1888 to Miss Harkness, Engels had already stated: "In my view realism means not only the faithful reproduction of detail but also the faithful reproduction of typical characters in typical circumstances . . The rebellion of the working class against the milieu of oppression surrounding them, their attempts — desperate, half conscious or unconscious — to recover their position as human beings, are a part of history and therefore must have their claim to a place in the sphere of realism."

Writers, literary theorists and critics have carried forward the discussion of this problem in many disputes since the 4th Writers' Conference. At the Soviet Union conference on questions of socialist realism, the Soviet writers, critics and literary theorists stated:

"Life formed the source for socialist realism, which is a stage of world literature reached in accordance with the laws of literary development, the outcome of the tireless striving of all progressive art."

Our opponents often claim that socialist realism levels out national features in art and rejects historically developed traditions. That is totally false. Socialist realism is an affirmation of life. Socialist realism is a creative method of artistic activity, and the future belongs to it because it educates writers as active participants in the struggle to build the socialist society.

In the last years it has become evident how the growing influence of socialist realism is extending to art all over the world. Works of socialist realism dealing with present-day themes are of direct assistance to the construction of socialism. They advance it because they help people to recognize the new and to see everything in context.

The stimulus the broad masses of the people receive from literary works of a socialist content works in two directions:

(1) The reader is prompted by the heroes of novels and artistic works or by the beauty of poetry to emulate them.

(2) The writing worker and reader is encouraged by them to try himself to represent in literary form the questions which concern him.

Our party's cultural conference initiated an ideological dispute about literary problems. The results so far from this development are that revisionism has been driven back in the literary and aesthetic spheres.

Some conferences last year already had positive results. But at the same time they showed weaknesses which have not yet been completely overcome among writers and artists. The fact is that many writers and artists still regard the most important question, the question of ideological clarity, as a secondary matter, and consider that concerning themselves with it would rather hinder their artistic work. But their inadequate familiarity with Marxist-Leninist theory is reflected in their artistic works; it produces superficiality and poverty of thought, sometimes even false revisionist tendencies.

A writer can achieve something worthwhile only if he knows the laws of development of society and is filled with a profound scientific conviction of the justice of the cause of socialism and communism and the certainty of its triumph.

[. . .]

The writer and the collective

In general the Fourth Congress of the Writers' Association took a correct line and set the correct basic tasks for the development of a socialist national literature. The error was that the problems were not pursued to their conclusion. Revisionist views were allowed to be put forward without being answered. For instance, Lukács's position was put forward, and there were other views which should have been discussed.

The second error was that the literary works of our writers were not discussed. This was characteristic of the Writers' Congress. That is, a general survey was given, but nothing was said about the main point, namely about the literature which had been produced and existed in manuscript. In the meantime that has in part happened.

We have made important progress. We could be further forward if we worked collectively and spoke about this in our organization. *Writers are not in a position to deal with the new problems of socialist society unless they discuss the problem of their own creative work with each other, as friends, within the Association.* It is not simply a question of writers studying the new social relationships in the working class and between people in the factory or in agriculture; *there are also new problems of writers' relationships to each other,* really creative relationships which will lead to great socialist works.

What is important at present? *It is important that our writers help with their specifically artistic works in their achievement of the great task of developing socialism in the German Democratic Republic.* The works of our writers should proclaim what is new and progressive in the German Democratic Republic.

(*Greif zur Feder, Kumpel! Protokoll der Autorenkonferenz des Mitteldeutschen Verlages Halle (Saale) am 24. April 1959 im Kulturpalast des Elektrochemischen Kombinats Bitterfeld,* Halle/Saale 1959, pp. 96 ff.)

D153 Resolutions passed at the Bitterfeld Conference, 1959:

(1) To develop further the movement of reading workers and to supplement it by a movement of writing workers.

(2) To give priority to the promotion of writers who take as their theme the literary treatment of problems of the socialist transformation in the GDR.

(3) To call on the publishers to redirect their work with authors and their publishing activities in this direction.

(4) To use the resources of the cultural fund so that support is given primarily to the artistic activity which assists socialist culture.

(5) To combine the proposals on the development of the arts and entertainment put forward in the discussion into a complete system of effective measures.

(6) To suggest to the cultural commission of the Central Committee of the SED that these measures should be extended to the other arts.

(Source as above, p. 117)

D154 From Kurt Hager's speech to the Tenth Meeting of the Central Committee of the SED, 28–9 April 1969:

Planning and guidance of intellectual and cultural processes

The practical development of the social system of socialism not only proves the burning relevance of the Marxist-Leninist recognition that social consciousness, ideology, the superstructure represents a powerful transforming and moving force in social development but also demonstrates what new basic laws determine the content of intellectual life in socialism and the direction in which it is developing. These laws include the planning and guidance of intellectual and cultural processes by the party and the socialist state. This is an essential, indispensable component of scientific leadership at all levels.

Planning and guidance of intellectual and cultural processes must be based on scientific forecasting of society's development and must be in accord with the planning and guidance of the other social processes, particularly with the economic developments and structural policies laid down in the long-term plan and with the development of the educational system. We have already followed these principles in previous years. The successful formation of a rich, varied and interesting intellectual life in all spheres, particularly since the 7th Party Congress of the SED, has refuted the view that intellectual and cultural processes cannot be planned. This is unaffected by the outcry of our opponents, for whom of course the ever stronger development of socialist humanism, socialist morality and the culture and educational system of the GDR is a thorn in their flesh.

The further development of the socialist consciousness of the working class and the other working classes and sections of our people can only take place as a result of planned leadership by the SED and the socialist state and with the involvement of all the forces of our people united in the National Front. Therefore the proper formation and practical implementation of a comprehensive system of ideological activity is one of the most important tasks facing the party in the period ahead.

We are aware that planning and guidance of the processes of intellectual and cultural development is a complicated task since the sharpest conflicts between socialism and imperialism take place in the sphere of ideology, as the remnants of bourgeois and petty-bourgeois ideology, habits and way of living survive the longest and as ideology is not one subsystem of socialist society among others but permeates all spheres of social life and is naturally also influenced by them.

At the same time however these are also the reasons why a properly functioning system of planning and guidance of intellectual and cultural processes and ideological work is of such great importance. In the 10th Meeting of the Central Committee of the SED we want to direct the attention of all party organizations to this important task in the further construction of socialism and lay down the measures required.

[. . .]

In the sphere of culture our greatest efforts are directed towards these areas and genres which play an outstanding part in developing the distinctiveness of socialist and national culture and socialist consciousness, and in moulding the long-term cultural needs of all working people. This applies above all to the literature of socialist realism.[3] This, in all its forms, is particularly suitable for dealing with the new problems of socialism with reference to the individual. It is outstandingly well able to portray the development of personality in socialist society and so to contribute to the development of new human relationships.

Working people's increased demand for education and reading material, the requirements of the theatres, of television and film production, of light entertainment and of amateur cultural activity, the need for lyrics for songs and popular music all call for the development and promotion of all the literary talent available in our country.

(Kurt Hager: *Grundfragen des geistigen Lebens im Sozialismus. Referat auf der 10. Tagung des ZK der SED, 28/29 April 1969*, Berlin 1969, pp. 60 ff., 66)

D155 From Erich Honecker's speech to a mass meeting of the Leipzig Region party organization, 10 March 1972:

We too understand the vocation and responsibility of the writer in socialism as that of a conscious, faithful and courageous comrade-in-arms of the working class, discovering and helping to shape the new reality and constantly seeking to get to know life in all its aspects and "use it as his material" — in all the richness it offers him. After all, no one is gripped by a mere cliché abstracted from life; what is moving and exciting in books and plays is what experiences can be shared and imagined in them, what gives clearer, more profound access to present, past and future. What is gripping is, as writers themselves say, the "whole ensemble" of various characters, all striving forward. Given that, it should not be impossible to find the right mixture of conflicts; and in my opinion while the field between bad and good is certainly not a narrow one, the field between good and better is considerably broader, and productive as well.

In its cultural policy too our party is taking Lenin's path, the path by which our writers and artists make a contribution valued by many people because of their closeness to the people and their party commitment, and because of their works' closeness to life, sense of reality and certainty about the future. This is a valued contribution which enriches working people's intellectual world, and which they respect and love. There is a great deal of free play here for personal initiative by our writers and artists and for their individual preferences, free play for thoughts and imagination, form and content. And everyone who is serious about his artistic work will employ it precisely the way in which in the development of socialist society we do everything for the benefit of the people.

Many questions have arisen in the sphere of literature and art and must now be answered in accordance with the decisions of the 8th Party Conference. There are questions concerning the development of our literary and art criticism in order to support and promote our artists' activities still better — and also to challenge them. There is the question of what we understand by contemporary creative work, and whether the whole width and depth of this concept is yet understood by everybody. Our criterion should be how works of art and literature affect the socialist consciousness of people today. It remains crucial that new works of art should constantly be produced which are more and more attuned to the demands of our socialist age and the requirements of working people.

Culture in socialism permeates all aspects of social and individual existence more and more, from the daily work in the industrial enterprises, the agricultural co-operatives and the educational and scientific establishments to life in the residential areas. It is precisely because we know that this does not happen by itself and does not happen to the same extent everywhere, precisely because this far-reaching and prolonged change needs constant, planned, sensitive guidance that we constantly draw the attention of our party organizations to the tasks connected with it.

(Erich Honecker: *Der VIII. Parteitag und unsere nächsten Aufgaben. Aus der Rede auf einer propagandistischen Großveranstaltung der Bezirksparteiorganisation der SED Leipzig am 10. März 1972*, Berlin 1972, pp.40 f.)

D156 From Erich Honecker's speech to the Ninth Plenum of the Central Committee of the SED, May 1973:

Certainly first attempts to track down what is new here, to uncover it and help to give it form are not always successful, particularly not when the attempt is made to impose one's own sorrows on society. The individual's loneliness and isolation from society as presented in various plays and films and their anonymity in respect of social circumstances already show clearly that the basic attitude of such works is in contradiction to the demands socialism makes of art and literature.[4]

(*Sonntag* Nr. 23, 10.6, 1973)

D157 The socialist state and culture:

(From the Constitution of the German Democratic Republic)

Article 18

(1) Socialist national culture is one of the foundations of socialist society. The German Democratic Republic fosters and protects socialist culture, which serves peace, humanism and the development of socialist society. It combats imperialist anti-culture, which serves psychological warfare and the degradation of man. Socialist society promotes the cultured life of the working people, cultivates the humanistic values of the national cultural heritage and of world culture and develops socialist national culture as the concern of all people.

(2) The promotion of the arts, the artistic interests and abilities of all working people, and the dissemination of artistic works and creations, are the obligation of the state and all social forces. Artistic work is based on close contact between artists and the life of the people.

(3) Physical culture, sports and tourism, as elements of socialist culture, serve the all-round physical and intellectual development of citizens.

(Panorama DDR: *Culture and Art in socialist society*, Dresden, 1975, pp. 54 ff)

D158 From the Act relating to the local assemblies and their agencies in the GDR of 12 July 1973:

§ 31 Culture

(1) The County Assemblies and Councils are responsible for the development of intellectual and cultural life. They encourage the creation of new socialist works of art, the preservation and dissemination of the cultural heritage. They work together with the FDGB, the FDJ, the Cultural Association of the GDR, the art associations and other mass organizations in the county.

(2) The County Assembly and the County Council are responsible for working out long-term plans to develop and disseminate art and literature and guarantee, together with artist, writers and cultural workers, that the plans are carried out. In organizing cultural life, they take account of the works of art of the Soviet Union and other socialist countries as well as progressive culture of other peoples.

(3) The County Council and County Assembly encourage the participation of citizens in cultural life and in folk art and culture. They are responsible, together with the local assemblies and District Councils, for the expansion and maintenance of the network of cultural institutions and memorials.

(Source as above)

D159 Nationalized industries and culture:

(From the decree on the tasks, rights and duties of the nationally owned enterprises, combined works and associations of nationally owned enterprises of 28 March 1973)

§ 5

(1) The nationally owned enterprises, combined works and associations of nationally owned enterprises work together with the local assemblies and their councils for the goal of increasing the political influence of the working class in their area and to guarantee political, economic, cultural and social development in their area which is harmoniously co-ordinated with the development of the various industrial branches and sectors.

§ 20

(2) The nationally owned enterprises . . . support the cultural and athletic activity of their staff, especially of the youth. The cultural, medical and social facilities as well as the sports facilities of the factory are to be used in such a way that the needs of the workers and other employees in the factory and the citizens in the residential areas can be better satisfied. Agreements are to be made with local government authorities on the joint creation, financing and use of such facilities.

(Source as above)

D160 Youth and Culture (From the Youth Act of the GDR of 28 January 1974):

§ 27

It is a desire and a task of the youth to make their lives cultured, to use their free time in a sensible way, to become culturally and artistically active and to creatively take part in the development of art and culture. The government encourages the youth in their striving to acquaint themselves with the socialist art and literature of the German Democratic Republic, the Soviet Union and other countries of the socialist community, the humanistic art and literature of the peoples of the world as well as the treasures of the proletarian-revolutionary and democratic-humanist legacy.

§ 30

The needs of the youth for a social life, dancing and entertainment, their striving for high-quality events which enrich their many-sided leisure time activities are to be encouraged and constantly to be better satisfied . . .

§ 31

(1) The government and economic officials, teachers and directors of cultural institutions encourage the artistic work of young people, especially the working-class youth, in all spheres.

§ 32

(1) The artists and cultural workers are called upon to create works of art in all artistic genres for the youth.

(Source as above)

D161 From the Programme of the SED: on the development of a socialist national culture, May 1976:

The Socialist Unity Party of Germany is pledged to a policy of promoting socialist culture in all spheres of social life, material and spiritual. It supports all efforts to enhance the material and spiritual values of socialist culture on the broadest possible scale and to make cultural life as diversified and stimulating as possible. A major concern is the systematic promotion of a truly socialist climate in all places of work and study.

The Party advocates the use of all the opportunities existing for the development of a cultured socialist life in urban and rural communities and holiday areas. It is necessary to provide more amenities for joint cultural experiences, sociability, entertainment and dancing as well as sporting activities.

An advanced socialist society is distinguished by a high standard of spiritual culture. The individual demand for artistic and aesthetic enjoyment is being linked more and more to the creative development of individual artistic talent. The Party will therefore promote people's creative impulses in the cultural sphere and amateur artistic activities in as many ways as possible.

The Socialist Unity Party of Germany supports all efforts aimed at the blossoming of socialist realism in art. Such art is deeply rooted in the realities of socialism and in the life of the people, and it is based on a firm commitment to peace, democracy and socialism and the rejection of imperialism, aggression and reaction. Thanks to the force which political commitment and intimate ties with the people lend to artistic expression, socialist realism in all its breadth and depth is able to influence national life and to mould socialist beliefs, attitudes and relations, a sense of beauty and attachment to the ideals of the working class.

The Party works to see the socialist content of the arts further enhanced. It encourages the quest for artistic discoveries contributing to the enrichment of socialist art and social reality. Artistic development calls for an atmosphere characterized by high spiritual, moral and aesthetic demands on artists and understanding towards them as well as by the encouragement of all talent.

The SED advocates the attainment of such a level in literature, the fine arts, music, the theatre, the cinema and television as well as in the work of museums and libraries so as to meet the rising demands of an advanced socialist society and do justice to the international position of the German Democratic Republic. The task of literary and art critics will be to promote this process in a sensitive but principled manner.

The socialist national culture of the German Democratic Republic includes the careful nurturing and assimilation of all humanist and progressive cultural achievements of the past. The socialist culture of the German Democratic Republic is indebted to the rich heritage built up throughout the history of the German people. Everything great and noble, humanist and revolutionary is preserved and continued in the German Democratic Republic with an eye to its contemporary relevance. The revolutionary cultural traditions of the German working-class movement and the rich cultural heritage of the German Democratic Republic itself are among the reasons for the patriotic feelings of pride we have for our socialist country.

The Socialist Unity Party of Germany will work for socialist culture to become rooted still more deeply in the international cultural heritage. The cultural achievements past and present of the Soviet Union and the other fraternal socialist countries are an especially constant source of inspiration. The humanist and democratic cultural achievements of the whole world are very important for the all-round education of working people. The treasures of world culture cherished in the German Democratic Republic are a vast potential for the enhancement of the richness and diversity of socialist culture. In comprehensively developing the socialist national culture and fully bringing out its patriotic and internationalist socialist content, the German Democratic Republic will make a valuable contribution to the international culture of socialism.

(*Programme of the Socialist Unity Party of Germany*, Dresden 1976, pp. 56 ff.)

D162 From the Central Committee's report to the Eleventh Party Congress of the SED, April 1986:

Comrades,

We can note that intellectual and cultural life has gained in substance and diversity. The values and ideals of socialism are determining cultural achievements in a wide range of areas to an ever greater extent. People's commitment to peace and their devotion to their socialist homeland and to the cause of proletarian internationalism, especially friendship with the Soviet Union and anti-imperialist solidarity, find their expression in a rich cultural outpouring, much esteemed by the consuming public. The socialist German national culture of the GDR is developing successfully, with Sorbian culture forming an integral part.

It remains our main concern to continue raising the cultural standards of the working class and increasing its influence on the development of socialist culture and art. The trade unions and the Free German Youth organization are making a major contribution to this objective by promoting an interesting intellectual and cultural life at workplace level and organizing other cultural activities. They are helping to develop a socialist climate of work and provide opportunities for political and job-related education, and leisure pursuits.

The arts festivals staged by individual factories and other firms to demonstrate the standard of cultural life form the widest possible democratic basis for the workers' arts festivals of the GDR, which take place under the auspices of the trade unions to promote the cause of socialism and peace and lend fresh momentum to cultural activities throughout the country. A new surge of initiative is needed to develop amateur art extensively in all its diversity. There must be more interesting and varied ways for people to indulge their specific interests and inclinations, to go in for do-it-yourself activities, technical and scientific hobbies, and artistic pastimes, whether on an organized, or a temporary and individual basis.

Many forces are involved in the development of our socialist national culture. The GDR League of Culture, the mass organization uniting citizens active or interested in cultural pursuits, has managed to increase its impact on society quite considerably. It will continue to enrich our intellectual and cultural life through the work of local branches, clubs for scholars, study circles, hobby groups, and societies.

We can state here once again that the continuity of our party's cultural policies since the 8th Congress and the clear orientation provided by the 10th Congress have served us well. Our party greatly values the arts for the invaluable contribution they are making to the development of the human personality, and to the public discussion of the main issues affecting human relations in a socialist society and the meaning and purpose of life in the world today. We always respect their specific aesthetic features and mode of functioning.

Our life calls for a socialist realism in literature and art that is distinguished by commitment, close ties with the people, and a wealth of socialist ideas, and that stimulates the thoughts, feelings, and actions of working people. In this context, I should like to emphasize that we need works of art that bolster socialism, and highlight the greatness and beauty of our often hard-won achievements, works of art whose main protagonists are the active men and women who shape history and without whose vitalism the new society would be inconceivable.

For all cultural workers who look upon the arts as a weapon in the struggle for social progress, it is a great challenge to discover and portray the sea changes that have taken place in the life of our people and of the individual, the things we have accomplished and those which remain to be done. The field is wide open here for artistic achievements which neither science nor journalism can replace. Yet especially in these contentious times, this requires adopting a clear stance. The position of an observer or critic of our society is ill-suited to this task. Given the responsibilities of the arts community in a socialist society, the only valid position is that of a fellow fighter, of a fervent protagonist who, with her/his own particular tools, spreads the ideas of peace and socialism among the masses.

All artistic endeavours designed to develop socialist realism more fully and bring out the entire scope and diversity of its conceptual and stylistic aspects ought to be supported more vigorously. This includes encouraging the unearthing of artistic phenomena in the everyday life of our socialist society.

The important thing is to depict those features of a socialist personality, those patterns of behaviour and thinking, those qualities and relationships which place working people apart, whether at the workplace or in their life experience as a whole. Consequently, the portrayal of working-class characters deserves pride of place. The artistic appropriation of socialist reality also accommodates a critical evaluation of patterns of behaviour and attitudes that impede the advance of socialism.

Our party favours a creative atmosphere in the development of the arts, a climate marked by exacting ideological, moral, and ethical demands, and devotion to principle but also geniality in dealing with writers and artists. The open and friendly spirit which has permeated our informed, and frequently critical, discussions has proved one of the most important conditions for strengthening the mutual trust existing between the arts community and our party.

By the same token, it is a matter of importance to encourage a dialogue on the arts amongst the socialist public at large, and to promote discussion between artists and their audiences, not least in the media. The standard of art criticism and art theory will have to be further improved so that critics and scholars can do more justice to their role in this public dialogue, primarily by stating more clearly which works and productions are commendable or flawed, and analysing their artistic weight in tandem with their ideological positions.

We continue to attach great importance to the fostering, preservation and dissemination of our humanitarian cultural heritage. Greater emphasis is to be laid on our anti-fascist and socialist cultural heritage and on cultural traditions which are closely linked with the growth and vigour of our workers' and farmers' state. The assimilation of our socialist heritage represents a major contribution to the development of the all-round personality and a corresponding way of living.

(*Report of the Central Committee of the Socialist Unity Party of Germany to the 11th Congress of the SED*, Rapporteur: Erich Honecker, Dresden 1986, pp. 83 ff.)

D163 From the Directives for the Five-Year Plan 1986–1990:

Culture and the arts must be accorded greater recognition as factors helping people to personally unfold, engage in creative activities, and pursue fulfilling pastimes. It is necessary to provide a rich array of cultural events in all towns and villages if the growing demands on cultural standards and attractiveness are to be met. It is of particular importance in this connection to raise the cultural levels of the working class and also to promote cultural activities for and by the young. The aesthetic principle of socialist realism needs to be enriched with new literary and artistic works conducive to the moulding of socialist patterns of life, morality and behaviour.

The task is to make more varied and effective use of all suitable facilities, regardless of status, to promote manifold cultural and intellectual activities.

Cultural establishments are to be modernized and given a new lease of life. Step by step, cultural facilities are to be set up in major new housing estates and areas with a high concentration of working-class people. Greater variety in top-quality dance functions, especially for the young, should be striven for.

Reconstruction and modernization of inner-city areas must include measures to increase the attraction of lending libraries, book shops, neighbourhood clubs and cultural centres.

Appropriate measures are to be taken to ensure that a wide range of high-quality books and brochures, records and cassettes are put on the market. The minimum annual production should be fixed at 6,500 titles breaking down into 150 million copies, and approx. 20 million records and cassettes. Sufficient supplies of high-quality paper must be available to ensure high standards of book printing and design.

Modernization and expansion work will begin at the wholesale bookselling facilities in Leipzig. In addition, the DEFA film studios will be refurbished and brought up to date.

More articles for leisure and amateur art activities must reach the market. The network of small galleries, art shops and workshops managed by the GDR's fine art trade association is to be expanded to offer professional and amateur visual artists more premises and better conditions for their work.

Substantial improvements must be achieved with regard to the supply of musical instruments to professional orchestras, music schools and similar establishments, amateur musicians, general education facilities and the general public. At the same time, it will be necessary to have an adequate quantity of repair workshops.

Facilities are to be modernized and enlarged at higher education and vocational training establishments for artists.

The reconstruction of Berlin's Platz der Akademie will be brought to completion. Reconstruction work will commence on the Museum island, including the New Museum, in the GDR capital. In Dresden, preparations will be made to preserve the structural substance of the former Royal Palace for future reconstruction. The Panorama Museum in Bad Frankenhausen, a memorial to the Peasants' War, should be ready.

The reconstruction of cultural facilities is to be funded from budget appropriations earmarked for maintenance efforts. To an increasing extent, local labour and materials are to be employed in the restoration and preservation of cultural establishments.

Improvements in programme quality will be needed if radio and television are to increase their impact on millions of viewers and listeners and meet their demands for information, knowledge and varied entertainment. Priority should be given to TV programmes for children and the young. There will be more radio programmes for the young, and the transmission time of some local radio stations will be extended.

Investment in this field has to be effected in a way that guarantees outstanding execution of all planned programmes. In tandem with this, the reception of radio and television programmes must be improved.

(*Directives issued by the 11th Congress of the SED for the Five-Year Plan for the GDR's national economic development 1986–1990*, Dresden 1986, pp. 118 ff.)

D164 From the report on the Tenth Writers' Congress of the GDR in Neues Deutschland, 27 November 1987:

[. . .] The delegates adopted a statement in which they profess their support for peace and for socialism. There was one vote against and five abstentions.[5]

[. . .]

Statement by the Tenth Writers' Congress

We profess our support for peace. Threatened by self-destruction, humankind is taking the first step from the utopia of disarmament to its realization. At this encouraging moment we confirm our solidarity with the German Democratic Republic which has peace as the highest precept of its national policy.

We profess our support for socialism. Our century, which has experienced two devastating world wars, has been characterized by the victory of the Great Socialist October Revolution. We confirm our solidarity with the Soviet Union, which has paved the way for the social liberation of humankind and the construction of a just society.

Our literature puts into words the world as it is and as it can be. In the present time of scientific-technical advance and intense effort directed at the productivity of socialist society, we confirm the proletarian-revolutionary and anti-fascist tradition of our association and the indispensible requirement for every humanistic culture that it should serve man and his environment, discover his riches and his potential, understand him in his happiness and his unhappiness, and portray him in his creative endeavour.
Berlin, 26 November 1987

(*Neues Deutschland* vol. 42 no. 279 of 27 November 1987)

D165 From the speech by Christoph Hein at the Tenth Writers' Congress of the GDR, November 1987:[6]

The authorization procedure, state supervision, or to put it more briefly and no less clearly, the censorship of publishing houses and books, of publishers and authors, is outdated, useless, paradoxical, inhumane, against the interests of the people, illegal and a punishable offence. I shall go on to substantiate that:

Censorship is outdated. It had its justification in the years after the Second World War, when German fascism had been destroyed militarily by the Allies but the intellectual battle for Germany, for the Germans, was still undecided. At that time censorship, like food rationing, had the task of imposing order on the general shortages, preventing chaos and making possible the work of reconstruction. Additionally, censorship was favoured by the historical situation of the time, namely what our modern historians attempt rather to conceal than to designate by the curiously wishy-washy formulations "those tragic events of the thirties in the Soviet Union" and "temporary infringements of the Leninist norms of party conduct". Censorship should have disappeared along with food rationing in the midfifties, at the latest in February 1956.

Censorship is useless, for it cannot prevent literature; at most it can delay its spread. We have repeatedly seen that books which were not authorized have had to be given authorization years later. And so we all know that books not available to us today, such as some of Stefan Heym's books or those by Monika Maron, will eventually be published in the GDR.

Censorship is paradoxical because it always brings about the opposite of its declared intention. The censored object does not disappear but instead becomes unignorable and is blown up into a political issue even where the book and the author are quite unsuitable and should have had quite the opposite expectation. Censorship then merely appears as an idea devised by the publisher's advertising department to increase sales.

Censorship is inhumane; it is harmful to authors, readers, publishers, and even the censors themselves. In the last ten years our country has lost many writers, irreplaceable people whose works we miss and whose encouragement and dissent were beneficial and helpful to us. Certainly these writers left the GDR for the most varied reasons. One of the reasons why these people and their country are missing each other — I know one side of that for certain, and I suspect the other; for as the English say "you can take the boy out of the country, but you can't take the country out of the boy" — one of the reasons is censorship.

And the author who is unable to keep the subsequent censorship apart from his work becomes its victim against his will even as he writes: he will practise self-censorship or betray the text, or direct his writing against censorship and here too betray the text, since he is unwillingly and perhaps also unwittingly changing his truth polemically.

Censorship deprives the reader of responsibility for his own decisions. He can either accept it and the restrictions it imposes or resist it and avoid it by undertaking the extra efforts necessary to read the unauthorized book. In either case his choice is determined by censorship.

Censorship destroys the publisher, it destroys his authority and his credibility. It forbids the publisher to be a publisher since it does not permit him to determine his programme of publications. What special wisdom distinguishes these people who award or withhold printing permits that they can take it on themselves to lay down rules for a reliable and capable person? — for no one else could ever become a publisher in our country. Censorship reduces the publisher's vocabulary, it reduces it by the weighty word No. A publisher must have the right to say no, no to a manuscript, no to a programme not in keeping with his publishing house. But as long as there exists a censorship which is independent of the publisher and determines his decisions, the publisher's No cannot be used, it is improper and immoral.

And censorship destroys the censor. When his function is to grant or withhold authorization, the most artistically sensitive individual becomes an instrument of the law. His vision and his senses cannot help being narrowed down in the effort to discover anything that may be disapproved

Literature and Culture 327

of. And like many colleagues I have seen examples where this limited vision produced nonsensical interpretations, absurd suspicions, and ambiguous misunderstandings which were imposed on quite unambiguous statements.

Censorship is against the interests of the people. It is a crime against the people's wisdom we hear praised so much. Readers of our books are quite able to form their own judgements. The idea that a civil servant could decide what is appropriate or beneficial for a people betrays only the presumption and arrogance of officials.

Censorship is illegal, for it is unconstitutional. It is incompatible with the current constitution of the GDR and in conflict with several of its articles.

And censorship is a punishable offence, as it greatly damages the standing of the GDR and is the equivalent of "public disparagement".

The authorization procedure — censorship — must vanish immediately and without replacement, to avert further damage to our culture and avoid harming further our public life, our dignity, our society and our state.

(*Die Zeit* no. 50 of 4 December 1987)

D166 From the catalogue of the Tenth Art Exhibition of the GDR 1987/88:

Ten major art exhibitions in Dresden have now documented over 40 years of the development of art in the German Democratic Republic. The initiators of the first exhibition in 1946 knew that for survival, nourishment for the mind, the emotions, and the senses was also necessary. On the occasion of the "10th" it may be asked whether there is any constant, unifying characteristic to be found in the quite different viewpoints that the catalogues of the individual exhibitions provide us with. And indeed the "1st" (1946), the "3rd" (1953), and the "7th" (1972–3) for example had hardly anything in common in their outward appearance; after all, radical social changes lay between them and also had consequences for aesthetic understanding, artistic attitudes, and for our visual relation to the world. In each case developments had taken place which must always be present when creative artists are working in periods of revolutionary transformation . . .

The dialogue between the artists and the public was conducted in various ways during these four decades. In response to the intellectual hunger of the first years, the relationship was initially rather an informative one; artists attempted, frequently in a didactic manner, to provide answers to the question how all these things could have happened and what was going to happen now. But as individuals found themselves and adopted their own attitudes, the relationship between the artists and their public took on features of a partnership where both took each other seriously in an attempt to find truths ... There was always the productive friction against what was on offer without which no progress can result. It was precisely those works which pointed forward in content and form which again and again became the focus of debate. Long years of experience with art in a living, public context advanced critical consciousness and the self-confidence of all involved. On the one hand we know today that excessively narrow standards were sometimes applied; however on the other the conviction grew that never before had art been taken seriously and used by such a large forum as a means of communication about values and the meaning of life. The painter Willi Sitte wrote in 1983, "It represents a considerable increase in true closeness to the people that in our country the most progressive art is constantly faced with such an interested public. It seems particularly valuable to me that our works are often received in a contradictory manner. Working people do not accept our works as proclamations of assured truths but as the artists' opinions, to which they quite naturally contrast their own opinions. I do not consider it to be a shortcoming if in a discussion about works of art someone does not find his view of the world and his perception of reality confirmed but feels himself to be challenged and even provoked. Here the new quality in the relationship between the artist and his public is evident."

There were also repeated discussions about what was worthy to be represented and how it was to be represented: should it only be the major subjects of the epoch, or the inconspicuous and everyday as well? Should conditions be shown as they should be, or as they really are? And should the conflicts in which we are embroiled be invoked in nightmare pictures or is it rather necessary to create counter-pictures of human beauty and hope? ...

In countries where the development of art is determined primarily by the capitalist market the art of our country was long seen as outdated and unfree, since critics there applied only their own criteria and overlooked the fact that really we had had violent disagreements about our art, about progress and regress, appropriateness or presumptuousness, and that these confirmed that our art fulfilled a need. In the meantime there have been exhibitions of GDR art all over the world, and not infrequently these have provoked great surprise at the distinctiveness of this art. The criticism that it ignored international artistic trends has given way to respect for its original and self-determined achievement.

Yet this art has not in fact grown up without taking a critical stance on developments in East and West and the great inheritance of European art. However, these influences were dealt with not as a trend but in individual, complex forms — and this long before the postmodern concept of historicism. In this country the continuation of artistic development is determined not by waves of fashion but by the deeply rooted conviction that art has a social function in a concrete area of influence.

Personal freedom to create such works, and a social atmosphere receptive to art, are social conditions made possible by the farsighted cultural policy which the party of the working class has carried on in alliance with artists. This has become so natural for us that we often do not even mention it any more. From the already legendary cultural meeting of the KPD in February 1946 to the 11th Party Congress of the SED it has been and is obvious to what extent the party attends to the development of a democratic and socialist culture and art.

Interest in art does not arise only through contact with works of art but is also promoted by the varied efforts of state institutions and social organizations. These include the developed network of museums and galleries in our country and the initiatives of the small galleries run by the League of Culture, the art trade, the towns and communities; and finally these include the activities of so many professional and honorary cultural workers and art scholars who have a commitment to such art. And the fact that around 20 per cent of the paintings, graphic works and sculptures accepted for the 10th Art Exhibition were produced on public commission proves that the social circumstances and the intellectual climate are favourable for art to flourish. The artists make use of this opportunity by taking on responsibility for quality and contributing their best to society: their individuality.

(Karl Max Kober/Peter Pachnicke: Preface to the *Katalog der X. Kunstausstellung der DDR, Dresden 1987/88*, Berlin 1987, pp. 11 ff.)

Notes

1. For the role of the writer and the intellectual cf. K Stuart Parkes, *Writers and Politics in West Germany*, Croom Helm, London 1986. The burning of books and harsh censorship are also indicative of the high status accorded to the influence exerted by writers and intellectuals throughout modern German history.
2. It should be noted that Marx, Engels and Lenin were extremely knowledgeable in literature and very often proved themselves to be excellent literary critics. Cf. Siegbert S. Prawer, *Karl Marx and World Literature*, OUP, Oxford 1976.
3. It is now almost impossible to define socialist realism. Especially during the last thirty years, both this term and socialist art itself have undergone tremendous changes. "Socialist realism" used to constitute a rigid ideological and formal framework within which artists had to operate, practically following a prescribed check-list of ingredients. This is no longer the case; GDR art is almost as varied and multi-faceted as western European art. See Michael Scriven and Dennis Tate (eds.), *European Socialist Realism*, Berg, Oxford 1988, pp. 1–10, 60–78.
4. "Sorrows" (*Leiden*) is a reference to Ulrich Plenzdorf's *Die neuen Leiden des jungen W.* ("The New Sorrows of Young W."), originally turned down as a film scenario, then published as a play and in a prose version in 1972: it was very popular, was widely discussed and condemned, and the original film scenario was published in the GDR only in 1986.

5. Dissent, and particularly its reporting, can be seen as indicating the influence of *glasnost*.
6. Hein's speech, and the fact that it was delivered in full, can be seen as another indication of greater openness; however *Neues Deutschland* published only a brief report of this (and of the other speeches delivered at the Congress). Long excerpts from the speech were first published by the West German *Die Zeit*, although perhaps significantly Hein subsequently complained that the excerpts chosen gave an unbalanced impression of his address.

Statistics

Territory

Area: 108,333 sq.km.

Borders: Baltic Sea in the north, Poland in the east (length 460 km), Czechoslovakia in the southeast (454 km), and the Federal Republic of Germany in the southwest and west (1,378 km).

Capital: Berlin (1.2 million inhabitants).

Major cities: (population in '000)
Leipzig 556, Dresden 520, Karl Marx Stadt 317, Magdeburg 289, Rostock 242, Halle 236, Erfurt 215, Potsdam 138, Gera 131, Schwerin 126, Cottbus 123, Zwickau 120, Jena 107, Dessau 104.

Administrative structure: 15 counties, 191 rural and 36 urban districts.

Longest river: Elbe, a 566 km stretch of which runs through the GDR.

Largest lake: Müritz, 117 sq.km.

Largest island: Rügen, 926 sq.km.

Highest mountain: Fichtelberg, 1,214 m.

Breakdown of land use: 58 per cent farmland (arable land, meadows, pastures and gardens); 27 per cent forest, 15 per cent built-up areas, roads, rivers and lakes, and waste land.

Located in the midst of GDR territory is West Berlin, a city whose political status is defined in the Quadripartite Agreement signed by the Soviet Union, the United States, France and Great Britain.

Population

Inhabitants: 16.7 million; 53 per cent of the population is female, 47 per cent is male.

Population density: 154 inhabitants per sq.km.

Age structure: 64 per cent of the population is of working age (women between 15 and 60, and men between 15 and 65), 19 per cent are children, and 17 per cent of retirement age.

Live births: 227,440 (1985).

Life expectancy: 69 years for men and 75 years for women.

Population distribution: 75 per cent of the population live in towns and 25 per cent in rural communities.

Source: Panorama der DDR, *GDR '85. Facts and Figures*, Berlin 1985

Age Structure

Year	under 6	6–15	15–20	20–45	45–65	over 65
1950	7.0	15.8	8.7	30.4	27.5	10.6
1960	9.3	12.0	6.8	30.4	27.6	13.8
1970	8.7	14.3	7.7	32.2	21.2	15.6
1980	7.7	11.8	8.5	35.8	20.5	15.7

Source: *Statistisches Jahrbuch der DDR*

Local Assemblies

The local assemblies are 15 county assemblies, 227 district and 7,567 community and borough assemblies which are responsible for all matters of local concern. They, therefore, closely co-operate with local citizens, as well as with industrial combines, enterprises, co-operatives and other institutions.

	People's Chamber	County Assemblies	District Assemblies Community and Borough Assemblies
Deputies	500 *	3,172 *	202,757 **
Composition according to social background (in per cent)			
Workers	47.2	50.3	50.5
Office workers	17.8	31.1	21.4
Members of production co-operatives (crafts-people's co-operatives not included)	10.4	11.9	22.9
Female deputies	32.4	38.7	37.7
Young deputies (between 18 and 25 years)	9.2	17.3	16.0

* 1981 elections,   ** 1984 elections
Source: Panorama der DDR, *GDR '85 Facts and Figures*, Berlin 1985

Mass participation

Millions of people are involved in decision-making:

206,000	are deputies of people's assemblies
450,000	co-operate in the commissions of local assemblies and their bodies
388,000	participate in the work of National Front committees
266,000	are active in people's control bodies
359,000	are involved in the administration of justice
614,000	are engaged in parents' committees and parent-teacher councils

Source: Panorama der DDR, *GDR '85 Facts and Figures*, Berlin 1985

Divorce rate

Year	Divorce no.	per 1000 marriages	per 100 weddings
1950	49,860	109	23
1960	25,540	—	15
1970	27,407	64	21
1980	44,794	107	33
1983	49,624	121	40

Source: *Statistisches Jahrbuch der DDR*

Membership of parties

Year	CDU	DBD	LDPD	NDPD	SED
1950	194,934	50,000	171,300	41,000	1,750,000
1966	110,000	80,000	80,000	110,000	1,769,912
1981	120,000	103,000	82,000	91,000	2,172,110

Source: R. Rytlewski, M. Opp de Hipt, *Die Deutsche Demokratische Republik in Zahlen 1945/49–1980*, Munich 1987

Membership of FDGB

Year	membership	% of women
1945	1,700,000	
1950	4,700,000	
1960	6,200,000	43.5
1970	7,090,000	48.0
1980	8,807,000	51.1
1982	9,123,000	51.5

Source: Statistisches Jahrbuch der DDR

Monthly take-home pay of GDR households 1980

average per household in Marks	1490
under 600 marks	3.7%
between 600 and 800 marks	7.3%
between 800 and 1000 marks	7.8%
between 1000 and 1200 marks	9.5%
between 1200 and 1400 marks	14.7%
between 1400 and 1600 marks	18.3%
between 1600 and 1800 marks	14.6%
between 1800 and 2000 marks	9.6%
between 2000 and 2200 marks	5.8%
more than 2200	8.7%

*Source: R. Rytlewski, M. Opp de Hipt, Die Deutsche Demokratische Republik
in Zahlen 1945/49–1980, Munich 1987*

Monthly expenditure of all households 1960–80

Food, drink, alcoholic beverages, tobacco	1960 1980	41.1% 35.7%
Commodities other than above, incl. shoes, clothing	1960 1980	28.2% 36.8%
Expenditure on services, incl. rent (in brackets), entertainment, leisure activities, holidays	1960 1980	11.2 (4) % 12.8 (2.7) %

Source: *Statistisches Jahrbuch der DDR*

Membership of other mass organizations

Organization	1950	1960	1970	1980
Democratic Women's League	1,021,038	1,322,723	1,300,000	1,400,000
Free German Youth	1,133,309	1,700,000	1,700,000	2,300,000
Culture League	194,734	173,678	193,345	226,593

Source: R. Rytlewski, M. Opp de Hipt, *Die Deutsche Demokratische Republik in Zahlen 1945/49–1980*, Munich 1987

Distribution of seats in parliament 1981–6

SED	127
CDU	52
LDPD	52
NDPD	52
DBD	52
FDGB	68
FDJ	40
DFD	35
KB	22
	500

Source: Rytlewski/Opp de Hipt (as above)

Leisure Statistics

Year	Theatres No.	Theatres Visitors	Cinemas No.	Cinemas Visitors	Museums No.	Museums Visitors
1951	77	14.0 Mill	1,494	189 Mill	—	—
1960	87	16.0	1,369	238	—	—
1970	101	12.3	858	91	552	19.8 Mill
1980	152	10.5	826	79	636	31.3 Mill

Source: Statistisches Jahrbuch der DDR

Trade between the FRG and the GDR (in Mill. Marks)

	from the FRG	from the GDR
1960	960	1122
1970	2416	1996
1980	5203	5579

Source: R. Rytlewski, M. Opp de Hipt, *Die Deutsche Demokratische Republik in Zahlen 1945/49–1980*, Munich 1987

Prices (in Marks) of selected goods 1981

Loaf of rye bread	1 kg	0.52	6 mins working time
Sugar	1 kg	1.59	19 mins
Butter	1 kg	10.00	119 mins
Potatoes	5 kg	1.04	12 mins
Men's shirt	1	45.00	9 hours
Men's shoes	1	130.00	26 hours
Men's suit	1	350.00	70 hours
Fridge	1	1425.00	282 hours
Bus fare	1	0.20	2 mins
Haircut (men)	1	1.80	21 mins

Source: Rytlewski/Opp de Hipt (as above)

Consumer durables per 100 households

	1962	1980
cars	5	37
motor bikes	26	50
TV sets	31	90
washing-machines	12	82
fridges	11	99
telephones	4	20

Source: Rytlewski/Opp de Hipt (as above)

Biographies

Ackermann, Anton (1905–73), real name Eugen Hanisch, politically active from 1919, member of the Communist Party from 1926, member of the Central Committee of the SED from 1950, member of the People's Chamber 1950–4, candidate member of Politburo 1950–3. Removed from all party posts in 1953.

Bahro, Rudolf (1935–), one of the best-known dissidents, former apparatchik, had his book *Die Alternative* published in West Germany 1977, jailed in 1978, released to go to West Germany one year later.

Bolz, Lothar (1903–), lawyer, emigration to Soviet Union during the Third Reich, co-founder of NDPD (1948), GDR Foreign Minister 1953–65.

Brandt, Willy (1913–), first Social Democrat Chancellor of West Germany (1969–74), before that mayor of West Berlin.

Felfe, Werner (1928–88), active political career from 1954 (FDJ), candidate member of Central Committee of SED (1954–63), full member since 1963, then secretary of Central Committee, candidate member of Politburo (1973–76). Full member since 1976. Rising star within the party apparatus before his recent death.

Fischer, Oskar (1923–), distinguished SED and FDJ party career since 1946, member of Central Committee, Minister of Foreign Affairs since 1975.

Grotewohl, Otto (1894–1964), distinguished political career as Social Democrat before 1933, briefly imprisoned by Nazis, chairman of the SPD in the Soviet Occupied Zone, co-president of SED until 1954, from 1949 to his death prime minister of GDR.

Hager, Kurt (1912–), joined Communist Party in 1930, arrested by Nazis and on release emigrated to France and UK, distinguished SED party career, chief ideologue, special interest in arts and culture.

Honecker, Erich (1912–), distinguished communist career before 1933, imprisonment during Nazi era, leader of FDJ 1946–55, since 1958 distinguished SED career, since 1971 First (General) Secretary of the SED, chair of National Defence Council, since 1976 chair of Council of State.

Honecker, Margot (1927–), early career within FDJ, married Erich Honecker 1953, since 1963 Minister of Education, only woman in cabinet.

Krenz, Egon (1937–), First Secretary of FDJ, since 1973 member of

Central Committee, since 1976 candidate member, now full member of Politburo, member of Council of State.

Loeser, Franz (1924–), after exile in the UK and university in the UK and USA return to the GDR in 1957, professor of moral philosophy at the Humboldt University in Berlin, eminent member of the SED, left the GDR in 1983.

Mielke, Erich (1907–), distinguished communist before 1933, distinguished SED career after 1946, Minister for State Security since 1957.

Mittag, Günter (1926–), distinguished career in SED and FDGB since 1946, secretary for economy in Central Committee, member of Politburo.

Pieck, Wilhelm (1876–1960), distinguished Communist Party politician before 1933, emigrated to France and Soviet Union, chair of KPD after 1945, co-chair of SED from 1946, President of GDR 1949–1960.

Seghers, Anna (1900–83), after 1945 leading writer of the GDR, chair of German Writers' Congress, influential doyenne.

Stoph, Willy (1914–), distinguished SED career, 1952 Minister of Interior, since 1956 Minister of Defence, 1964–73 chair of Council of Ministers, 1973–6 chair of Council of State, since 1976 again chair of Council of Ministers.

Tisch, Harry (1927–), distinguished FDGB and SED career, chair of FDGB since 1975, member of Central Committee and Politburo, member of Council of State.

Ulbricht, Walter (1893–1973), distinguished communist career before 1933, emigrated to Soviet Union, after 1945 SED and union activity, from 1950 to 1971 General Secretary of SED, chair of Council of State 1960–73, chair National Defence Council 1960–71.

Select Bibliography

Sources used

Abusch, Alexander, *Humanismus und Realismus in der Literatur*, Leipzig, Reclam 1972

Bahro, Rudolf, *The Alternative in Eastern Europe*, tr. David Fernbach, London, NLB 1978

Bundesvorstand des FDGB (ed.), *Geschichte des freien deutschen Gewerkschaftbundes*, Berlin, Verlag Tribüne 1985

——, *Protokoll des 3. Kongresses des freien deutschen Gewerkschaftbundes*, Berlin, Verlag Tribüne 1950

Christians and Churches in the GDR, Dresden, Verlag Zeit im Bild 1980

Deuerlein, Ernst (ed.), *DDR 1945–1970*, Munich, dtv 1972

Directives for the Five-Year Plan for the GDR's national economic development 1976–1980, issued by the 9th Congress of the Socialist Unity Party, Dresden, Verlag Zeit im Bild, n.d. [1976]

Directives for the Five-Year Plan for the GDR's national economic development 1981–85, issued by the 10th Congress of the Socialist Unity Party, Dresden, Verlag Zeit im Bild, n.d. [1981]

Directives for the Five-Year Plan for the GDR's national economic development 1986–90, issued by the 11th Congress of the Socialist Unity Party, Dresden, Verlag Zeit im Bild, n.d. [1986]

Fischbeck, Helmut, *Literaturpolitik und Literaturkritik in der DDR*, Frankfurt, Diesterweg 1976

Five-Year Plan Act: The Development of the GDR's national economy in the period 1986–1990, adopted on 27 November 1986, Dresden, Panorama DDR n.d. [1986]

GDR '86: Facts and Figures, Dresden, Verlag Zeit im Bild 1986

The German Democratic Republic, Dresden, Panorama DDR 1984

Hager, Kurt, *Grundfragen des geistigen Lebens im Sozialismus*, Berlin, Dietz Verlag 1969

Honecker, Erich, *Der VIII. Parteitag und unsere nächsten Aufgaben*, Berlin, Dietz Verlag 1972

——, *Report of the Central Committee to the 9th Congress of the Socialist Unity Party of Germany*, Dresden, Verlag Zeit im Bild n.d. [1976]

——, *Report of the Central Committee of the Socialist Unity Party of Germany to the 10th Congress of the SED*, Dresden, Verlag Zeit im Bild n.d. [1981]

——, *Report of the Central Committee of the Socialist Unity Party of Germany to the 11th Congress of the SED*, Dresden, Verlag Zeit im Bild n.d. [1986]

100 Years of August Bebel's "Women and Socialism": Women in the GDR, Dresden, Verlag Zeit im Bild 1978

Kosing, Alfred, *Wörterbuch der Marxistisch-Leninistischen Philosophie*, Berlin, Dietz Verlag 1986

Kühn, Werner, Heinz Knapp, *Culture and Art in Socialist Society*, Dresden, Panorama DDR 1975

Laws and justice in a socialist society, Dresden, Verlag Zeit im Bild 1978

Lenin, V.I., *Selected Works*, London, Lawrence & Wishart 1971

——, *The Essentials of Lenin in Two Volumes*, vol. II, London, Lawrence & Wishart 1947

Loeser, Franz, *Die unglaubwürdige Gesellschaft*, Cologne, Bund Verlag 1984

Ministerium für Kultur der DDR; Verband Bildender Künstler der DDR (eds.), *X. Kunstausstellung der Deutschen Demokratischen Republik Dresden 1987/88*, Berlin 1987

Neues Deutschland, 1945– [journal]

The planned socialist economy of the German Democratic Republic, Dresden, Verlag Zeit im Bild 1977

Politische ökonomie: Lehrbuch, Berlin, Dietz Verlag 1955

Programme of the Socialist Unity Party of Germany, Dresden, Verlag Zeit im Bild n.d. [1976]

Report by the Central Statistical Office of the GDR on the fulfilment of the National Plan in the first half of 1987, Dresden, Verlag Zeit im Bild n.d. [1987]

Rytlewski, Ralf, Manfred Opp de Hipt, *Die Deutsche Demokratische Republik in Zahlen 1945/49–1980*, Munich, Verlag C.H. Beck 1987

Schweitzer, C.C. et al. (eds.), *Politics and Government in the Federal Republic of Germany: Basic Documents*, Leamington Spa, Berg Publishers 1984

Seghers, Anna, *Über Kunstwerk und Wirklichkeit*, vol. 1, Berlin, Akademie Verlag 1975

A success for the politics of common sense and realism, Dresden, Verlag Zeit im Bild n.d. [1987]

Steininger, Rolf, *Deutsche Geschichte 1945–1961*, 2 vols., Frankfurt, Fischer 1986

Theses concerning Martin Luther, Dresden, Verlag Zeit im Bild n.d. [1983]

Thomas, Rüdiger, *Modell DDR*, Munich, Carl Hanser Verlag 1981

Ulbricht, Walter, *Die gegenwärtige Lage und die neuen Aufgaben der Sozialistischen Einheitspartei Deutschlands*, Berlin, Dietz Verlag 1952

——, *Die gegenwärtige Lage und die neuen Aufgaben der Sozialistischen Einheitspartei Deutschlands*, Berlin, Dietz Verlag 1952

——, *Über Gewerkschaften*, vol. 2, Berlin, Tribüne-Verlag 1953
——, *Zur Geschichte der neuesten Zeit*, vol. I. 1, Berlin, Dietz Verlag 1955
Die Verfassung der Deutschen Demokratischen Republik, Dresden, Verlag
    Zeit im Bild 1968
Weber, Hermann, *DDR: Dokumente zur Geschichte der Deutschen De-
    mokratischen Republik 1945–1985*, Munich, dtv 1986
Wilharm, Irmgard (ed.), *Deutsche Geschichte 1962–1983*, 2 vols., Frank-
    furt, Fischer 1985
Die Zeit, 1946–

Bibliographies

Brewer, Jim, et al., "A working bibliography for the study of the GDR",
    New German Critique no. 2 (1974), pp. 121–51.
Dennis, Mike, Martin McCauley, "A selected bibliography of articles and
    books in the social sciences published in the German Democratic Re-
    public in 1983", *East Central Europe* 1–2 (1984), pp. 129–45
——, Martin Watson, "A selected bibliography of articles and books in the
    social sciences and humanities published in the German Democratic
    Republic in 1984", *East Central Europe* 1 (1985), pp. 65–98
Hersch, Gisela, *A Bibliography of German Studies 1945–1971*, Blooming-
    ton, Indiana, London, Indiana University Press 1972
Price, Arnold H., *East Germany: a selected bibliography*, Washington
    D.C., Library of Congress 1967
Wallace, Ian, *East Germany: The German Democratic Republic*, Oxford,
    Santa Barbara, Denver, Clio Press 1987

Document Collections

Docker, Günther, Jens A. Bräckner, Ralph Freiberg (eds.), *The Federal
    Republic of Germany and the German Democratic Republic in Inter-
    national Relations*, Dobbs Ferry, New York, Oceana 1979, 3 vols.
Honecker, Erich, *The German Democratic Republic*, New York, Inter-
    national Publishers 1979
McCardle, Arthur W., A. Bruce Boenau (eds.), *East Germany — A New
    German Nation under Socialism?*, Lanham, New York, London, Univer-
    sity Press of America 1984
von Oppen, Beate Ruhm (ed.), *Documents on Germany under Occupation
    1945–1954*, London, Oxford University Press 1955
Ulbricht, Walter, *Whither Germany*, Berlin, German Institute of Contem-
    porary History 1966

——, *On Questions of Socialist Construction in the GDR*, Dresden, Verlag Zeit im Bild 1968

Weber, Hermann, *DDR: Dokumente zur Geschichte der Deutschen Demokratischen Republik*, Munich, dtv 1986

General Works

Childs, David, *The GDR: Moscow's German Ally*, London, Allen & Unwin 1983

——(ed.), *Honecker's Germany*, London, Allen & Unwin 1985

Edwards, Gwyneth E., *GDR Society and Social Institutions: Facts and Figures*, London, Macmillan 1985

Keefe, Eugene K., *East Germany: A Country Study*, Washington D.C., Department of Army 1982

Krisch, Henry, *The German Democratic Republic: The Search for Identity*, Boulder/Colorado, London, Westview Press 1985

Mellor, Roy E.H., *The Two Germanies: A Modern Geography*, London, New York, Sydney, Harper & Row 1978

Scharf, C. Bradley, *Politics and Change in East Germany: An Evaluation of Socialist Democracy*, Boulder/Colorado, London, Westview Press 1984

Verlag Zeit im Bild (DDR-8012 Dresden, Julian-Grimau-Allee) publishes small volumes in English on aspects of the GDR at regular intervals. The publisher supplies copies on request.

The most authoritative West German account to date is:

Bundesministerium für innerdeutsche Beziehungen (ed.), *DDR Handbuch*, 2 vols., Cologne, Verlag Wissenschaft und Politik 1985

Further Reading

Chapter 1: The Origins:

Calleo, David, *The German Problem Reconsidered: Germany and the World Order 1870 to the Present*, Cambridge, CUP 1978

Dorpalen, Andreas, *German History in Marxist Perspective: The East German Approach*, London, Tauris 1985

Heitzer, Heinz, *GDR: An historical outline*, Dresden, Verlag Zeit im Bild 1985

Krisch, Henry, *German Politics under Soviet Occupation: The Unification of the Communist and Social Democratic Parties in the Soviet Zone*, New York, University of Columbia Press 1974

McCauley, Martin, *The German Democratic Republic since 1945*, London, Macmillan 1983

Sandford, Gregory W., *From Hitler to Ulbricht: The Communist Reconstruction of East Germany 1945–46*, Princeton, Princeton University Press 1983

Steele, Jonathan, *Socialism With a Human Face: The State that Came in from the Cold*, London, Jonathan Cape 1977

Chapter 2: The State, the Constitution, and Party-Political Life:

Asmus, Ronald, "The GDR and the German Nation", *International Affairs* 80 no. 3 (1984), pp. 403–18

von Beyme, Klaus, Hartmut Zimmermann (eds.), *Policymaking in the German Democratic Republic*, Aldershot, Gower 1984

Christopher, Inge, "The Written Constitution — the Basic Law of a Socialist State", in David Childs (ed.), *Honecker's Germany*, London, Allen & Unwin 1985, pp. 15–31.

Krisch, Henry, "Nation Building and Regime Stability in the DDR", *East Central Europe* 3, no. 1 (1976), pp. 15–29

McCauley, Martin, "Official and Unofficial Nationalism in the GDR", *GDR Monitor* 5 (1981), pp. 13–20

——, "Legitimation in the German Democratic Republic", in Paul G. Lewis (ed.), *Eastern Europe: Political Crisis and Legitimation*, London, Sydney, Croom Helm 1984, pp. 42–67

Chapter 3: Public Opinion, Mass Organizations, and the Organization of the Masses:

Brayne, Mark, "Luther: One of the Greatest Sons of the German People", *GDR Monitor* 3 (1980), pp. 35–43

Goeckel, Robert F., "The Luther Anniversary in East Germany", *World Politics* 37 no. 1 (1984), pp. 112–33

Hebblethwaite, Peter, "The GDR: Servant or Subservient Church?", *Religion in Communist Lands* 6 no. 2 (1978), pp. 97–100

Mushaben, Joyce Mary, "Swords to Plowshares: the Church, the State and the East German Peace Movement", *Studies in Comparative Communism* 17 no. 2 (1984), pp. 123–35

Oeser, Hans-Christian, "The Multi-Party System in the GDR — its Character and Function", *GDR Monitor* 6 (1981/82), pp. 10–20

Ramet, Pedro, "Church and Peace in the GDR", *Problems of Communism* 33 no. 4 (1984), pp. 44–57

Rueschemeyer, Marilyn, "Integrating Work and Personal Life: An Analysis of Three Professional Work Collectives in the German Democratic Republic", *GDR Monitor* 8 (1982/83), pp. 27–45

Sandford, John, *The Sword and the Ploughshare: Autonomous Peace Initiatives in East Germany*, London, Merlin Press 1983

——, "The Press in the GDR: Principles and Practice", in Graham Bartram, Anthony Waine (eds.), *Culture and Society in the GDR*, Dundee, *GDR Monitor* Special Series No. 2 1984, pp. 27–36

Smith, Roland, "The Church in the German Democratic Republic", in D. Childs (ed.), *Honecker's Germany*, London, Allen & Unwin 1985, pp. 66–81

Ward, Caroline, "Church and State in East Germany", *Religion in Communist Lands* 6 no. 2 (1978), pp. 89–96

Williamson, Roger, "East Germany: the Federation of Protestant Churches", *Religion in Communist Lands* 9 no. 1 (1981), pp. 6–17

Chapter 4: Economic and Social Policy

Berghahn, Volker R., *Modern Germany: Society, Economy and Politics in the Twentieth Century*, Cambridge, CUP 1987 (2nd edn)

Böhme, Helmut, *An Introduction to the Social and Economic History of Germany*, Oxford, Basil Blackwell 1978

Boot, Pieter A., "The GDR Economy between East and West: Problems and Opportunities", in Margy Gerber et al. (eds.), *Studies in GDR Culture and Society 6: Selected Papers from the Eleventh New Hampshire Symposium on the German Democratic Republic*, Lanham, New York, London, University Press of America 1986, pp. 17–30

Bryson, Philip J., *The Consumer under Socialist Planning: the East German Case*, New York, Praeger 1984

Burrington, Douglas, "Planning Higher and Further Education in the GDR", *GDR Monitor* 6 (1981/82), pp. 1–9

Collier, Irwin L. (ed.), *Workshop on the GDR Economy: Proceedings*, Washington D.C., American Institute for Contemporary German Studies 1986

Dennis, Michael, "Women and Political Leadership Positions in the GDR", *GDR Monitor* 3 (1980), 25-34

——, "Women and Work in the GDR", in Ian Wallace (ed.), *The GDR under Honecker 1971–1981*, Dundee, *GDR Monitor* Special Series No. 1 1981, 97–106

Dölling, Irene, "Social and Cultural Changes in the Lives of GDR Women - Changes in their Self-Conception", in Margy Gerber et al. (eds.), *Studies in GDR Culture and Society 6: Selected Papers from the Eleventh New Hampshire Symposium on the German Democratic Republic*, Lanham,

New York, London, University of America Press 1986, pp. 81–92

Freeman, Verna, "From Collectivization to Co-operation: A Study of Recent Trends in East German Agriculture", *GDR Monitor* 1 (1979), pp. 39–49

Frowen, Stephen F., "The Economy of the GDR", in David Childs (ed.), *Honecker's Germany*, London, Allen & Unwin 1985, pp. 32–49

Greenberg, Robert A., "Maternal and Child Health Care in the German Democratic Republic", in Margy Gerber et al. (eds.), *Studies in GDR Culture and Society 2: Proceedings of the Seventh International Symposium on the German Democratic Republic*, Washington D.C., University Press of America 1982, pp. 261–78

Kolinsky, Eva (ed.), *Youth in East and West Germany*, Modern German Studies 1, Aston University, Association for Modern German Studies 1985

Lemke, Christiane, "Youth and Youth Policy in GDR Society", in Margy Gerber et al. (eds.), *Studies in GDR Culture and Society 3: Selected Papers from the Eighth International Symposium on the German Democratic Republic*, Lanham, New York, London, University Press of America 1983, pp. 101–10

McCauley, Martin, "Social Policy under Honecker", in Ian Wallace (ed.), *The GDR under Honecker 1971–1981*, Dundee, *GDR Monitor* Special Series No. 1 1981, pp. 3–20

Page, John, "Education under the Honeckers", in David Childs (ed.), *Honecker's Germany*, London, Allen & Unwin 1985, pp. 50–65

Roads to Victory, Leipzig, Verlag Zeit im Bild 1974

Shaffer, Harry G., *Women in the Two Germanies: A Comparative Study of a Socialist and a Non-Socialist Society*, New York, Pergamon 1981

Stahnke, Arthur A., "Progress and the GDR Economy: GDR Economic Performance and its Measurement", in Margy Gerber et al. (eds.), *Studies in GDR Culture and Society 6: Selected Papers from the Eleventh New Hampshire Symposium on the German Democratic Republic*, Lanham, New York, London, University Press of America 1986, pp. 1–16

Sudan, Christel, "Women in the GDR", *New German Critique* 13 (1978), pp. 69–81.

Chapter 5: The Judiciary, Security and Defence

Christopher, Inge, "Citizen Participation in the GDR's Judicial System: A Case Study in Socialist Democracy", *GDR Monitor* 15 (1986), pp. 1–16

Forster, Thomas M., *The East German Army: The Second Power in the Warsaw Pact*, 5th edn, London, Allen & Unwin 1980

Neugebauer, Gero, "The Military and Society in the GDR", in Margy Gerber et al. (eds.), *Studies in GDR Culture and Society 5: Selected Papers from the Tenth New Hampshire Symposium on the German*

Democratic Republic, Lanham, New York, London, University Press of America 1985, pp. 81–93

Chapter 6: Foreign Relations

Asmus, Ronald D., "East and West Germany: Continuity and Change", *World Today* 40 (1984), pp. 142–51

——, "The Dialectics of Detente and Discord: The Moscow — East Berlin — Bonn Triangle", *Orbis* 4 (1985), pp. 743–74

Davis, Geoffrey, "Erkennt Ihr, warum wir Euch lieben? The GDR and the States of Southern Africa in the 1980s", in Ian Wallace (ed.), *The GDR in the 1980s*, Dundee, *GDR Monitor* Special Series No. 4 1984, pp. 43–70

Glass, George A., "East Germany in Black Africa: A New Special Role?", *World Today* 36 (1980), pp. 305–12

Kusin, Vladimir V., "Gorbachev and Eastern Europe", *Problems of Communism* (Jan./Feb. 1986), pp. 39–53

McAdams, A. James, *East Germany and Detente: Building Authority after the Wall*, Cambridge, CUP 1985

McCauley, Martin, "The German Democratic Republic and the Soviet Union", in David Childs (ed.), *Honecker's Germany*, London, Allen & Unwin 1985, pp. 147–65

Marsh, Paul, "Foreign Policy Making in the German Democratic Republic", in Hannes Adomeit, Robert Boardman (eds.), *Foreign Policy Making in Communist Countries*, Farnborough, Saxon House 1979, pp. 79–111

Minnerup, Günter, "The GDR and the German Question in the 1980s", in Ian Wallace (ed.), *The GDR in the 1980s*, Dundee, *GDR Monitor* Special Series No. 4 1984, pp. 3–13

Schulz, Eberhard, et al. (eds.), *GDR Foreign Policy*, Armonk/New York , London, M.E. Sharpe 1982

Sodaro, Michael, "The GDR and the Third World: Supplicant and Surrogate", in Michael Radu (ed.), *Eastern Europe and the Third World. East vs. South*, New York, Praeger 1981, pp. 106–41.

Starrels, J.M., "The GDR's Relations with the Advanced Industrial Countries of the West", in Viola Harms Drath (ed.), *Germany in World Politics*, New York, Cyrco Press 1979, pp. 78–96

Valenta, Jim, Shannon Butler, "East German Security Policies in Africa", in Michael Radu (ed.), *Eastern Europe and the Third World. East vs. South*, New York, Praeger 1981, pp. 142–68

Volkmer, Werner, "Political Culture and the Nation in the GDR", *GDR Monitor* 11 (1984), pp. 12–23

Whetton, Lawrence L., *Germany East and West*, New York and London, New York University Press 1980

Chapter 7: Literature and Culture

Dennis, Michael, "Sports Participation in the GDR", *GDR Monitor 7* (1982), pp. 10–22

Gransow, Volker, "The Politics of Leisure in the GDR", in Ian Wallace (ed.), *The GDR under Honecker 1971–1981*, Dundee, *GDR Monitor* Special Series No. 1 1981, pp. 21–29

Stephan, Alexander, "Cultural Politics in the GDR under Honecker", in Ian Wallace (ed.), *The GDR under Honecker 1971–1981*, Dundee, *GDR Monitor* Special Series No. 1 1981, pp. 31–42

Wallace, Ian (ed.), *The Writer and Society in the GDR*, Hutton Press, Tayport/Scotland 1984

Notes on the Editors

Jürgen K.A. Thomaneck

Senior Lecturer in German at Aberdeen University, he was educated at the universities of Kiel, Tübingen, and Aberdeen. He graduated from Kiel and received his Dr.phil from Kiel, and his M.Ed. from Aberdeen. His research and teaching interests are in sociolinguistics and language teaching, history and politics, and specifically GDR studies. He has published widely in these areas including a book on *Police and Public Order in Europe* (with J. Roach). He is also an active trade unionist and a Grampian Region Councillor.

James Mellis

Lecturer in German at Aberdeen University. Educated at the universities of Aberdeen and Mainz (MA Ph.D Aberdeen), and Lecturer 1970 to 1975 at Glasgow University. His research and teaching interests are in language teaching and in various aspects of literature, including cultural policies in the GDR.

Index